Preface

It took a long time in the history of humankind before it occurred to anyone that mathematics is useful – even vital – in the understanding of nature. Western thought was dominated from antiquity to the Renaissance, turn by turn, by Plato and Aristotle. Plato taught that reality consists of idealised "forms", and our world was a flawed, inadequate shadow of reality – hardly worthy of passing notice, let alone study. Aristotle thought that the intricacies of nature could never be described by the abstract simplicity of mathematics. Galileo recognized and used the power of mathematics in his study of nature, and with his discovery, modern science was born.

A large fraction of classical, and also quantum, physics uses a common type of mathematics. Certain partial differential equations occur over and over again in different fields. The methods of solution of these equations and the special functions, which arise, are thus generally useful tools which should be known to all physicists. The purpose of this book *"Mathematical Methods in Physics-II (PHE-05)"* is to provide a guide to the study of this part of mathematics and to show how it is used in various applications. The book is strictly based on IGNOU syllabus.

In this book, introductions and solved practical problems are given in each chapter, which will give you better understanding of chapters. Best point is that we have included previous years solved papers to help students to understand the unique examination structure.

We hope that this book will not only helpful for students but also for teachers.

We wish you great success. Feedback in this regard is solicited.

– GPH Panel of Expert

Acknowledgement

Our compliments go to the **GullyBaba Publishing House (P) Ltd.,** and its meticulous team who have been enthusiastically working towards the perfection of the book.

Their teamwork, initiative and research have been very encouraging. Had it not been for their unflagging support, this work wouldn't have been possible. The creative freedom provided by them along with their aim of presenting the best to the reader has been a major source of inspiration in this work. Hope that this book would be successful.

– GPH Panel of Expert

Publisher's Note

The present book of the PHE series is targeted for examination purpose as well as enrichment. With the advent of technology and the Internet, there has been no dearth of information available to all; however, finding the relevant and qualitative information, which is focused, is an uphill task.

We at **GullyBaba Publishing House (P) Ltd.,** have taken this step to provide quality material which can accentuate in-depth knowledge about the subject. GPH books are a pioneer in the effort of providing unique and quality material to its readers. With our books, you are sure to attain success by making use of this powerful study material. Provided book is just a reference book based on the syllabus of particular University/Board. For a profound information, see the textbooks recommended by the University/Board.

Our site **gullybaba.com** is a vital resource for your examination. The publisher wishes to acknowledge the significant contribution of the Team Members and our experts in bringing out this publication and highly thankful to Almighty God, without His blessings, this endeavor wouldn't have been successful.

– Publisher

MATHEMATICAL METHODS IN

Physics-II

<u>PHE-05</u>

For

Bachelor of Science [B.Sc.]

Useful For

Delhi University (DU), IGNOU, Berhampur University (Odisha), University of Kashmir, Sambalpur University (Odisha), University of Kalyani (West Bengal), Gurukula Kangri Vishwavidyalaya (Uttarakhand), Himachal Pradesh University, Cooch Behar Panchanan Barma University (West Bengal), Ranchi University, University of Culcutta, Pune University, University of Mumbai, Andhra University, School of Open Learning (DU), Gondwana University (Maharashra), Babasaheb Bhimrao Ambedkar University (Lucknow), Dr. Babasaheb Ambedkar Marathwada University (Aurangabad), University of Madras, Netaji Subhas Open University (Kolkata), Odisha State Open University, all other Indian Universities.

Closer to Nature  We use Recycled Paper

GULLYBABA PUBLISHING HOUSE (P) LTD.
ISO 9001 & ISO 14001 CERTIFIED CO.

Published by:

GullyBaba Publishing House Pvt. Ltd.

Regd. Office:
2525/193, 1st Floor, Onkar Nagar-A,
Tri Nagar, Delhi-110035
(From Kanhaiya Nagar Metro Station Towards Old Bus Stand)
Ph. 011-27387998, 27384836, 27385249

Branch Office:
1A/2A, 20, Hari Sadan,
Ansari Road, Daryaganj,
New Delhi-110002
Ph. 011-23289034
011-45794768

E-mail: hello@gullybaba.com, Website: GullyBaba.com

New Edition

Author: GullyBaba.Com Panel

ISBN: 978-93-82688-79-2

FREE HOME DELIVERY of GPH Books

You can get GPH books by VPP/COD/Speed Post/Courier.
You can order books by Email/SMS/WhatsApp/Call.
For more details, visit gullybaba.com/faq-books.html

Topics Covered

Contents

Question Papers

1

First Order Ordinary Differential Equations

AN OVERVIEW

In mathematics, an ordinary differential equation (abbreviated ODE) is an equation containing a function of one independent variable and its derivatives.

First-degree first-order ODEs contain only dy/dx equated to some function of x and y, and can be written in either of two equivalent standard forms

$$\frac{dy}{dx} = F(x, y), \quad \text{or} \quad A(x, y)dx + B(x, y)dy = 0,$$

Phenomena in many disciplines are modelled by first-order ordinary differential equations (odes). Some examples include Mechanical Systems, Electrical Circuits, Population Models, Newton's Law of Cooling, Compartmental Analysis, etc.

Differential equation: In many physical situation, e.g. bending of beams, oscillations of mechanical systems and electrical circuits, etc., we come across equations which contain, besides the dependent and independent variables, differential coefficients of the dependent variable with respect to the independent variable or variables. These equations are called Differential Equations. Thus, a differential equation is an equation which involves differential coefficient of a dependent variable with respect to independent variable or variables.

Ordinary Differential Equation: Differential equation which involves only one independent variable is called an Ordinary Differential Equation. Thus, the differential equations

$$\frac{dy}{dx} = m \qquad \qquad \text{...(i)}$$

$$\frac{d^2y}{dx^2} = k^2 y \qquad \qquad \text{...(ii)}$$

$$\frac{d^2y}{dx^2} + 2x\frac{dy}{dx} + \sqrt{\left(1 + \frac{dy}{dx}\right)^2} = 0 \qquad \qquad \text{...(iii)}$$

are all examples of ordinary differential equations. They involve only one independent variable x.

Partial Differential Equation: The equation which involves partial derivatives with respect to one or more independent variables is called a Partial Differential Equation.

$$\text{Thus, } \frac{\partial y}{\partial x} = k^2 \frac{\partial y}{\partial t} \qquad \qquad \text{...(iv)}$$

$$\frac{\partial^2 y}{\partial t^2} = k^2 \frac{\partial y^2}{\partial x^2} \qquad \qquad \text{...(v)}$$

are partial differential equations involving two independent variables t and x.

Order of Differential Equation: The order of differential equation is the highest order of the derivative in the equation. If a differential equation contains *n*th and lower derivatives, it is said to be of *n*th order. Thus, differential equations (ii), (iii) and (v) are of second order while those in (i) and (iv) are of first order.

Degree of Differential Equation: The degree of a differential equation is the degree of the highest order derivative when the equation has been made rational and integral as far as the derivatives are concerned. Thus, equation (iii) must be squared to rationalise it and then we find that the greatest degree of $\dfrac{d^2y}{dx^2}$, the highest order derivative, is two. Hence, the equation is of second degree. The equation (iii) is an ordinary differential equation of second order and second degree.

Linear and non-linear Differential Equation: An ordinary differential equation is called linear differential equation when the following conditions are fulfiled:

- The unknown function and its derivatives occur only to the first degree

- In the equation, there are no products involving either the unknown function and its derivatives or two or more derivatives.

- There are no transcendental functions involving the unknown function or any of its derivatives.

An nth-order ordinary differential equation, linear in y, may be expressed as

$$a_n(x)y^{(n)} + a_{n-1}(x)y^{(n-1)} + \dots + a_1(x)y' + a_0(x)y = f(x) \qquad \dots\text{(vi)}$$

Here f and coefficients $a_0, a_1, \dots, a_n$ are functions of x only, on some interval of x, and $a_n(x) \neq 0$ on that interval.

In writing Eq. (vi), we have adopted the notation $y' = \dfrac{dy}{dx}, y'' = \dfrac{d^2y}{dx^2}, \dots, y^{(n)} = \dfrac{d^ny}{dx^n}.$

A differential equation that is not linear is said to be **non-linear differential equation.**

Note: Any function which cannot be expressed as a solution of a polynomial equation of the form $P_0(x)u^n + P_1(x)u^{n-1} + \dots P_{n-1}(x)u + P_n(x) = 0$ is called a transcendental function. The logarithmic, trigonometric, hyperbolic functions and their corresponding inverses are examples of transcendental functions.

Homogeneous and non-homogeneous ordinary differential Equation:

A differential equation of the form $\dfrac{dy}{dx} = \dfrac{f(x,y)}{g(x,y)}$ $\qquad \dots\text{(vii)}$

Where $f(x, y)$ and $g(x, y)$ are homogeneous functions of x and y of the same degree, is called a homogeneous differential equation.

And non-homogeneous equations of the first degree in x and y are of the form: $\dfrac{dy}{dx} = \dfrac{ax + by + c}{Ax + By + C}$ $\qquad \dots\text{(viii)}$

This is called non-homogeneous differential equation, which is not homogeneous.

Solution of a differential equation: A function $y = \phi(x)$ is called a solution of differential equation in y on some interval, say, $a \leq x \leq b$, if $\phi(x)$ is defined and differentiable throughout that interval and is such that the equation becomes an identity when y is replaced by $\phi(x)$ in the differential equation.

Explicit Solution: Consider an equation, y=Sinx   ...(ix)

In this equation, we have y given as an explicit function of x. Such a solution is called an explicit solution.

Implicit Solution: Consider $y^2 + x = 4$ ...(x)

In this equation, we have an implicit relation between x and y. So, it is a implicit solution. In other words, a solution of a D.E. in the form $G(x, y) = 0$ is called an implicit solution.

General Solution: Consider the differential equation $y' = \cos x$ ...(xi)

We may easily verify that each of the functions y = sinx, y = sinx+5, y = sinx-9 is a solution of Eq(xi).

We can express them generally as y = sinx+c   ...(xii)

Where c is arbitrary constant.   Then Eq(xii) is called a general solution of Eq(xi). Hence, a solution involving arbitrary constants is known as the general solution.

Particular Solution: Now putting y = 0 and x = 0 in equation (xii), than we get 0 = 0 + c or c = 0 and y = sinx. Therefore, by imposing a condition on Eq(xii), we can assign a specific value to c. The solution thus obtained is called a particular solution. Thus, a definite value can be assigned to each arbitrary constant appearing in a general solution, and then we get a particular solution.

Existence and Uniqueness of a Particular solution: There are two points about existence and uniqueness of a particular solution:

(a) If the conditions on the solution of a differential equation, or its derivatives, are specified for a single value of the independent variable, they are called initial conditions. The differential equation with its initial conditions is called an Initial-Value Problem (IVP).

(b) If the conditions on the solution of a differential equation, or its derivatives are specified for two or more values of the independent variable, they are called boundary conditions. The differential equation with its boundary conditions is called a boundary- value problem (BVP).

Example:

- $y' + 2y = 3$, with the initial condition $y(0) = 1$, is a first, order initial-value problem.

- $y'' + 3y = 0$, with the initial conditions $y(1) = 2$, and $y'(1) = -8$, is a second-order initial-value problem.

- $y'' - 2y' + 6y = x^3$ with the boundary conditions $y(0) = 2$, $y(1) = -1$ is a second-order boundary-value problem.

General Properties of the solutions of Linear ODEs: Let us consider the following ODEs

$$a_2(x)y'' + a_1(x)y' + a_0(x)y = 0 \qquad \ldots(xiii)$$

and

$$a_2(x)y'' + a_1(x)y' + a_0(x)y = f(x) \qquad \ldots(xiv)$$

Eqs. (xiii) and (xiv) are both linear second order ODEs. The former is homogeneous and the latter is non-homogeneous.

Properties of the solutions of linear ODEs are as follows:

- $y = 0$ is a solution of Eq. (xiii). This is called the trivial solution.

- If y_1 and y_2 are linearly independent solutions of Eq. (xiii), then $u = c_1 y_1 + c_2 y_2$ is also a solution of Eq. (xiii), where c_1 and c_2 are constants.

- If y_1 is a solution of (xiii) and y_2 is a solution of (xiv), then $z = y_1 + y_2$ is a solution of (xiv).

- The difference $(y_1 - y_2)$ of two solutions y_1 and y_2 of (xiv) is a solution of (xiii).

Method of separation of variables: When the equation $M\, dx + N\, dy = 0$ can be put in the form $f_1(x)dx + f_2(y)dy = 0$ then it can be easily solved by integrating each term separately. Hence, by direct integration, the solution of this differential equation is given by $\int f_1(x)dx + \int f_2(y)dy = c$ where c is an arbitrary constant.

Solution by the method of substitution: First, we shall take up the case where substitution can be done by mere inspection of the equation. For example, let us consider the ODE, $\dfrac{dy}{dx} = \cos(x + y)$. The given equation is non-separable because of the factor $(x + y)$. So we put, $u = x + y$

$$\therefore \frac{du}{dx} = 1 + \frac{dy}{dx} \quad \text{or} \quad \frac{dy}{dx} = \frac{du}{dx} - 1$$

$$\text{Hence, } \frac{du}{dx} = 1 + \cos u = 2\cos^2\frac{u}{2}$$

$$\therefore \qquad \frac{du}{2\cos^2\dfrac{u}{2}} = dx$$

Thus, we have separated the variables u and x. Now, the above equation may be rewritten as $\dfrac{1}{2}\sec^2\dfrac{u}{2}du - dx = 0$ or

$$\frac{1}{2}\int \sec^2\frac{u}{2}du - \int dx = c$$

or $\tan\dfrac{u}{2} - x = c$ or $\tan\dfrac{x+y}{2} - x = c$

This is the required solution.

Method for solving Homogeneous Differential Equations of the first order: This case includes equations which are of the from $\dfrac{dy}{dx} = \dfrac{f(x,y)}{\phi(x,y)}$ where $f(x,y)$ and $\phi(x,y)$ are both homogenous functions of the same degree. These equations can be put in the form $\dfrac{dy}{dx} = F\left(\dfrac{y}{x}\right)$.

In such cases, the substitution $y = vx$ changes them to the variable separable form, for $\dfrac{dy}{dx} = v + x\dfrac{dv}{dx}$ gives $v + x\dfrac{dv}{dx} = F(v)$ or $x\dfrac{dv}{dx} = F(v) - v$.

Method for solving non-homogenous differential equations of the first degree in x and y:- These can be put in the form $\dfrac{dy}{dx} = \dfrac{ax+by+c}{a'x+b'y+c'}$ ...(xv)

In this, the substitutions $x = X + h$ and $y = Y + k$ where h, k are constants, give $\dfrac{dY}{dX} = \dfrac{aX+bY}{a'X+bY'}$ ...(xvi)

provided that

$$\left.\begin{array}{l} ah + bk + c = 0 \\ a'h + b'k + c' = 0 \end{array}\right\} \qquad ..(xvii)$$

and

Relations (xvii) determine the constants h and k. With these values of h and k, (xv) transforms to the form (xvi), which is the homogeneous form and can be integrated by the method of solving homogeneous differential equation. Equations (xvii) give $h = \dfrac{bc'-cb'}{ab'-ba'}, k = \dfrac{ca'-ac'}{ab'-ba'}$

Clearly if $ab'-ba' \neq 0$ only then this method is successful. But if $ab'-ba' = 0$, i.e. $\dfrac{a}{a'} = \dfrac{b}{b'}$, this method fails.

Special Case. If $\dfrac{a}{a'} = \dfrac{b}{b'} = \dfrac{1}{m}$ (say), the eq. (xv) takes the form

$$\frac{dy}{dx} = \frac{ax + by + c}{m(ax + by) + c'} \text{ where m is any number.}$$

In such cases, the substitutions $ax + by = v, a + b\dfrac{dy}{dx} = \dfrac{dv}{dx}$ transform the differential equation to variables separable form.

Exact equations: A differential equation obtained from its primitive by direct differentiation and without any further elimination or reduction is called an exact differential equation. Thus, xdx - ydy = 0 is an exact differential equation because it is obtained from its primitive $x^2 - y^2 = a^2$ directly by differentiation. Hence, a differential equation $Mdx + Ndy = 0$ is exact if there exists a function $u(x,y)$ such that $du = Mdx + Ndy$ and $u(x,y) = c$ is its primitive.

Note: The necessary and sufficient condition for the ordinary differential equation $Mdx + Ndy = 0$ to be exact is $\dfrac{\partial M}{\partial y} = \dfrac{\partial N}{\partial x}$.

Method for solving an exact equation: The procedure for solving an exact equation are as follows:

Step 1: Write the differential equation in the form

$$M (x, y)\, dx + N (x, y)\, dy = 0 \text{ and check to make sure that } \frac{\partial M}{\partial y} = \frac{\partial N}{\partial x}$$

Step 2: Evaluate (i) $z(x,y) = \int M(x,y)\, dx + f(y)$ or (ii) $z(x,y) = \int N(x,y)\, dy + g(x)$ (treating y and x, as constants in the integration processes (i) and (ii), respectively).

Step 3: Evaluate the arbitrary functions f (y) or g (x) that occur in Step 2 by putting $\dfrac{\partial z}{\partial y} = N(x,y)$ or $\dfrac{\partial z}{\partial x} = M(x,y)$.

Step 4: Write a solution in the form z (x, y) = C.

First order Linear Differential Equations: A differential equation in which the dependent variable and its derivative appear in first degree only is called a first order linear differential equation.

Thus, a linear differential equation is of the form $\dfrac{dy}{dx} + Py = Q$, where P and Q are functions of x (or constants) only and it is said to be linear in y.

To solve it, let us multiply it by a function R of x only so that

$$R\frac{dy}{dx}+RPy=RQ$$

Let R be such that the left hand side of above equation be $\frac{d}{dx}(Ry)$.

$$R\frac{dy}{dx}+RPy=\frac{d}{dx}(Ry) \Rightarrow R\frac{dy}{dx}+RPy=R\frac{dy}{dx}+y\frac{dR}{dx}$$

$$\therefore \quad RP=\frac{dR}{dx} \text{ or } \frac{dR}{R}=Pdx \text{ or } \log R=\int Pdx$$

$$\therefore \quad R=e^{\int Pdx}.$$

Hence, we have determined the function R and it is called the Integrating factor, denoted by I.F.

$$\therefore \quad \text{I.F}=e^{\int Pdx}$$

Hence, equation $R\frac{dy}{dx}+RPy=RQ$ becomes $\frac{d}{dx}(Ry)=RQ$

This, on integration, gives $Ry=\int RQ\,dx+c$

$$y\times \text{I.F.}=\int Q\times \text{I.F.}dx+c \text{ or } ye^{\int Pdx}=\int Q\,e^{\int Pdx}dx+c$$

which is the required solution.

Equations reducible to first order: Here, we shall consider two cases, each corresponding to a second order ODE.

(1) If a second order ODE in x and y is devoid of y, then it can be expressed as $F(y'',y',x)=0$ ...(xviii)

We make the substitution $w=y'=\frac{dy}{dx}$. Thus, Eq. (xviii) takes the form of a first order ODE $F(w',w,x)=0$ ...(xix)

To illustrate this technique, we consider the ODE

$$y''+2y'=0 \tag*{...(xx)}$$

We put $w=y'$, so that $\frac{dw}{dx}+2w=0$ ...(xxi)

We can solve this equation by the method of separation of variables.

(2) If a second order ODE in x and y is devoid of x, then it can be expressed as $F(y'',y',y)=0$ ...(xxii)

We again make the substitution $w=y'$. Then we express y'' as follows:

$$y''=\frac{dy'}{dx}=\frac{dw}{dx}=\frac{dw}{dy}\frac{dy}{dx}=w\frac{dw}{dy}$$

Thus, Eq. (xxii) becomes $F\left(w\dfrac{dw}{dy}, w, y\right)$ ...(xiii)

which is a first order ODE in w with y as the independent variable.

To illustrate this method, we consider the following ODE

$$yy'' + (y')^2 = 0 \qquad \text{...(xxvi)}$$

We put $w = y'$, so that $y'' = w\dfrac{dw}{dy}$ so, we get

$$yw\dfrac{dw}{dy} + w^2 = 0 \qquad \text{...(xxv)}$$

Now this can be solved by the method of separation of variables.

Solved Practical Problems

Q1. Ten equations from various areas of physics are listed below. Identify the ordinary and partial differential equations.

(i) $\dfrac{d^2y}{dt^2} = -g$

Ans. ODEs.

(ii) $y = u_0t - \dfrac{1}{2}gt^2$

Ans. Neither ordinary not partial.

(iii) $\dfrac{d^2\theta}{dt^2} + \dfrac{g}{l}\theta = 0$

Ans. ODEs.

(iv) $\dfrac{\partial^2 T}{\partial x^2} + \dfrac{\partial^2 T}{\partial y^2} = 0$

Ans. PDEs.

(v) $L\dfrac{d^2q}{dt^2} + R\dfrac{dq}{dt} + \dfrac{q}{C} = E(t)$

Ans. ODEs.

(vi) $\dfrac{\partial^2 u}{\partial x^2} + \dfrac{\partial^2 u}{\partial y^2} + \dfrac{\partial^2 u}{\partial z^2} = \dfrac{1}{\alpha^2}\dfrac{\partial u}{\partial t}$

Ans. PDEs.

(vii) $u = A\sin(x - \omega t) + B\cos(x - \omega t)$

Ans. Neither ordinary not partial.

(viii) $\dfrac{dT}{dt} = K(T - T_0)$

Ans. ODEs.

(ix) $m\dfrac{dv}{dt} = mg - kv$

Ans. ODEs.

(x) $\dfrac{1}{r}\dfrac{\partial}{\partial\theta}\left(r\dfrac{\partial u}{\partial r}\right) + \dfrac{1}{r^2}\left(\dfrac{\partial^2 u}{\partial\theta^2}\right) + \dfrac{\partial^2 u}{\partial z^2} = 0$

Ans. PDEs.

Q2. **Obtain the integrating factor and solve the equation:** $x\dfrac{dy}{dx} - 2y = x^4$.

[Dec-2012,Q.No.-1(b)]

Ans. Given equation is $x\dfrac{dy}{dx} - 2y = x^4$

On dividing by x, we get $\dfrac{dy}{dx} - \dfrac{2}{x}y = x^3$ ...(i)

Compare eq. (i) with $\dfrac{dy}{dx} + Py = Q$, we get $P = \dfrac{-2}{x}$, $Q = x^3$

Hence, $\text{I.F.} = e^{\int Pdx} = e^{\int \frac{-2}{x}dx} = e^{-2\int\frac{1}{x}dx} = e^{-2\log x} = e^{\log x^{-2}} = x^{-2}$

$\Rightarrow$ $\text{I.F.} = \dfrac{1}{x^2}$

Now multiplying eq. (i) by $\dfrac{1}{x^2}$, we get $\dfrac{1}{x^2}\dfrac{dy}{dx} - \dfrac{2}{x}.\dfrac{1}{x^2}y = x$

$\Rightarrow$ $\dfrac{d}{dx}\left(\dfrac{1}{x^2}y\right) = x$

Integrating, we get $\dfrac{y}{x^2} = \dfrac{x^2}{2} + c$

$\Rightarrow$ $y = \dfrac{x^4}{2} + cx^2$

$\Rightarrow$ $y = \dfrac{x^4 + 2cx^2}{2}$

$\Rightarrow$ $2y = x^4 + 2cx^2$

$\Rightarrow$ $2y = x^2(x^2 + 2c)$

$\Rightarrow$ $y = \dfrac{x^2}{2}(x^2 + 2c)$ is the required solution.

Q3. Solve: $\dfrac{dy}{dx} + \dfrac{x-y-2}{x-2y-3} = 0$.

Ans. Here $\dfrac{dy}{dx} = -\dfrac{x-y-2}{x-2y-3}$.

Putting, $x = X + h$, $y = Y + k$, $\dfrac{dy}{dx} = \dfrac{dY}{dX}$, we get

$$\dfrac{dY}{dX} = -\dfrac{(X-Y)+h-k-2}{(X-2Y)+h-2k-3} \qquad \text{...(i)}$$

where $\left. \begin{array}{l} h-k-2=0, \\ h-2k-3=0 \end{array} \right\} \qquad \text{...(ii)}$

Solving equations (ii), we get $h = 1$, $k = -1$.

Hence, (i) gives, $\dfrac{dY}{dX} = -\dfrac{X-Y}{X-2Y}$

which is in homogeneous form. Hence, substituting $Y = vX$, we get

$$v + X\dfrac{dv}{dX} = -\dfrac{X-vX}{X-2vX} = \dfrac{v-1}{1-2v} \;\Rightarrow\; X\dfrac{dv}{dX} = \dfrac{v-1}{1-2v} - v = \dfrac{2v^2-1}{1-2v}.$$

Hence, $\dfrac{1-2v}{2v^2-1}dv = \dfrac{dX}{X} \;\Rightarrow\; \left(\dfrac{1}{2v^2-1} - \dfrac{2v}{2v^2-1}\right)dv = \dfrac{dX}{X}.$

This, on integration, gives

$$\dfrac{1}{2\sqrt{2}}\log\dfrac{\sqrt{2}v-1}{\sqrt{2}v+1} - \dfrac{1}{2}\log(2v^2-1) = \log X + \log c$$

where $X = x - h = x - 1, Y = y - k = y + 1, v = \dfrac{Y}{X} = \dfrac{y+1}{x-1}.$

Q4. Show that the following equation is exact: $e^y\, dx + (xe^y + 2y)\, dy = 0$.

[June-2010,Q.No.-1(a)]

Ans. Given equation is $e^y\, dx + (xe^y + 2y)\, dy = 0$ $\qquad$ ...(i)

Compare Eq (i) with $Mdx + Ndy = 0$, we get

$M = e^y \quad , \quad N = xe^y + 2y$

$\Rightarrow \qquad \dfrac{\partial M}{\partial y} = e^y \quad , \quad \dfrac{\partial N}{\partial x} = e^y$

$\Rightarrow \qquad \dfrac{\partial M}{\partial y} = \dfrac{\partial N}{\partial x}$

Therefore, given equation is exact.

Q5. (a) Verify that $x^2 + y^2 - 1 = 0$ is a solution of the differential equation $yy' = -x$ on the interval $[-1, 1]$. State whether this solution is implicit or explicit.

Ans. Differentiating both sides of the equation $x^2 + y^2 - 1 = 0$ with respect to x, we get $2x + 2yy' = 0$ or $yy' + x = 0$, which is the given differential equation. Hence, $x^2 + y^2 - 1 = 0$ is a solution. It is implicit.

(b) Verify that $y = Ax + \cos A$, for constant A is the solution of the ODE $y = xy' + \cos y'$ Identify the type of the solution (i.e. whether general or particular).

Ans. It is given that $y = Ax + \cos A$

$$\therefore \quad y' = \frac{dy}{dx} = A$$

Thus, on replacing A by y', the given equation becomes $y = y'x + \cos y'$, which is the given ordinary differential equation.

Hence, $y = Ax + \cos A$ is a solution of the given ODE. As A is an arbitrary constant, it is a general solution.

Q6. Obtain the integrating factor of the following equation and solve it: $\dfrac{dy}{dx} + \dfrac{1}{x} y = 3x$ **[June-2012,Q.No.-1(b)]**

Ans. Given equation is $\dfrac{dy}{dx} + \dfrac{1}{x} y = 3x$ ...(i)

Compare (i) with $\dfrac{dy}{dx} + Py = Q$ we get

$$P = \frac{1}{x}, \quad Q = 3x$$

Hence, $\text{I.F.} = e^{\int P dx} = e^{\int \frac{1}{x} dx} = e^{\log x} \Rightarrow \text{I.F.} = x$

Now multiplying Eq. (i) by x, we get $x\dfrac{dy}{dx} + y = 3x^2$

or $\dfrac{d}{dx}(xy) = 3x^2$

Integrating, we have $xy = 3\int x^2 + c$

$\Rightarrow xy = x^3 + c$ or $y = x^2 + cx^{-1}$ is the required solution.

Q7. Solve the equation $\dfrac{dy}{dx} = -\dfrac{5(y^2+2)}{xy}$.

Ans. Comparing f(x, y) of this equation with the form $\left(f(x,y) = \dfrac{M(x)}{N(y)}\right)$, we

get $M(x) = -\dfrac{5}{x}, N(y) = \dfrac{y}{y^2+2}$

So, we can rewrite it in the form $5\displaystyle\int\dfrac{dx}{x} + \int\dfrac{y\,dy}{y^2+2} = C$

or $5ln\big|x\big| + \dfrac{1}{2}ln\big|y^2+2\big| = C$

$\therefore ln\big|x\big|^5\big|y^2+2\big|^{\frac{1}{2}} = C$

or $x^5(y^2+2)^{\frac{1}{2}} = C_1$, where $C_1 = \exp(C)$ is the required solution.

Q8. Obtain the integrating factor and solve:

$$x\dfrac{dy}{dx} + y = 3x^2 \qquad\qquad \textbf{[June-2010,Q.No.-1(b)]}$$

Ans. Given equation is $x\dfrac{dy}{dx} + y = 3x^2$

On dividing by x, we get $\dfrac{dy}{dx} + \dfrac{1}{x}y = 3x$ \qquad ...(i)

Compare (i) with $\dfrac{dy}{dx} + Py = Q$ we get $P = \dfrac{1}{x}, \qquad Q = 3x$

Hence, I.F. $= e^{\int Pdx} = e^{\int\frac{1}{x}dx} = e^{\log x} = x$

Now multiplying Eq. (i) by x, we get $x\dfrac{dy}{dx} + y = 3x^2$

$\Rightarrow \qquad \dfrac{d}{dx}(xy) = 3x^2$

Integrating, we get $xy = 3\displaystyle\int x^2\,dx + c$ or $xy = x^3 + c$

$\Rightarrow y = x^2 + cx^{-1}$ is the required solution.

Q9. (a) Find the general solution of the ODE (y + 1) y' + x = 0.
Ans. We have (y + 1) y' + x = 0, this is a separable equation.

Using the method of separation of variables, we have
$\displaystyle\int(y+1)dy = -\int x\,dx$ or $\dfrac{1}{2}y^2 + y = -\dfrac{x^2}{2} + C$ or $y^2 + x^2 + 2y = 2C$ or

$(y+1)^2 + x^2 = 2C+1$

This is the equation of family of concentric circles centred at $(0, -1)$ and of radius $\sqrt{2C+1}$

(b) Solve the IVP $y' = -2xy, y(0) = 3$

Ans. Given IVP is: $y' = -2xy, y(0) = 3$ also a separable ODE.

Here, $\int \dfrac{dy}{y} = -2\int x\,dx + C$

or $\ln|y| = -x^2 + C$ or $y = C_1 e^{-x^2}$ where $C_1 = \ln|C|$

From the initial condition, we have $C_1 = 3$ and the particular solution is $y = 3e^{-x^2}$.

Q10. Obtain the integrating factor and solve: $x\dfrac{dy}{dx} - 3y = x^4$

[Dec-2010,Q.No.-1(b)]

Ans. Given equation is $x\dfrac{dy}{dx} - 3y = x^4$

$$\Rightarrow \qquad \dfrac{dy}{dx} - \dfrac{3y}{x} = x^3 \qquad\qquad \text{...(i)}$$

Compare (i) with $\dfrac{dy}{dx} + Py = Q$ we get $P = \dfrac{-3}{x}$, $Q = x^3$

Hence, I.F. $= e^{-3\int \frac{1}{x}dx} = e^{-3\log x} = e^{\log x^{-3}} = x^{-3}$

$\Rightarrow$ I.F. $= \dfrac{1}{x^3}$

Now multiplying Eq. (i) by $\dfrac{1}{x^3}$, we get

$$\dfrac{1}{x^3}\dfrac{dy}{dx} - \dfrac{3}{x^4}y = 1 \quad \Rightarrow \quad \dfrac{d}{dx}\left(\dfrac{1}{x^3}y\right) = 1$$

Integrating, we get $\dfrac{1}{x^3}y = \int 1\,dx + c$

$$\Rightarrow \dfrac{y}{x^3} = x + c \Rightarrow y = x^4 + cx^3 \text{ is the required solution.}$$

Q11. Identify the homogeneous first order ODEs from the following:

(i) $x^2\dfrac{dy}{dx} = y^2 - 3xy + 5x^2$

Ans. $x^2\dfrac{dy}{dx} = y^2 - 3xy + 5x^2 \quad\Rightarrow\quad \dfrac{dy}{dx} = \dfrac{y^2}{x^2} - \dfrac{3xy}{x^2} + \dfrac{5x^2}{x^2}$

$$\Rightarrow \frac{dy}{dx} = \left(\frac{y}{x}\right)^2 - 3\left(\frac{y}{x}\right) + 5$$

Hence, this equation is in the form of $\frac{dy}{dx} = F\left(\frac{y}{x}\right)$

Hence, it is homogeneous equation.

(ii) $\left(x^2 + y^2\right)dx + \left(x + y\right)dy = 0$

Ans. $\left(x^2 + y^2\right)dx + (x+y)\,dy = 0 \Rightarrow \frac{dy}{dx} = -\frac{(x^2 + y^2)}{(x+y)}$

This equation cannot be expressed in the form of $\frac{dy}{dx} = F\left(\frac{y}{x}\right)$

Hence, it is not a homogeneous equation.

(iii) $\left\{y + x\sin\left(y/x\right)\right\}dx - xdy = 0$

Ans. $\left\{y + x\sin\left(\frac{y}{x}\right)\right\}dx - xdy = 0 \Rightarrow -xdy = -\left\{y + x\sin\left(\frac{y}{x}\right)\right\}dx$

$$\Rightarrow \frac{xdy}{dx} = \left\{y + x\sin\left(\frac{y}{x}\right)\right\} \Rightarrow \frac{dy}{dx} = \frac{y}{x} + \sin\left(\frac{y}{x}\right)$$

Hence, it is homogenous equation.

Q12. **Show that the ordinary differential equation of the form:** $(e^x + y - 1)\,dx + (3e^y + x - 7)\,dy = 0$ **is an exact equation and hence solve it.** [June-2011,Q.No.-1(c)]

Ans. Given ODE is $(e^x + y - 1)\,dx + (3e^y + x - 7)\,dy = 0$

Compare this equation with $Mdx + Ndy = 0$, we get

$M = e^x + y - 1, \quad N = 3e^y + x - 7$

$$\Rightarrow \frac{\partial M}{\partial y} = 1, \quad \frac{\partial N}{\partial x} = 1 \Rightarrow \frac{\partial M}{\partial y} = \frac{\partial N}{\partial X}$$

Hence, given ODE is an exact equation.

Now the solution is, $\int M\,dx + \int (N \sim x)dy = c$ or

$\int (e^x + y - 1)dx + \int (3e^y - 7)dy = c$

$\Rightarrow (e^x + yx - x) + 3e^y - 7y = c$

$\Rightarrow e^x + 3e^y + xy - x - 7y = c$ where c is constant

Q13. Solve the ODEs:

(a) $\left(x - 2y - 1\right) = \left(x - 2y + 7\right)y'$

Ans. By inspection, we can substitute x - 2y = v

Differentiating it w.r.t x, we get $1 - 2\dfrac{dy}{dx} = \dfrac{dv}{dx}$ or $y' = \dfrac{1}{2}(1 - v')$

Substituting this in the original ODE, we get $(v - 1) = \dfrac{v + 7}{2}\left(1 - \dfrac{dv}{dx}\right)$

or $\dfrac{dv}{dx} = 1 - \dfrac{2v - 2}{v + 7} = \dfrac{-v + 9}{v + 7}$

Using the method of separation of variables, we have

$$\int \frac{v + 7}{v - 9}\,dv = -\int dx + C \quad \text{or} \quad \int\left(1 + \frac{16}{v - 9}\right)dv = -\int dx + c$$

or $v + 16 \, ln\left|v - 9\right| = -x + C$

Since $v = x - 2y$, we get the general solution in the form

$x - 2y + 16\,ln\left|x - 2y - 9\right| = -x + C$ or $2x - 2y + 16\,ln\left|x - 2y - 9\right| = C$

(b) $(1 + \cos\theta)dr = r\sin\theta\,d\theta$

Ans. We have $(1 + \cos\theta)dr = r\sin\theta\,d\theta$

$$\therefore \frac{dr}{r} - \frac{\sin\theta\,d\theta}{1 + \cos\theta} = 0 \quad \text{or} \quad \int\frac{dr}{r} + \int\frac{(-\sin\theta)d\theta}{1 + \cos\theta} = ln\left|C\right|$$

or $ln\left|r\right| + ln\left|1 + \cos\theta\right| = ln\left|C\right|$ $\left[\because \dfrac{d}{d\theta}(1 + \cos\theta) = -\sin\theta\right]$

$\therefore\ r(1 + \cos\theta) = C$

Q14. Solve the equation: $xy\,dy = -3\,(y^2 + 4)dx$ **.[June-2011,Q.No.-1(a)]**

Ans. Given equation is $xy\,dy = -3(y^2 + 4)\,dx$

Using method of separation of variables:- $\displaystyle\int\frac{y}{y^2 + 4}\,dy = -3\int\frac{1}{x}\,dx$

Integrating $\displaystyle\int\frac{y}{y^2 + 4}\,dy = -3\cdot\int\frac{1}{x}\,dx$

$\Rightarrow \dfrac{1}{2}\log\,(y^2 + 4) = -3\log x + \log c \ \Rightarrow\ \log\,(y^2 + 4)^{1/2} = \log x^{-3} + \log c$

$\Rightarrow \sqrt{y^2 + 4} = cx^{-3} \ \Rightarrow\ \sqrt{y^2 + 4} = c/x^3$ or $y^2 + 4 = c^2/x^6$

is the required solution.

Q15. Solve the differential equation $\left(x^2 + y^2\right)dx - xy\,dy = 0$ **.**

Ans. We can rearrange the equation as $\dfrac{dy}{dx} = \dfrac{x^2 + y^2}{xy} = \dfrac{x}{y} + \dfrac{y}{x}$

Now, this form suggests a substitution, $\dfrac{y}{x} = v$ where v is a function of

x. Thus, we get $y = vx$ and $\dfrac{dy}{dx} = v + x\dfrac{dv}{dx}$

$$\therefore \quad v + x\dfrac{dv}{dx} = \dfrac{1}{v} + v \text{ or } v\,dv - \dfrac{dx}{x} = 0$$

Thus v and x are separated. On integrating, we get $\dfrac{v^2}{2} - ln|x| = C$

or $x = C_1 \exp\left(v^2/2\right) = C_1 \exp\left(y^2/2x^2\right)$

Q16. Solve the equation $\dfrac{y'}{y+1} = \dfrac{1}{x}$ 								[Dec-2011,Q.No.-1(a)]

Ans. Given equation is $\dfrac{y'}{y+1} = \dfrac{1}{x} \Rightarrow y' = (y+1)\dfrac{1}{x}$

$$\Rightarrow \dfrac{dy}{dx} = \dfrac{(y+1)}{x} \Rightarrow \dfrac{dy}{y+1} = \dfrac{1}{x}\,dx$$

Integrating, we have $\displaystyle\int\dfrac{dy}{y+1} = \int\dfrac{1}{x}\,dx$ or $\log(y+1) = \log x + \log c \Rightarrow$

$y + 1 = cx$ is the required solution.

Q17. Solve the equation $L\dfrac{di}{dt} + Ri = E_0 \sin\omega t$

Ans. We may rewrite the equation as $\dfrac{di}{dt} + \dfrac{R}{L}i = \dfrac{E_0}{L}\sin\omega t$

$$\therefore \text{Integrating factor} = \exp\left[\int\dfrac{R}{L}dt\right] = e^{Rt/L}$$

On multiplying the ODE by this factor, we get

$$e^{Rt/L}\left[\dfrac{di}{dt} + \dfrac{Ri}{L}\right] = \dfrac{E_0}{L}e^{Rt/L}\sin\omega t$$

$$\therefore \dfrac{d}{dt}\left(ie^{Rt/L}\right) = \dfrac{E_0}{L}e^{Rt/L}\sin\omega t$$

$$\therefore ie^{Rt/L} = \dfrac{E_0}{L}\int e^{Rt/L}\sin\omega t\,dt + C$$

where C is an arbitrary constant.

$$\therefore \text{ The required solution is } i = \dfrac{E_0 \sin(\omega t - \theta)}{\sqrt{R^2 + \omega^2 L^2}}$$

Q18. Solve the equation $x^2 y' - 2xy = \dfrac{1}{x}$.   **[Dec-2011,Q.No.-1(b)]**

Ans. Given equation is $x^2 y' - 2xy = \dfrac{1}{x} \Rightarrow x^2 \dfrac{dy}{dx} - 2xy = \dfrac{1}{x}$

On dividing by x^2, we get $\dfrac{dy}{dx} - 2 \cdot \dfrac{1}{x} y = \dfrac{1}{x^3}$ ...(i)

Compare with $\dfrac{dy}{dx} + Py = Q$ we get, $P = \dfrac{-2}{x}$, $Q = 1/x^3$

$\Rightarrow$ I.F. $= e^{\int \frac{-2}{x} dx} = e^{-2\int \frac{1}{x} dx} = e^{-2\log x} = e^{\log x^{-2}} = x^{-2} = \dfrac{1}{x^2}$ $\Rightarrow$ I.F. $= \dfrac{1}{x^2}$

Now multiplying Eq. (i) by $\dfrac{1}{x^2}$ we get $\dfrac{1}{x^2} \dfrac{dy}{dx} - 2 \cdot \dfrac{1}{x} \cdot \dfrac{1}{x^2} y = \dfrac{1}{x^5}$

$\Rightarrow \dfrac{d}{dx}\left(y \cdot \dfrac{1}{x^2} \right) = \dfrac{1}{x^5}$

Integrating, we get $y \cdot \dfrac{1}{x^2} = \int \dfrac{1}{x^5} + c$ or $\dfrac{y}{x^2} = \dfrac{x^{-5+1}}{-5+1} + c$ or $\dfrac{y}{x^2} = -\dfrac{1}{4} \cdot \dfrac{1}{x^4} + c$

$\Rightarrow y = \dfrac{-1}{4x^2} + cx^2$ is the required solution.

Q19. Show that the differential equation $3x(xy - 2)dx + (x^3 + 2y)dy = 0$ is exact. Hence, solve it.

Ans. Here, $M = 3x^2 y - 6x$, $N = x^3 + 2y$

$\therefore \dfrac{\partial M}{\partial y} = 3x^2, \dfrac{\partial N}{\partial x} = 3x^2$, i.e. $\dfrac{\partial M}{\partial y} = \dfrac{\partial N}{\partial x}$

So the equation is exact. Now, we have to solve the ODE. Since the ODE is exact, there exists a function z (x, y), such that $dz(x,y) = Mdx + Ndy = 0$.

$z = \int M(x,y)dx + f(y) = \int (3x^2 y - 6x)dx + f(y) = x^3 y - 3x^2 + f(y)$

Since $\dfrac{\partial z}{\partial y} = N(x,y)$, we have $x^3 + \dfrac{df}{dy} = x^3 + 2y$

$\therefore \dfrac{df}{dy} = 2y$ or $f(y) = y^2 + k,$

where k is an arbitrary constant.

Thus, $z = x^3 y - 3x^2 + y^2 + k$

Hence, the required solution is $x^3 y - 3x^2 + y^2 + k = C = a$ constant

or $x^3 y - 3x^2 + y^2 = a$ constant.

Q20. Solve the equation $(2y+2)dx+2xdy=0$　　　[June-2013,Q.No.-1(a)]

Ans. Given equation is $(2y+2)dx+2xdy=0$ or $2xdy=-(2y+2)dx$

or $\dfrac{dy}{dx}=\dfrac{-(2y+2)}{2x}$　　$\Rightarrow$　$\dfrac{dy}{dx}=\dfrac{-2(y+1)}{2x}$　　$\Rightarrow$　$\dfrac{dy}{dx}=\dfrac{-y-1}{x}$

$\Rightarrow$　$\dfrac{dy}{y+1}=\dfrac{-1}{x}dx$　$\Rightarrow$　$\dfrac{dy}{y+1}+\dfrac{1}{x}dx=0$

Integrating, we get $\log(y+1)+\log(x)=\log c$

$\Rightarrow$　　$x(y+1)=c$ is the required solution.

Q21. Solve $xy'+2y=x^3$

Ans. The given ODE may be expressed as $y'+\dfrac{2}{x}y=x^2$

The integrating factor $=\exp\left(\int\dfrac{2}{x}dx\right)=\exp\left[2ln|x|\right]=\exp\left[ln|x^2|\right]=x^2$

Thus, we have $\dfrac{d}{dx}(x^2y)=x^4$ or $x^2y=\int x^4dx+C$ or $x^2y-\dfrac{x^5}{5}=C$ is the

required solution.

Q22. Solve $3e^x\tan y\,dx+(1-e^x)\sec^2 y\,dy=0$.

Ans. We have, $3e^x\tan y\,dx+(1-e^x)\sec^2 y\,dy=0$.

or $\dfrac{3\,e^x}{1-e^x}dx+\dfrac{\sec^2 y}{\tan y}dy=0$.

Integrating, we obtain $-3\log(1-e^x)+\log\tan y=\log c$.

Hence, $\dfrac{\tan y}{(1-e^x)^3}=c$ or $\tan y=c(1-e^x)^3$ is the required solution.

Q23. Solve $\dfrac{dy}{dx}=e^{x+y}+x^2e^y$

Ans. We have, $\dfrac{dy}{dx}=e^{x+y}+x^2e^y$.

Or $\dfrac{dy}{dx}=e^x.e^y+x^2e^y=(e^x+x^2)e^y$

$\Rightarrow$　　$(e^x+x^2)dx=e^{-y}dy$.

Integrating, we obtain $e^x+\dfrac{1}{3}x^3=-e^{-y}+c$, c being an arbitrary constant.

Hence, $e^x+e^{-y}+\dfrac{1}{3}x^3=c$ is the required solution.

Q24. Solve $\left(x^2 - yx^2\right)dy + \left(y^2 + xy^2\right)y\,dx = 0.$

Ans. Given, $\left(x^2 - yx^2\right)dy + \left(y^2 + xy^2\right)y\,dx = 0.$

or $x^2(1-y)dy + y^3(1+x)dx = 0$ or $\dfrac{1+x}{x^2}dx + \dfrac{1-y}{y^3}dy = 0.$

Integrating, we obtain $\displaystyle\int\left(\dfrac{1}{x^2} + \dfrac{1}{x}\right)dx + \int\left(\dfrac{1}{y^3} - \dfrac{1}{y^2}\right)dy = c$

or $\quad -\dfrac{1}{x} + \log x - \dfrac{1}{2y^2} + \dfrac{1}{y} = c$

Hence, $2xy^2\log x - 2y^2 + 2xy - 2cxy^2 - x = 0$ is the required solution.

Q25. Solve $x\dfrac{dy}{dx} - y = \sqrt{x^2 + y^2}.$

Ans. We have $x\dfrac{dy}{dx} - y = \sqrt{x^2 + y^2}.$

The given equation may be written as $\dfrac{dy}{dx} = \dfrac{y + \sqrt{x^2 + y^2}}{x}.$ ...(i)

Put $y = Vx$ so that $\dfrac{dy}{dx} = V + x\dfrac{dV}{dx}.$

Now (i) becomes $V + x\dfrac{dV}{dx} = \dfrac{Vx + \sqrt{x^2 + V^2x^2}}{x} = V + \sqrt{1 + V^2}$

$\Rightarrow \quad x\dfrac{dV}{dx} = \sqrt{1 + V^2} \Rightarrow \dfrac{dV}{\sqrt{1 + V^2}} = \dfrac{dx}{x}.$

Q26. Solve $(x - y)^2\dfrac{dy}{dx} = a^2.$

Ans. We have $(x - y)^2\dfrac{dy}{dx} = a^2.$ ...(i)

Put $x - y = z \Rightarrow 1 - \dfrac{dy}{dx} = \dfrac{dz}{dx} \Rightarrow \dfrac{dy}{dx} = 1 - \dfrac{dz}{dx}$

Using in (i), $z^2\left(1 - \dfrac{dz}{dx}\right) = a^2 \Rightarrow 1 - \dfrac{dz}{dx} = \dfrac{a^2}{z^2}$

$\Rightarrow \dfrac{dz}{dx} = \dfrac{z^2 - a^2}{z^2} \Rightarrow \displaystyle\int\dfrac{z^2\,dz}{z^2 - a^2} = \int dx + c,\ c$ being a constant.

$\Rightarrow x + c = \displaystyle\int\dfrac{z^2 - a^2 + a^2}{z^2 - a^2}dz = \int\left(1 + \dfrac{a^2}{z^2 - a^2}\right)dz$

$= z + a^2 \cdot \dfrac{1}{2a}\log\dfrac{z - a}{z + a},\ z = x - y.$

Hence, $\dfrac{a}{2}\log\dfrac{x - y - a}{x - y + a} - y = c$ is the required solution.

Q27. Solve $(x+y)^2 \dfrac{dy}{dx} = a^2.$

Ans. We have $(x+y)^2 \dfrac{dy}{dx} = a^2.$ ...(i)

Put $x+y = z \Rightarrow 1 + \dfrac{dy}{dx} = \dfrac{dz}{dx}.$ ...(ii)

From (i) and (ii), we obtain $z^2\left(\dfrac{dz}{dx} - 1\right) = a^2$ or $\dfrac{dz}{dx} = \dfrac{a^2}{z^2} + 1 = \dfrac{a^2 + z^2}{z^2}.$

$$\therefore \quad \int \dfrac{z^2 dz}{a^2 + z^2} = \int dx + c \Rightarrow x + c = \int\left(1 - \dfrac{a^2}{a^2 + z^2}\right)dz$$

$$= z - a^2\left(\dfrac{1}{a}\tan^{-1}\dfrac{z}{a}\right) = z - a\,\tan^{-1}\dfrac{z}{a}$$

$$\therefore \quad x + c = x + y - a\tan^{-1}\dfrac{x+y}{a}.$$

Hence, $y = c + a\tan^{-1}\dfrac{x+y}{a}$ is the required solution.

Integrating, we obtain $\log\left[V + \sqrt{1+V^2}\right] = \log x + \log c$

or $V + \sqrt{1+V^2} = cx$ or $\dfrac{y}{x} + \sqrt{1 + \dfrac{y^2}{x^2}} = cx.$

Hence, $y + \sqrt{x^2 + y^2} = c\,x^2$ is the required solution.

Q28. Solve $(x^2 + xy)dy = (x^2 + y^2)dx.$

Ans. We have $(x^2 + xy)dy = (x^2 + y^2)dx.$ $\Rightarrow \dfrac{dy}{dx} = \dfrac{x^2 + y^2}{x^2 + xy}$

$$\Rightarrow V + x\dfrac{dV}{dx} = \dfrac{1+V^2}{1+V} \quad \left(y = Vx, \dfrac{dy}{dx} = V + x\dfrac{dV}{dx}\right)$$

$$\Rightarrow x\dfrac{dV}{dx} = \dfrac{1+V^2}{1+V} - V = \dfrac{1-V}{1+V} \Rightarrow \dfrac{1+V}{1-V}dV = \dfrac{dx}{x}.$$

Integrating, we obtain $\int\dfrac{V+1}{V-1}dV + \int\dfrac{dx}{x} + \log c = 0$

$$\Rightarrow \int\left(1 + \dfrac{2}{V-1}\right)dV + \log x + \log c = 0 \Rightarrow V + 2\log(V-1) + \log cx = 0$$

$$\Rightarrow V + \log\left[cx(V-1)^2\right] = 0, \ V = y/x.$$

Hence, $y + x\log\left[\dfrac{c}{x}(y-x)^2\right] = 0$ is the required solution.

Q29. Solve $x\log x\dfrac{dy}{dx}+y=2\log x.$

Ans. Dividing by x log x, we obtain $\dfrac{dy}{dx}+\dfrac{1}{x\log x}\cdot y=\dfrac{2}{x}.$

Here, $P=\dfrac{1}{x\log x},Q=\dfrac{2}{x}.$

Now, $\int P\,dx=\int\dfrac{dx}{x\log x}=\log\left(\log x\right).$

$\therefore$ I.F. $=e^{\int P\,dx}=e^{\log(\log x)}=\log x.$

Hence, the required solution is

$$y\log x=\int\dfrac{2}{x}\log x\,dx+c=\left(\log x\right)^{2}+c.$$

Q30. Solve $\left(x^{3}+y^{3}\right)dx=\left(x^{2}y+xy^{2}\right)dy.$

Ans. We have $\left(x^{3}+y^{3}\right)dx=\left(x^{2}y+xy^{2}\right)dy.$ $\Rightarrow$ $\dfrac{dy}{dx}=\dfrac{x^{3}+y^{3}}{x^{2}y+xy^{2}}$

$\Rightarrow$ $V+x\dfrac{dV}{dx}=\dfrac{1+V^{3}}{V+V^{2}}$ $\left(y=Vx,\dfrac{dy}{dx}=V+x\dfrac{dV}{dx}\right)$

$\Rightarrow$ $x\dfrac{dV}{dx}=\dfrac{1+V^{3}}{V+V^{2}}-V=\dfrac{1-V^{2}}{V+V^{2}}=\dfrac{(1-V)(1+V)}{V(1+V)}$ $\Rightarrow$ $\dfrac{V\,dV}{(1-V)}=\dfrac{dx}{x}.$

Integrating, we obtain $\int\dfrac{V\,dV}{(V-1)}+\int\dfrac{dx}{x}+\log c=0$

$\Rightarrow$ $\int\left(1+\dfrac{1}{V-1}\right)dV+\log x+\log c=0$ $\Rightarrow$ $V+\log(V-1)+\log x+\log c=0$

$\Rightarrow$ $\dfrac{y}{x}+\log\left[\left(\dfrac{y}{x}-1\right).x.c\right]=0.$

Hence, $y+x\log\left[c(y-x)\right]=0$ is the required solution.

Q31. Solve $\left(4y+3x\right)dy+\left(y-2x\right)dx=0.$

Ans. We have $\dfrac{dy}{dx}=\dfrac{2x-y}{3x+4y}$ or $V+x\dfrac{dV}{dx}=\dfrac{2x-Vx}{3x+4Vx},$ where $y=Vx$

or $x\dfrac{dV}{dx}=\dfrac{2-V}{3+4V}-V=\dfrac{2-4V-4V^{2}}{3+4V}$ or $\int\dfrac{(3+4V)dV}{4V^{2}+4V-2}+\int\dfrac{dx}{x}=0.$ ...(i)

Put $2V^{2}+2V-1=t\Rightarrow\left(4V+2\right)dV=dt.$

Thus (i) becomes

or $\dfrac{1}{2}\int \dfrac{dt}{t} + \int \dfrac{dV}{4V^2 + 4V - 2} + \log x + \log c = 0$

or $\dfrac{1}{2}\log\left(2V^2 + 2V - 1\right) + \int \dfrac{dV}{\left(2V+1\right)^2 - 3} + \log x + \log c = 0$

or $\dfrac{1}{2}\log\left[\dfrac{2y^2}{x^2} + \dfrac{2y}{x} - 1\right] + \dfrac{1}{4\sqrt{3}}\log\dfrac{2V+1-\sqrt{3}}{2V+1+\sqrt{3}} + \log x + \log c = 0$

or $\log c + 2\sqrt{3}\log\left(\dfrac{2y^2 + 2xy - x^2}{x^2}\right) + 4\sqrt{3}\log x = \log\dfrac{2V+1+\sqrt{3}}{2V+1-\sqrt{3}}$

$$\therefore \quad c\left(\dfrac{2y^2 + 2xy - x^2}{x^2}\right)^{2\sqrt{3}} \cdot (x)^{4\sqrt{3}} = \dfrac{2V+1+\sqrt{3}}{2V+1-\sqrt{3}}.$$

Hence, $c\left(2y^2 + 2xy - x^2\right)^{2\sqrt{3}} = \dfrac{\left(\sqrt{3}+1\right)x + 2y}{\left(1-\sqrt{3}\right)x + 2y} \quad \left(\because V = \dfrac{y}{x}\right)$

is the required solution.

Q32. Show that the following equation is exact and then solve it:

$$\left(x + \dfrac{2}{y}\right)dy + y\,dx = 0 \qquad \text{[Dec-2010,Q.No.-1(a)][Dec-2012, Q.No.-1(a)]}$$

Ans. Given equation is $\left(x + \dfrac{2}{y}\right)dy + ydx = 0$

Comparing with Mdx + Ndy = 0, we have

$$M = y \quad , \quad N = x + \dfrac{2}{y}$$

$$\Rightarrow \quad \dfrac{\partial M}{\partial y} = 1 \ , \qquad \dfrac{\partial N}{\partial x} = 1$$

Hence, $\dfrac{\partial M}{\partial y} = \dfrac{\partial N}{\partial x}$

Therefore, given equation is exact.

Now, the solution is $\int Mdx + \int (N \sim x)\, dy = c$

$$\Rightarrow \quad \int ydx + \int \dfrac{2}{y}\, dy = c$$

$$\Rightarrow \quad yx + 2\log y = c \ \text{ is the required solution.}$$

Q33. Solve the following:

(i) $\dfrac{dy}{dx} = \dfrac{x - 2y + 5}{2x + y - 1}.$

Ans. On putting $x = X + h, y = Y + k$, the given equation becomes

$$\dfrac{dY}{dX} = \dfrac{(X+h) - 2(Y+k) + 5}{2(X+h) + (Y+k) - 1} \quad \text{or} \quad \dfrac{dY}{dX} = \dfrac{X - 2Y + (h - 2k + 5)}{2X + Y + (2h + k - 1)} \qquad \text{...(i)}$$

Choose h and k so that $h - 2k + 5 = 0$ and $\quad 2h + k - 1 = 0.$ ...(ii)

From (i) and (ii), we obtain $\dfrac{dY}{dX} = \dfrac{X - 2Y}{2X + Y},$ ...(iii)

which is a homogeneous equation. We substitute $Y = VX$, so that $\dfrac{dY}{dX} = V + X\dfrac{dV}{dX}$. Putting in (iii), we get $V + X\dfrac{dV}{dX} = \dfrac{1 - 2V}{2 + V}$

or $X\dfrac{dV}{dX} = \dfrac{1 - 2V}{2 + V} - V = \dfrac{1 - 4V - V^2}{2 + V}$ or $\displaystyle\int \dfrac{V + 2}{V^2 + 4V - 1} dV + \int \dfrac{dX}{X} = \log c$

or $\dfrac{1}{2}\displaystyle\int \dfrac{dt}{t} + \log X = \log c \qquad \begin{bmatrix} t = V^2 + 4V - 1 \\ \Rightarrow dt = 2(V + 2)dV \end{bmatrix}$

or $\dfrac{1}{2}\log t + \log X = \log c$ or $tX^2 = k, k = c^2$

or $\left(V^2 + 4V - 1\right)X^2 = k$ or $Y^2 + 4XY - X^2 = k.$ ...(iv)

Solving (ii) for h and k, we obtain

$h = -3/5, k = 11/5$ and so $X = x + (3/5), Y = y - (11/5).$

Putting in (iv) and simplifying, the required solution is

$x^2 - y^2 - 4xy + 10x + 2y = a.$

(ii) $\left(3y - 7x + 7\right)dx + \left(7y - 3x + 3\right)dy = 0$

Ans. We have $\dfrac{dy}{dx} = \dfrac{7x - 3y - 7}{7y - 3x + 3}.$ ...(v)

Putting $x = X + h, y = Y + k$ in (v), we obtain

$$\dfrac{dY}{dX} = \dfrac{(7X - 3Y) + (7h - 3k - 7)}{(7Y - 3X) + (7k - 3h + 3)}. \qquad \text{...(vi)}$$

Choose h and k so that $7h - 3k - 7 = 0$ and $7k - 3h + 3 = 0.$ ...(vii)

From (vi) and (vii), $\dfrac{dY}{dX} = \dfrac{7X - 3Y}{7Y - 3X}$ or $V + X\dfrac{dV}{dX} = \dfrac{7 - 3V}{7V - 3},$ where

$Y = VX$

or $X\dfrac{dV}{dX} = \dfrac{7(1-V^2)}{7V-3}$ or $\displaystyle\int\dfrac{(7V-3)dV}{V^2-1} + 7\int\dfrac{dX}{X} = \log c$

or $\dfrac{7}{2}\log(V^2-1) - \dfrac{3}{2}\log\dfrac{V-1}{V+1} + 7\log X = \log c$ or $\left[(V^2-1)^7\left(\dfrac{V+1}{V-1}\right)^3\right]^{1/2} .X^7 = c$

or $(V+1)^5(V-1)^2 X^7 = c$, $V = Y/X$ or $(X+Y)^5(Y-X)^2 = c.$ ...(viii)

Solving (vii) for h and k, we get $h = 1, k = 0.$

$\therefore\ x = X + h = X + 1 \Rightarrow X = x - 1, y = Y + k = Y.$

Putting in (viii), $(x+y-1)^5(y-x+1)^2 = c.$ This is the required solution.

Q34. Obtain the general solution of the first order ODE $2y'-4y = 16e^x$

Ans. We can see that given ODE is a linear non-homogeneous first order ODE. Rewriting the equation in the standard form, we get $y' - 2y = 8e^x$

We note that $p(x) = -2$. So the integrating factor is

$v(x) = \exp\left[-\int 2dx\right] = \exp(-2x)$

Multiplying the given ODE (in standard form) by e^{-2x}, we get

$e^{-2x}y' - 2ye^{-2x} = 8e^{-x}$ or $\dfrac{d}{dx}(ye^{-2x}) = 8e^{-x}$ or $d[ye^{-2x}] = 8e^{-x}dx$

Integrating both sides yields $ye^{-2x} = -8e^{-x} + C$

Hence, the general solution is $y = -8e^x + Ce^{2x}$

Thus, the required solutions are $x = a\sin(\omega t + \delta)$ and $x = a\cos(\omega t + \delta)$

Q35. Solve $\dfrac{dy}{dx} + y\sec x = \tan x.$

Ans. Comparing with general equation $\dfrac{dy}{dx} + Py = Q,$

We get $P = \sec x, Q = \tan x.$

Now $\displaystyle\int P\,dx = \int\sec x\,dx = \log(\sec x + \tan x).$

We know I.F.$= e^{\int P\,dx} = e^{\log(\sec x + \tan x)} = \sec x + \tan x.$

The solution is given by

$y(\sec x + \tan x) = \displaystyle\int\tan x(\sec x + \tan x)dx + c = \int\tan x\sec x\,dx + \int\tan^2 x\,dx + c$

$= \sec x + \displaystyle\int(\sec^2 x - 1)dx + c$

Hence, $y(\sec x + \tan x) = \sec x + \tan x - x + c$ is the required solution.

Q36. Solve $(x+1)\dfrac{dy}{dx} - ny = e^x(x+1)^{n+1}$

Ans. The given equation can be written as $\dfrac{dy}{dx} - \dfrac{n}{x+1}y = e^x(x+1)^n$.

Now $\int P\,dx = -n\int \dfrac{dx}{x+1} = -n\log(x+1) = \log(x+1)^{-n}$.

$\therefore$ I.F. $= e^{\int P\,dx} = (x+1)^{-n}$. The solution is given by

$$y(x+1)^{-n} = \int e^x(x+1)^n(x+1)^{-n}\,dx + c = e^x + c$$

Hence, $y = (e^x + c)(x+1)^n$ is the required solution.

Q37. Show that the ODE $(4x^3 + 6e^y + 2y\cos 2x)dx + (3y^2 + 6xe^y + \sin 2x)dy = 0$ **is an exact equation and hence solve it.**   **[June-2013,Q.No.-1(b)]**

Ans. Given equation is $(4x^3 + 6e^y + 2y\cos 2x)dx + (3y^2 + 6xe^y + \sin 2x)dy = 0$

Comparing given equation with the equation Mdx + Ndy = 0,

We have $M = 4x^3 + 6e^y + 2y\cos 2x$ and $N = 3y^2 + 6xe^y + \sin 2x$

Now $\dfrac{\partial M}{\partial y} = 6e^y + 2\cos 2x$ and $\dfrac{\partial N}{\partial x} = 6e^y + 2\cos 2x$

$\Rightarrow \qquad \dfrac{\partial M}{\partial y} = \dfrac{\partial N}{\partial x}$

Hence, given equation is an exact equation

Now, its solution is $\int M\,dx + \int (N \sim x)\,dy = c$

$\Rightarrow \quad \int (4x^3 + 6e^y + 2y\cos 2x)\,dx + \int (3y^2)\,dy = c$

$\Rightarrow \qquad x^4 + 6xe^y + y\sin 2x + y^3 = c$ is the required solution.

The main aim of GPH book is to provide knowledge as well as good marks in exams.

$$\Diamond \; \Diamond \; \Diamond$$

Chapter

2

Second Order Ordinary Differential Equations with Constant Coefficients

An Overview

A second order linear homogeneous ordinary differential equation with constant coefficients can be expressed as

$$a_2 y'' + a_1 y' + a_0 y = 0$$

This equation implies that the solution is a function whose derivatives keep the same form as the function itself and do not explicitly contain the independent variable x, since constant coefficients are not capable of correcting any irregular formats or extra variables. An elementary function which satisfies this restriction is the exponential function $e^{\lambda x}$.

Substitute the exponential function $e^{\lambda x}$ into the above differential equation, the characteristic equation of this differential equation is obtained

$$a_2 \lambda^2 + a_1 \lambda + a_0 = 0$$

This characteristic equation has two roots λ_1 and λ_2.

Linearly Independent solutions and the Wronskian: We know that a second order linear ODE can be written as

$$\frac{d^2 y}{dx^2} + p_1(x)\frac{dy}{dx} + p_0(x)y = g(x) \qquad \text{...(i)}$$

the function $g(x)$ is termed as the forcing function and $p_1(x)$ and $p_0(x)$ are coefficient functions. These are continuous over the interval where the solution exists.

if y_1 and y_2 are linearly independent solutions of the homogeneous equation $y'' + p_1(x)y' + p_0(x)y = 0$ ...(ii)

then their linear combination $y = C_1 y_1 + C_2 y_2$ ...(iii)

where C_1 and C_2 are arbitrary constants, is a general solution of Eq. (ii). For example, we know that $y_1 = \sin\omega t$ and $y_2 = \cos\omega t$ are linearly independent solutions of the ODE for an undamped harmonic oscillator: $\frac{d^2 y}{dt^2} + \omega^2 y = 0$. So the general solution of this equation is $y(t) = C_1 \sin\omega t + C_2 \cos\omega t$

We say that two solutions y_1 and y_2 are linearly independent on an interval if the identity $C_1 y_1 + C_2 y_2 = 0$ ...(iv)

is satisfied only when $C_1 = C_2 = 0$. For, if C_1 and C_2 were non-zero constants, Eq. (iv) would yield $y_2/y_1 = $ constant, i.e. y_1 and y_2 would be proportional on some interval. Then, by definition, y_1 and y_2 would be linearly dependent functions on that interval. In other words, linear independence of y_1 and y_2 means that the ratio y_2/y_1 is not a constant. This implies that the differential of this ratio $\dfrac{y'_2 y_1 - y'_1 y_2}{y_1^2}$ ...(v)

is not identically equal to zero. Therefore, we can write the condition of linear independence of two solutions y_1 and y_2 as

$$W(y_1, y_2) = \begin{vmatrix} y_1 & y_2 \\ y'_1 & y'_2 \end{vmatrix} \neq 0 \qquad \text{...(vi)}$$

The determinant $W(y_1, y_2)$ is called the Wronski determinant or the Wronskian of the given differential equation. We may, therefore, conclude that two solutions y_1 and y_2 are linearly independent on an interval [a, b], if and only if, their Wronskian is non-zero for $a \leq x \leq b$.

For a harmonic oscillator, this means that

$$W(x) = \begin{vmatrix} \sin\omega t & \cos\omega t \\ \omega\cos\omega t & -\omega\sin\omega t \end{vmatrix} = -\omega$$

showing that $\sin\omega t$ and $\cos\omega t$ are linearly independent. We also say that y_1 and y_2 are linearly dependent solutions on an interval I, if and only if their Wronskian is zero for some $x = x_0$ in I.

Particular integral and complementary function: We know that the equation of motion of a forced damped harmonic oscillator is

$$my'' + \gamma y' + ky = F_0\cos\omega t$$

which is usually rewritten as $y'' + 2by' + \omega_0^2 y = f_0\cos\omega t$ ...(vii)

where $2b = \gamma/m$, $\omega_0^2 = k/m$ and $f_0 = F_0/m$.

Physically, the actual motion of this system is a sum of two oscillations: one of the frequency of damped oscillations and the other of the frequency of the driving force. Mathematically, we express it as

$$y(t) = y_1 + y_2 \qquad\qquad ...(viii)$$

where y_1 is a solution of the homogeneous equation

$$y_1'' + 2by_1' + \omega_0^2 y_1 = 0 \qquad\qquad ...(xi)$$

On substituting Eq. (viii) in Eq. (vii) and using Eq. (ix) in the resultant expression,   we   will   find   that y_2 satisfies   the   equation

$$y_2'' + 2by_2' + \omega_0^2 y_2 = f_0\cos\omega t$$

In the language of mathematics, y_1 is called the complementary function and y_2 is called the particular integral. We can write the general solution of a second order non-homogeneous linear differential equation with constant coefficients as the sum of a complementary function and the particular integral: $y(x) = y_c(x) + y_p(x)$ ...(x)

We know that the solution of a second order differential equation consists only two arbitrary constants. This implies that the particular integral will not contain any arbitrary constant.

Homogeneous   linear   equations   with   constant   coefficients: A homogeneous   linear   ordinary   differential   equation   with   constant coefficients can be expressed in the form

$$ay'' + by' + cy = 0 \qquad\qquad ...(xi)$$

where a, b and c are real constants.

                    Mathematical Methods in Physics-II [PHE-05]

We know that the solution of the first order homogeneous linear ordinary differential equation $(y'+y=0)$ is an exponential function of the form

$$y = A\exp(-kx)$$

Let us, therefore, seek a solution of Eq.(xi) of the form

$$y = A\exp(mx) \qquad\qquad ...(xii)$$

where dimensions of m are inverse of those of x. This ensures that the power of exponential is dimensionless.

Substituting this and its derivatives $y' = Am\exp(mx)$

and $y'' = Am^2\exp(mx)$ in Eq. (11), we will obtain

$$\left(am^2 + bm + c\right)A\exp(mx) = 0$$

Since $A\exp(mx)$ is finite, this equation will be satisfied only if

$$am^2 + bm + c = 0 \qquad\qquad ...(xiii)$$

This quadratic equation is called the characteristic equation (or auxiliary equation). Its roots are

$$m_1 = \frac{-b+\sqrt{b^2-4ac}}{2a} \quad \text{and} \quad m_2 = \frac{-b-\sqrt{b^2-4ac}}{2a}$$

For example, the auxiliary equation for $y''+5y'-7y=0$ is $m^2+5m-7=0$

so we will agree that $y_1(x) = A\exp(m_1x)$ $\qquad\qquad$ ...(xiv)

and $y_2(x) = A\exp(m_2x)$ $\qquad\qquad$ ...(xv)

are solutions of Eq. (xi). Using the principle of superposition, we can write its most general solution as

$$y(x) = C_1\exp(m_1x) + C_2\exp(m_2x) \qquad\qquad ...(xvi)$$

for a suitable choice of constants C_1 and C_2 determined by initial or boundary conditions.

The Wronskian of these solutions is

$$W(x) = \begin{vmatrix} A\exp(m_1x) & A\exp(m_2x) \\ m_1A\exp(m_1x) & m_2A\exp(m_2x) \end{vmatrix}$$

$$= (m_2 - m_1)B\exp[(m_1 + m_2)x] \qquad\qquad ...(xvii)$$

where B is a constant. This shows that for $m_1 \neq m_2$, the solutions will be linearly independent.

We must have noticed that the process of solving a homogeneous linear second order ordinary differential equation with constant coefficients using an exponential function as a solution reduces for finding the roots of a quadratic equation. The roots of this equation can be

- real and distinct for $b^2 - 4ac > 0$ or $b^2 > 4ac$

- real and equal when $b^2 - 4ac = 0$, or $b^2 = 4ac$ and

- complex conjugate for $b^2 - 4ac < 0$ or $b^2 < 4ac$

Distinct Real Roots: For distinct real roots, $\exp(m_1 x)$, and $\exp(m_2 x)$ are linearly independent and the general solution is given by
$y = C_1 \exp(m_1 x) + C_2 \exp(m_2 x)$

$$= \exp\left[-\left(\frac{bx}{2a}\right)\right]\left[C_1 \exp(\alpha x) + C_2 \exp(-\alpha x)\right] \qquad \text{...(xviii)}$$

Where $\alpha = \dfrac{\sqrt{b^2 - 4ac}}{2a}$

The constants C_1 and C_2 can be determined by using given initial and boundary conditions.

Repeated Real Roots: When a second order differential equation has two equal roots, we obtain the correct form of the second solution by assuming that

$$y_2 = u(x)\exp(mx) \qquad \text{...(xix)}$$

is a root of the auxiliary equation eq.(xiii). Differentiating eq. (xix) with respect to x, we get $y_2' = u'\exp(mx) + mu\exp(mx)$

and $y_2'' = u''e^{mx} + 2mu'e^{mx} + m^2 u e^{mx}$

Substituting these in Eq. (xi), we have

$$\left(am^2 + bm + c\right)u(x)e^{mx} + (2ma + b)e^{mx}u' + ae^{mx}u'' = 0$$

The first term in this expression vanishes in view of Eq. (xiii). The coefficient of u' is zero since m = − b/2a in this case. Hence, the above expression simplifies to $\exp(mx)au'' = 0$

Multiplying by exp(-mx) and integrating, we will get u' = K

where K is an arbitrary constant of integration. Integration again, we will get $u = Kx + C$

Hence, the desired solution is $y_2 = xe^{mx} = xe^{-bx/2a}$ ...(xx) where the arbitrary constants K and C have been dropped (since we are seeking only a second linearly independent solution). Hence, the general solution of a second order differential equation, when auxiliary equation has repeated real roots, is $y(x) = C_1 e^{-bx/2a} + C_2 x e^{-bx/2a}$

$$= (C_1 + C_2 x)\exp\left(-\frac{bx}{2a}\right) \qquad \qquad \text{...(xxi)}$$

To test the $e^{-bx/2a}$ and $xe^{-bx/2a}$ are linearly independent, we can compute their Wronskian

$$W(x) = \begin{vmatrix} \exp\left(-\dfrac{bx}{2a}\right) & x\exp\left(-\dfrac{bx}{2a}\right) \\[2ex] -\dfrac{b}{2a}\exp\left(-\dfrac{bx}{2a}\right) & -\dfrac{b}{2a}x\exp\left(-\dfrac{bx}{2a}\right) + \exp\left(-\dfrac{bx}{2a}\right) \end{vmatrix}$$

$$= e^{-(bx/a)} > 0 \text{ for } a \le x \le b \qquad \qquad \text{...(xxii)}$$

It implies that $e^{-(bx/a)}$ and $xe^{-bx/2a}$ are acceptable solutions. The arbitrary constants C_1 and C_2 occurring in Eq.(xxi) can be determined using specified initial or boundary conditions. We may, therefore, conclude as follows:

When the auxiliary equation for a second order ODE with constant coefficients has repeated real roots $(m_1 = m_2 = m)$, the general solution is given by $y = (C_1 + C_2 x)\exp(mx)$ where C_1 and C_2 are arbitrary constants.

Complex Roots: We know that complex roots of a real polynomial equation always occur in conjugate pairs. That is, if $m_1 = \alpha + i\beta$ is one of the roots, then $m_2 = \alpha - i\beta$ is also a root.

The general solution as a linear combination of two linearly independent solutions as $y = A\exp(m_1 x) + B\exp(m_2 x)$

$$= Ae^{(\alpha + i\beta)x} + Be^{(\alpha - i\beta)x} = e^{\alpha x}\left(Ae^{i\beta x} + Be^{-i\beta x}\right) \qquad \text{...(xxiii)}$$

we will note that this solution is complex. To express it as a real solution, we use Euler's formula: $e^{\pm i\theta} = \cos\theta \pm i\sin\theta$ ...(xxiv)

This gives $y = e^{\alpha x}[A(\cos\beta x + i\sin\beta x) + B(\cos\beta x - i\sin\beta x)]$

$$= e^{\alpha x}[(A + B)\cos\beta x + (A - B)i\sin\beta x]$$

By letting $C_1 = A + B$ and $C_2 = (A - B)i$, we can write

$$y = e^{\alpha x}(C_1 \cos\beta x + C_2 \sin\beta x) \qquad \qquad \text{...(xxv)}$$

Putting $C_1 = C\cos\phi$ and $C_2 = C\sin\phi$, we can rewrite Eq.(xxv) as

$$y = Ce^{\alpha x}\cos(\beta x - \phi)$$

where C and ϕ are arbitrary constants. These are related to C_1 and C_2 by

$$C = \sqrt{C_1^2 + C_2^2} \quad \text{and} \quad \tan\phi = \frac{C_2}{C_1}$$

We will note that when the roots of characteristic equation are complex, they generate solutions of the form of a product of an exponential and a trigonometric function. Therefore, we may conclude as follows:

If the characteristic equation of a second order ODE has complex roots of the form $m = \alpha \pm i\beta$, the general solution is of the form

$$y = Ce^{\alpha x}\cos(\beta x - \phi) \qquad \qquad \text{...(xxvi)}$$

Note: We know that the differential equation governing the motion of an undamped spring-mass system is $\dfrac{d^2x}{dt^2} + \omega_0^2 x = 0$ where $\omega_0^2 = k/m$. The characteristic equation for this case is $m^2 + \omega_0^2 = 0$

which has roots $m_1 = i\omega_0$ and $m_2 = -i\omega_0$.

Hence, the general solution is $x(t) = C_1\cos\omega_0 t + C_2\sin\omega_0 t$.

Non-homogeneous linear equations with constant coefficients: A non-homogeneous linear ordinary differential equation with constant coefficients can be expressed in the form $ay'' + by' + cy = g(x)$ where a, b and c are real constants.

It should be noted that the "complementary solution" is never actually a solution of the given non-homogeneous equation. It is merely taken from the corresponding homogeneous equation as a component that, when coupled with a particular solution, gives us the general solution of a non-homogeneous linear equation. On the other hand, the particular solution is necessarily always a solution of the said non-homogeneous equation. Indeed, in a slightly different context, it must be a "particular" solution of a certain initial value problem that contains the given equation and whatever initial conditions that would result in $C_1 = C_2 = 0$.

In the case of non-homogeneous equations with constant coefficients, the complementary solution can be easily found from the roots of the characteristic polynomial.

Therefore, the only task remaining is to find the particular solution Y, which is any one function that satisfies the given non-homogeneous equation. There are two general approaches to find Y:

(a) The Method of Undetermined Multipliers:

The Method of Undetermined Coefficients (sometimes referred to as the method of Judicious Guessing) is a systematic way to determine the general form/type of the particular solution $Y(x)$ based on the non-homogeneous term $g(x)$ in the given equation. The basic idea of this method is to first construct the general form of the particular integral from the forcing function. Then we determine coefficients for y_p that allow it to satisfy the given differential equation.

We tabulate below the form of $y_P(x)$ depending on the form of $g(x)$:

Table 2.1

Form of forcing function	Nature of the root of auxiliary equation	Form of particular integral
$A\, e^{kx}$	When k is not a root k is single root k is double root	$C\, e^{kx}$ $C\, x\, e^{kx}$ $C\, x^2 e^{kx}$
Polynomial $A\, x^n\, (n = 0,1,...)$	$k = 0$ is not a root $k = 0$ is single root $k = 0$ is double root	$C_0 + C_1 x + C_2 x^2 + ...$ $x(C_0 + C_1 x + ...)$ $x^2(C_0 + C_1 x + C_2 x^2 + ..)$
$A \cos kx$ $A \sin kx$	ik is not a root ik is a single root	$C \cos kx + D \sin kx$ $x(C \cos kx + D \sin kx)$

From the table, we will note that if $g(x)$ is of the form given in column 1, the corresponding PI will be of the form given in column 3. The form of PI will also be determined by the nature of the root of the auxiliary equation as given in column 2. Note also that if a term in $g(x)$ is a solution of the homogeneous equation corresponding to the given non-homogeneous ODE, the form of y_p is modified as follows: y_p is multiplied by x or x^2 depending on whether root of the auxiliary equation is a single or a double root. This is termed the Modification rule.

In the method of undetermined multipliers, the particular integral is constructed from the forcing function. The arbitrary constant (s) is (are) determined by solving equations obtained on comparing coefficients of like terms on the two sides of the given equation.

(b) The Method of Variation of Parameters:
The solution of $y'' + Py' + Qy = R$ by the method of variation of the parameters is given by the following steps:

Step 1: Find the C.F., i.e. $c_1 y_1 + c_2 y_2$ of the given equation.

Step 2: Find the Wronskian of the solutions y_1 and y_2:

$$W = \begin{vmatrix} y_1 & y_2 \\ y_1' & y_2' \end{vmatrix}$$

Step 3: P.I. $= u_1 y_1 + u_2 y_2$, where u_1 and u_2 are given by

$$u_1' = -\frac{y_2 R}{W}, \quad u_2' = \frac{y_1 R}{W} \text{ or } u_1 - \int \frac{y_2 R}{W} dx, \; u_2 = \int \frac{y_1 R}{W} dx$$

Step 4: The complete solution of $y'' + Py' + Qy = R$ is given by

$$y = C.F + P.I.$$

Solved Practical Problems

Q1. The solutions of the equation $y'' + 4y = 0$ are given by $y_1 = \sin 2x$ and $y_2 = \cos 2x$. Are these solutions linearly independent?

Ans. The Wronskian for these functions is

$$W(x) = \begin{vmatrix} \sin 2x & \cos 2x \\ 2\cos 2x & -2\sin 2x \end{vmatrix} = -2\sin^2 2x - 2\cos^2 2x = -2$$

Since, $W(x) \neq 0$ for all x, the functions sin2x and cos2x are linearly independent.

Q2. Solve: $\dfrac{d^2 y}{dx^2} + 4\dfrac{dy}{dx} + 4y = 0$ 　　　　　　　　[June-2010,Q.No.-1(c)]

Ans. Given, $\dfrac{d^2 y}{dx^2} + 4\dfrac{dy}{dx} + 4y = 0$

Auxiliary equation will be $m^2 + 4m + 4 = 0$ or $m^2 + 2m + 2m + 4 = 0$ or $m(m+2) + 2(m+2) = 0$

or $(m+2)(m+2) = 0 \Rightarrow m = -2, -2$

Hence, C.F. $= (c_1 + c_2 x) e^{-2x}$

Since, R.H.S of given equation is zero.

Therefore, its P.I. $= 0$

Since, $y = C.F. + P.I. \Rightarrow y = (c_1 + c_2 x) e^{-2x}$ is the required solution of given equation.

Q3. Solve by using variation of parameters:

$$\frac{d^2 y}{dx^2} - 2\frac{dy}{dx} = e^x \sin x.$$

Ans. To solve this we follow the following steps:

Step 1: The auxiliary equation is $m^2 - 2m = 0$ or $m = 0, 2$.

$$\therefore \; C.F. = c_1 e^{0x} + c_2 e^{2x} = c_1 + c_2 e^{2x}.$$

Step 2: Let $y_1 = 1$, $y_2 = e^{2x}$.

Their Wronskian is $W = \begin{vmatrix} y_1, & y_2 \\ y_1', & y_2' \end{vmatrix} = \begin{vmatrix} 1 & e^{2x} \\ 0 & 2e^{2x} \end{vmatrix} = 2e^{2x} \neq 0.$

Step 3. $P.I. = u_1 y_1 + u_2 y_2$, where

$$u_1 = -\int \frac{y_2 R}{W} dx = -\frac{1}{2}\int \frac{e^{2x}.e^x \sin x\, dx}{e^{2x}} = -\frac{1}{2}\int e^x \sin x\, dx,$$

Q4. **Solve the initial value problem** $y'' + 6y' + 9y = 0;$ $y(0) = 2$ **and** $y'(0) = 1$

Ans. The auxiliary equation corresponding to the given ODE is

$$m^2 + 6m + 9 = 0$$

which has a double root $m = -3$.

Hence, the general solution is $y(x) = (C_1 + C_2 x)e^{-3x}$ ...(i)

The condition y (0) = 2 gives $2 = C_1$ ...(ii)

Differentiate (i) with respect to x gives $\dfrac{dy}{dx} = C_2 e^{-3x} - 3(C_1 + C_2 x)e^{-3x}$

Using the condition $\dfrac{dy(0)}{dx} = 1$, we get $1 = C_2 - 3C_1$

or $C_2 = 1 + 3C_1 = 1 + 6 = 7$ ...(iii)

Hence, the desired solution is $y(x) = (2 + 7x)e^{-3x}$.

Q5. **Solve the equation** $y'' + 3y' + 2y = 0$ **subject to the initial conditions** $y(0) = 1$ **and** $y'(0) = 2.$

Ans. Given $y'' + 3y' + 2y = 0$ subject to the initial conditions y(0) = 1 and y'(0) = 2.

In this case, the auxiliary equation is $m^2 + 3m + 2 = 0$ which has roots $m = -1$ and $m = -2$. Therefore, the general solution is

$$y = C_1 e^{-x} + C_2 e^{-2x}$$ ...(i)

To determine C_1 and C_2, we first use the condition at x = 0, y = 1. This gives $1 = C_1 + C_2$ ...(ii)

Further, since $y' = -C_1 e^{-x} - 2C_2 e^{-2x}$

we find that $y'(0) = 2 = -C_1 - 2C_2$ ...(iii)

We can readily solve (ii) and (iii) for C_1 and C_2 to obtain $C_1 = 4$ and $C_2 = -3$. Hence, the desired particular solution is $y = 4e^{-x} - 3e^{-2x}$.

Q6. **Find the particular solution of**

$$\frac{d^2y}{dx^2}+3\frac{dy}{dx}=4\sin x.$$

[Dec-2012,Q.No.-1(e)]

Ans. Given equation is $\dfrac{d^2y}{dx^2}+3\dfrac{dy}{dx}=4\sin x$ ...(1)

Let, particular solution of given equation is

$$Y_p = A\sin x + B\cos x$$

$$\Rightarrow \qquad \frac{dY_p}{dx} = A\cos x - B\sin x \qquad\qquad ...(i)$$

and $\dfrac{d^2Y_p}{dx^2} = -A\sin x - B\cos x$ ...(ii)

Now putting (i) and (ii) in equation (1), we get

$$-A\sin x - B\cos x + 3A\cos x - 3B\sin x = 4\sin x$$

or $\sin x(-A-3B)+\cos x(3A-B)=4\sin x$

Comparing the coefficient of sinx and cosx, we get

$$-A-3B=4 \quad \text{and} \quad 3A-B=0$$

Hence, we find $A = \dfrac{-2}{5}$ and $B = \dfrac{-6}{5}$

Since, $Y_p = A\sin x + B\cos x$

Hence, particular solution is $\dfrac{-2}{5}\sin x - \dfrac{6}{5}\cos x$

Q7. **Consider a spring-mass system, which is damped by a viscous force which can be modelled so that it is linearly proportional to velocity. What differential equation describes its motion and what are its acceptable solutions?**

Ans. We know that viscous force opposes motion. Hence, the differential equation describing the motion of a damped spring-mass system is

$$M\frac{d^2x}{dt^2}+\gamma\frac{dx}{dt}+kx=0 \quad \text{or} \quad \frac{d^2x}{dt^2}+2b\frac{dx}{dt}+\omega_0^2x=0 \qquad ...(i)$$

where $2b = \gamma/M$ and $\omega_0^2 = k/M$

The characteristic equation as $m^2+2bm+\omega_0^2=0$ which has roots $m_1=-b+\sqrt{b^2-\omega_0^2}$ and $m_2=-b-\sqrt{b^2-\omega_0^2}$. These roots depend on damping and determine the motion of the oscillator. Depending on the value of $\left(b^2 - \omega_0^2\right)^{1/2}$, we have three possibilities.

Case 1:   If $b > \omega_0$, $\sqrt{b^2 - \omega_0^2}$ is positive and we have two real distinct roots.

Case 2:   If $b = \omega_0$, $b^2 - \omega_0^2 = 0$ and we have real repeated roots.

Case 3:   If $b < \omega_0$, $b^2 - \omega_0^2$ is negative and $\sqrt{b^2 - \omega_0^2}$ is imaginary, i.e. we have a complex conjugate pair of roots.

These cases are as follows:

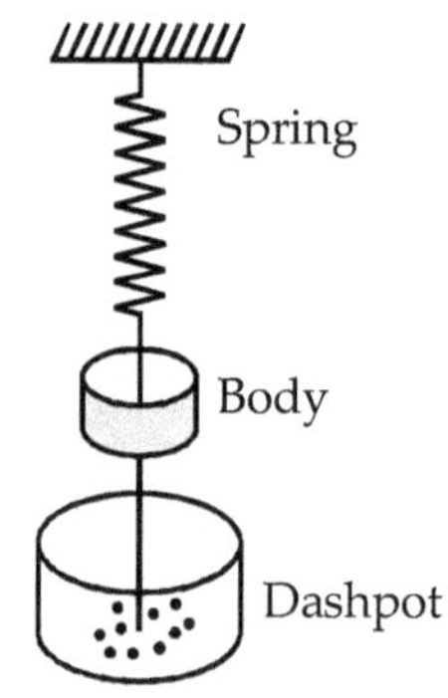

Fig. 2.2: A damped spring-mass system

Case 1:   When the roots are real and distinct, the system is said to be heavily damped and the general solution of Eq.(i) is given by

$$x(t) = \exp(-bt)\left[C_1 \exp(\beta t) + C_2 \exp(-\beta t)\right] \qquad \ldots(ii)$$

where $\beta = \sqrt{b^2 - \omega_0^2}$.

This represents non-oscillatory behaviour. The system is said to be heavily damped and such a motion is called dead beat.

Case 2:   When we have repeated real roots, the general solution of Eq. (i) is given by $x(t) = (C_1 + C_2 t)\exp(-bt)$ $\qquad \ldots(iii)$

Note that here C_1 has dimensions of length and C_2 those of velocity. As before, these constants can be determined by specifying initial conditions. We can easily verify that $C_1 = 0$ and $C_2 = v_0$ so that the complete solution is

$$x(t) = v_0 t \exp(-bt) \qquad \ldots(iv)$$

Such a system is said to be critically damped.

Case 3:   When the roots are imaginary, let us write

$\sqrt{b^2 - \omega_0^2} = \sqrt{-1}\left(\omega_0^2 - b^2\right)^{1/2} = i\omega_d$ where $i = \sqrt{-1}$ and $\omega_d = \sqrt{\omega_0^2 - b^2}$ is a real positive quantity. Hence, the displacement is given by

$$x(t) = \exp(-bt)\left[C_1 \exp(i\omega_d t) + C_2 \exp(-i\omega_d t)\right]$$

$$= C\exp(-bt)\cos(\omega_d t + \phi) \qquad \qquad \text{...(v)}$$

where $C = \sqrt{C_1^2 + C_2^2}$ and $\phi = \cos^{-1}\left(\dfrac{C_1 + C_2}{2\sqrt{C_1 C_2}}\right)$.

We will note that Eq. (v) represents oscillatory motion whose amplitude decreases exponentially at a rate governed by b. Such a system is said to be weakly damped.

Q8.　Determine the particular integral of $y'' + 3y' + 2y = \exp(2x)$.

Ans. Since the driving function is exp(2x), we assume the PI to be of the form $y_p = A\exp(2x)$. We substitute y_p and its derivatives $y' = 2A\exp(2x)$

And $y'' = 4A\exp(2x)$ in the given equation and solve for A. This gives

$$A = \frac{1}{12}.$$

Thus, $y_p = \dfrac{1}{12}\exp(2x)$ is a PI of the given equation.

Q9.　Find the PI of the equation $y'' - y = x + \dfrac{x^2}{2}$.

Ans. Assume that the PI is of the form $y_p = C_0 + C_1 x + C_2 x^2$ 　　　　...(i)

Substituting it and its second derivative $\dfrac{d^2 y_p}{dx^2} = 2C_2$

in the given ODE, we would get $2C_2 - \left(C_0 + C_1 x + C_2 x^2\right) = x + \dfrac{x^2}{2}$ 　　...(ii)

From (i) and (ii), we have $C_0 = -1, C_1 = -1$ and $C_2 = -\dfrac{1}{2}$.

Therefore, $y_p(x) = -\dfrac{x^2}{2} - x - 1$

Q10. Find the general solutions of the following differential equations:

(i)　$y'' + y = x^2$

Ans. The solution of the homogeneous equation $\dfrac{d^2 y}{dx^2} + y = 0$ is found to be

$$y_c(x) = C_1 \cos x + C_2 \sin x$$

A particular integral is assumed to have the form $y_p(x) = Ax^2 + Bx + C$

This is substituted into the original differential equation to give

$$2A + Ax^2 + Bx + C = x^2$$

Equating coefficients of the various powers of x, we have

Coefficient of x^0: $2A + C = 0$

Coefficient of x^1: $B = 0$

Coefficient of x^2: $A = 1$

These equations are solved simultaneously to give the particular solution

$$y_p(x) = x^2 - 2.$$

Finally, the general solution is $y(x) = y_c(x) + y_p(x)$
$$= C_1 \cos x + C_2 \sin x + x^2 - 2.$$

(ii) $y'' + 4y = 3\cos x$

Ans. The solution of the corresponding homogeneous equation $y'' + 4y = 0$ which has root $\pm 2i$, is $y_c = C_1 \sin 2x + C_2 \cos 2x$.

To find a particular solution of the given equation, we assume that the general from of y_p is $y_p = A \sin x + B \cos x$

Substituting y_p and y''_p into the given differential equation, we obtain

$$(-A \sin x - B \cos x) + 4(A \sin x + B \cos x) = 3 \cos x$$

Expanding and collecting like terms yields $3A = 0$, and $3B = 3$ which has the solution $A = 0$ and $B = 1$.

Hence, $y_p = \cos x$ and the general solution is

$$y = C_1 \sin 2x + C_2 \cos 2x + \cos x.$$

Q11. Solve $\dfrac{d^2y}{dx^2} - 2\dfrac{dy}{dx} + y = 0$ **[Dec-2010,Q.No.-1(f)]**

Ans. Given, $\dfrac{d^2y}{dx^2} - 2\dfrac{dy}{dx} + y = 0$

Auxiliary equation will be $m^2 - 2m + 1 = 0$

$$\Rightarrow \quad m = \frac{2 \pm \sqrt{4-4}}{2} \quad \Rightarrow \quad m = \frac{2}{2} \pm 0 \quad \Rightarrow \quad m = 1, 1$$

$\Rightarrow$ Complementary function, C.F. $=(c_1 + c_2 x)e^x$

Since, R.H.S of given equation is zero.

Therefore, its P.I. $= 0$

Since, $y = $ C.F.$+$P.I. $\Rightarrow y = (c_1 + c_2 x)e^x$ is the required solution.

Q12. Find the general solution of the differential equation

$$y'' + 4y = 2\sin 2x$$

Ans. The solution of the homogeneous equation is

$$y_c(x) = C_1 \cos 2x + C_2 \sin 2x$$

Since, the forcing function is itself a solution of the corresponding homogeneous equation, using the modification rule, we assume a solution of the form $y_p(x) = Ax\cos 2x + Bx\sin 2x$

Substituting this into the original differential equation, we get

$$-2A\sin 2x + 2B\cos 2x - 2A\sin 2x + 2B\cos 2x - 4Ax\cos 2x$$

$$-4Bx\sin 2x + 4Ax\cos 2x + 4Bx\sin 2x = 2\sin 2x$$

Equating coefficients of different trigonometric functions, we get

coefficient of sin 2x: $-2A - 2A = 2$

coefficient of cos 2x: $2B + 2B = 0$

coefficient of x sin 2x: $-4B + 4B = 0$

coefficient of x cos 2x: $-4A + 4A = 0$

These equations require that $A = -\dfrac{1}{2}$ and $B = 0$.

Thus, $y_p(x) = -\dfrac{1}{2}x\cos 2x$.

A general solution is then $y(x) = y_c(x) + y_p(x)$

$$= C_1 \cos 2x + C_2 \sin 2x - \frac{1}{2}x\cos 2x$$

Q13. A heavily damped oscillator in its equilibrium position is suddenly kicked so that at t = 0, x = 0 and $\dfrac{dx}{dt} = v_0$. Compute the particular solution and interpret the resulting expression for displacement.

Ans. Here, the particular solution is

$$x(t) = \exp(-bt)\left[C_1 \exp(\beta t) + C_2 \exp(-\beta t)\right] \qquad \qquad ...(i)$$

At $t = 0$, $x = 0$. This gives $0 = C_1 + C_2$ or $C_1 = -C_2$

Differentiate the given expression with respect to time. The result is

$$\frac{dx}{dt} = -b\exp(-bt)\left[C_1\exp(\beta t) + C_2\exp(-\beta t)\right]$$

$$+\exp(-bt)\left[\beta C_1\exp(\beta t) - \beta C_2\exp(-\beta t)\right]$$

Using the condition $\dfrac{dx(0)}{dt} = v_0$, we find that

$$v_0 = -b\left(C_1 + C_2\right) + \beta\left(C_1 - C_2\right) \quad \text{or} \quad C_1 = \frac{v_0}{2\beta} = -C_2$$

Hence, $x(t) = \dfrac{v_0}{2\beta}\exp(-bt)\left[\exp(\beta t) - \exp(-\beta t)\right] = \dfrac{v_0}{\beta}\exp(-bt)\sinh(\beta t)$

This shows that the resultant motion of a heavily damped oscillator is determined by the interplay of a decaying exponential and a hyperbolic function.

Q14. The motion of a damped harmonic oscillator is described by the equation $m\dfrac{d^2x}{dt^2} + \gamma\dfrac{dx}{dt} + kx = F_0\cos\omega t$. Obtain the particular integral.

Ans. The given differential equation is $m\ddot{x} + \gamma\dot{x} + kx = F_0\cos\omega t$ ...(i)

where dot over x denotes derivative with respect to time.

The corresponding homogeneous equation is $m\ddot{x} + \gamma\dot{x} + kx = F_0\cos\omega t$

$m\ddot{x} + \gamma\dot{x} + kx = 0$

which is the same as the equation describing damped vibration without a forcing function. Its solution depends upon the sign of $\gamma^2 - 4mk$.

Thus, if $\gamma^2 - 4mk > 0$ then $x_c(t) = C_1 e^{-(\alpha-\beta)t} + C_2 e^{-(\alpha+\beta)t}$

If $\gamma^2 - 4mk = 0$ then $x_c(t) = e^{-\alpha t}(C_1 t + C_2)$

If $\gamma^2 - 4mk < 0$ then

$x_c(t) = e^{-\alpha t}(C_1\cos\omega' t + C_2\sin\omega' t) = Ce^{-\alpha t}\cos(\omega' t - \delta)$

where $\alpha = \gamma/2m$, $\beta = \dfrac{1}{2m}\sqrt{\gamma^2 - 4mk}$, $\omega' = \dfrac{1}{2m}\sqrt{4mk - \gamma^2}$, $C = \sqrt{C_1^2 + C_2^2}$

and $\tan\delta = C_2/C_1$.

Since, no constant multiple of the driving function $F_0\cos\omega t$ is a term of $x_c(t)$, the particular solution is of the form $x_p(t) = A\cos\omega t + B\sin\omega t$

Differentiating twice with respect to time, we get

$$\dot{x}_p(t) = -\omega A \sin\omega t + \omega B \cos\omega t \quad \text{and} \quad \ddot{x}_p(t) = -\omega^2 A \cos\omega t - \omega^2 B \sin\omega t$$

Substituting these in (i) and collecting the coefficient of sine and cosine terms, we have

$$[(k - m\omega^2)A + \omega\gamma B]\cos\omega t + [-\omega\gamma A + (k - m\omega^2)B]\sin\omega t = F_0 \cos\omega t$$

Equating the coefficients of the sine and cosine terms on both sides of this equality, we get $-\omega\gamma A + (k - m\omega^2)B = 0$ and $(k - m\omega^2)A + \omega\gamma B = F_0$

Solving these for A and B, we will get $A = \dfrac{F_0(k - m\omega^2)}{(k - m\omega^2)^2 + \omega^2\gamma^2}$

and $B = \dfrac{\gamma\omega F_0}{(k - m\omega^2)^2 + \omega^2\gamma^2}$

We know that $\sqrt{k/m} = \omega_0$. we can write A and B as

$$A = \frac{F_0\, m(\omega_0^2 - \omega^2)}{m^2\left(\omega_0^2 - \omega^2\right)^2 + \omega^2\gamma^2} \quad \text{and} \quad B = \frac{\gamma\omega F_0}{m^2\left(\omega_0^2 - \omega^2\right)^2 + \omega^2\gamma^2}$$

We choose to write $x_p(t)$ in the form $\quad x_p(t) = C \cos(\omega t - \delta)$

where $C = F_0 / \sqrt{m^2(\omega_0^2 - \omega^2)^2 + \omega^2\gamma^2}$ and $\tan\delta = \omega\gamma / m(\omega_0^2 - \omega^2)$.

For large values of t, the motion is essentially described by $x_p(t)$. For this reason, $x_p(t)$ is called the steady-state solution.

Q15. Obtain the particular integral of $\dfrac{d^2 y}{dx^2} + \dfrac{dy}{dx} = \sin x$.

[Dec-2010,Q.No.-1(c)]

Ans. Given equation is $\dfrac{d^2 y}{dx^2} + \dfrac{dy}{dx} = \sin x$　　　　　　　　...(i)

Let the solution is $\quad y_p = A \sin x + B \cos x$

$$\Rightarrow \frac{dy_p}{dx} = A\cos x - B\sin x \text{ or } \frac{d^2 y_p}{dx^2} = -A\sin x - B\cos x$$

Substituting these in Eq. (i), we get

$$-A\sin x - B\cos x + A\cos x - B\sin x = \sin x$$

or $(-A - B)\sin x + (-B + A)\cos x = \sin x$

On equating the coefficients of $\sin x$ and $\cos x$, we get

$-A - B = 1$　　　　　　　　　　　　　　...(i)

$-B + A = 0$　　　　　　　　　　　　　　...(ii)

$\Rightarrow \quad A = -1/2, \ B = -1/2$

Now $\quad y_p = A\sin x + B\cos x$

$\Rightarrow \quad y_p = \dfrac{-1}{2}\sin x - \dfrac{1}{2}\cos x \Rightarrow y_p = \dfrac{-1}{2}(\sin x + \cos x)$ is the required

particular integral.

Q16. Using variation of parameters, solve $\dfrac{d^2 y}{dx^2} + y = x$.

Ans. The given equation is $\left(D^2 + 1\right) y = x, D = \dfrac{d}{dx}$.

Step 1: The auxiliary equation is $m^2 + 1 = 0$ or $m = \pm i$.

   $\therefore \quad$ C.F $= c_1 \cos x + c_2 \sin x$.

Step 2: Let $y_1 = \cos x, y_2 = \sin x$.

The Wronskian of y_1 and y_2 is $W = \begin{vmatrix} y_1 & y_2 \\ y_1' & y_2' \end{vmatrix} = \begin{vmatrix} \cos x & \sin x \\ -\sin x & \cos x \end{vmatrix} = 1 \neq 0$

Step 3: P.I. $= u_1 y_1 + u_2 y_2$, where $u_1 = -\int \dfrac{y_2 R}{W} dx = -\int x \sin x \, dx$,

$u_2 = \int \dfrac{y_1 R}{W} dx = \int x \cos x \, dx.$ $(\because W = 1, R = x)$

Integrating by parts, we obtain $u_1 = -[x(-\cos x) + \int \cos x \, dx] = x\cos x - \sin x,$

$u_2 = [x\sin x - \int \sin x \, dx] = x\sin x + \cos x.$

$\therefore$ P.I. $= u_1 y_1 + u_2 y_2 = (x\cos x - \sin x)\cos x + (x\sin x + \cos x)\sin x$

$= x(\cos^2 x + \sin^2 x) = x.$

Step 4: Hence, $y = $ C.F. $+$ P.I. $= c_1 \cos x + c_2 \sin x + x$ is the required solution.

Q17. Using the method of variation of parameters, solve $y'' - 3y' + 2y = 2$.

Ans. Using this method we follows the following steps:

Step 1: The auxiliary equation is $m^2 - 3m + 2 = 0$ or $(m-1)(m-2) = 0$ or $m = 1, 2$.

   $\therefore$ C.F. $= c_1 e^x + c_2 e^{2x}$.

Step 2: Let $y_1 = e^x, y_2 = e^{2x}$.

The Wronskian of y_1 and y_2 is

$$W = \begin{vmatrix} y_1 & y_2 \\ y_1' & y_2' \end{vmatrix} = \begin{vmatrix} e^x & e^{2x} \\ e^x & 2e^{2x} \end{vmatrix} = e^{2x} e^x = e^{3x} \neq 0.$$

Step 3: $\text{P.I} = u_1 y_1 + u_2 y_2$, where $u_1 = -\int \dfrac{y_2 R}{W}\,dx = -\int \dfrac{2e^{2x}dx}{e^{3x}} = -2\int e^{-x}\,dx = 2e^{-x}$,

$$u_2 = \int \dfrac{y_1 R}{W}\,dx = \int \dfrac{2e^x\,dx}{e^{3x}} = 2\int e^{-2x}\,dx = -e^{-2x}.$$

$$\therefore\ \ \text{P.I.} = u_1 y_1 + u_2 y_2 = 2e^{-x}e^x - e^{-2x}e^{2x} = 2 - 1 = 1.$$

Step 4: Hence, $y = \text{C.F.} + \text{P.I.} = c_1 e^x + c_2 e^{2x} + 1$ is the required solution.

$$u_2 = \int \dfrac{y_1 R}{W}\,dx = \dfrac{1}{2}\int \dfrac{1.e^x \sin x\,dx}{e^{2x}} = \dfrac{1}{2}\int e^{-x}\sin x\,dx.$$

Integrating by parts, we see that $\int e^x \sin x\,dx = e^x \sin x - \int e^x \cos x\,dx$

$$= e^x \sin x - [e^x \cos x + \int e^x \sin x\,dx]\ \ \therefore\ \ \int e^x \sin x\,dx = \dfrac{1}{2}e^x(\sin x - \cos x).$$

Similarly, $\int e^{-x}\sin x\,dx = -\dfrac{1}{2}e^{-x}(\sin x + \cos x)$.

$$\therefore\ \text{P.I.} = u_1 y_1 + u_2 y_2 = -\dfrac{1}{4}e^x(\sin x - \cos x) - \dfrac{1}{4}e^{-x}e^{2x}(\sin x + \cos x)$$

$$= -\dfrac{1}{2}e^x \sin x.$$

Hence, $y = c_1 + c_2 e^{2x} - \dfrac{1}{2}e^x \sin x$ is the required solution.

Q18. Solve the differential equations

(i) $\dfrac{d^2 y}{dx^2} + y = \sec x$

Ans. Since two linearly independent solutions of the corresponding homogeneous equation are cos x and sin x, the general solution of the given equation is $y = C_1 \cos x + C_2 \sin x + y_p$

where $y_p = u\cos x + v\sin x$ and u' and v' are respectively given by

$$\dfrac{du}{dx} = \dfrac{\begin{vmatrix} 0 & \sin x \\ \sec x & \cos x \end{vmatrix}}{\begin{vmatrix} \cos x & \sin x \\ -\sin x & \cos x \end{vmatrix}} \quad \text{and} \quad \dfrac{dv}{dx} = \dfrac{\begin{vmatrix} \cos x & 0 \\ -\sin x & \sec x \end{vmatrix}}{\begin{vmatrix} \cos x & \sin x \\ -\sin x & \cos x \end{vmatrix}}$$

Therefore, $\dfrac{du}{dx} = -\tan x$ and $\dfrac{dv}{dx} = 1$, from which it readily follows that $u = \ln|\cos x|$ and $v = x$.

The general solution is, therefore,

$$y = C_1 \cos x + C_2 \sin x + \ln|\cos x|\cos x + x\sin x$$

(ii) $\dfrac{d^2y}{dx^2} - y = x\,e^x$

Ans. The corresponding homogeneous equation $y'' - y = 0$ has the general solution $y = C_1 e^x + C_2 e^{-x}$.

Because of the nature of the driving function, y_p could not be found by the method of undetermined coefficients. In the method of variation of parameters, we put $y_1 = e^x$ and $y_2 = e^{-x}$ in the expressions for u' and v' to obtain

$$u' = \frac{\begin{vmatrix} 0 & e^{-x} \\ xe^x & -e^{-x} \end{vmatrix}}{\begin{vmatrix} e^x & e^{-x} \\ e^x & -e^{-x} \end{vmatrix}} \quad \text{and} \quad v' = \frac{\begin{vmatrix} e^x & 0 \\ e^x & xe^x \end{vmatrix}}{\begin{vmatrix} e^x & e^{-x} \\ e^x & -e^{-x} \end{vmatrix}}$$

Therefore, $u' = x/2$ and $v' = \dfrac{-x\exp(2x)}{2}$ from which it readily follows that $u = x^2/4$ and $v = -(xe^{2x}/4) + (e^{2x}/8)$. The general solution is then

$$y = C_1 e^x + C_2 e^{-x} + \frac{1}{4}x^2 e^x - \frac{x}{4}e^x + \frac{1}{8}e^x$$

Finally, we note that $C_1 e^x$ and $\dfrac{1}{8}e^x$ can be combined as $(C_1 + \dfrac{1}{8})e^x = Ce^x$ and general solution may be written as

$$y = C_1 e^x + C_2 e^{-x} - \frac{1}{4}xe^x + \frac{1}{4}x^2 e^x$$

Q19. What do mean by linearly independent solutions of an ordinary differential equation? Show that the solutions of an undamped harmonic oscillator $y'' + \alpha y = 0$ are linearly independent.

[June-2011,Q.No.-1(d)]

Ans. Two solutions y_1 and y_2 of an ODE are linearly independent on an interval [a, b], if and only if, their Wronskian is non-zero for $a \le x \le b$.

For a harmonic oscillator $y'' + \alpha y = 0$,

$$W(x) = \begin{vmatrix} \sin\omega t & \cos\omega t \\ \omega\cos\omega t & -\omega\sin\omega t \end{vmatrix} = -\omega \neq 0$$

Hence, solutions of an undamped harmonic oscillator are linearly independent. To get success in your studies, read only GPH book.

Q20. Use method of variation of parameters to solve

$$\frac{d^2y}{dx^2} - 3\frac{dy}{dx} + 2y = \frac{e^x}{1+e^x}.$$

Ans. Using this method we follows the following steps:

Step 1: The auxiliary equation is $m^2 - 3m + 2 = 0 \Rightarrow m = 1, 2.$

$$\therefore \ \text{C.F.} = c_1 e^x + c_2 e^{2x}$$

Step 2: Let $y_1 = e^x$, $y_2 = e^{2x}$.

Their Wronskian is $W = \begin{vmatrix} y_1 & y_2 \\ y_1' & y_2' \end{vmatrix} = \begin{vmatrix} e^x & e^{2x} \\ e^x & 2e^{2x} \end{vmatrix} = e^{3x} \neq 0.$

Step 3: P.I. $= u_1 y_1 + u_2 y_2$, where

$$u_1 = -\int \frac{y_2 R}{W} dx = -\int \frac{e^{2x}}{e^{3x}}\left(\frac{e^x}{1+e^x}\right) dx = -\int \frac{dx}{1+e^x}$$

$$= -\int \frac{e^{-x}}{e^{-x}+1} dx = \log(e^{-x}+1),$$

$$u_2 = \int \frac{y_1 R}{W} dx = \int \frac{e^x}{e^{3x}}\left(\frac{e^x}{1+e^x}\right) dx = \int \frac{dx}{e^x(1+e^x)} = -x - e^{-x} + \log(1+e^x)$$

$$\therefore \ \text{P.I.} = u_1 y_1 + u_2 y_2 = e^x \log(e^{-x}+1) - xe^{2x} - e^x + e^{2x}\log(1+e^x).$$

Step 4: Hence, $y = \text{C.F.} + \text{P.I.}$ is the required solution.

Q21. Use the method of variation of parameters to solve $\dfrac{d^2y}{dx^2} - y = \dfrac{2}{1+e^x}.$

Ans. Using this method we follows the following steps:

Step 1: The auxiliary equation is $m^2 - 1 = 0$ or $m = \pm 1.$

$$\therefore \ \text{C.F.} = c_1 e^x + c_2 e^{-x}.$$

Step 2: Let $y_1 = e^x$, $y_2 = e^{-x}$.

Their Wronskian is $W = \begin{vmatrix} y_1 & y_2 \\ y_1' & y_2' \end{vmatrix} = \begin{vmatrix} e^x & e^{-x} \\ e^x & -e^{-x} \end{vmatrix} = -2 \neq 0.$

Step 3: P.I. $= u_1 y_1 + u_2 y_2$, where

$$u_1 = -\int \frac{y_2 R}{W} dx = \frac{1}{2}\int e^{-x}\left(\frac{2}{1+e^x}\right) dx = \int \frac{dx}{e^x(1+e^x)},$$

$$u_2 = \int \frac{y_1 R}{W} dx = -\frac{1}{2}\int e^x\left(\frac{2}{1+e^x}\right) dx = -\int \frac{e^x \, dx}{1+e^x}. \quad \therefore \ u_2 = -\log(1+e^x).$$

Now $u_1 = \int \dfrac{dt}{t^2(1+t)}$, where $t = e^x \Rightarrow dx = dt/t$

Let $\dfrac{1}{t^2(1+t)} = \dfrac{A}{t} + \dfrac{B}{t^2} + \dfrac{C}{1+t}$.

Then $1 = At(1+t) + B(1+t) + Ct^2$.

$\therefore\ t = 0 \Rightarrow B = 1, t = -1 \Rightarrow C = 1$.

Comparing the coefficients of t^2, we obtain $0 = A + C \Rightarrow A = -1$.

$\therefore\ u_1 = -\int\dfrac{dt}{t} + \int\dfrac{dt}{t^2} + \int\dfrac{dt}{1+t} = -\log e^x - \dfrac{1}{e^x} + \log(1+e^x)$

$= -x - e^{-x} + \log(1+e^x).$

$\therefore \text{P.I.} = u_1 y_1 + u_2 y_2 = -xe^x - 1 + e^x \log(1+e^x) - e^{-x} \log(1+e^x)$

Step 4: Hence, $y = \text{C.F.} + \text{P.I.}$ is the required solution.

Q22. Solve by the method of undetermined coefficients:

$$\dfrac{d^2y}{dx^2} + 2\dfrac{dy}{dx} + y = x - e^x.$$

Ans. The auxiliary equation is $m^2 + 2m + 1 = 0$ or $(m+1)^2 = 0$.

$\therefore\ \text{C.F} = (c_1 + c_2 x)e^{-x}.$

Let the trial solution be $Y = Ax + B + Ce^x$.

$\therefore\ DY = A + Ce^x$ and $D^2Y = Ce^x$

The equation $D^2Y + 2DY + Y = x - e^x$ becomes

$Ce^x + 2A + 2Ce^x + Ax + B + Ce^x = x - e^x$ or $Ax + 4Ce^x + (2A+B) = x - e^x$.

Comparing the coefficients of like terms, we obtain

$A = 1,\ \ 4C = -1 \Rightarrow C = -1/4,\ \ 2A + B = 0 \Rightarrow B = -2.$

$\therefore\ Y = x - 2 - \dfrac{1}{4}e^x.$

Hence, the complete solution is $y = (c_1 + c_2 x)e^{-x} + x - 2 - \dfrac{1}{4}e^x.$

Q23. By the method of undetermined coefficients, solve $\dfrac{d^2y}{dx^2} + 4y = x^2.$

Ans. The auxiliary equation is $m^2 + 4 = 0$ or $m = \pm 2i$.

$\therefore\ \text{C.F.} = c_1 \cos 2x + c_2 \sin 2x.$

Let the trial solution be $Y = Ax^2 + Bx + C.$

$\therefore\ DY = 2Ax + B,\ D^2Y = 2A. \ (D = d/dx)$

Putting the values of D^2Y and Y in $D^2Y + 4Y = x^2$, we get

$$2A + 4(Ax^2 + Bx + C) = x^2 \quad \text{or} \quad 4Ax^2 + 4Bx + (2A + 4C) = x^2.$$

Equating the coefficients of like powers of x, we get

$4A = 1, \; 4B = 0, \; 2A + 4C = 0$

or $A = \dfrac{1}{4}, B = 0$ and $C = -\dfrac{1}{8}.$

Thus, $Y = \dfrac{1}{4}x^2 - \dfrac{1}{8}.$

Hence, the required solution is $y = C.F. + Y$ or

$$y = c_1 \cos 2x + c_2 \sin 2x + \frac{1}{8}(2x^2 - 1).$$

Q24. By the method of undetermined coefficients, solve

$$(D^2 + 2)y = e^x + 2.$$

Ans. The auxiliary equation is $m^2 + 2 = 0$ or $m = \pm\sqrt{2}\,i.$

$\therefore$ C.F. $= c_1 \cos \sqrt{2}x + c_2 \sin \sqrt{2}x.$

Let the trial solution be $Y = Ae^x + B.$

$\therefore$ $DY = Ae^x, \; D^2y = Ae^x.$

Now $D^2Y + 2Y = e^x + 2$ becomes $Ae^x + 2(Ae^x + B) = e^x + 2.$

Equating the coefficients of like terms, we obtain

$$3A = 1, \; 2B = 2 \text{ or } A = \frac{1}{3}, B = 1.$$

$\therefore Y = \dfrac{1}{3}e^x + 1.$

Hence, the required solution is $y = C.F. + Y$ or

$$y = c_1 \cos\sqrt{2}x + c_2 \sin\sqrt{2}x + \frac{1}{3}e^x + 1.$$

Q25. Solve the equation $y'' - 4y' + 4y = 0$　　　　　**[Dec-2011,Q.No.-1(d)]**

Ans. Given equation is $y'' - 4y' + 4y = 0$

$$\Rightarrow \quad \frac{d^2y}{dx^2} - 4\frac{dy}{dx} + 4y = 0$$

putting $\dfrac{d}{dx} = D \;\Rightarrow\; D^2y - 4Dy + 4y = 0 \;\Rightarrow\; (D^2 - 4D + 4)\,y = 0$

Here, Auxiliary equation is $m^2 - 4m + 4 = 0$

$$\Rightarrow \quad m^2 - 2m - 2m + 4 = 0 \;\Rightarrow\; m(m-2) - 2(m-2) = 0$$

$$\Rightarrow (m-2)(m-2) = 0 \quad \Rightarrow \quad m = 2, 2$$

$$\Rightarrow \text{C.F.} = (c_1 x + c_2) e^{2x} = c_1 x e^{2x} + c_2 e^{2x}$$

Since, R.H.S. of given equation is zero. Hence, its particular integral is zero.

Therefore, the required solution is $y = c_1 x e^{2x} + c_2 e^{2x}$.

Q26. Using the method of undetermined coefficients, solve
$$\frac{d^2 y}{dx^2} - 2\frac{dy}{dx} + 3y = x^2 + \cos x.$$

Ans. The auxiliary equation is $m^2 - 2m + 3 = 0$ or $m = \dfrac{2 \pm \sqrt{4-12}}{2} = 1 \pm \sqrt{2}\, i$.

$$\therefore \text{C.F.} = e^x(c_1 \cos\sqrt{2}\,x + c_2 \sin\sqrt{2}\,x).$$

Let the trial solution be $Y = Ax^2 + Bx + C + E \cos x + F \sin x$.

$$\therefore DY = 2Ax + B - E\sin x + F\cos x, \quad D^2Y = 2A - E\cos x - F\sin x.$$

The equation $D^2Y - 2DY + 3Y = x^2 + \cos x$ becomes

$$2A - E\cos x - F\sin x - 2(2Ax + B - E\sin x + F\cos x)$$

$$+3(Ax^2 + Bx + C + E\cos x + F\sin x) = x^2 + \cos x$$

or $3Ax^2 + (3B-4A)x + (3C+2A-2B) + (2E-2F)\cos x + (2E+2F)\sin x$

$$= x^2 + \cos x.$$

Comparing the coefficients of like terms, we obtain

$$3A = 1 \left(\Rightarrow A = \frac{1}{3}\right), \quad 3B - 4A = 0 \left(\Rightarrow B = \frac{4}{9}\right), \quad 3C + 2A - 2B = 0 \left(\Rightarrow C = \frac{2}{27}\right),$$

$$2E - 2F = 1 \text{ and } 2E + 2F = 0 \Rightarrow E = \frac{1}{4}, \quad F = -\frac{1}{4},$$

$$\therefore \ Y = \frac{1}{3}x^2 + \frac{4}{9}x + \frac{2}{27} + \frac{1}{4}(\cos x - \sin x).$$

Hence, $y = \text{C.F.} + Y$ is the required solution.

The Book you can believe most – GPH book.

Chapter

3

Second Order Ordinary Differential Equations with Variable Coefficients

An Overview

The general form of the second order ordinary differential equations with variable coefficients is

$$P(x)y'' + Q(x)y' + R(x)y = 0$$

In many physical and engineering problems, we have to solve second order ordinary differential equations with variable coefficients. For example, we have to solve such equations to study the field distribution around a charged sphere or a cylinder, and energy production in a reactor. Similarly, when we wish to know how high a vertical column of uniform cross-section can be extended upward until it buckles under its own weight, we have to solve a second order ODE with variable coefficients.

One of the most elegant and efficient methods of solving such ODEs is the power series method. This is so particularly because it facilities numerical computations. Even so, it has limited utility when coefficients of the given differential equation are not well defined at some point. In such cases, we use an extension of the power series method, called the Frobenius' method.

Power Series: An infinite series of the form

$$\sum_{n=0}^{\infty} a_n x^n = a_0 + a_1 x + a_2 x^2 + a_3 x^3 + \ldots \qquad \ldots(i)$$

is called a power series in x. In general, a power series in $(x - x_0)$ is an

infinite series $\sum_{n=0}^{\infty} a_n (x - x_0)^n = a_0 + a_1(x - x_0) + a_2(x - x_0)^2 + \ldots$

For example, the exponential function has the power series

$$e^x = \sum_{n=0}^{\infty} \frac{x^n}{n!} = 1 + x + \frac{x^2}{2!} + \ldots \qquad \ldots(ii)$$

Note that $y = e^{x^2}$ is a solution of the first order differential equation

$$\frac{dy}{dx} - 2xy = 0. \qquad \ldots(iii)$$

This solution can be written as $y = e^{x^2} = \sum_{n=0}^{\infty} \frac{x^{2n}}{n!}$,

which is a power series solution of (iii).

It can be easily verified that eq. (ii) converges for all real values of x, by Ratio Test. The power series (1) converges (absolutely) for $|x| < R$, where

$$R = \lim_{n \to \infty} \left| \frac{a_n}{a_{n+1}} \right|, \text{ provided the limit exists.}$$

R is called the radius of convergence of eq. (i).

The interval $(-R, R)$ is called the interval of convergence.

Since $R = \infty$ for the power series (ii), therefore, its interval of convergence is $(-\infty, \infty)$, i.e. the real line.

Remarks:

(a) A power series represents a continuous function within its interval of convergence.

(b) A power series can be differentiated term wise within its interval of convergence.

$$\text{Let } f(x) = \sum_{n=0}^{\infty} a_n x^n, |x| < R. \text{ Then } f'(x) = \sum_{n=1}^{\infty} n a_n x^{n-1},$$

$$f''(x) = \sum_{n=2}^{\infty} n(n-1) a_n x^{n-2} \text{ etc.}$$

Power Series Expansion of Some Simple Functions Analytic at x = 0: For the particular case of $x_0 = 0$, familiar examples of analytic functions are given in table 3.1.

Table 3.1

Function	Power Series	Radius of Convergence
$\dfrac{1}{1-x}$	$\displaystyle\sum_{n=0}^{\infty} x^n = 1 + x + x^2 + \ldots$	$\|x\| < 1$
e^x	$\displaystyle\sum_{n=0}^{\infty} \dfrac{x^n}{n!} = 1 + x + \dfrac{x^2}{2!} + \ldots$	$\|x\| < \infty$
$\sin x$	$x - \dfrac{x^3}{3!} + \dfrac{x^5}{5!} - \ldots$	$\|x\| < \infty$
$\cos x$	$1 - \dfrac{x^2}{2!} + \dfrac{x^4}{4!} - \ldots$	$\|x\| < \infty$

Ordinary and singular points of y″+ Py′ +Qy = 0: A point $x = x_0$ is called an ordinary point of the differential equation

$$\frac{d^2 y}{dx^2} + P(x)\frac{dy}{dx} + Q(x)y = 0, \qquad\qquad \ldots\text{(iv)}$$

if both $P(x)$ and $Q(x)$ are analytic at x_0 (i.e. each has a power series expansion in $(x - x_0)$ with a positive radius of convergence).

If either $P(x)$ or $Q(x)$ is not analytic at x_0, then $x = x_0$ is called a singular point of (iv).

Singular points are further classified as regular or irregular singular points.

A singular point $x = x_0$ of the differential eq. (iv) is said to be a regular singular point (RSP) if both $(x - x_0)P(x)$ and $(x - x_0)^2 Q(x)$ are analytic at x_0 (i.e. each has a power series expansion in $(x - x_0)$ with a positive radius of convergence).

A singular point, which is not regular, is called an irregular singular point.

Power series solutions of y″ + p(x)y′ + q(x)y = 0: The power series method is used to seek a power series solution to certain differential equations. In general, such a solution assumes a power series with unknown coefficients, then substitutes that solution into the differential equation to find a recurrence relation for the coefficients.

Solutions Around Ordinary Points: If $x = 0$ is an ordinary point of a differential equation, then the power series expansion of the general solution has the form $y = \sum\limits_{n=0}^{\infty} a_n x^n$. $\qquad\qquad$ ...(v)

The undetermined coefficients $a_2, a_3, a_4, \ldots\ldots$ may be determined in terms of a_0 and a_1 by substituting the values of y from (v) and its derivatives

$$y' = \sum_{n=1}^{\infty} n a_n x^{n-1}, y'' = \sum_{n=2}^{\infty} n(n-1) a_n x^{n-2} \qquad\qquad ...(vi)$$

in the given differential equation and then equating the coefficients of like powers of x.

Solutions Around Regular Singular Point (Frobenius Method): Consider the differential equation with polynomial coefficients:

$$y'' + P(x)y' + Q(x)y = 0. \qquad\qquad ...(vii)$$

If $x = 0$ is a regular singular point (RSP) of (vii), then

$$xP(x) = p_0 + p_1 x + p_2 x^2 + \ldots, \text{ and } x^2 Q(x) = q_0 + q_1 x + q_2 x^2 + \ldots$$

$$\therefore \quad \lim_{x \to 0} xP(x) = p_0, \lim_{x \to 0} x^2 Q(x) = q_0.$$

For $0 < x < R$, we take the solution of (vii) as

$$y = x^r \sum_{n=0}^{\infty} a_n x^n = \sum_{n=0}^{\infty} a_n x^{n+r} \ (a_0 \neq 0), \qquad\qquad ...(viii)$$

where r is given by the equation $r(r-1) + r p_0 + q_0 = 0$

or $\qquad r^2 + (p_0 - 1)r + q_0 = 0.$ $\qquad\qquad$ ...(ix)

The quadratic eq. (ix) in r is called the indicial equation.

This quadratic eq. (ix) may be obtained by substituting the series (viii) into (vii), and then equating to zero the coefficient of the term containing the smallest power of x (assuming $a_0 \neq 0$).

Let r_1 and r_2 be the real roots of the indicial eq. (ix), $r_1 \geq r_2$.

Then the following three cases arise:

Case I: $\quad$ Let $r_1 - r_2$ be not an integer.

We substitute the series (viii) in (vii) and divide throughout by x^r. Then on equating to zero the coefficients of various powers of x, a recurrence relation is obtained. In this case, we get two linearly independent solutions y_1 and y_2 by taking $r = r_1$ and r_2 respectively in (8), and using the recurrence relation for both the values of r.

Case II: $\quad$ Let $r_1 = r_2.$

In this case, one solution $y_1(x)$ can be obtained by taking $r = r_1$ in the recurrence relation (as done in case I). To find the other linearly independent solution $y_2(x)$, we may take $a_0 = 1$, and write (viii)　　(using　　recurrence　　relation)　　as　　follows:

$$y(r,x) = x^r \sum_{n=0}^{\infty} a_n(r)x^n = \sum_{n=0}^{\infty} a_n(r)\, x^{n+r},$$

taking r as variable. Then $y_2(x) = \dfrac{\partial\, y(r,x)}{\partial r}\bigg|_{r=r_1}$

Case III:　Let $r_1 - r_2$, be a positive integer.

Note that $r_1 > r_2$, and so Frobenius method will always generate a solution $y_1(x)$ corresponding to $r = r_1$ (as in *Case I or II*) and it may generate another linearly independent solution $y_2(x)$ corresponding to the smaller root r_2. Otherwise, we proceed like

Case II and take $y_2(x) = \dfrac{\partial}{\partial r}[(r - r_2)\, y(r,x)]\bigg|_{r=r_2}$

Solved Practical Problems

Q1.　Determine whether $x = 0$ is an ordinary point or a RSP of the differential equation $x^2 \dfrac{d^2y}{dx^2} + 2\dfrac{dy}{dx} + xy = 0$.

Ans. Here, $P(x) = \dfrac{2}{x^2}, Q(x) = \dfrac{1}{x}$ are not analytic at $x=0$

Thus, $x=0$ is not an ordinary point. Further $x\, P(x) = \dfrac{2}{x}$, which is not analytic at $x=0$ and $x^2 Q(x) = x$, which is analytic at $x=0$.

Hence, $x = 0$ is not a RSP, and so $x=0$ is an irregular singular point

Q2.　Determine the singular point of the following equation and specify its nature:

$$x^2 \dfrac{d^2 y}{dx^2} - 2x\dfrac{dy}{dx} + \left(x^2 + 2\right) y = 0$$

Obtain the indicial equation and determine its roots.

[Dec-2012,Q.No.-2]

Ans. Given equation is $x^2 \dfrac{d^2y}{dx^2} - 2x\dfrac{dy}{dx} + \left(x^2 + 2\right)y = 0$

On dividing by x^2, we get $\dfrac{d^2y}{dx^2} - \dfrac{2}{x}\dfrac{dy}{dx} + \dfrac{(x^2+2)}{x^2}y = 0$

Compare with $\dfrac{dy}{dx} + Py = Q \Rightarrow \qquad P(x) = \dfrac{-2}{x}$, $Q(x) = \dfrac{x^2+2}{x^2}$

Hence, $xP(x) = -2$ and $x^2Q(x) = (x^2+2)$

Now, $\lim\limits_{x\to 0} xP(x) = -2 = b(x)$

and $\lim\limits_{x\to 0} x^2Q(x) = 2 = c(x)$

Since, $x\,P(x)$ and $x^2Q(x)$ or $b(x)$ and $c(x)$ are both analytic.

Hence, $x = 0$ is Regular Singular Point (RSP).

Now $y(x) = \sum\limits_{n=0}^{\infty} a_n x^{n+r}$

$\Rightarrow \qquad y'(x) = \sum\limits_{n=0}^{\infty} a_n(n+r)x^{n+r-1}$

and $y''(x) = \sum\limits_{n=0}^{\infty} a_n(n+r)(n+r-1)x^{n+r-2}$

Substituting these values in given equation, we get

$$\sum\limits_{n=0}^{\infty} a_n(n+r)(n+r-1)x^{n+r} - 2\sum\limits_{n=0}^{\infty} a_n(n+r)x^{n+r} + \sum\limits_{n=0}^{\infty} a_n x^{n+r+2} + 2\sum\limits_{n=0}^{\infty} a_n x^{n+r} = 0$$

Now equating the coefficients of the lowest power of x, i.e. x^{n+r} to zero. Then, we have $a_0\left[r(r-1) - 2r + 2\right] = 0$

For $a_0 \neq 0$, the indicial equation takes the form, $r(r-1) - 2r + 2 = 0$

or $r^2 - r - 2r + 2 = 0$ or $r^2 - 2r - r + 2 = 0$ or $r(r-2) - 1(r-2) = 0$ or

$(r-2)(r-1) = 0$

$\Rightarrow \qquad r = 1, 2$

Hence, required roots are 1 and 2.

Q3. Determine whether x=0 is an ordinary point or a regular singular point of the differential equation $2x^2\dfrac{d^2y}{dx^2} + 7x(x+1)\dfrac{dy}{dx} - 3y = 0$

Ans. Dividing the given equation by $2x^2$, we obtain

$$p(x) = \dfrac{7(x+1)}{2x}, Q(x) = -\dfrac{3}{2x^2}$$

Since both $P(x)$ and $Q(x)$ have x in their denominators, so they are not analytic at x=0

Thus, x=0 is not an ordinary point and so the point x=0 is a singular point. Now, $(x-0)P(x) = xP(x) = \frac{7}{2}(x+1) = \frac{7}{2} + \frac{7}{2}x$, and $x^2 Q(x) = -\frac{3}{2}$

It follows that $xP(x)$ and $x^2 Q(x)$ are analytic at $x = 0$.

Hence, $x = 0$ is a regular singular point.

Q4. Find a power series solution of the initial-value problem

$$(x^2 - 1)y'' + 3xy' + xy = 0, y(0) = 4, y'(0) = 6.$$

Ans. Since, the initial values of y and its first derivative are prescribed at $x = 0$ (which is an ordinary point of the given differential equation), therefore we shall find the solution near $x = 0$.

Thus, we have $y = \sum_{n=0}^{\infty} a_n x^n, y' = \sum_{n=1}^{\infty} na_n x^{n-1}, y'' = \sum_{n=2}^{\infty} n(n-1)a_n x^{n-2}$.

Now $y(0) = 4 \Rightarrow a_0 = 4$ and $y'(0) = 6 \Rightarrow a_1 = 6$.

$$\therefore \quad (x^2 - 1)\sum_{n=2}^{\infty} n(n-1)a_n x^{n-2} + 3x\sum_{n=1}^{\infty} na_n x^{n-1} + x\sum_{n=0}^{\infty} a_n x^n = 0$$

or $\sum_{n=2}^{\infty} n(n-1)a_n x^n - \sum_{n=2}^{\infty} n(n-1)a_n x^{n-2} + \sum_{n=1}^{\infty} 3n\,a_n x^n + \sum_{n=0}^{\infty} a_n x^{n+1} = 0$

By changing the index n in the second and last summations to $(n + 2)$ and $(n - 1)$ respectively, we obtain

$$\sum_{n=2}^{\infty} n(n-1)a_n x^n - \sum_{n=0}^{\infty} (n+2)(n+1)a_{n+2} x^n + \sum_{n=1}^{\infty} 3n\,a_n x^n + \sum_{n=1}^{\infty} a_{n-1} x^n = 0$$

or $-2a_2 - 6a_3 x + 3a_1 x + a_0 x$

$$+ \sum_{n=2}^{\infty} \{n(n-1)a_n - (n+2)(n+1)a_{n+2} + 3na_n + a_{n-1}\} x^n = 0.$$

Thus, $-2a_2 = 0 \Rightarrow a_2 = 0$,

$-6a_3 + 3a_1 + a_0 = 0 \Rightarrow a_3 = 11/3$, since $a_0 = 4, a_1 = 6$,

and $n(n-1)a_n - (n+2)(n+1)a_{n+2} + 3na_n + a_{n-1} = 0, n \geq 2$

or $a_{n+2} = \dfrac{n(n+2)a_n + a_{n-1}}{(n+1)(n+2)}, n \geq 2$.

$\therefore a_4 = \dfrac{1}{2}, a_5 = \dfrac{11}{5},$ and so on.

Hence, $y = 4 + 6x + \dfrac{11}{3}x^3 + \dfrac{1}{2}x^4 + \dfrac{11}{4}x^5 + ...$ is the required solution of the given initial value problem in powers of x.

Q5. Find the singular points and determine those, which are singular points of the differential equation

$$x^2(x-2)^2 \frac{d^2y}{dx^2} + 2(x-2)\frac{dy}{dx} + (x+1)y = 0.$$

Ans. Here, $P(x) = \dfrac{2}{x^2(x-2)}$ and $Q(x) = \dfrac{x+1}{x^2(x-2)^2}$

$\therefore$ $x = 0$ and $x = 2$ are both singular points.

Now, $xP(x) = \dfrac{2}{x(x-2)}$ which is not analytic at x=0,

and $x^2 Q(x) = \dfrac{x+1}{(x-2)^2}$ which is analytic at x=0.

Since, x=0 is not a RSP, x=0 is an irregular singular point.

Further, $(x-2)P(x) = \dfrac{2}{x^2}$, which is analytic at x = 2,

Since $x^2 = (2+x-2)^2 = 2^2\left[1 + \dfrac{1}{2}(x-2)\right]^2$ implies

$\dfrac{2}{x^2} = \dfrac{1}{2}\left[1-(x-2)+3(x-2)^2 - .....\right]$, and $(x-2)^2 Q(x) = \dfrac{x+1}{x^2}$, which is also analytic at x = 2.

Hence, x=2 is a RSP.

Q6. Using the power series method, find the general solution near x=0 of the equation $(x^2+1)\dfrac{d^2y}{dx^2} + x\dfrac{dy}{dx} - xy = 0$.

Ans. Here $P(x) = \dfrac{x}{x^2+1}$, $Q(x) = -\dfrac{x}{x^2+1}$, are both analytic at x=0.

Thus, x = 0 is an ordinary point.

Now $y = \displaystyle\sum_{n=0}^{\infty} a_n x^n$

$\Rightarrow$ $y' = \displaystyle\sum_{n=1}^{\infty} na_n x^{n-1}$ and $y'' = \displaystyle\sum_{n=2}^{\infty} n(n-1)a_n x^{n-2}$

Now, substituting y, y', y'' from above, we get

$$\left(x^2+1\right)\sum_{n=2}^{\infty}n(n-1)a_n x^{n-2}+x\sum_{n=1}^{\infty}na_n x^{n-1}-x\sum_{n=0}^{\infty}a_n x^n=0$$

or $\displaystyle\sum_{n=2}^{\infty}n(n-1)a_n x^n+\sum_{n=2}^{\infty}n(n-1)a_n x^{n-2}+\sum_{n=1}^{\infty}na_n x^n-\sum_{n=0}^{\infty}a_n x^{n+1}=0$

Replacing n by n + 2 in the second summation and n by $n-1$ in the last summation, we get

$$\sum_{n=2}^{\infty}n(n-1)a_n x^n+\sum_{n=0}^{\infty}(n+2).(n+1)a_{n+2}x^n+\sum_{n=1}^{\infty}na_n x^n-\sum_{n=1}^{\infty}a_{n-1}x^n=0$$

$$\sum_{n=2}^{\infty}n(n-1)a_n x^n+(2a_2+6a_3 x)+\sum_{n=2}^{\infty}(n+2).(n+1)a_{n+2}x^n+\left(a_1 x+\sum_{n=2}^{\infty}na_n x^n\right)-a_0 x-\sum_{n=2}^{\infty}a_{n-1}x^n=0$$

or

$$2a_2+\left(6a_3+a_1-a_0\right)x+\sum_{n=2}^{\infty}\left\{n(n-1)a_n+(n+2)(n+1)a_{n+2}+na_n-a_{n-1}\right\}x^n=0$$

or $\quad 2a_2+\left(6a_3+a_1-a_0\right)x+\displaystyle\sum_{n=2}^{\infty}\left\{(n+2)(n+1)a_{n+2}+n^2a_n-a_{n-1}\right\}x^n=0$

Equating the constant term and the coefficients of various powers of x to zero, we obtain $2a_2=0$, i.e. $a_2=0$,

$$6a_3+a_1-a_0=0,\ \text{i.e.}\ a_3=\frac{1}{6}(a_0-a_1),$$

$$(n+2)(n+1)a_{n+2}+n^2a_n-a_{n-1}=0,\ \text{for all}\ n\geq 2$$

or $\ a_{n+2}=\dfrac{a_{n-1}-n^2a_n}{(n+2)(n+1)}$ for all $n\geq 2$

The above relation is called a recurrence relation.

Putting n=2, 3,........; we obtain

$$a_4=\frac{1}{12}a_1,\ \text{since}\ a_2=0;$$

$$a_5=-\frac{9}{20}a_3\ \text{or}\ a_5=-\frac{9}{20}\times\frac{1}{6}(a_0-a_1)=-\frac{3}{40}(a_0-a_1)\ \text{and so on.}$$

Putting the values of a_3,a_4,a_5, etc. in $y=\displaystyle\sum_{n=0}^{\infty}a_n x^n$, we obtain

$$y=a_0+a_1 x+\frac{1}{6}(a_0-a_1)x^3+\frac{1}{12}a_1 x^4-\frac{3}{40}(a_0-a_1)x^5+....$$

Hence, $\quad y = a_0\left(1+\dfrac{1}{6}x^3 - \dfrac{3}{40}x^5 + ...\right) + a_1\left(x - \dfrac{1}{6}x^3 + \dfrac{1}{12}x^4 + \dfrac{3}{40}x^5 - ...\right).$

is the required general solution near $x = 0$, where a_0 and a_1 are arbitrary constants.

Q7. Find the general solution of $\left(1+x^2\right)y'' + xy' - y = 0$ near $x=0$.

Ans. Since $x = 0$ is an ordinary point.

Now, we have $\left(1+x^2\right)\sum_{n=2}^{\infty} n(n-1)a_n x^{n-2} + x\sum_{n=1}^{\infty} na_n x^{n-1} - \sum_{n=0}^{\infty} a_n x^n = 0$

or $\sum_{n=2}^{\infty} n(n-1)a_n x^{n-2} + \sum_{n=2}^{\infty} n(n-1)a_n x^n + \sum_{n=1}^{\infty} na_n x^n - \sum_{n=0}^{\infty} a_n x^n = 0$

By changing n to $n+2$ in the first summation, we obtain

$\sum_{n=2}^{\infty}(n+2)(n+1)a_{n+2}x^n + \sum_{n=2}^{\infty} n(n-1)a_n x^n + a_1 x + \sum_{n=2}^{\infty} na_n x^n - a_0 - a_1 x - \sum_{n=2}^{\infty} a_n x^n = 0$

or $\left(2a_2 - a_0\right) + 6a_3 x + \sum_{n=2}^{\infty}\{(n+2)(n+1)a_{n+2} + n(n-1)a_n + na_n - a_n\}x^n = 0$

or $\left(2a_2 - a_0\right) + 6a_3 x + \sum_{n=2}^{\infty}\{(n+2)(n+1)a_{n+2} + \left(n^2 - 1\right)a_n\}x^n = 0$

Equating to zero the coefficients of various powers of x, we obtain

$2a_2 - a_0 = 0 \Rightarrow a_2 = \dfrac{1}{2}a_0, a_3 = 0$

and $(n+2)(n+1)a_{n+2} + \left(n^2 - 1\right)a_n = 0$, for all $n \geq 2$

or $a_{n+2} = -\dfrac{(n-1)}{n+2}a_n, n \geq 2$

$\therefore \quad a_5 = 0, a_7 = 0, a_9 = 0......$ $\qquad\qquad \left(\because a_3 = 0\right)$

and $\qquad\qquad a_4 = -\dfrac{1}{4}a_2 = -\dfrac{1}{8}a_0, a_6 = -\dfrac{1}{2}a_4 = \dfrac{1}{16}a_0 .....$

Hence, the general solution of the given differential equation near $x = 0$ is

$y = a_0 y_1(x) + a_1 y_2(x),$ where $\quad y_1(x) = 1 + \dfrac{1}{2}x^2 - \dfrac{1}{8}x^4 + \dfrac{1}{15}x^6 .....,$ and

$y_2(x) = x$ are two linearly independent solutions, a_0 and a_1 are arbitrary constants. For excellent score, read GPH book.

Q8. Obtain the singular point of the following ODE and specify its nature:

$$x\frac{d^2y}{dx^2} - 2\frac{dy}{dx} + xy = 0$$

Determine the indicial equation and its roots.

[June-2012, Q.No.-2]

Ans. Given ODE is $x\dfrac{d^2y}{dx^2} - 2\dfrac{dy}{dx} + xy = 0$ ...(i)

On dividing by x, we get $\dfrac{d^2y}{dx^2} - \dfrac{2}{x}\dfrac{dy}{dx} + y = 0$

Compare with $\dfrac{dy}{dx} + Py = Q \Rightarrow \quad P(x) = -\dfrac{2}{x} \quad$ and $\quad Q(x) = 1$

Now, $xP(x) = -2$ and $x^2Q(x) = x^2$

Here, $\lim\limits_{x \to 0} xp(x) = -2 = b(x)$ and $\lim\limits_{x \to 0} x^2Q(x) = 0 = c(x)$

Since, $b(x)$ and $c(x)$ are analytic at $x = 0$.

Thus, $x = 0$ is a regular singular point (RSP).

Now $y(x) = \sum\limits_{n=0}^{\infty} a_n x^{n+r}$

$\Rightarrow \quad y'(x) = \sum\limits_{n=0}^{\infty} a_n(n+r)x^{n+r-1}$

and $y''(x) = \sum\limits_{n=0}^{\infty} a_n(n+r)(n+r-1)x^{n+r-2}$

on substituting these in given equation (i), we get,

$$x\sum_{n=0}^{\infty} a_n(n+r)(n+r-1)x^{n+r-2} - 2\sum_{n=0}^{\infty} a_n(n+r)x^{n+r-1} + x\sum_{n=0}^{\infty} a_n x^{n+r} = 0$$

$$\Rightarrow \sum_{n=0}^{\infty} a_n(n+r)(n+r-1)x^{n+r-1} - 2\sum_{n=0}^{\infty} a_n(n+r)x^{n+r-1} + \sum_{n=0}^{\infty} a_n x^{n+r+1} = 0$$

For indicial equation, we equate the coefficients of the lowest power of x, i.e. x^{r-1} to zero. Thus,

$$a_0\left[r(r-1) - 2r\right] = 0$$

For $a_0 \neq 0$, indicial equation takes form, $r(r-1) - 2r = 0$ or $r^2 - r - 2r = 0$ or $r^2 - 3r = 0$ or $r(r-3) = 0$

$\Rightarrow r = 0,\ 3$ Hence, required roots are 0 and 3.

Q9. Find the indicial equation of each of the following differential equations, for a solution near x = 0:

(i) $8x^2y'' + 2xy' + y = 0.$

Ans. Here, $P(x) = \dfrac{1}{4x}, Q(x) = \dfrac{1}{8x^2}.$

Neither of these functions is analytic at $x = 0$.

Since, $xP(x) = \dfrac{1}{4}$ and $x^2Q(x) = \dfrac{1}{8}$ are both analytic at $x = 0$, so $x = 0$ is a regular singular point. We have $p_0 = \dfrac{1}{4}, q_0 = \dfrac{1}{8}$.

Therefore, the indicial equation is $r^2 + (p_0 - 1)r + q_0 = 0$

$$\Rightarrow r^2 + (\dfrac{1}{4} - 1)r + \dfrac{1}{8} = 0 \Rightarrow 8r^2 - 6r + 1 = 0$$

$$\Rightarrow (4r - 1)(2r - 1) = 0 \Rightarrow r_1 = \dfrac{1}{2}, \ r_2 = \dfrac{1}{4}.$$

(ii) $2x^2y'' + x(2x + 1)y' - y = 0.$

Ans. Here, $x\,P(x) = x + \dfrac{1}{2} \to \dfrac{1}{2}$ as $x \to 0$, $x^2Q(x) = -\dfrac{1}{2}$.

Thus, $p_0 = \dfrac{1}{2}$ and $q_0 = -\dfrac{1}{2}$.

The indicial equation is $r^2 + (p_0 - 1)r + q_0 = 0$ or $r^2 + (\dfrac{1}{2} - 1)r - \dfrac{1}{2} = 0$

$$\Rightarrow 2r^2 - r - 1 = 0 \Rightarrow r_1 = 1, r_2 = -\dfrac{1}{2}.$$

(iii) $3x^2y'' - xy' + y = 0.$

Ans. Here, $x\,P(x) = -\dfrac{1}{3}$ and $x^2Q(x) = \dfrac{1}{3}$, therefore $x = 0$ is a RSP.

The indicial equation is $r(r - 1) - \dfrac{1}{3}r + \dfrac{1}{3} = 0 \Rightarrow (r - 1)(r - \dfrac{1}{3}) = 0$

$$\Rightarrow r_1 = 1, r_2 = \dfrac{1}{3}.$$

(iv) $2x^2y'' + x(x - 1)y' + y = 0.$

Ans. Here, $xP(x) = -\dfrac{1}{2} + \dfrac{1}{2}x \to -\dfrac{1}{2}$ as $x \to 0$, and $x^2Q(x) = \dfrac{1}{2}$.

The indicial equation is $r(r - 1) - \dfrac{1}{2}r + \dfrac{1}{2} = 0$ or $(r - 1)(r - \dfrac{1}{2}) = 0$ or

$r_1 = 1, \ r_2 = \dfrac{1}{2}.$

(v) $x^2y'' + xy' + x^2y = 0.$

Ans. Here, $x\,P(x) = 1$ and $x^2Q(x) = x^2 \to 0$ as $x \to 0$.

$\therefore r(r - 1) + r = 0$, i.e. $r^2 = 0$ is the indicial equation.

Thus, $r_1 = r_2 = 0.$

(vi) $x^2 y'' + xy' + (x^2 - 1)y = 0.$

Ans. Here, $x\,P(x) = 1$ and $x^2 Q(x) = x^2 - 1 \to -1$ as $x \to 0$.

$\therefore\ r(r-1) + r - 1 = 0$ or $r^2 - 1 = 0$ is the indicial equation having roots 1 and -1.

Q10. (i) Find the general power series solution of the Legendre's equation $(1 - x^2)\dfrac{d^2 y}{dx^2} - 2x\dfrac{dy}{dx} + m\,(m+1)y = 0$ **near x = 0 where m is an arbitrary constant.**

Ans. Since $x = 0$ is an ordinary point, so we have a solution of the form

$$y = \sum_{n=0}^{\infty} a_n x^n. \text{ Also } y' = \sum_{n=1}^{\infty} na_n x^{n-1}, y'' = \sum_{n=2}^{\infty} n(n-1)x^{n-2}.$$

Putting these relations in the given equation, we obtain

$$\sum_{n=2}^{\infty} n(n-1)a_n x^{n-2} - \sum_{n=2}^{\infty} n(n-1)a_n x^n - \sum_{n=1}^{\infty} 2na_n x^n + \sum_{n=0}^{\infty} m(m+1)a_n x^n = 0$$

or $\displaystyle\sum_{n=0}^{\infty} (n+1)(n+2)a_{n+2}x^n - \sum_{n=2}^{\infty} n(n-1)a_n x^n - \sum_{n=1}^{\infty} 2na_n x^n + \sum_{n=0}^{\infty} m(m+1)a_n x^n = 0$

or $[m(m+1)a_0 + 2a_2] + [(m-1)(m+2)a_1 + 6a_3]\,x$

$$+ \sum_{n=2}^{\infty} [(n+1)\,(n+2)a_{n+2} + (m-n)(m+n+1)a_n]\,x^n = 0.$$

Equating coefficients of various powers of x to zero, we obtain

$$m(m+1)a_0 + 2a_2 = 0,\ (m-1)(m+2)a_1 + 6a_3 = 0,$$

$$(n+1)(n+2)a_{n+2} + (m-n)(m+n+1)a_n = 0, n \geq 2$$

or $a_2 = -\dfrac{m(m+1)}{2!}a_0,\ a_3 = -\dfrac{(m-1)\,(m+2)}{3!}a_1,$

$$a_{n+2} = -\dfrac{(m-n)\,(m+n+1)}{(n+1)(n+2)}a_n \text{ for } n \geq 2. \text{ (Recurrence relation) ...(i)}$$

Putting $n = 2$ and 3 in the above relation, we obtain

$$a_4 = -\dfrac{(m-2)(m+3)}{4.3}a_2 = \dfrac{m(m-2)(m+1)\,(m+3)}{4!}a_0,$$

$$a_5 = -\dfrac{(m-3)(m+4)}{5.4}a_3 = \dfrac{(m-1)(m-3)(m+2)(m+4)}{5!}a_0,$$

and so on. Thus, for $|x| < 1,$ we obtain two linearly independent power series solutions: $y_1(x) = a_0 \left[1 - \dfrac{m(m+1)}{2!}x^2 + \dfrac{m(m-2)(m+1)(m+3)}{4!}x^4 - ... \right],$

$$y_2(x)=a_1\left[x-\frac{(m-1)(m+2)}{3!}x^3+\frac{(m-1)(m-3)(m+2)(m+4)}{5!}x^5-...\right].$$

Hence, the general solution is $y=y_1(x)+y_2(x)$.

(ii) **Show also that if m is a positive integer, then one of the two linearly independent power series solutions of the Legendre's equation, near x = 0 is a polynomial of degree m**

Ans. If m is a positive integer, then on taking n = m in the recurrence relation (i), we get $a_{m+2}=0$. Consequently, the recurrence relation gives

$$a_{m+4}=0, a_{m+6}=0, \text{ and so on.}$$

It follows that if m is odd, then all the odd coefficients $a_n=0$ for n > m, and if m is even, then all the even coefficients $a_n=0$ for n > m. Hence, one of the solutions $y_1(x)$ or $y_2(x)$ (depending on whether m is even or odd) will contain only a finite number of terms till x^m, and so it will be polynomial of degree m.

Q11. The equation y″ - 2xy′ + 2my = 0 plays a particularly important role in statistics. Its solutions are known as Hermite polynomials. Obtain the coefficients of the power series solution of this equation.

Ans. We would readily recognise that x = 0 is an ordinary point of the given equation. So we assume a solution of the form $y(x)=\sum\limits_{n=0}^{\infty}a_n x^n$

Then $y'(x)=\sum\limits_{n=1}^{\infty}na_n x^{n-1}$ and $y''(x)=\sum\limits_{n=2}^{\infty}n(n-1)a_n x^{n-2}$

Substituting these in the given equation, we find that

$$\sum_{n=2}^{\infty}n(n-1)a_n x^{n-2}-2\sum_{n=1}^{\infty}na_n x^{n}+2m\sum_{n=0}^{\infty}a_n x^{n}=0$$

In the expanded form, $(2a_2+6a_3 x+12a_4 x^2+...+n(n-1)a_n x^{n-2}+...)$

$-2(a_1 x+2a_2 x^2+3a_3 x^3+...+na_n x^n+...)+2m(a_0+a_1 x+a_2 x^2+...+a_n x^n+...)=0$

Collecting the coefficients of each power of x, we get

$$(2a_2+2ma_0)+(6a_3-2a_1+2ma_1)x+(12a_4-4a_2+2ma_2)x^2+...$$

$$+[(n+2)(n+1)a_{n+2}-2na_n+2ma_n]x^n+...=0$$

Next, we equate the coefficient of each power of x to zero. The result is

Coefficient of x^0 : $2a_2+2ma_0=0 \Rightarrow a_2=-\dfrac{2m\,a_0}{2\times1}$

Coefficient of x^1 : $6a_3 + (2m-2)a_1 = 0 \Rightarrow a_3 = \dfrac{2(1-m)}{3 \times 2} a_1$

Coefficient of x^2 : $12a_4 + (2m-4)a_2 = 0 \Rightarrow a_4 = \dfrac{(2-m)}{3 \times 2} a_2 = -\dfrac{2m(2-m)}{4 \times 3} a_0$

Coefficient of x^n : $(n+2)(n+1)\, a_{n+2} - 2(n-m)a_n = 0$

or $a_{n+2} = \dfrac{2(n-m)}{(n+2)(n+1)} a_n$

Q12. Use Frobenius method to solve the equation

$$\frac{d^2y}{dx^2} + \frac{1}{4x}\frac{dy}{dx} + \frac{1}{8x^2}y = 0,\ x > 0.$$

Ans. We have $8x^2y'' + 2xy' + y = 0$.

Clearly, $x = 0$ is a RSP and the indicial equation is $8r^2 - 6r + 1 = 0$, having roots $r_1 = \dfrac{1}{2},\ r_2 = \dfrac{1}{4}$.

Since $r_1 - r_2 = \dfrac{1}{4}$ is not an integer, we take

$$y = x^r \sum_{n=0}^{\infty} a_n x^n,\ \text{where } a_0 \neq 0 \qquad\qquad \text{...(i)}$$

$$\Rightarrow y = \sum_{n=0}^{\infty} a_n x^{n+r},\ y' = \sum_{n=0}^{\infty} (n+r)a_n x^{n+r-1},\ \text{and}$$

$$y'' = \sum_{n=0}^{\infty} (n+r)(n+r-1)a_n x^{n+r-2}.$$

The given differential equation now reduces to

$$\sum_{n=0}^{\infty} 8(n+r)(n+r-1)a_n x^{n+r} + \sum_{n=0}^{\infty} 2(n+r)a_n x^{n+r} + \sum_{n=0}^{\infty} a_n x^{n+r} = 0$$

or $x^r \sum_{n=0}^{\infty} \left\{ 8(n+r)^2 - 6(n+r) + 1 \right\} a_n x^n = 0$

Dividing by x^r and equating all the coefficients to zero, we get

$(8r^2 - 6r - 1)a_0 = 0 \Rightarrow 8r^2 - 6r + 1 = 0\ (\because a_0 \neq 0)$

(This is the indicial equation as obtained above.)

and $\{8(n+r)^2 - 6(n+r) + 1\}a_n = 0$, for $n \geq 1$.

The above equation is satisfied by both the values of r, viz. $\dfrac{1}{2}$ and $\dfrac{1}{4}$

by choosing $a_n = 0$ for $n \geq 1$. Thus, by (1) $y_1(x) = x^{1/2} \sum_{n=0}^{\infty} a_n x^n = a_0\sqrt{x}, x > 0$

and $y_2(x) = x^{1/4} \sum_{n=0}^{\infty} a_n x^n = a_0 x^{1/4}$.

Hence, the general solution is $y = c_1 y_1(x) + c_2 y_2(x) = a\, x^{1/2} + b\, x^{1/4}$.

where $a = a_0 c_1$, $b = a_0 c_2$ are arbitrary constants.

Q13. Find the general solution of $2x^2 y'' + (x^2 - x)y' + y = 0, x > 0$, near x = 0, using Frobenius method.

Ans. Here, $x\, P(x) = -1 + \frac{1}{2}x \to -1$ as $x \to 0, x^2 Q(x) = \frac{1}{2}$.

Here x = 0 is a RSP and the indicial equation is $r(r-1) - \frac{1}{2}r + 1 = 0$ or $2r^2 - 3r + 1 = 0$.

Its roots are $r_1 = 1, r_2 = \frac{1}{2}$. We notice that the difference between these two roots is not an integer. We take $y = x^r \sum_{n=0}^{\infty} a_n x^n = \sum_{n=0}^{\infty} a_n x^{n+r}$.

Substituting y and its first two derivatives in the given differential equation, we obtain

$$\sum_{n=0}^{\infty} 2(n+r)(n+r-1)a_n x^{n+r} + \sum_{n=0}^{\infty} (n+r)a_n x^{n+r+1}$$

$$-\sum_{n=0}^{\infty} (n+r)a_n x^{n+r} + \sum_{n=0}^{\infty} a_n x^{n+r} = 0.$$

Dividing throughout by x^r and on combining terms, we obtain

$$\sum_{n=0}^{\infty} \{2(n+r)^2 - 3(n+r) + 1\} a_n x^n + \sum_{n=0}^{\infty} (n+r)a_n x^{n+1} = 0.$$

Changing n to $n-1$ in the second summation, we obtain

$$(2r^2 - 3r + 1)a_0 + \sum_{n=1}^{\infty} \{2(n+r)^2 - 3(n+r) + 1\} a_n x^n$$

$$+ \sum_{n=1}^{\infty} (n+r-1) a_{n-1} x^n = 0$$

or $(2r^2 - 3r + 1)a_0 + \sum_{n=1}^{\infty} [\{2(n+r)^2 - 3(n+r) + 1\}a_n + (n+r-1)a_{n-1}]x^n = 0$.

Equating the coefficients of various powers of x to zero, we obtain

$(2r^2 - 3r + 1)a_0 = 0 \Rightarrow 2r^2 - 3r + 1 = 0,$ $(\because a_0 \neq 0)$

and $\{2(n+r)^2 - 3(n+r)+1\}a_n +(n+r-1)a_{n-1} =0$, for $n \geq 1$.   ...(i)

For $r = r_1 = 1$, the above recurrence relation gives $a_n = -\dfrac{a_{n-1}}{2n+1}, \geq 1$.

$\therefore \ a_1 = -\dfrac{1}{3}a_0, \ a_2 = \dfrac{a_0}{3.5}, \ a_3 = -\dfrac{a_0}{3.5.7}$, and so on

Thus, $y_1(x) = x^1 \displaystyle\sum_{n=0}^{\infty} a_n x^n = a_0 x \left(1 - \dfrac{1}{3}x + \dfrac{1}{3.5}x^2 - \dfrac{1}{3.5.7}x^3 + ...\right)$

$\therefore \ y_1(x) = a_0 \displaystyle\sum_{n=0}^{\infty} (-1)^n \dfrac{x^{n+1}}{1.3.5......(2n+1)}, x > 0.$

Similarly, for $r = r_2 = 1/2$, the recurrence relation (i) gives

$a_n = -\dfrac{a_{n-1}}{2n}$ for $n \geq 1$.

$\therefore \ a_1 = -\dfrac{1}{2}a_0, \ a_2 = \dfrac{a_0}{2^2 2!}, \ a_3 = -\dfrac{a_0}{2^3 3!},....$

Thus, a second linearly independent solution is

$y_2(x) = x^{1/2} \displaystyle\sum_{n=0}^{\infty} a_n x^n$, for $x > 0$

$= a_0 \sqrt{x} \left(1 - \dfrac{1}{2}x + \dfrac{1}{2^2 2!}x^2 - \dfrac{1}{2^3 3!}x^3 + ...\right)$

$= a_0 \sqrt{x} \displaystyle\sum_{n=0}^{\infty} (-1)^n \dfrac{x^n}{2^n n!}.$

$\therefore \quad y_2(x) = a_0 \sqrt{x}\, e^{-x/2}$, for $x > 0$.

Hence, the general solution is $y = c_1 y_1(x) + c_2 y_2(x)$, where c_1 and c_2 are arbitrary constants.

Q14. Obtain the singular point of $x^2 \dfrac{d^2 y}{dx^2} + x\dfrac{dy}{dx} + (x^2 - 4)\, y = 0$ **and determine the indicial equation and its roots.**

[June-2010,Q.No.-2(a)]

Ans. Given equation is $x^2 \dfrac{d^2 y}{dx^2} + x\dfrac{dy}{dx} + (x^2 - 4)\, y = 0$ ...(i)

On dividing by x^2, we get $\dfrac{d^2 y}{dx^2} + \dfrac{1}{x}\dfrac{dy}{dx} + \dfrac{(x^2 - 4)}{x^2}\, y = 0$

Compare with $\dfrac{dy}{dx} + Py = Q$, we get $P(x) = \dfrac{1}{x}, \quad Q(x) = \dfrac{x^2 - 4}{x^2}$

Now, $xP(x) = x \cdot \dfrac{1}{x}$ and $x^2 Q(x) = \dfrac{x^2 - 4}{x^2} \cdot x^2$

$\Rightarrow xP(x) = 1$ and $x^2 Q(x) = x^2 - 4$

Here, $\displaystyle\lim_{x \to 0} xP(x) = 1 = b(x)$ and $\displaystyle\lim_{x \to 0} x^2 Q(x) = -4 = c(x)$

Since, $b(x)$ and $c(x)$ are both analytic. Hence $x = 0$ is regular singular point (RSP).

Now, $y(x) = \displaystyle\sum_{n=0}^{\infty} a_n x^{n+r} \Rightarrow y'(x) = \displaystyle\sum_{n=0}^{\infty} a_n (n+r) x^{n+r-1}$

and $y''(x) = \displaystyle\sum_{n=0}^{\infty} a_n (n+r)(n+r-1) x^{n+r-2}$

Substituting these values in Eq (i), we get

$$\sum_{n=0}^{\infty} a_n (n+r)(n+r-1) x^{n+r} + \sum_{n=0}^{\infty} a_n (n+r) x^{n+r} + \sum_{n=0}^{\infty} a_n x^{n+r+2} - 4\sum_{n=0}^{\infty} a_n x^{n+r} = 0$$

Now equating the coefficients of the lowest power of x, i.e. x^{n+r} to zero. This gives $a_0 \left[r(r-1) + r - 4 \right] = 0$

For $a_0 \neq 0$, the indicial equation takes the form, $r(r-1) + r - 4 = 0$

$\Rightarrow r^2 - r + r - 4 = 0 \Rightarrow r^2 - 4 = 0 \Rightarrow (r+2)(r-2) = 0 \Rightarrow r = 2, -2$

Hence, required roots are 2 and –2.

Q15. Show that $x = 0$ is a regular singular point of $(2x + x^3)\dfrac{d^2y}{dx^2} - \dfrac{dy}{dx} - 6xy = 0$ and find its solution about $x = 0$.

Ans. Here, $P(x) = -\dfrac{1}{2x + x^3}, Q(x) = -\dfrac{6x}{2x + x^3}$.

Now, $\displaystyle\lim_{x \to 0} x\, P(x) = \lim_{x \to 0} \left(-\dfrac{1}{2 + x^2} \right) = -\dfrac{1}{2} \Rightarrow p_0 = -\dfrac{1}{2}$,

and $\displaystyle\lim_{x \to 0} x^2 Q(x) = \lim_{x \to 0} \left(-\dfrac{6x^2}{2 + x^2} \right) = 0 \Rightarrow q_0 = 0.$

Thus, $x = 0$ is a RSP of the given equation.

The indicial equation is $r^2 + (p_0 - 1)r + q_0 = 0$ or $r^2 - (3/2)r = 0$.

Its roots are $r_1 = 3/2, r_2 = 0$.

Since $r_1 - r_2 = 3/2$ is not an integer, we take

$$y = x^r \sum_{n=0}^{\infty} a_n x^n, \text{ where } a_0 \neq 0 \qquad \qquad \text{...(i)}$$

$$\Rightarrow y = \sum_{n=0}^{\infty} a_n x^{n+r}, \quad y' = \sum_{n=0}^{\infty} (n+r) a_n x^{n+r-1} \text{ and}$$

$$y'' = \sum_{n=0}^{\infty} (n+r)(n+r-1) a_n x^{n+r-2}.$$

The given differential equation now reduces to

$$\sum_{n=0}^{\infty} (2x + x^3)(n+r)(n+r-1) a_n x^{n+r-2} - \sum_{n=0}^{\infty} (n+r) a_n x^{n+r-1} - \sum_{n=0}^{\infty} 6 a_n x^{n+r+1} = 0$$

or $\displaystyle \sum_{n=0}^{\infty} \{(n+r)(n+r-1) - 6\} a_n x^{n+r+1} + \sum_{n=0}^{\infty} \{2(n+r)(n+r-1) - (n+r)\} a_n x^{n+r-1} = 0.$

Dividing throughout by x^{r-1}, we obtain

$$\sum_{n=0}^{\infty} \{2(n+r)(n+r-1) - (n+r)\} a_n x^n + \sum_{n=0}^{\infty} \{(n+r)(n+r-1) - 6\} a_n x^{n+2} = 0.$$

Equating the coefficients of various powers of x, we get

$$(2r^2 - 3r) a_0 = 0 \Rightarrow 2r^2 - 3r = 0 \qquad \qquad (\because a_0 \neq 0),$$

$$\{2(1+r)r - (1+r)\} a_1 = 0 \Rightarrow a_1 = 0,$$

$$\{2(r+2)(r+1) - (r+2)\} a_2 + \{r(r-1) - 6\} a_0 = 0, \qquad \qquad \text{...(i)}$$

$$\{2(r+3)(r+2) - (r+3)\} a_3 + \{(r+1)r - 6\} a_1 = 0 \Rightarrow a_3 = 0$$

$$\{2(r+4)(r+3) - (r+4)\} a_4 + \{(r+2)(r+1) - 6\} a_2 = 0, \qquad \qquad \text{...(ii)}$$

and so on. It is easy to verify that $a_1 = a_3 = a_5 = ... = 0.$

From (i), $(r+2)(2r+1) a_2 + (r+2)(r-3) a_0 = 0 \Rightarrow a_2 = -\left(\dfrac{r-3}{2r+1}\right) a_0.$

Similarly, from (ii), $a_4 = \left(\dfrac{r-1}{2r+5}\right) \cdot \left(\dfrac{r-3}{2r+1}\right) a_0$, etc.

$$\therefore \quad y = a_0 x^r (1 + a_2 x^2 + a_4 x^4 + ...)$$

or $\displaystyle y = a_0 x^r \left[1 - \frac{r-3}{2r+1} x^2 + \frac{(r-1)(r-3)}{(2r+1)(2r+5)} x^4 - .... \right].$

Putting $r = 0$ and $3/2$ and taking $a_0 = a$ and b respectively in the above relation, the required solution is

$$y = a\left(1 + 3x^2 + \frac{3}{5} x^4 - ....\right) + bx^{3/2}\left(1 + \frac{3}{8} x^2 - \frac{3}{128} x^4 + ...\right).$$

Q16. Find the general solution of $x^2 y'' - xy' + y = 0$ near $x = 0$.

Ans. Here, $P(x) = -1/x, Q(x) = 1/x^2$

$$\Rightarrow \qquad xP(x) = -1 \text{ and } x^2 Q(x) = 1.$$

Thus, $x = 0$ is a RSP, and $r(r-1) - r + 1 = 0$ or $(r-1)^2 = 0$ is the indicial equation having equal roots $r_1 = r_2 = 1$.

Substituting $y = x^r \sum\limits_{n=0}^{\infty} a_n x^n$ and its first two derivatives in the given differential equation and simplifying, we obtain $x^r \sum\limits_{n=0}^{\infty} (n + r - 1)^2 a_n x^n = 0$.

Dividing by x^r and equating the coefficients of various powers of x to zero, we obtain $(r-1)^2 a_0 = 0 \Rightarrow (r-1)^2 = 0$, since $a_0 \neq 0$ and $(n+r-1)^2 a_n = 0$, for $n \geq 1$.

Taking $r = 1$, we obtain $n^2 a_n = 0$, for $n \geq 1$

$\therefore \quad a_n = 0$, for $n \geq 1$. Also $r = 1$

Thus, $y_1(x) = a_0 x$ is a solution.

To find the second solution $y_2(x)$, we take

$$y(r,x) = x^r \sum\limits_{n=0}^{\infty} a_n x^n = a_0 x^r. \qquad (\because a_n = 0 \text{ for } x \geq 1)$$

$$\therefore \quad \frac{\partial y(r,x)}{\partial r} = a_0 x^r \log x, \text{ for } x > 0.$$

Now, $y_2(x) = \dfrac{\partial y(r,x)}{\partial r}\bigg|_{r=1} = a_0 x \log x.$

The general solution is $y = c_1 y_1(x) + c_2 y_2(x) = ax + bx \log x$, where a and b are arbitrary constants.

Q17. Find the general solution of the Bessel's equation of order one: $x^2 y'' + xy' + (x^2 - 1)y = 0, x > 0$ near $x = 0$.

Ans. Here, $x P(x) = 1$ and $x^2 Q(x) = -1 + x^2 \to -1$ as $x \to 0$.

$\therefore x = 0$ is a RSP and the indicial equation is

$r(r-1) + r - 1 = 0 \Rightarrow (r-1)(r+1) = 0 \Rightarrow r_1 = 1, r_2 = -1.$

Here $r_1 - r_2 = 2$ is a positive integer. We take

$$y = x^r \sum\limits_{n=0}^{\infty} a_n x^n, a_0 \neq 0. \qquad \qquad \text{...(i)}$$

Substituting this value of y and its first two derivatives in the given equation, we obtain

$$\sum_{n=0}^{\infty}(n+r)(n+r-1)a_n x^n + \sum_{n=0}^{\infty}(n+r)a_n x^n + \sum_{n=0}^{\infty}a_n x^{n+2} - \sum_{n=0}^{\infty}a_n x^n = 0$$

or $\sum_{n=0}^{\infty}\{(n+r)^2 - 1\}a_n x^n + \sum_{n=2}^{\infty}a_{n-2}x^n = 0,$ which gives

$$(r^2 - 1)a_0 = 0 \Rightarrow r = 1, -1 \qquad\qquad (\because a_0 \neq 0)$$

$$[(1+r)^2 - 1]\,a_1 = 0 \Rightarrow a_1 = 0$$

and $\{(n+r)^2 - 1\}a_n + a_{n-2} = 0,$ for $n \geq 2.$ ...(ii)

For r = 1, we obtain $a_n = \dfrac{-1}{n\,(n+2)}a_{n-2},$ for $n \geq 2.$

Now, $a_1 = 0$ implies $0 = a_3 = a_5 = a_7 = ...$

Also, $a_2 = -\dfrac{1}{2.4}a_0 = -\dfrac{1}{2^2.1!2!}a_0,$

$a_4 = -\dfrac{1}{4.6}a_2 = \dfrac{1}{2^4 2!3!}a_0,$ and so on.

Thus, $y_1(x) = a_0 x\left(1 - \dfrac{1}{2^2 1!2!}x^2 + \dfrac{1}{2^4 2!3!}x^4 - ....\right)$

or $y_1(x) = a_0\, x \sum_{n=0}^{\infty}\dfrac{(-1)^n}{2^{2n}\,n!\,(n+1)!}x^{2n}.$

Note: If we substitute $r = r_2 = -1$ in the recurrence relation (ii), then

$$a_n = -\dfrac{1}{n(n-2)}a_{n-2},$$ which fails to define $a_2.$

So we do not get the second solution $y_2(x)$ from this recurrence relation. We shall now obtain $y_2(x).$

From the recurrence relation (ii), we obtain $0 = a_1 = a_3 = a_5 = ...$

and $a_2 = \dfrac{-1}{(r+3)(r+1)}a_0,$ $a_4 = \dfrac{1}{(r+5)(r+3)^2(r+1)}a_0, ...$

Thus, $y(r,x) = a_0\left[x^r - \dfrac{1}{(r+3)(r+1)}x^{r+2} + \dfrac{1}{(r+5)(r+3)^2(r+1)}x^{r+4} - ...\right]$

Now $r - r_2 = r + 1 \Rightarrow (r - r_2)y(r,x) = (r+1)y(r,x)$

or $(r - r_2)y(r,x) = a_0 \left[(r+1)x^r - \dfrac{1}{r+3}x^{r+2} + \dfrac{1}{(r+5)\,(r+3)^2}x^{r+4} - \ldots \right]$

Using $\dfrac{\partial}{\partial r}(x^{r+k}) = x^{r+k}\log x$ (for $x > 0$), we obtain

$\dfrac{\partial}{\partial r}[(r - r_2)y(r,x)] = a_0 \left[x^r + (r+1)x^r \log x + \dfrac{1}{(r+3)^2}x^{r+2} \right.$

$-\dfrac{1}{(r+3)}x^{r+2}\log x - \dfrac{1}{(r+5)^2(r+3)^2}x^{r+4}$

$\left. -\dfrac{2}{(r+5)(r+3)^3}x^{r+4} + \dfrac{1}{(r+5)(r+3)^2}x^{r+4}\log\,x + \ldots \right]$

Thus, $y_2(x) = \dfrac{\partial}{\partial r}\left[(r - r_2)\,y\,(r,x)\right]_{r=r_2=-1}$

$= a_0 \left(x^{-1} + 0 + \dfrac{1}{4}x - \dfrac{1}{2}x\log\,x - \dfrac{1}{64}x^3 - \dfrac{2}{32}x^3 + \dfrac{1}{16}x^3\log\,x + \ldots \right)$

$= \left(-\dfrac{1}{2}\log x \right)a_0 \times \left(1 - \dfrac{1}{8}x^2 + \ldots \right) + a_0 \left(x^{-1} + \dfrac{1}{4}x - \dfrac{5}{64}x^3 + \ldots \right)$

$= -\dfrac{1}{2}\log x\,y_1(x) + a_0\,x^{-1}\left(1 + \dfrac{1}{4}x^2 - \dfrac{5}{64}x^4 + \ldots \right).$

Hence, the general solution is $y = c_1\,y_1(x) + c_2\,y_2(x)$.

Q18. Determine the two Frobenius series solutions around $x = 0$ for the ODE $x^2 y'' + \left(x^2 + \dfrac{5}{36} \right)y = 0$

Ans. Let us first rewrite the given ODE in the standard form on dividing

by $x^2 : y'' + \left(\dfrac{x^2 + \dfrac{5}{36}}{x^2} \right)y = 0$ $\hspace{2cm}$ ...(i)

Here $p(x) = 0$ and $q(x) = \dfrac{x^2 + (5/36)}{x^2}$. We will easily recognise that the point $x = 0$ is a singularity. Further, since $\lim\limits_{x \to 0} x^2 q(x) = 5/36$, we may logically conclude that $x = 0$ is a regular singular point of the given differential equation. By assuming a solution of the form $y(x) = \sum\limits_{m=0}^{\infty} a_m x^{m+r}$ and substituting it in (i), we will obtain

$$\sum_{m=0}^{\infty} a_m(m+r)(m+r-1)x^{m+r} + \sum_{m=0}^{\infty} a_m x^{m+r+2} + \dfrac{5}{36}\sum_{m=0}^{\infty} a_m x^{m+r} = 0$$

To obtain the indicial equation, we equate the sum of the coefficients of x^r to zero. This yields $a_0\left[r(r-1)+\dfrac{5}{36}\right]=0$

For $a_0\neq 0$, we find that $r(r-1)+\dfrac{5}{36}=0$ is the required indicial equation. We can readily verify that the two distinct roots are 5/6 and 1/6. Moreover, these do not differ by an integer.

To determine a_n corresponding to $r=5/6$, let us equate the sum of the coefficients of $x^{r+1},x^{r+2},\ldots x^{n+r}$ to zero:

$$\text{Coefficient of } x^{r+1}:\quad a_1\left[r(r+1)+\frac{5}{36}\right]=0$$

Since the bracketed term does not vanish for $r=r_1=5/6$, this equality will hold only if we choose $a_1=0$.

$$\text{Similarly, coefficient of } x^{r+2}:\quad a_2(r+1)(r+2)+a_0+\frac{5}{36}a_2=0$$

or

$$a_2=-\frac{a_0}{(r+1)(r+2)+\dfrac{5}{36}}$$

$$\text{Coefficient of } x^{m+r}:\quad a_m(m+r)(m+r-1)+a_{m-2}+\frac{5}{36}a_m=0$$

or $a_m\left[(m+r)(m+r-1)+\dfrac{5}{36}\right]=-a_{m-2}$

On substituting $r=r_1=5/6$, we will find that

$$a_m\left[\left(m+\frac{5}{6}\right)\left(m-\frac{1}{6}\right)+\frac{5}{36}\right]=-a_{m-2}$$

or $a_m=-\dfrac{a_{m-2}}{m\left(m+\dfrac{2}{3}\right)}$ 　　　　　　　　　　...(ii)

Since $a_1=0$, this recurrence relation implies that all odd coefficients will vanish. To evaluate even coefficients, let us introduce the change $m=2p$. This means that $a_{2p}=-\dfrac{a_{2p-2}}{2p\left(2p+\dfrac{2}{3}\right)}=-\dfrac{3}{4}\dfrac{a_{2p-2}}{p(3p+1)}$

Hence, with

$$p=1:\qquad a_2=-\frac{3}{4}\left(\frac{a_0}{1\times4}\right)$$

$p = 2:$ $\qquad a_4 = -\dfrac{3}{4}\left(\dfrac{a_2}{2\times 7}\right) = \left(\dfrac{3}{4}\right)^2 \dfrac{a_0}{1\times 2\times 4\times 7} = \left(\dfrac{3}{4}\right)^2 \dfrac{a_0}{2!\,4\times 7}$

Similarly, we can write

$p = 3:$ $\qquad a_6 = -\left(\dfrac{3}{4}\right)^3 \dfrac{a_0}{3!\,4\times 7\times 10}$

$$a_{2p} = (-1)^P \left(\dfrac{3}{4}\right)^P \dfrac{a_0}{p!\,1\times 4\times 7\times 10 \,.....(3p+1)}$$

Hence, one of the solutions of the given equation is

$$y_1(x) = a_0 x^{5/6}\left[1 - \dfrac{3}{16}x^2 + \dfrac{9}{16}\cdot\dfrac{x^4}{2\times 4\times 7} - ... + (-1)^P\left(\dfrac{3}{4}\right)^P \dfrac{x^{2P}}{p!\,1\times 4\times 7...(3p+1)}\right]$$

This can be expressed in a compact from as

$$y_1(x) = a_0 x^{5/6}\left[1 + \sum_{p=1}^{\infty}(-1)^P\left(\dfrac{3}{4}\right)^P \dfrac{x^{2P}}{p!\,1\times 4\times 7....(3p+1)}\right]$$

For $r = r_2 = 1/6$ also, all odd coefficients will vanish and similarly,

we   can   verify   that $y_2(x) = d_0 x^{1/6} + \sum\limits_{p=1}^{\infty} d_{2p} x^{2P+(1/6)}$ where

$$d_{2p} = (-1)^P\left(\dfrac{3}{4}\right)^P \dfrac{d_0}{p!\,2\times 5\times 8 ...(3p-1)}$$

Q19. Obtain the general solution of the following ODE using the power series method $(x^2 + 1)\,y'' - 2x\,y' + 2y = 0$.   **[June-2011,Q.No.-2(a)]**

Ans. Given ODE is $(x^2 + 1)y'' - 2xy' + 2y = 0$ ...(i)

Dividing eq. (1) by $x^2 + 1$, we get $\quad y'' - \dfrac{2x}{x^2+1}y' + \dfrac{2}{x^2+1}y = 0$ ...(ii)

or $\quad \dfrac{d^2y}{dx^2} - \dfrac{2x}{x^2+1}\dfrac{dy}{dx} + \dfrac{2}{x^2+1}y = 0$

Compare this equation with $\quad \dfrac{d^2y}{dx^2} + P(x)\dfrac{dy}{dx} + Q(x)y = 0$

$\Rightarrow \quad P(x) = \dfrac{-2x}{x^2+1}, \quad Q(x) = \dfrac{2}{x^2+1}$

are both analytic at $x = 0$. Thus, $x = 0$ is an ordinary point.

Now, $\quad y = \sum\limits_{n=0}^{\infty} a_n x^n$ ...(i)

$y' = \sum\limits_{n=1}^{\infty} na_n x^{n-1}$ and $y'' = \sum\limits_{n=2}^{\infty} n(n-1)\,a_n x^{n-2}$ ...(ii) & ...(iii)

Substituting y, y' and y'' from (i), (ii) and (iii) in eq. (i), we obtain,

$$(x^2+1)\sum_{n=2}^{\infty} n(n-1)a_n x^{n-2} - 2x\sum_{n=1}^{\infty} na_n x^{n-1} + 2\sum_{n=0}^{\infty} a_n x^n = 0$$

$$\Rightarrow \sum_{n=2}^{\infty} n(n-1)a_n x^{n-2} + \sum_{n=2}^{\infty} n(n-1)a_n x^n - 2\sum_{n=1}^{\infty} a_n x^n + 2\sum_{n=0}^{\infty} na_n x^n = 0$$

By changing n to $n+2$ in first summation, we obtain,

$$\sum_{n=0}^{\infty}(n+2)(n+1)a_{n+2}x^n + \sum_{n=2}^{\infty} n(n-1)\,a_n x^n - 2a_1 x - 2\sum_{n=2}^{\infty} na_n x^n$$

$$+2a_0 + 2a_1 x + 2\sum_{n=2}^{\infty} a_n x^n = 0$$

$$\Rightarrow (2a_2+2a_0)+6a_3 x + \sum_{n=2}^{\infty}\{(n+2)(n+1)a_{n+2}+n(n-1)a_n - 2na_n + 2a_n\}x^n = 0$$

$$\Rightarrow (2a_2+2a_0)+6a_3 x + \sum_{n=2}^{\infty}\{(n+2)(n+1)a_{n+2} + (n-2)(n-1)a_n\}x^n = 0$$

Now comparing the coefficients of various powers of x, we obtain,

$$2a_2 + 2a_0 = 0 \Rightarrow a_2 + a_0 = 0 \Rightarrow a_2 = -a_0$$

and $a_3 = 0$ and $(n+2)(n+1)a_{n+2} + (n-2)(n-1)a_n = 0$

$$\Rightarrow a_{n+2} = \frac{-(n-2)(n-1)\,a_n}{(n+2)(n+1)} \qquad\qquad \text{...(iii)}$$

eq. (iii) is called recurrence relation.

$$\therefore\ a_5=0,\ a_7=0,\ a_9=0.... \qquad\qquad (\because a_3 = 0)$$

and $a_4 = 0,\ a_6 = 0....$

Hence, solution is $y(x) = a_0 + a_1 x + a_2 x^2 + a_3 x^3 + a_4 x^4 + ...$

$$\Rightarrow y(x) = a_0 + a_1 x - a_0 x^2 \Rightarrow y(x) = a_0(1-x^2) + a_1 x \Rightarrow$$

$y(x) = a_0 y_1(x) + a_1 y_2(x)$

Q20. Use the Frobenius method to solve the equation
$$x^2 y'' + xy' + (x^2 - \tfrac{1}{4})y = 0,\ x > 0.$$

Ans. Here, $x = 0$ is a RSP. The indicial equation is $r^2 - \dfrac{1}{4} = 0$, therefore

$r_1 = \dfrac{1}{2}, r_2 = -\dfrac{1}{2}$. Note that $r_1 - r_2 = 1$ (a positive integer), but still we can find

two linearly independent solutions.

Substituting $y = x^r \sum_{n=0}^{\infty} a_n x^n$, and its first two derivatives in the given

equation, we obtain $(r^2 - \dfrac{1}{4})a_0 = 0$,

$$\{(r+1)^2 - \frac{1}{4}\} \, a_1 = 0, \text{ and } \{(r+n)^2 - \frac{1}{4}\} a_n + a_{n-2} = 0, \text{ for } n \geq 2. \quad \text{...(i)}$$

Now $r = \frac{1}{2} \Rightarrow 0 = a_1 = a_3 = a_5 = ...$

and $a_2 = -\frac{1}{3!} a_0, \, a_4 = \frac{1}{5!} a_0, \, ...$

$$\therefore \quad y_1(x) = a_0 \sqrt{x} \left(1 - \frac{x^2}{3!} + \frac{x^4}{5!} - ... \right)$$

Again $r = -\frac{1}{2} \Rightarrow (-\frac{1}{2} + 1)^2 - \frac{1}{4} = 0.$

Taking $a_1 \neq 0$, we obtain, from (i), $\quad a_3 = -\frac{1}{3!} a_1, \quad a_5 = \frac{1}{5!} a_1, ...$

$$a_2 = -\frac{1}{2!} a_0, \, a_4 = \frac{1}{4!} a_0, ...$$

Thus, $y_2(x) = a_0 x^{-1/2} \left(1 - \frac{x^2}{2!} + \frac{x^4}{4!} - .... \right) + a_1 x^{-1/2} \left(x - \frac{x^3}{3!} + \frac{x^5}{5!} ..... \right)$

or $y_2(x) = x^{-1/2}(a_0 \cos x + a_1 \sin x).$

This is a complete solution of the given equation, where a_0 and a_1 are arbitrary constants.

Q21. Like Legendre's equation, another ODE that arises in advanced studies in physics and applied mathematics is the Bessel's equation of order m:

$$x^2 \, y'' + xy' + (x^2 - m^2) y = 0$$

Use Frobenius' method to solve this equation.

Ans. The family of ODEs $x^2 y'' + xy' + (x^2 - m^2)y = 0$ is known as Bessel's equations. The parameter m is real and non-negative. We would readily note that $x = 0$ is a regular singular point of the equation. So we assume that $y(x) = \sum_{n=0}^{\infty} a_n x^{n+r}$ ...(i)

Substitute $y(x)$ and its derivatives in the given equation. This yields

$$\sum_{n=0}^{\infty} (n+r)(n+r-1) \, a_n x^{n+r} + \sum_{n=0}^{\infty} (n+r) a_n x^{n+r} + \sum_{n=0}^{\infty} a_n x^{n+r+2} - \sum_{n=0}^{\infty} m^2 a_n x^{n+r} = 0$$

Changing the first summation so that the exponent on x is n+r and collecting other series, we have

$$\sum_{n=0}^{\infty} [(n+r)(n+r-1) + (n+r) - m^2] \, a_n x^{n+r} + \sum_{n=2}^{\infty} a_{n-2} x^{n+r} = 0 \quad \text{...(ii)}$$

The smallest power of x is $x^r (n = 0)$. Equating the coefficient of x^r to zero, we get $[r(r-1)+r-m^2] a_0 = 0$

Since $a_0 \neq 0$, we have the indicial equation

$$r^2 - m^2 = 0 \qquad \qquad \text{...(iii)}$$

which has roots $r_1 = m$ and $r_2 = -m$.

Depending on the value of m, the solutions can differ vastly:

$$y_1(x) = \sum_{n=0}^{\infty} a_n x^{n+m} \qquad \qquad \text{...(iv)}$$

and

$$y_2(x) = \sum_{n=0}^{\infty} b_n x^{n-m} \qquad \qquad \text{...(v)}$$

To find y_1, let us write (ii) in the expanded form

$$x^r [(r^2 - m^2) a_0 + \{(r+1)^2 - m^2\} a_1 x$$

$$+ \{(r+2)^2 - m^2\} a_2 x^2 + ... + \{(n+r)^2 - m^2\} a_n x^n + ...]$$

$$+ x^r [a_0 x^2 + a_1 x^3 + a_2 x^4 + ... + a_{n-2} x^n + ...] = 0$$

Equating the coefficient of each power of x to zero, we get

Coefficient of $x^r \quad : \quad (r^2 - m^2) a_0 = 0$

Coefficient of $x^{r+1} \quad : \quad \left[(r+1)^2 - m^2 \right] a_1 = 0$

Coefficient of $x^{r+2} \quad : \quad \left[(r+2)^2 - m^2 \right] a_2 - a_0 = 0 \Rightarrow a_2 = -\dfrac{1}{(r+2)^2 - m^2} a_0$

Coefficient of $x^{r+n} \quad : \quad [(n+r)^2 - m^2] a_n + a_{n-2} = 0 \Rightarrow a_n = -\dfrac{1}{(n+r)^2 - m^2} a_{n-2}$

For $r = m$, we find that $a_1 = 0$ since the bracketed quantity does not vanish. Then recurrence relation implies that $a_3 = a_5 = a_7 = 0 = ...$, i.e. all odd subscripted coefficients vanish. For even subscripted coefficients, we find that $a_2 = -\dfrac{a_0}{(m+2)^2 - m^2} = -\dfrac{a_0}{(m+2-m)(m+2+m)} = -\dfrac{a_0}{2^2(m+1)}$

Similarly, $a_4 = -\dfrac{a_2}{2^2 \times 2(m+2)} = \dfrac{a_0}{2^4 \times 2(m+1)(m+2)}$

$$a_6 = -\dfrac{a_4}{2^2 \times 3(m+3)} = -\dfrac{a_0}{2^6 \times 3 \times 2(m+1)(m+2)(m+3)}$$

In general, $a_{2n} = \dfrac{(-1)^n a_0}{2^{2n} n!(m+1)(m+2)...(m+n)} \qquad n = 0, 1, 2,...$

The solution corresponding to $r_2 = -m$ is found by simply replacing m by –m provided m is not an integer.

Q22. Using the power series method, obtain the recurrence relation for the following equation: $y'' - 2xy' + 2ny = 0$.   **[June-2013,Q.No.-2(a)]**

Ans. Given equation is $y'' - 2xy' + 2ny = 0$

Here $P(x) = -2x$ and $Q(x) = 2n$ are both analytic at $x = 0$ Thus, $x = 0$ is an ordinary point.

Now, $\displaystyle y = \sum_{n=0}^{\infty} a_n x^n \;\Rightarrow\; y' = \sum_{n=1}^{\infty} n a_n x^{n-1}$ and $\displaystyle y'' = \sum_{n=2}^{\infty} n(n-1) a_n x^{n-2}$

On substituting y, y', y'' in given equation, we get

$$\sum_{n=2}^{\infty} n(n-1) a_n x^{n-2} - 2\sum_{n=1}^{\infty} n a_n x^n + 2n\sum_{n=0}^{\infty} a_n x^n = 0$$

Replacing n by n + 2 in first summation, we get

$$\sum_{n=0}^{\infty} (n+2)(n+1) a_n x^n - 2\sum_{n=1}^{\infty} n a_n x^n + 2n\sum_{n=0}^{\infty} a_n x^n = 0$$

$$\Rightarrow \qquad 2a_0 + \sum_{n=1}^{\infty} (n+2)(n+1) a_n x^n - 2\sum_{n=1}^{\infty} n a_n x^n + 0 + 2n\sum_{n=1}^{\infty} a_n x^n = 0$$

$$\Rightarrow \qquad 2a_0 + \sum_{n=1}^{\infty} \left[(n+2)(n+1) a_n - 2n a_n + 2n a_n \right] x^n = 0$$

Equating the constant term and the coefficients of various powers of x to zero, we obtain $2a_0 = 0 \;\Rightarrow\; a_0 = 0$ and $\left[(n+2)(n+1) - 2n + 2n \right] a_n = 0$

$$\Rightarrow \quad (n+2)(n+1) a_n = 0 \;\Rightarrow\; a_n = 0$$

This is the required recurrence relation of the given equation.

The main aim of GPH book is to provide knowledge as well as good marks in exams.

◈ ◈ ◈

Some Applications of ODEs in Physics

AN OVERVIEW

There are many real life applications of differential equations. In addition to the general, every-day uses, many of the equations that describe major concepts in physics and engineering are differential equations: Newton's Second Law (sometimes simply expressed as "force equals mass times acceleration") is a differential equation, as is his law of cooling. The Einstein field equations that describe his general theory of relativity also rely on differential equations. When physicists describe waves of light, sound and water, they use differential wave equations. Although, these are all real-world applications of differential equations.

Mathematical Modelling: A mathematical model is a description of a system using mathematical concepts and languages. The process of developing a mathematical model is termed mathematical modelling.

In other words, the process of mimicking reality by using the language of mathematics is known as mathematical modelling.

The various steps in the mathematical modelling process are as follows:

Step 1: Specify the real problem

Step 2: Set up the model

Step 3: Formulate the mathematical problem

Step 4: Solve the mathematical problem

Step 5: Interpret the solution

Step 6: Compare with reality

Applications of first order ODEs in Newtonian Mechanics: We know that the mechanics is the study of motion of objects and the effect of forces acting on objects. Newtonian mechanics deals with the motion of objects that are large compared to atoms, and move with speeds much less than the speed of light. A model for Newtonian mechanics can be based on Newton's laws of motion. Here we shall consider two specific examples on (i) motion under resistive forces that depend on velocity and (ii) velocity of escape.

(i) Motion under velocity-dependent resistive forces:

To explain this, we consider the following example:

A packet of mass 60 kg is dropped from rest from a helicopter hovering at a height of 750m. It falls on the earth under the influence of gravity. A force due to air resistance also acts on the packet opposite to the force of gravity (Fig. 4.1). It is proportional to the packet's velocity with a proportionality constant k. Determine when the packet will hit the ground. What will its velocity be when it hits the ground?

Let us solve it stepwise.

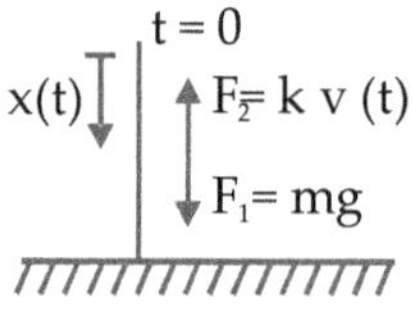

Fig. 4.1: Packet at an instant t

Step I: The specific problem here is to find velocity and the position of the packet as a function of time. We can then plug in the numbers in these functions to get the required answers.

Step II: We use Newton's second law of motion to model this situation. Two forces act on the packet along the vertical; a constant force of gravity $F_1 (= mg)$, where m is the mass of the packet and the velocity dependent force due to air resistance $F_2 (=kv)$. Let us choose the positive x-axis along the vertical in the downward direction (Fig. 4.1). Since F_2 acts opposite to F_1, the magnitude of the net force acting on the object is $F = mg - kv$ (t)

Step-III: From Newton's second law, the equation of motion of the packet is

$$ma = m\frac{d^2x}{dt^2} = mg - kv$$

$$\text{or } m\frac{dv}{dt} = mg - kv, \quad \left[\because v(t) = \frac{dx}{dt}\right] \qquad \text{...(i)}$$

Eq. (i) is a first order ODE and we can solve it using the method of separation of variables.

Step-IV: The particular solution v (t) of Eq. (i) corresponding to the given initial conditions is $v(t) = \dfrac{mg}{k}t - \dfrac{mg}{k}\exp(-kt/m)$ ...(ii)

and by integrating $v = \dfrac{dx}{dt}$ its particular solution is

$$x(t) = \frac{mg}{k}t - \frac{m^2g}{k^2}(1-e^{-kt/m}) \qquad \text{...(iii)}$$

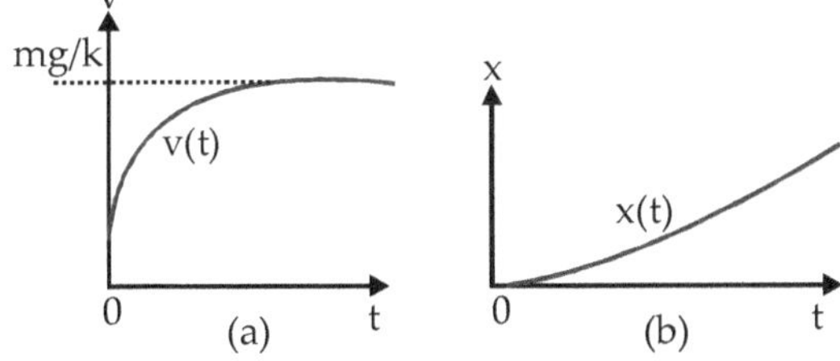

Fig. 4.2: (a) The speed and (b) the position of the falling packet as a function of time.

Step V: The solutions given in Eqs. (ii) and (iii) are sketched in Fig. 4.2. To find the time t_1, taken by the packet to fall 750m, we put $x(t_1) = 750\,\text{m}$, $g = 9.81\text{ms}^{-2}$. Let us assume a value for k. Let

$k = 60 \text{ kgs}^{-1}$. Substituting these values in Eq. (iii), we get

$$750\,m = \frac{60\text{kg} \times 9.81\text{ms}^{-2}}{60\text{kgs}^{-1}} t_1\,s - \frac{(60)^2\text{kg}^2 \times 9.81\text{ms}^{-2}}{(60)^2\text{kg}^2\text{s}^{-2}}(1 - \exp[-60\text{kgs}^{-1}\,t_1\,s/60\text{kg}])$$

or
$$750\,m = (9.81\text{ms}^{-1})t_1\,s - 9.81m(1 - e^{-t_1})$$

or
$$750 = 9.81t_1 - 9.81\,(1 - e^{-t_1})$$

or
$$t_1 + e^{-t_1} = \frac{750}{9.81} + 1 = \frac{759.81}{9.81} = 77.5$$

We cannot solve this equation explicitly for t_1. But we can use an approximation. Since for $t_1 = 77.5$, e^{-t_1} is very small ($\sim$ zero), we can neglect this term and obtain in our approximation $t_1 \approx 77.5$ s. The speed of

the packet at $t_1 = 77.5$ s will be $v\,(77.5s) = \dfrac{60\text{kg} \times 9.81\text{ms}^{-2}}{60\text{kgs}^{-1}} = 9.81\text{ms}^{-1}$.

(ii) Velocity of escape from the earth

We will first consider an example for this:

A projectile is fired from the earth in the radial direction. Find the minimum initial velocity of the projectile which will enable it to escape from the earth's gravitational pull. Neglect the air resistance and the gravitational attraction of other heavenly bodies.

Solution of this example is below:

From Newton's law of gravitation, we know that the gravitational force on the projectile is given by $\vec{F} = -\dfrac{GMm}{r^2}\,\hat{r} = m\,a\,(r)\hat{r}$ ...(iv)

where $\vec{r}\,(= r\,\hat{r})$ is the displacement of the projectile from the centre of the earth. Here M and m are the masses of the earth and the projectile, respectively (Fig. 4.3). Therefore, the magnitude of the acceleration of the projectile is $a(r) = \dfrac{dv(r)}{dt} = -\dfrac{GM}{r^2}$ ...(v)

where v is the speed of the projectile. Let us Now express a (r) in terms of the magnitude of velocity and distance. Since v is also a function of r, we can write $a(r) = \dfrac{dv(r)}{dt} = \dfrac{dv}{dr}\dfrac{dr}{dt} = v\dfrac{dv}{dr}, \quad \left(\because v = \dfrac{dr}{dt}\right)$ ...(vi)

So Eq. (v) becomes $v\dfrac{dv}{dr} = -\dfrac{GM}{r^2}$ ...(vii)

Using the method of separation of variables we get

$$\int v\, dv = -GM\int \frac{dr}{r^2} + C'$$

Thus, the general solution is $v^2 = \dfrac{2GM}{r} + C$ 				...(viii)

Let the initial speed of the projectile be $v = v_0$ at $r = R$.

Thus, $C = v_0^2 - \dfrac{2GM}{R}$ and the particular solution becomes

$$v^2 = \frac{2GM}{r} + v_0^2 - \frac{2GM}{R} \qquad ...(ix)$$

Now, in order that the projectile escapes from the earth, v should remain positive for all values of r. On examining the right-hand side of Eq. (ix), we find that v>0 always, if and only if, $v_0^2 - \dfrac{2GM}{R} \geq 0$ 	...(x)

For, if $v_0^2 - \dfrac{2GM}{R} < 0$, then there will be a value of r for which v = 0. In such a situation, the projectile would stop, its velocity $\vec{v}$ would change from positive to negative and it would return to the earth.

Thus, if a projectile is launched with an initial velocity v_0, such that $v_0 \geq \sqrt{2GM/r}$, it will escape from the earth. The minimum velocity of projectile [with magnitude $v_e(= \sqrt{2GM/R})$] is called the velocity of escape.

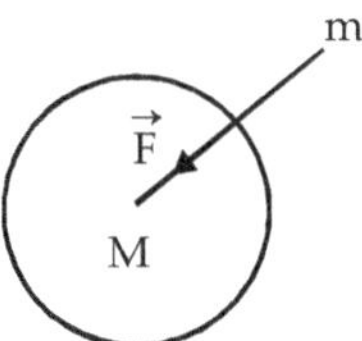

Fig. 4.3: Gravitational force $\vec{F}$ on a projectile at a distance r from the centre of the earth

Applications of Second Order ODEs in Rotational Mechanical Systems:

Let us consider a mechanical system in which the only motion is rotation about a fixed axis.

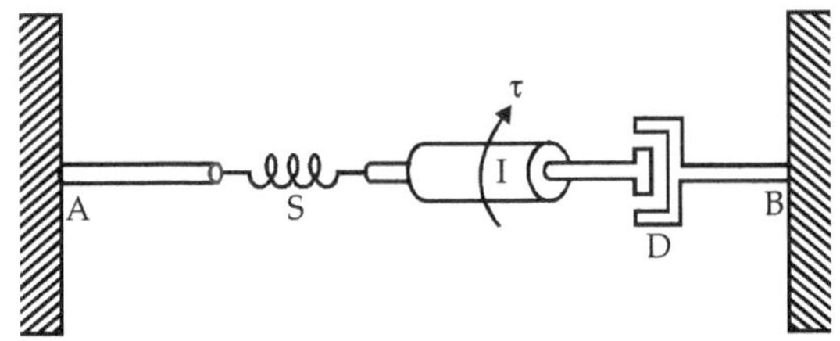

Fig. 4.4: Rotational mechanical system consisting of a spring (S) governed by Hooke's Law, an inertial cylindrical element (I) and a damping element (D). AB is the axis of rotation.

This system consists of a linear spring S, an inertial cylindrical element having a constant moment of inertia I and a linear damper D (Fig. 4.6). The brakes in automobiles and the suspension type galvanometer can be modelled by similar systems. For this system, we have to deal with angular quantities only.

Let us set up a coordinate system about the fixed axis of rotation AB. Let θ be the angular displacement with $\theta = 0$ corresponding to the fixed axis. Now suppose an external torque τ is applied to the inertial element (the cylinder) as shown in the figure.

The rotational analogue of Newton's second law tells us that the net external torque on the cylinder equals the rate of change of its angular momentum, i.e.
$$\tau_{ext} = \frac{d\vec{L}}{dt} = I\frac{d^2\vec{\theta}}{dt^2} \quad \left[\because \vec{L} = I\vec{\omega} = I\frac{d\vec{\theta}}{dt}\right] \qquad \text{...(xi)}$$

The net external torque on the inertial element is

$$\tau_{ext} = \vec{\tau} + \vec{\tau}_K + \vec{\tau}_B \qquad \text{...(xii)}$$

where $\vec{\tau}_K$ is the torque applied by the spring and $\vec{\tau}_B$ is the torque due to the damper D. These are, respectively, given as $\vec{\tau}_K = -K\vec{\theta}$ ...(xiii)

where K is the stiffness constant of the spring

and $\vec{\tau}_B = -B\vec{\omega} = -B\dfrac{d\vec{\theta}}{dt}$ ...(xiv)

Then, we have $I\dfrac{d^2\vec{\theta}}{dt^2} = \vec{\tau} - B\dfrac{d\vec{\theta}}{dt} - K\vec{\theta}$ ...(xv)

Since $\vec{\theta} = \theta\,\widehat{AB}$ and $\widehat{AB}$ is a constant vector in the direction of the axis of rotation, therefore, we can write Eq. (xv) as

$$I\frac{d^2\theta}{dt^2} + B\frac{d\theta}{dt} + K\theta = \tau \qquad \text{...(xvi)}$$

This is a non-homogeneous linear second order ODE. The mathematical model of the system is complete if we specify two initial conditions like the following: $\theta(t_0) = C_0$, $\theta'(t_0) = C_1$.

Applications of Second Order ODEs in Planetary Orbits: Let us Consider the motion of a planet of mass m in the gravitational field of the sun of mass M. Let us assume the sun to be stationary and neglect the effect of the gravitational field of other planets on this planet. We can model this system by Newton's second law from which we have

$$\vec{F} = m\vec{a} \quad \text{or} \quad -\frac{GMm}{r^2}\hat{r} = m\vec{a}. \qquad \text{...(xvii)}$$

where $\hat{r}$ is the unit vector pointing from the sun to the planet (Fig. 4.5). Since $\vec{F}$ is a central force, the planet's angular momentum is constant. Therefore, its motion is restricted to a plane and it is convenient to use plane polar coordinates to solve this equation. In the plane polar coordinate system, acceleration $\vec{a}$ is given as

$$\vec{a} = (\ddot{r} - r\dot{\theta}^2)\hat{r} + (r\ddot{\theta} + 2\dot{r}\dot{\theta})\hat{\theta}$$

On substituting $\vec{a}$ in Eq. (vii), we get two differential equations

$$m(\ddot{r} - r\dot{\theta}^2) = -\frac{GMm}{r^2} \qquad \qquad ...(xviii)$$

$$m(r\ddot{\theta} + 2\dot{r}\dot{\theta}) = 0. \qquad \qquad ...(xix)$$

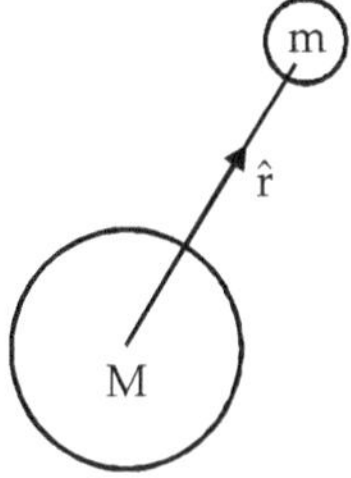

Fig. 4.5: Force of gravitation on the earth due to the sun is $F = -\dfrac{GMm}{r^2}\hat{r}$

We can multiply Eq. (19) by r and write it as $\dfrac{d}{dt}(mr^2\dot{\theta}) = 0$

which gives on integration $mr^2\dot{\theta} = \text{constant}$

The term $mr^2\dot{\theta}$ is nothing but the magnitude of the angular momentum of the planet about the sun. We know that $\vec{L} = \vec{r} \times \vec{p} = mr\hat{r} \times (r\hat{r} + r\dot{\theta}\hat{\theta}) = mr^2\dot{\theta}(\hat{r} \times \hat{\theta}) = mr^2\dot{\theta}\hat{k}$, where $\hat{k}$ is a unit vector normal to both $\hat{r}$ and $\hat{\theta}$. Thus, $mr^2\dot{\theta} = L$.

We now have to solve Eq. (xviii) to determine the path of the planet in space, i.e. the shape of its orbit. Thus, we have to find r as a function of θ. To do this, we first have to eliminate t from Eqs. (xviii) and (xix). Let us make the substitutions $r = \dfrac{1}{u}$ and $\dfrac{d\theta}{dt} = \dfrac{L}{mr^2} = \dfrac{L}{m}u^2$

in Eqs. (xviii) and (xix). Then, differentiating r with respect to t, we get

$$\frac{dr}{dt} = -\frac{1}{u^2}\frac{du}{dt} = -\frac{1}{u^2}\left(\frac{du}{d\theta}\right)\left(\frac{d\theta}{dt}\right) = -\frac{L}{m}\left(\frac{du}{d\theta}\right)$$

Differentiating again, we get $\dfrac{d^2r}{dt^2} = -\dfrac{L}{m}\left(\dfrac{d^2u}{d\theta^2}\right)\left(\dfrac{d\theta}{dt}\right) = \dfrac{-L^2}{m^2}u^2\dfrac{d^2u}{d\theta^2}$

Thus, Eq. (xviii) becomes $-\dfrac{L^2}{m}u^2\left(\dfrac{d^2u}{d\theta^2}+u\right) = -\dfrac{GMm}{r^2} = -GMm\,u^2$

or $\dfrac{d^2u}{d\theta^2}+u = \dfrac{GMm^2}{L^2} = A$ ...(xx)

This is again a non-homogeneous linear second order ODE. But we can remove the non-homogeneity in this equation by substituting $u' = u - A$. Eq. (xx) then becomes $\dfrac{d^2u'}{d\theta^2}+u' = 0$ ...(xxi)

Its general solution is $u' = B\cos(\theta-\theta_0)$ or $u = A + B\cos(\theta-\theta_0)$

Now shifting the origin of θ-axis, we can put $\theta_0 = 0$.

Thus, we get $u = A + B\cos\theta$, or $\dfrac{1}{r} = A + B\cos\theta$ ...(xxii)

This is the equation of a conic section (ellipse, parabola or hyperbola) with focus at r = 0 (Fig. 4.6). The shape of the orbit is determined by the relation between A and B. For A > B, orbit is an ellipse; B = A, orbit is a parabola;

0 < A < B, orbit is a hyperbola.

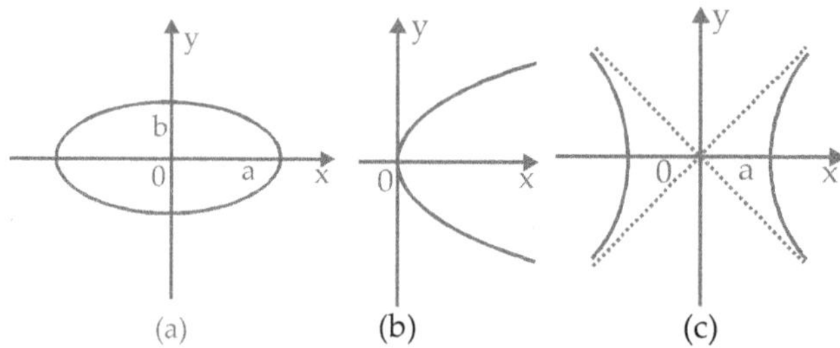

Fig. 4.6: (a) Ellipse; (b) parabola; (c) hyperbola.

The constant B can be determined for planetary orbits using energy considerations. It is given by $B^2 = \dfrac{m^2(GmM)^2}{L^4} + \dfrac{2mE}{L^2}$

Coupled differential equations: Many physical situations can be described in terms of coupled differential equations. Coupled differential equations used for modelling physical systems like coupled oscillators, coupled electric circuits, charged particles in electric and magnetic fields.

Coupled Oscillators: Consider two identical pendulums, each having a mass m suspended on a rigid massless rod of length L. The masses are connected by a spring of stiffness constant k. Its natural length equals the distance between the masses when neither is displaced from the equilibrium.

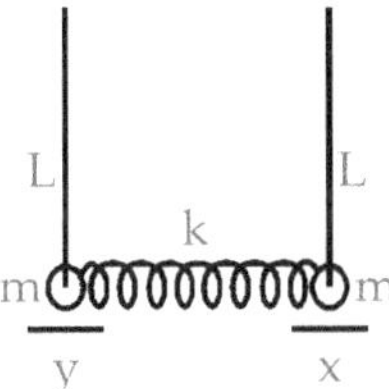

Fig. 4.7: Two identical pendulums coupled by a spring of stiffness k. Each light rigid rod of length L supports a mass m. The natural length of the spring is equal to the separation of the masses at zero displacement.

Such a system can be used to model the vibration of two atoms set in a crystal lattice. The atoms experience a mutual coupling force. Assume that the amplitude of oscillations is small and these are restricted in the plane of the paper. If x and y are the displacements of the masses, then the equations of motion are

$$m\ddot{x} = -mg\frac{x}{L} - k(x-y) \qquad \text{...(xxiii)}$$

and $$m\ddot{y} = -mg\frac{y}{L} + k(x-y) \qquad \text{...(xxvi)}$$

These are the differential equations representing the normal simple harmonic motion of each pendulum plus a coupling term $k\,(x-y)$ from the spring. Writing $\omega_0 = \sqrt{\dfrac{g}{L}}$, where ω_0 is the natural angular frequency of each

pendulum, gives $$\ddot{x} + \omega_0^2 x = -\frac{k}{m}(x-y) \qquad \text{...(xxv)}$$

$$\ddot{y} + \omega_0^2 y = +\frac{k}{m}(x-y) \qquad \text{...(xxvi)}$$

We can see that these ODEs are coupled together. Each of them involves x and y, and so cannot be solved independently. We can solve these equations by uncoupling them. With the choice of suitable coordinates X and Y, we can obtain two independent equations in X and Y. Let

$$X = x + y, \quad Y = x - y$$

Adding these given equations, we get $(\ddot{x} + \ddot{y}) + \omega_0^2(x+y) = 0$

Since $X = x+y$, $\dot{X} = \dot{x}+\dot{y}$ and $\ddot{X} = \ddot{x}+\ddot{y}$

Thus, the above differential equation becomes $\ddot{X} + \omega_0^2 X = 0$

which has the well known solution of the from

$X = A\cos\omega_0 t + B\sin\omega_0 t$, where $\omega_0^2 = g/L$.

A and B can be determined from given initial conditions.

Now subtracting eq. (xxvi) from (xxv),

we get $(\ddot{x}-\ddot{y}) = -\omega_0^2(x-y) - \dfrac{2k}{m}(x-y)$

Again since $Y = x-y$, $\dot{Y} = \dot{x}-\dot{y}$ and $\ddot{Y} = \ddot{x}-\ddot{y}$, we get $\ddot{Y} = -\omega_0^2 Y - \dfrac{2kY}{m}$

or $\ddot{Y} + \left(\omega_0^2 + \dfrac{2k}{m}\right)Y = 0$. The solution of this equation is

$$Y = C\cos\omega t + D\sin\omega t \ \text{ with } \omega^2 = \omega_0^2 + \dfrac{2k}{m} .$$

Coupled Electrical Circuits: In fig. 4.8, we can see that two loops in an electrical circuit joined together by a resistive coupling. Applying Kirchoff's law to the left and right loops, respectively, we get

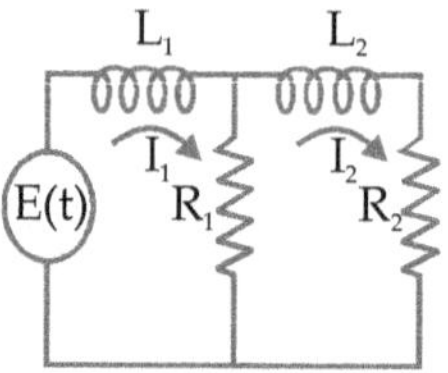

Fig. 4.8: Resistively coupled RL electrical circuits

$$L_1\dfrac{dI_1}{dt} + R_1(I_1 - I_2) = E(t) \qquad\qquad\text{...(xxvii)}$$

$$L_2\dfrac{dI_2}{dt} + R_2 I_2 + R_1(I_2 - I_1) = 0 \qquad\qquad\text{...(xxviii)}$$

Here, we have used the fact that the current in R_1 is $(I_1 - I_2)$ relative to the left loop and $(I_2 - I_1)$ relative to the right loop. These are once again coupled equations. We can eliminate either I_1 or I_2 from these equations. Let us rewrite Eqs. (xxvii) and (xxviii) as follows:

$$L_1\dfrac{dI_1}{dt} + R_1 I_1 - R_1 I_2 = E(t) \qquad\qquad\text{...(xix)}$$

and $-R_1 I_1 + L_2\dfrac{dI_2}{dt} + (R_1 + R_2)I_2 = 0.$ $\qquad\qquad\text{...(xxx)}$

Multiplying Eq. (xix) by R_1 and operating on Eq. (xxx) by $\left(L_1\dfrac{d}{dt}+R_1\right)$, we get

$$R_1L_1\frac{dI_1}{dt}+R_1^2I_1-R_1^2I_2=R_1\,E(t)\ -R_1L_1\frac{dI_1}{dt}-R_1^2I_1+L_1L_2\frac{d^2I_2}{dt^2}+R_1L_2\frac{dI_2}{dt}$$

$$+(R_1+R_2)L_1\frac{dI_2}{dt}+R_1(R_1+R_2)I_2=0.$$

Adding the two equations, we get

$$L_1L_2\frac{d^2I_2}{dt^2}+(R_1L_2+R_1L_1+R_2L_1)\frac{dI_2}{dt}+R_1R_2I_2=R_1E(t) \qquad \text{...(xxxi)}$$

Eq. (xxxi) is a second order non-homogeneous linear ODE with constant coefficients.

Charged-Particle Motion in Electric and Magnetic Fields: We know that a particle of charge q moving in an applied electric field $\vec{E}$ and a magnetic field $\vec{B}$ is acted upon by the force

$$\vec{F}=q\,(\vec{E}+\vec{v}\times\vec{B}) \qquad \text{...(xxxii)}$$

From Newton's second law of motion, its equation of motion is

$$m\frac{d\vec{v}}{dt}=q(\vec{E}+\vec{v}\times\vec{B}). \qquad \text{...(xxxiii)}$$

We will consider only constant electric and magnetic fields, i.e. the fields which are constant in time and uniform in space.

Uniform electrostatic field

Consider the situation in which the applied magnetic field is zero. Then Eq. (xxxiii) simplifies to $\quad \dfrac{d\vec{v}}{dt}=\dfrac{q}{m}\,\vec{E} \qquad \text{...(xxxiv)}$

Since $\vec{E}$ is constant, we get upon direct successive integrations

$$\vec{v}(t)=\frac{q\vec{E}}{m}t+\vec{v}_0 \qquad \text{...(xxxv)}$$

and $\quad \vec{r}(t)=\dfrac{q\vec{E}}{2m}t^2+\vec{v}_0\,t+\vec{r}_0 \qquad \text{...(xxxvi)}$

Here $\vec{v}_0$ and $\vec{r}_0$ are constants of integration which can be determined from the given initial conditions.

Thus, the charged particle moves with a constant acceleration $\dfrac{q\vec{E}}{m}$ in the direction of $\vec{E}$ when $q>0$ and in the opposite direction when $q<0$.

Uniform magnetostatic field

When the applied electric field is zero, Eq. (xxxiii) becomes

$$m\frac{d\vec{v}}{dt} = q(\vec{v}\times\vec{B}) \qquad\qquad \text{...(xxxvii)}$$

Let us use the Cartesian coordinate system to solve this equation. Let the z-axis be along $\vec{B}$, i.e. $\vec{B} = B\hat{k}$. We can simplify Eq. (xxxvii) as follows:

$$m\frac{d}{dt}(v_x\hat{i}+v_y\hat{j}+v_z\hat{k}) = q(v_x\hat{i}+v_y\hat{j}+v_z\hat{k})\times B\hat{k} = -qBv_x\hat{j}+qBv_y\hat{i}$$

Taking each component separately, we have

$$m\frac{dv_x}{dt} = qBv_y \qquad\qquad \text{...(xxxviii)}$$

$$m\frac{dv_y}{dt} = -qBv_x \qquad\qquad \text{...(xxxix)}$$

$$m\frac{dv_z}{dt} = 0. \qquad\qquad \text{...(xxxx)}$$

Now, Eqs. (xxxviii) and (xxxix) are coupled together. We can solve these equations by uncoupling them. Differentiating Eq. (xxxviii) and using Eq. (xxxix) we get

$$m\frac{d^2v_x}{dt^2} = qB\frac{dv_y}{dt} = -\frac{q^2B^2}{m}v_x \quad \text{or} \quad \frac{d^2v_x}{dt^2}+\omega_c^2 v_x = 0, \text{ where } \omega_c = \frac{qB}{m}$$

The solution of this equation is $v_x = C_1\sin\omega_c t + C_2\cos\omega_c t$.

C_1 and C_2 have the dimensions of speed. For the sake of convenience, we can rewrite v_x as $v_x = v_\perp \sin(\omega_c t+\phi)$,

where $C_1 = v_\perp\cos\phi$, $C_2 = v_\perp\sin\phi$. Now from Eq. (xxxviii) we have for v_y:

$$v_y = \frac{1}{\omega_c}\frac{dv_x}{dt} = \frac{1}{\omega_c}\omega_c v_\perp\cos(\omega_c t+\phi) = v_\perp\cos(\omega_c t+\phi)$$

Note that $v_x^2 + v_y^2 = v_\perp^2$. v_z is found by simply integrating Eq. (xxxx):

$$v_z = v_\parallel$$

where $v_\parallel$ is an arbitrary constant having the dimension of speed. It is the component of $\vec{v}$ parallel to the z-axis. Thus, we have

$$\vec{v} = v_\perp\left[\sin(\omega_c t+\phi)\hat{i}+\cos(\omega_c t+\phi)\hat{j}\right]+v_\parallel\hat{k} \qquad\qquad \text{...(xxxxi)}$$

Since $\vec{v} = \dfrac{d\vec{r}}{dt}$ we can integrate $\vec{v}$ with respect to t, we have

$$\vec{r} = \frac{v_\perp}{\omega_c}\left[-\cos(\omega_c t+\phi)\hat{i}+\sin(\omega_c t+\phi)\hat{j}\right]+v_\parallel t\hat{k}+R_0 \qquad\qquad \text{...(xxxxii)}$$

where $\vec{R}_0$ is a constant vector of integration. This is a general solution of Eq. (xxxvii).

Solved Practical Problems

Q1. A sinusoidally varying source of emf is applied to a series RC circuit. Determine the current through the circuit as a function of time.

Ans.

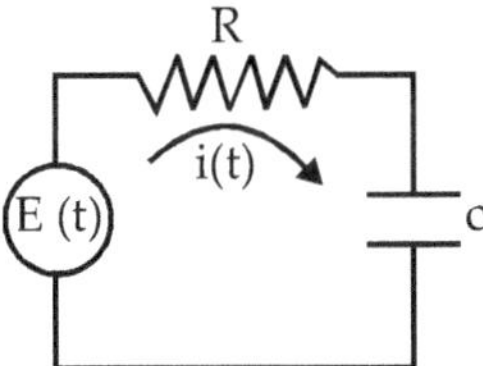

Fig. 4.9: A series circuit (in which the resistor and capacitor are connected in series)

Using Kirchoff's law, we can model the circuit by the following differential equation: $\quad Ri(t) + \dfrac{q(t)}{C} = E(t)$ ...(i)

Since E (t) varies sinusoidally, we have $E(t) = E_0 \sin \omega t$

Since $i(t) = \dfrac{dq}{dt}$, on dividing Eq. (i) by R, we get

$$\frac{dq}{dt} + \frac{q}{RC} = \frac{E_0}{R} \sin \omega t \qquad \text{...(ii)}$$

Now, we can write down the solution of Eq. (ii) as

$$q(t) = \frac{E_0}{R} e^{-t/RC} \int e^{t/RC} \sin \omega t \, dt + C' e^{-t/RC}$$

or $\quad q(t) = \dfrac{E_0 C}{\sqrt{1 + \omega^2 R^2 C^2}} \sin(\omega t - \theta) + C_1 e^{-t/RC}$ ...(iii)

where $\quad \theta = \tan^{-1}(\omega CR)$ ...(iv)

Hence, $\quad i(t) = \dfrac{dq}{dt} = \dfrac{E_0 \omega C}{\sqrt{1 + \omega^2 R^2 C^2}} \cos(\omega t - \theta) + C_2 e^{-t/RC}$ ...(v)

The second term on the right hand side of Eq. (v) decreases exponentially as t increases. It is called the transient term. The first term represents the steady state current which is sinusoidal.

Q2. A godown for storing cement has to be built. It will have no external heating or cooling arrangement. How can it be designed so that its temperature changes by a specified amount in a given period of time?

Ans. Let us follow the modelling cycle stepwise to solve this 'real world' problem.

Step 1: Specify the real problem

We have to answer the following question: How long does it take to change the building temperature by a specific amount?

Step 2: Set up a model

Our model must describe the 24-h temperature variation inside the building as a function of time and the outside temperature. In the simplest model, we can view the building as a single entity, i.e. we do not take individual rooms into account. We can immediately see that the inside temperature T and time t are the two main variables. We have to find T(t), i.e. the temperature inside the building at time t. Following factors that affect T(t) are

    (a)   The heat produced by people, lights, machines inside the building will increase T(t). Let H (t) be the rate of increase in T(t) due to this factor.

    (b)   The effect of outside temperature $T_s(t)$ on T(t).

Having identified the variables, we must find relationship between them. To model the effect of $T_s(t)$ on T(t), we can apply Newton's law of cooling, If $T_s(t) < T(t)$ at all times. We get that the rate of change in the inside temperature T(t) is proportional to the difference between T(t) and the outside temperature $T_s(t)$. Thus, the time rate of change in T(t) due to $T_s(t)$ is $\{-K[T(t) - T_s(t)]\}$. K is a positive constant which depends on the physical properties of the building, such as the number of doors and windows, colour scheme, type of insulation, etc. K does not depend on T_s, T or t. Note that K has the dimension of reciprocal of time. The minus sign is used to show that the temperature of the building will decrease. We can now formulate the mathematical problem and solve it.

Step 3: Formulate the mathematical problem

From our model, we get the following first order ODE:

$$\frac{dT(t)}{dt} = K[\,T_s(t) - T(t)\,] + H(t)$$

$$...(i)$$

Step 4: Solve the mathematical problem

Eq. (i) is a first order linear non-homogeneous ODE. We rewrite Eq. (i) in the standard form $\dfrac{dT(t)}{dt} + P(t)T(t) = Q(t)$ ...(ii)

where $P(t) = K, \quad Q(t) = KT_s(t) + H(t)$ ...(iii)

The integrating factor is $\exp\left(\int K\,dt\right) = e^{Kt}$. The solution of Eq. (ii) is

$$T(t) = e^{-Kt}\left[\int e^{Kt}[\,KT_s(t)+H(t)\,]\,dt+C\right] \qquad \text{...(iv)}$$

Let us simplify our model further to solve Eq. (iv). Let H (t) be negligibly small and $T_s(t)$ be a constant T_{s0}. So with $H(t)=0$ and $T_s(t)=T_{s0}$, we get

$$T(t) = e^{-Kt}\left[\int e^{Kt}KT_{s0}\,dt+C\right] = e^{-kt}\,[T_{s0}\,e^{Kt}+C] = T_{s0}+Ce^{-Kt} \qquad \text{...(v)}$$

Eq. (v) is a general solution of Eq. (i) in our simplified model. We can check the solution by substituting Eq. (v) into Eq. (i) with H (t) = 0 and $T_s(t) = T_{s0}$.

Let us now specify the initial condition to determine C and get a particular solution.

Let $T = T_0$ at $t = 0$. Then $T_0 = T_{s0}+C$, or $C=T_0-T_{s0}$

Thus, the particular solution is $T(t) = T_{s0}+(T_0-T_{s0})e^{-Kt} \qquad \text{...(vi)}$

Let us now interpret this solution.

Step 5: Interpret the solution

Since $T_{s0}<T_0$, $T(t)$ decreases exponentially from T_0. As t increases, the exponential term falls off and T(t) tends to T_{s0} (see Fig. 4.11). Now, choose the problem we specified in Step 1. Let us determine the time it takes for the temperature difference $(T-T_{s0})$ to change from (T_0-T_{s0}) to $\left(\dfrac{T_0-T_{s0}}{e}\right)$. This time is called the time constant of the building. From Eq. (vi) at $t = 0, T-T_{s0} = T_0-T_{s0}$ and at $t = \dfrac{1}{K}, T-T_{s0} = \dfrac{T_0-T_{s0}}{e}$.

So the time constant of the building is 1/K. Thus, we can interpret the solution as follows: The building temperature decreases exponentially with a time constant 1/K.

A typical value of the time constant of a building is 2 to 4 h. It can be made much shorter if the windows are open or if there are fans circulating the air. It can be made much longer if the building is well insulated.

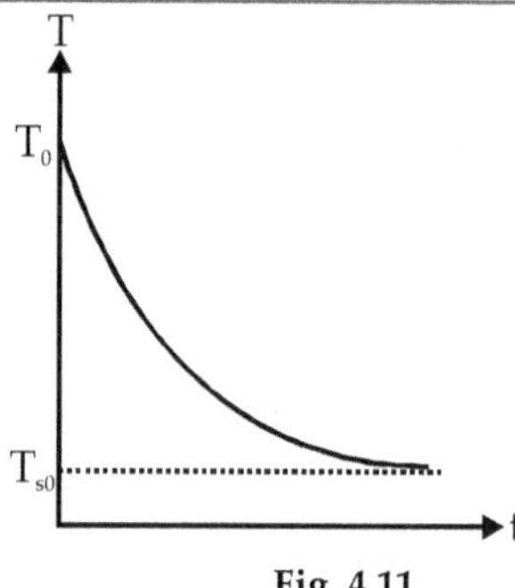

Fig. 4.11

Step 6: Compare with reality

This can be done by collecting data on several similar buildings and comparing the results of this model for different time constants.

Step 7: Use the results

This simple model may be used to design buildings like warehouses, godowns or garages. The model can be further refined to take into account the heat inside or time variation of outside temperature. The effect of external heating (heaters) and cooling (coolers or air conditioners) can also be incorporated.

Q3.   **A particle falls under gravity in a pool of water. A resistive force directly proportional to its velocity acts on it opposite to the force of gravity. Write its equation of motion. Solve it to obtain the particle's velocity as a function of time.**   **[Dec-2011, Q.No.-1(e)]**

Ans. We use Newton's second law of motion for this situation. Two forces act on the packet along the vertical; a constant force of gravity $F_1 = mg$, where m is the mass of the particle and the velocity dependent force due to resistance $F_2 = kv$. Since F_2 acts opposite to F_1, the magnitude of the net force acting on the object is $F = mg - kv(t)$.

From Newton's second law, the equation of the motion of the particle is

$$ma = m\frac{d^2x}{dt^2} = mg - kv$$

or $m\dfrac{dv}{dt} = mg - kv, \quad \left[\because v(t) = \dfrac{dx}{dt}\right]$

Now $\dfrac{dv}{dt} = g - \dfrac{k}{m}v \;\Rightarrow\; \dfrac{dv}{dt} + \dfrac{k}{m}v = g$ ...(i)

Now, it is a linear first order D.E.

Compare (i) with $\dfrac{dv}{dt} + Pv = Q$, we get

$$P = k/m \quad , \quad Q = g \quad \Rightarrow \quad I.F. = e^{\int Pdv} = e^{\frac{k}{m}\int 1dv} = e^{\frac{k}{m}v}$$

Now, multiplying eq. (i) by $e^{kv/m}$, we get $\dfrac{d}{dt}\left[ve^{kv/m}\right] = g\,e^{kv/m}$

Integrating, we have $ve^{kv/m} = g\int e^{kv/m} + c$

or $ve^{kv/m} = g\dfrac{m}{k}e^{kv/m} + c \quad \Rightarrow \quad v = \dfrac{gm}{k} + c\,e^{-kv/m}$ is the required solution

Q4. A steel casting at a temperature of $20°C$ is put into an oven that has a temperature of $200°C$. One minute later, the temperature of the casting is $30°C$. Determine the temperature profile of the casting. How long will it take the temperature of the casting to reach $190°C$?

Ans. We know that the rate at which heat is absorbed by the object is $\dfrac{dQ}{dt} = ms\dfrac{dT}{dt}$, where m is the object's mass, and s, its specific heat. If T is the temperature of the object at any instant t, then $\dfrac{dT}{dt}$ is the time rate of change of temperature. Since the rate at which heat is absorbed by an object is proportional to the temperature difference of the object and its surroundings we have $\dfrac{dQ}{dt} \propto (T_s - T)$ or $ms\dfrac{dT}{dt} = C'(T_s - T)$

or $\dfrac{dT}{dt} = \dfrac{C'}{ms}(T_s - T) = K(T_s - T)$, where K^{-1} has the dimensions of time.

Now the difference between the temperature of the oven and the casting is $(200 - T)°C$. So the first order ODE describing the given system is

$$\dfrac{dT}{dt} = K[200 - T]°C \text{ with the boundary conditions that}$$

when (i) $t = 0$ min, $T = 20°C$ and when (ii) $t = 1$ min, $T = 30°C$.

The solution of this equation is obtained as follows:

$$\int\dfrac{dT}{200-T} = K\int dt + C$$

$$-ln|200 - T| = Kt + C \text{ or } 200 - T = C_1\exp[-Kt] \text{ or}$$

$$T°C = 200°C - C_1\exp[-Kt]$$

where C_1 is a constant of integration having the dimensions of temperature. Using the boundary conditions, we get

(i) $20°C = 200°C - C_1$, at $t = 0$ min, $\therefore C_1 = 180°C$

(ii) $30°C = 200°C - (180°C)\exp[-K\text{min}^{-1} \times 1\text{min}]$, at $t = 1$ min

or $e^{-K} = \dfrac{170}{180} = \dfrac{17}{18}$,

$\therefore K = -ln\left|\dfrac{17}{18}\right| = 0.057$

Thus, the particular solution is $T°C = 200°C - 180°C \exp[(-0.057)t]$.

To find the time t at which $T = 190°C$ we have to solve the following equation: $190°C = 200°C - 180°C \exp[-0.57t]$

or $\exp[-.057t] = \dfrac{1}{18}$ or $t = \dfrac{ln|1/18|}{-0.057} = 50$ min.approx.

Q5. **Show that the particular solution v (t) of $m\dfrac{dv}{dt} = mg - kv$ corresponding to the given initial conditions is $v(t) = \dfrac{mg}{k} - \dfrac{mg}{k}\exp(-kt/m)$. Determine x (t) by integrating $v = \dfrac{dx}{dt}$ and show that its particular solution is $x(t) = \dfrac{mg}{k}t - \dfrac{m^2g}{k^2}(1 - e^{-kt/m})$**

Ans. We have $m\dfrac{dv}{dt} = mg - kv$

Using the method of separation of variables, we get

$$\int \dfrac{dv}{g - \dfrac{k}{m}v} = \int dt + C$$

Let $w = g - \dfrac{k}{m}v$, $dw = -\dfrac{k}{m}dv$ we get $\int \dfrac{dw}{w} = -\dfrac{k}{m}\int dt + C'$

or $w = C_1 \exp\left(-\dfrac{k}{m}t\right)$ or $v = \dfrac{mg}{k} - \dfrac{m}{k}C_1\exp\left(-\dfrac{k}{m}t\right)$

The given initial condition is that at $t = 0$, $v = 0$ and we get $\dfrac{m}{k}C_1 = \dfrac{mg}{k}$ or $C_1 = g$

Thus, the particular solution is $v = \dfrac{mg}{k} - \dfrac{mg}{k}\exp\left(-\dfrac{k}{m}t\right)$.

Integrating $v = \dfrac{dx}{dt}$, we get $x(t) = \dfrac{mg}{k}t + \dfrac{m^2g}{k^2}\exp\left(-\dfrac{k}{m}t\right) + C_2$

To determine C_2 we use the given initial condition that at $t = 0$, $x = 0$.

$$\therefore C_2 = -\frac{m^2 g}{k^2} \quad \text{and} \quad x(t) = \frac{mg}{k}t - \frac{m^2 g}{k^2}\left[1 - \exp\left(-\frac{k}{m}t\right)\right].$$

Q6. Solve the equation $I\dfrac{d^2\theta}{dt^2} + B\dfrac{d\theta}{dt} + K\theta = \tau,$ **given that** $\tau = \tau_0 \cos\omega t, \theta(0) = 0, \theta'(0) = 0.$ **If** $B = 0,$ **what is the resonance frequency** ω_0 **and the solution** $\theta(t)$ **for the system?**

Ans. For $\tau = \tau_0 \cos\omega t$, given equation becomes

$$I\frac{d^2\theta}{dt^2} + B\frac{d\theta}{dt} + K\theta = \tau_0 \cos\omega t$$

This is a non-homogeneous linear second order ODE. We know that a general solution of given equation has the form $\theta(t) = \theta_c(t) + \theta_p(t)$, where the particular integral is $\theta_p(t) = A_1 \cos\omega t + A_2 \sin\omega t$. Using the method of undetermined coefficients, we can see that A_1 and A_2 satisfy the equations $(-\omega^2 I + K)A_1 + \omega B A_2 = \tau_0$ and $(-\omega^2 I + K)A_2 - \omega B A_1 = 0$.

Solving these equations, we get

$$A_1 = \frac{\tau_0(K - \omega^2 I)}{(K - \omega^2 I)^2 + \omega^2 B^2}, \quad A_2 = \frac{\omega B \tau_0}{(K - \omega^2 I)^2 + \omega^2 B^2}$$

$$\therefore \theta(t) = \theta_c(t) + \frac{\tau_0}{(K - \omega^2 I)^2 + \omega^2 B^2}[(K - \omega^2 I) \cos\omega t + B\omega \sin\omega t]$$

$\theta_p(t)$ can be simplified further by letting $\cos\phi = \dfrac{K - \omega^2 I}{f(\omega)}$ and

$\sin\phi = \dfrac{B\omega}{f(\omega)}$, where $f(\omega) = [(K - \omega^2 I)^2 + \omega^2 B^2]^{1/2}$

Thus, $\theta_p(t) = \dfrac{\tau_0}{f(\omega)}[\cos\phi \cos\omega t + \sin\phi \sin\omega t] = \dfrac{\tau_0}{f(\omega)}\cos(\omega t - \phi)$

Thus $\theta_p(t)$ is a periodic function of period $\dfrac{2\pi}{\omega}$. As we know, the

complementary function $\theta_c(t)$ is the solution of $I\dfrac{d^2\theta}{dt^2} + B\dfrac{d\theta}{dt} + K\theta = 0$.

The general solution of this homogeneous second order ODE is

$$\theta_c(t) = C_1 e^{\lambda_1 t} + C_2 e^{\lambda_2 t}$$

where λ_1 and λ_2 are the roots of $I\lambda^2 + B\lambda + K = 0$

$$\therefore \lambda_1 = \frac{-B+\sqrt{B^2-4IK}}{2I}, \quad \lambda_2 = \frac{-B-\sqrt{B^2-4IK}}{2I}$$

Thus, $\theta(t) = C_1 e^{-(\alpha-\beta)t} + C_2 e^{-(\alpha+\beta)t} + \dfrac{\tau_0}{f(\omega)}\cos(\omega t - \phi)$,

where $\alpha = \dfrac{B}{2I}, \beta = \dfrac{1}{2I}\sqrt{B^2-4IK}$

From the initial conditions, we get

$$\theta(0) = 0 = C_1 + C_2 + \frac{\tau_0}{f(\omega)}\cos\phi$$

$$\theta'(0) = 0 = C_1\lambda_1 + C_2\lambda_2 + \frac{\tau_0\omega}{f(\omega)}\sin\phi$$

Thus, $C_1 = \dfrac{\tau_0[\lambda_2\cos\phi - \omega\sin\phi]}{f(\omega)(\lambda_1 - \lambda_2)}, \quad C_2 = \dfrac{\tau_0[\lambda_1\cos\phi - \omega\sin\phi]}{f(\omega)(\lambda_2 - \lambda_1)}$

We can see that as $t \to \infty, \theta_c(t) \to 0$, i.e. it is a transient function.

Now, we determine the solution for $B = 0$.

For $B = 0, \lambda_1 = i\sqrt{\dfrac{K}{I}} = i\omega_0, \lambda_2 = -i\sqrt{\dfrac{K}{I}} = -i\omega_0,$ where $\omega_0 = \sqrt{\dfrac{K}{I}}$ and $i = \sqrt{-1}.$

$$f(\omega) = (K - \omega^2 I) = I(\omega_0^2 - \omega^2), \quad \cos\phi = 1, \sin\phi = 0, \text{ i.e. } \phi = 0^\circ.$$

$$\therefore C_1 = \frac{-i\omega_0\tau_0}{(K-\omega^2 I)(i\omega_0 + i\omega_0)} = -\frac{\tau_0}{2(K-\omega^2 I)} = -\frac{\tau_0}{2I(\omega_0^2 - \omega^2)}$$

and $C_2 = \dfrac{i\omega_0\tau_0}{(K-\omega^2 I)(-2i\omega_0)} = -\dfrac{\tau_0}{2I(\omega_0^2 - \omega^2)}$

Thus, $\theta(t) = -\dfrac{\tau_0}{2I(\omega_0^2-\omega^2)}[e^{i\omega_0 t} + e^{-i\omega_0 t}] + \dfrac{\tau_0\cos\omega t}{I(\omega_0^2-\omega^2)}$

$$= \frac{\tau_0}{I(\omega_0^2-\omega^2)}\left[\cos\omega t - \cos\omega_0 t\right]$$

Thus, ω_0 is the resonance frequency of the system given by $\omega_0 = \sqrt{K/I}$

Q7. Find the particular solutions fo $\vec{v} = v_\wedge\left[\sin(\omega_c t+\phi)\hat{i} + \cos(\omega_c t+\phi)\hat{j}\right] + v_P\hat{k}$

and $\vec{r} = \dfrac{v_\wedge}{\omega_c}\left[-\cos(\omega_c t+\phi)\hat{i} + \sin(\omega_c t+\phi)\hat{j}\right] + v_P t\hat{k} + R_0$ given that

$B = 10^{-2}$ tesla, $q = 1.6\times10^{-19}$ C, $m = 1.6\times10^{-24}$ kg and

(i) $\vec{v}(0) = (2000\,\mathrm{m\,s}^{-1})\hat{i},\ \vec{r}(0) = 2\mathrm{m}\hat{j}$

(ii) $\vec{v}(0) = (2000\,\mathrm{m\,s}^{-1})(\hat{i}+\hat{k}),\ \vec{r}(0) = 2\mathrm{m}\hat{j}$

Ans. From the given values of q, B and m, we can compute:

$$\omega_c = \frac{qB}{m} = \frac{(1.6\times10^{-19}\,\mathrm{C})(10^{-2}\,\mathrm{tesla})}{1.6\times10^{-24}\,\mathrm{kg}} = 10^3\,\mathrm{rad\ s}^{-1}$$

(i) $\vec{v}(0) = (2000\,\mathrm{m\,s}^{-1})\hat{i},\ \vec{r}(0) = 2\mathrm{m}\hat{j}$

Applying the initial condition for $\vec{v}$ to equation

$$\vec{v} = v_{\perp}\left[\sin(\omega_c t + \phi)\hat{i} + \cos(\omega_c t + \phi)\hat{j}\right] + v_{\parallel}\hat{k} \qquad \ldots(i)$$

we get, $\vec{v}(0) = (2000\,\mathrm{m\,s}^{-1})\hat{i} = v_{\perp}\sin\phi\,\hat{i} + v_{\perp}\cos\phi\,\hat{j} + v_{\parallel}\hat{k}.$

Now, we know that $\vec{a} = \vec{b},$ iff $a_x = b_x, a_y = b_y, a_z = b_z.$

This gives us, $v_{\perp}\sin\phi = 2000\,\mathrm{m\,s}^{-1}, v_{\perp}\cos\phi = 0, v_{\parallel} = 0.$

Since $v_{\perp}$ has to be non-zero, we get $\phi = 90°$ and $v_{\perp} = 2000\,\mathrm{ms}^{-1}.$

Thus, $\vec{v}(t) = 2000\,\mathrm{m\,s}^{-1}(\cos\omega_c t\,\hat{i} - \sin\omega_c t\,\hat{j}),\ \omega_c = 10^3\,\mathrm{rad\,s}^{-1}.$

Next, we apply the initial condition for $\vec{r}$ to equation

$$\vec{r} = \frac{v_{\perp}}{\omega_c}[-\cos(\omega_c t + \phi)\hat{i} + \sin(\omega_c t + \phi)\hat{j}] + v_{\parallel}t\hat{k} + \vec{R}_0 \qquad \ldots(ii)$$

keeping in mind that $\phi = 90°$:

$$\vec{r}(0) = 2\mathrm{m}\hat{j} = \frac{v_{\perp}}{\omega_c}\hat{j} + \vec{R}_0 = \frac{2000\,\mathrm{m\,s}^{-1}}{10^3\,\mathrm{rad\,s}^{-1}}\hat{j} + \vec{R}_0 = 2\,\mathrm{m}\hat{j} + \vec{R}_0$$

$$\therefore \vec{R}_0 = 0$$

Thus, $\vec{r}(t) = 2\,\mathrm{m}(\sin\omega_c t\,\hat{i} + \cos\omega_c t\,\hat{j}),\ \omega_c = 10^3\,\mathrm{rad\,s}^{-1}.$

This gives the position vector of a particle moving clockwise in a circle of radius 2 m

(ii) Now $\vec{v}(0) = (2000\,\mathrm{ms}^{-1})(\hat{i}+\hat{k}),\ \vec{r}(0) = 2\mathrm{m}(\hat{j}).$ From Eq. (i), we get

$$\vec{v}(0) = 2000\,\mathrm{m\,s}^{-1}(\hat{i}+\hat{k}) = v_{\perp}[\sin\phi\,\hat{i} + \cos\phi\,\hat{j}] + v_{\parallel}\hat{k}$$

$$\therefore \phi = 90°,\ v_{\perp} = 2000\,\mathrm{ms}^{-1},\ v_{\parallel} = 2000\,\mathrm{m\,s}^{-1},$$

Thus, $\vec{v}(t) = 2000\,\mathrm{m\,s}^{-1}(\cos\omega_c t\,\hat{i} - \sin\omega_c t\,\hat{j}) + 2000\,\mathrm{m\,s}^{-1}\hat{k}$

From Eq. (ii), we get $\vec{r}(0) = 2m\,\hat{j} = \dfrac{v_\perp}{\omega_c}\hat{j} + \vec{R}_0 = \dfrac{2000\,\text{m s}^{-1}}{10^3\,\text{rad s}^{-1}}\hat{j} + \vec{R}_0$

$\therefore \vec{R}_0 = 0$.

Thus, $\vec{r}(t) = 2m\left(\sin\omega_c t\,\hat{i} + \cos\omega_c t\,\hat{j}\right) + (2000\,\text{m s}^{-1})t\,\hat{k}$.

In this case, the position vector and the velocity of the particle have a z component also, which is constant.

Q8. **A radioactive sample decays at a rate proportional to the number of nuclei present in it at a given time. Write down the equation of radioactive decay and solve it. Given that the number of nuclei at $t = 0$ is N_0.** **[June-2011,Q.No.-1(e)]**

Ans. Let N denotes number of nuclei present at time t.

Then the Differential equation of radioactive decay is

$$\dfrac{dN}{dt} = kN \quad\Rightarrow\quad \dfrac{dN}{N} = k\,dt$$

Integrating, we get $\displaystyle\int\dfrac{dN}{N} = k\int dt \;\Rightarrow\; \log N = kt + \log c$

$$\Rightarrow\quad N = c e^{kt}$$

Since $N = N_0$ when $t = 0$

$\therefore c = N_0 \;\Rightarrow\; N = N_0 e^{kt}$ is the required solution.

Q9. **A beam of length L is supported at its ends and weighs w kg/ unit length. The ODE governing the deflection of the beam is** $C\dfrac{d^2y}{dx^2} = w\left(\dfrac{x^2}{2} - \dfrac{Lx}{2}\right)$ **where C is a constant which depends on the elasticity of the material of the beam and its geometry. Solve this equation given that $y = 0$ when $x = 0$ and $y = 0$ when $x = L$.**

Ans. This equation can be solved by simple integration

$$C\dfrac{dy}{dx} = w\left[\dfrac{x^3}{2\times 3} - \dfrac{Lx^2}{2\times 2}\right] + C_1 \text{ and } Cy = w\left[\dfrac{x^4}{2\times 3\times 4} - \dfrac{Lx^3}{2\times 2\times 3}\right] + C_1 x + C_2$$

Applying the boundary conditions, we get that $C_2 = 0$

and $w\left[\dfrac{L^4}{24} - \dfrac{L^4}{12}\right] + C_1 L = 0$ or $C_1 = -\dfrac{1}{L}\left(-\dfrac{wL^4}{24}\right) = \dfrac{wL^3}{24}$

Thus, $Cy = w\left[\dfrac{x^4}{24} - \dfrac{Lx^3}{12}\right] + \dfrac{wL^3}{24}x$.

Q10. Solve $L_1L_2\dfrac{d^2I_2}{dt^2}+(R_1L_2+R_1L_1+R_2L_1)\dfrac{dI_2}{dt}+R_1R_2I_2 = R_1E(t)$ **for** $I_2(t)$

given $L_1 = L_2 = 2H$, $R_1 = 3\Omega$, $R_2 = 8\Omega$ **and E (t) = 6V. Assume the initial current in the circuits to be zero. Determine** $I_1(t)$ **from equation** $-R_1I_1+L_2\dfrac{dI_2}{dt}+(R_1+R_2)I_2 = 0.$

Ans. We have $L_1 = L_2 = 2H$, $R_1 = 3\Omega, R_2 = 8\Omega$ and E (t) = 6V.

Therefore, the equation

$$L_1L_2\frac{d^2I_2}{dt^2}+(R_1L_2+R_1L_1+R_2L_1)\frac{dI_2}{dt}+R_1R_2I_2 = R_1E(t) \text{ becomes}$$

$$\frac{4d^2I_2}{dt^2}+[6+6+16]\frac{dI_2}{dt}+24I_2 = 18 \text{ or } \frac{d^2I_2}{dt^2}+\frac{7dI_2}{dt}+6I_2 = \frac{9}{2}$$

Here we have not written the units explicitly in the ODE. We can remove the non-homogeneity of this ODE by substituting $I' = I_2-\dfrac{3}{4}$ in it.

Thus, we get $\dfrac{d^2I'}{dt^2}+\dfrac{7dI'}{dt}+6I' = 0$

The characteristic equation for this homogeneous second order ODE is

$\lambda^2+7\lambda+6 = 0$ which has the roots $\lambda_1 = -6$, $\lambda_2 = -1$.

Hence, the solution is $I' = C_1e^{-6t}+C_2e^{-t}$ or $I_2 = \dfrac{3}{4}+C_1e^{-6t}+C_2e^{-t}$

Now, we can get I_1 from equation $-R_1I_1+L_2\dfrac{dI_2}{dt}+(R_1+R_2)I_2 = 0$,

i.e. $-3I_1+\dfrac{2dI_2}{dt}+11I_2 = 0$

Substituting for I_2, we have

$$-3I_1+2(-6C_1e^{-6t}-C_2e^{-t})+11\left(\frac{3}{4}+C_1e^{-6t}+C_2e^{-t}\right)= 0$$

or $I_1 = \dfrac{11}{4}-\dfrac{C_1}{3}e^{-6t}+3C_2e^{-t}$

Now it is given that at t = 0, $I_1(t) = 0$, $I_2(t) = 0$.

These initial conditions give us two equations for C_1 and C_2 :

$$C_1+C_2+\frac{3}{4} = 0 \text{ and } \frac{-C_1}{3}+3C_2+\frac{11}{4} = 0$$

Thus, $C_1 = \dfrac{3}{20}$ and $C_2 = -\dfrac{9}{10}$

The particular solutions for I_1 and I_2 (in amperes) are

$$I_1 = (2.75 - 0.05e^{-6t} - 2.7e^{-t}) \text{ and } I_2 = (0.75 + 0.15e^{-6t} - 0.9e^{-t})$$

Q11. Given figure shows a very long strip of thickness D and length L in a furnace attached to a hot wall which is maintained at a temperature of 200°C. Heat is conducted steadily along the strip and is lost from the sides by convection to the surrounding air.

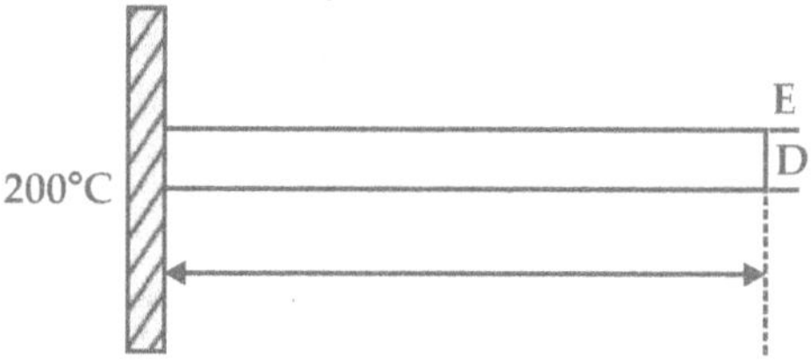

The strip temperature θ, assumed to depend only on the distance x along the strip, is modelled by the differential equation $C\dfrac{d^2\theta}{dx^2} = 2H(\theta - \theta_{air})$ where C and H are constants, and $\theta_{air} = 70°C$.

Assuming that the strip is long enough so that the end E is at the same temperature as the surrounding air, we have the boundary conditions $\theta = 200°C$ when $x = 0$, $\theta = 70°C$ when $x \to \infty$. Solve the equation for the given boundary conditions.

Ans. This is non-homogeneous second order ODE. We can remove its non-homogeneity. By making the substitution $\phi = \theta - \theta_{air}$, we get

$$\frac{d^2\phi}{dx^2} - k^2\phi = 0, \ k^2 = \frac{2H}{C}$$

We can write down the solution of this equation as $\phi = C_1 e^{kx} + C_2 e^{-kx}$

or $\theta = \theta_{air} + C_1 e^{kx} + C_2 e^{-kx}$

Now we apply the boundary conditions.

At $x = 0$, $\theta = 200°C$.

$$C_1 + C_2 = 200°C - 70°C = 130°C \hspace{3cm} ...(i)$$

As $x \to \infty$, $\theta = 70°C$

Now, as $x \to \infty$, $e^{kx} \to \infty$, i.e. the solution for θ tends to infinity, as $x \to \infty$. But the temperature of the thin strip tends to a finite value $(70°C)$

as $x \to \infty$. Therefore, the term containing e^{kx} in the general solution for θ is physically unacceptable. Hence, we put $C_1 = 0$ in (i). Thus, $C_1 = 0$, $C_2 = 130°C$ and the particular solution is $\theta = 70°C + 130°Ce^{-kx}$.

Q12. A long suspended telephone wire hangs under its own weight. Determine the differential equation governing the shape that the hanging wire assumes and obtain its general solution.

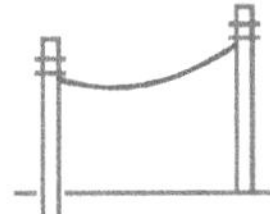

Ans. Consider the portion of the wire between its lowest point P and a point Q, close to P. Let us choose a two-dimensional Cartesian coordinate system such that P lies at its origin and the segment PQ lies in the xy plane (Fig. 4.12).

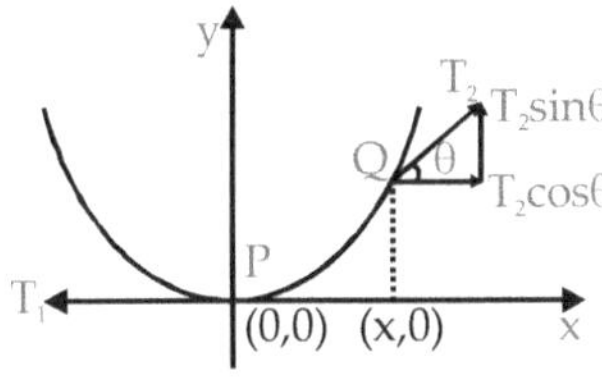

Fig. 4.12

Three forces are acting on the segment PQ of the wire; the force due to gravity $\vec{F}\,(= m\,\vec{g})$ and the tensions $\vec{T}_1$ and $\vec{T}_2$ in the wire at P and Q, respectively. If λ_m is the linear mass density of the wire (measured in kg m^{-1}), and s is the length of the segment, $m = \lambda_m s$ and $\vec{F} = \lambda_m s\vec{g}$. We can resolve $\vec{T}_2$ into two components; $T_2 \cos\theta$ and $T_2 \sin\theta$. Since the wire is in equilibrium, the net force acting on it is zero. The condition of equilibrium of forces gives us $T_1 = T_2 \cos\theta$ and $\lambda_m sg = T_2 \sin\theta$ which yields $\tan\theta = \dfrac{\lambda_m sg}{T_1}$.

Since $\dfrac{dy}{dx}$ gives the slope at Q, we can also write

$$\frac{dy}{dx} = \frac{\lambda_m sg}{T_1} \qquad \text{...(i)}$$

Differentiating (i), we get $\dfrac{d^2 y}{dx^2} = \dfrac{\lambda_m g}{T_1}\dfrac{ds}{dx}$

We can relate ds with dx and dy. The infinitesimal arc segment ds about Q is given by $(ds)^2 = (dx)^2 + (dy)^2$ or $\dfrac{ds}{dx} = \sqrt{1 + \left(\dfrac{dy}{dx}\right)^2}$ ...(ii)

Differentiating (i) and using (ii), we get the differential equation

$$\frac{d^2y}{dx^2} = \frac{\lambda_m g}{T_1}\left(\frac{ds}{dx}\right) \quad \text{or} \quad \frac{d^2y}{dx^2} = K\sqrt{1+\left(\frac{dy}{dx}\right)^2}, \quad \text{where } K = \frac{\lambda_m g}{T_1}$$

Now let $\dfrac{dy}{dx} = u$ so that $\dfrac{du}{dx} = K\sqrt{1+u^2}$

Using the method of separation of variables, we get

$$\int\frac{du}{\sqrt{1+u^2}} = K\int dx + C_1$$

or $\sinh^{-1} u = Kx + C_1$ or $u = \sinh(Kx+C_1)$ or $\dfrac{dy}{dx} = \sinh(Kx+C_1)$

Thus, $y = \int \sinh(Kx+C_1)dx + C_2$ or $y = K\cosh(Kx+C_1)+C_2$

Q13. Let E (t) be zero in the circuit of following Figure. The capacitor will discharge its charge through the resistor. Let its initial charge be q_0. Determine the charge q (t) on it in terms of q_0, t, C and R.

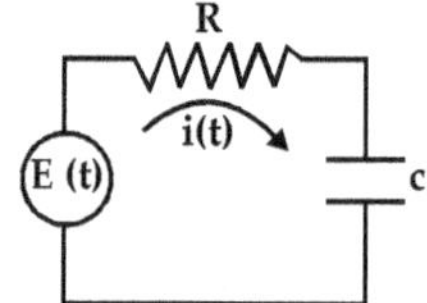

Ans. For E (t) = 0, equation $\dfrac{dq}{dt} + \dfrac{q}{RC} = \dfrac{E_0}{R}\sin\omega t$ becomes $\dfrac{dq}{dt} = -\dfrac{q}{RC}$.

Its general solution is $q = C_1 \exp(-t/RC)$

It is given that at $t = 0$, $q = q_0$

$\therefore C_1 = q_0$ and $q = q_0 \exp(-t/RC)$

(RC) is called the time constant of the circuit. At $t = RC$, the charge on the capacitor is $\dfrac{q_0}{e}$, i.e. RC is the time at which the charge on the capacitor is $\dfrac{1}{e}$ of its initial value.

Q14. A particle of mass m falls freely under gravity in a liquid that offers a resistive force proportional to its velocity:

$$f_{res} = -y\frac{dx}{dt}$$

Set up the equation of motion and solve it.　　　　[June-2012,Q.No.-3]

Ans. Given equation is $f_{res} = -y\dfrac{dx}{dt}$

By Newton's second law, $f_{res} = m\dfrac{d^2x}{dt^2} \Rightarrow m\dfrac{d^2x}{dt^2} = -y\dfrac{dx}{dt}$

Putting $\dfrac{dx}{dt} = V$, $\dfrac{d^2x}{dt^2} = \dfrac{dV}{dt}$, we get

$$m\dfrac{dV}{dt} = -yV$$

$$\Rightarrow \dfrac{dV}{V} = \dfrac{-y}{m}dt$$

Integrating, we get $\displaystyle\int\dfrac{dV}{V} = \int\dfrac{-y}{m}dt \Rightarrow \log V = \dfrac{-y}{m}t + \log C$

$$\Rightarrow \log V - \log C = \dfrac{-y}{m}t \Rightarrow \log\dfrac{V}{C} = \dfrac{-y}{m}t \Rightarrow \dfrac{V}{C} = \exp.\left(\dfrac{-y}{m}t\right)$$

$$\Rightarrow V = C\exp.\left(\dfrac{-y}{m}t\right) \Rightarrow \dfrac{dx}{dt} = C\exp.\left(\dfrac{-y}{m}t\right) \Rightarrow dx = C\int\exp.\left(\dfrac{-y}{m}t\right)dt$$

Again Integrating, we get $x = C\,\dfrac{\exp.\left(\dfrac{-y}{m}t\right)}{-y\big/m} + C_1$

$$\Rightarrow x = -\dfrac{mC}{y}\exp.\left(\dfrac{-y}{m}t\right) + C_1 \text{ is the required solution.}$$

The main aim of GPH book is to provide knowledge as well as good marks in exams.

◈ ◈ ◈

An Introduction to Partial Differential Equations

An Overview

A partial differential equation (PDE) is a differential equation that contains unknown multivariable functions and their partial derivatives.

A partial differential equation (PDE) for the function $u(x_1, \ldots x_n)$ is an equation of the form

$$F\left(x_1, \ldots\ldots, x_n, u, \frac{\partial u}{\partial x_1}, \ldots\ldots, \frac{\partial u}{\partial x_n}, \frac{\partial^2 u}{\partial x_1 \partial x_1}, \ldots\ldots \frac{\partial^2 u}{\partial x_1 \partial x_n} \ldots\ldots\right)$$

PDEs can be used to describe a wide variety of phenomena such as sound, heat, electrostatics, electrodynamics, fluid flow, or elasticity. These seemingly distinct physical phenomena can be formalised similarly in terms of PDEs. Just as ordinary differential equations often model one-dimensional dynamical systems, partial differential equations often model multidimensional systems.

Limits and Continuity to functions of more than one variable: Suppose $f(x, y)$ is a real single valued function of x and y. L is said to be the limit of $f(x, y)$ as the point (x, y) approaches, (x_0, y_0), if $f(x, y)$ approaches the value L, as (x, y) approaches (x_0, y_0).

It is written as $\qquad \lim_{(x,y)\to(x_0,y_0)} f(x,y) = L$ $\qquad\qquad$ ...(i)

Now (x, y) can approach (x_0, y_0) along any one of an infinite number of curves passing through (x_0, y_0). The limit (L) of a function $f(x, y)$ is said to exit, only if the function always approaches the value L, irrespective of the curve along which (x, y) approaches (x_0, y_0). Thus intuitively, we can say that L is the limit of $f(x, y)$ as (x, y) approaches (x_0, y_0), if $f(x, y)$ is as close to L as we wish whenever (x, y) is close enough to (x_0, y_0). We may like to study Fig. 5.1 which shows the geometric interpretation of this limit.

This concept can be extended to functions of three or more variables. For instance, intuitively L is the limit of $f(x, y, z)$ as (x, y, z) approaches (x_0, y_0, z_0) if $f(x, y, z)$ is as close to L as we wish whenever (x, y, z) is close enough to (x_0, y_0, z_0). It is not possible to represent this limit pictorially because that would require four dimensions.

Let f be a function of two variables and let $\lim_{(x,y)\to(x_0,y_0)} f(x,y) = L$. Then the concept of the limit as explained above implies that $f(x, y)$ must approach L as (x, y) approaches (x_0, y_0) along each line (or curve) through (x_0, y_0). Thus, to show that $\lim_{(x,y)\to(x_0,y_0)} f(x,y) = L$ does not exist, it is enough to show that $f(x, y)$ approaches different numbers as (x, y) approaches (x_0, y_0) along different lines (curves) through (x_0, y_0). This idea can be extended to functions of more than two variables.

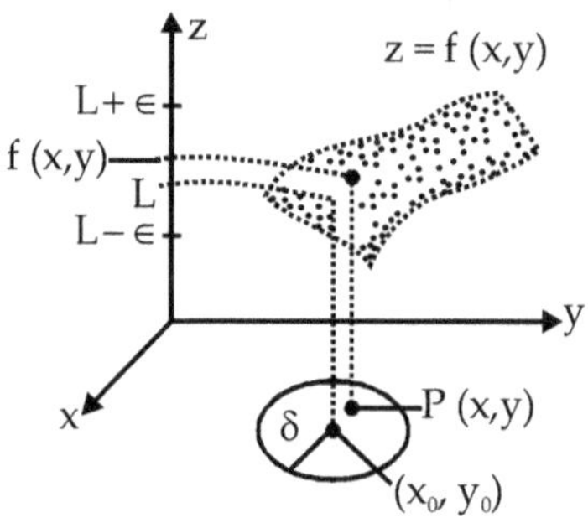

Fig. 5.1

Now, we can define the continuity of such functions:

A function f of two variables is continuous at (x_0, y_0) if $\lim\limits_{(x,y)\to(x_0,y_0)} f(x,y) = f(x_0,y_0)$. A function f of three variables is continuous at (x_0, y_0, z_0) if $\lim\limits_{(x,y,z)\to(x_0,y_0,z_0)} f(x,y,z) = f(x_0,y_0,z_0)$.

Partial derivatives: The partial derivative w.r.t. x of a function $z = f(x, y)$ at (x, y) is defined as $\lim\limits_{\Delta x \to 0} \dfrac{f(x+\Delta x, y) - f(x,y)}{\Delta x}$ provided the limit exists and is finite. It is denoted as $\dfrac{\partial z}{\partial x}$ or $\dfrac{\partial f}{\partial x}$ or f_x.

The partial derivative w.r.t. y of a function $z = f(x, y)$ at (x, y) is defined as $\lim\limits_{\Delta y \to 0} \dfrac{f(x, y+\Delta y) - f(x,y)}{\Delta y}$ provided the limit exists and is finite. It is denoted as $\dfrac{\partial z}{\partial y}$ or $\dfrac{\partial f}{\partial y}$ or f_y.

Note: It is clear from the definition that $\dfrac{\partial z}{\partial x}$ is the derivative of $z = f(x, y)$ w.r.t. x, regarding y as a constant and $\dfrac{\partial z}{\partial y}$ is the derivative of $z = f(x, y)$ w.r.t. y, regarding x as a constant.

For Example:

If $z = e^{-x/y} + \tan^{-1}\left(\dfrac{x}{y}\right)$, find $\dfrac{\partial z}{\partial x}$ and $\dfrac{\partial z}{\partial y}$.

We have $\dfrac{\partial z}{\partial x} = e^{-x/y}\left(-\dfrac{1}{y}\right) + \dfrac{1}{1+\dfrac{x^2}{y^2}} \cdot \dfrac{1}{y} = -\dfrac{1}{y}e^{-x/y} + \dfrac{y}{x^2+y^2}$

Now, $\dfrac{\partial z}{\partial y} = e^{-x/y}\left(\dfrac{x}{y^2}\right) + \dfrac{1}{1+\dfrac{x^2}{y^2}}\left(-\dfrac{x}{y^2}\right) = \dfrac{x}{y^2}e^{-x/y} - \dfrac{x}{x^2+y^2}$.

Second order partial derivatives: The first order partial derivatives $\dfrac{\partial z}{\partial x}$ and $\dfrac{\partial z}{\partial y}$ are generally functions of x and y and so we can again find their partial derivatives as given below:

- $\dfrac{\partial}{\partial x}\left(\dfrac{\partial z}{\partial x}\right)$, denoted by $\dfrac{\partial^2 z}{\partial x^2}$ or f_{xx} or f_{x^2}

- $\dfrac{\partial}{\partial y}\left(\dfrac{\partial z}{\partial x}\right)$, denoted by $\dfrac{\partial^2 z}{\partial y \partial x}$ or f_{yx}

- $\dfrac{\partial}{\partial x}\left(\dfrac{\partial z}{\partial y}\right)$, denoted by $\dfrac{\partial^2 z}{\partial x \partial y}$ or f_{xy}

- $\dfrac{\partial}{\partial y}\left(\dfrac{\partial z}{\partial y}\right)$, denoted by $\dfrac{\partial^2 z}{\partial y^2}$ or f_{yy} or f_{y^2}

We call $\dfrac{\partial^2 z}{\partial x^2}, \dfrac{\partial^2 z}{\partial y^2}, \dfrac{\partial^2 z}{\partial x \partial y}$ and $\dfrac{\partial^2 x}{\partial y \partial x}$ as the second order partial derivatives of $z = f(x, y)$.

For Example:

If $z = \tan^{-1}\left(\dfrac{y}{x}\right)$, *verify that* $\dfrac{\partial^2 z}{\partial x^2} + \dfrac{\partial^2 z}{\partial y^2} = 0$.

We have $\dfrac{\partial z}{\partial x} = \dfrac{1}{1 + \dfrac{y^2}{x^2}}\left(\dfrac{-y}{x^2}\right) = -\dfrac{y}{x^2 + y^2} = -y\left(x^2 + y^2\right)^{-1}$

$$\therefore \dfrac{\partial^2 z}{\partial x^2} = y\left(x^2 + y^2\right)^{-2}.2x = \dfrac{2xy}{\left(x^2 + y^2\right)^2},$$

Now $\dfrac{\partial z}{\partial y} = \dfrac{1}{1 + \dfrac{y^2}{x^2}}.\dfrac{1}{x} = \dfrac{x}{x^2 + y^2}.$

$$\therefore \dfrac{\partial^2 z}{\partial y^2} = -\dfrac{2xy}{\left(x^2 + y^2\right)^2}. \text{ Hence, } \dfrac{\partial^2 z}{\partial x^2} + \dfrac{\partial^2 z}{\partial x^2} = 0$$

Higher Order Partial Derivatives

If $f(x, y)$ is a real-valued function defined in a neighbourhood of (a, b) having both the partial derivatives at all the points of the neighbourhood.

Then, $f_{xx}(a,b) = \lim\limits_{h \to 0} \dfrac{f_x(a+h,\ b) - f_x(a,b)}{h}$

$f_{xy}(a,b) = \lim\limits_{k \to 0} \dfrac{f_x(a,\ b+k) - f_x(a,b)}{k}$

$f_{yx}(a,b) = \lim\limits_{h \to 0} \dfrac{f_y(a+h,\ b) - f_y(a,b)}{h}$

$f_{yy}(a,b) = \lim\limits_{k \to 0} \dfrac{f_y(a,\ b+k) - f_y(a,b)}{k}$

provided each one of these limits exists.

We also denote the second order partial derivatives of f by

$$f_{xx} = \dfrac{\partial^2 f}{\partial x^2} ; f_{xy} = \dfrac{\partial^2 f}{\partial x \partial y}$$

$$f_{yy} = \dfrac{\partial^2 f}{\partial y^2} ; f_{yx} = \dfrac{\partial^2 f}{\partial y \partial x}$$

If we want to indicate the particular point at which the second order partial derivatives are taken, then we write

$$\left(\frac{\partial^2 f}{\partial x^2}\right)_{(a,b)}, \ \frac{\partial^2 f\ (a,b)}{\partial x^2}, \ f_{xx}\ (a,b), \ \left(\frac{\partial^2 f}{\partial x\ \partial y}\right)_{(a,b)}$$

$$\frac{\partial^2 f\ (a,b)}{\partial x\ \partial y}, \ f_{xy}\ (a,b), \text{ and so on.}$$

Differentiability of Functions From $R^n \to R, n > 2$

Let f be a real-valued function defined in a neighbourhood of the point a= $(a_1, a_2, \ldots\ldots a_n)$. The function f is said to be differentiable at the point a if there exist constants $A_1, A_2, \ldots\ldots A_n$ (depending on the function and the point a) such that

$$f(a_1 + h_1\ldots\ldots a_n + h_n) - f(a_1\ldots\ldots, a_n) = \sum_{i=1}^{n} h_i A_i + \sum_{i=1}^{n} h_i \phi_i (h_1 \ldots\ldots h_n)$$

where each $\phi_i \to 0$ as $(h_1, h_2 \ldots\ldots h_n) \to (0, 0, \ldots\ldots 0)$.

As in the case of two variables, we have the following results:

(i) $\quad A_i = \dfrac{\partial f}{\partial x_i}$ at $(a_1, \ldots.a_n)$.

(ii) $\quad$ If f is differentiable at a, then f is continuous at a.

(iii) $\quad$ F is differentiable at a if and only if

$$f(a + h) - f(a) = \sum_{i=1}^{n} h_i A_i + |h| \phi(h_1, h_2, \ldots h_n)$$

where $\phi(h_1, h_2, \ldots\ldots h_n) \to 0$ as $h \to 0$,

$h = (h_1, h_2, \ldots\ldots h_n)$ and $|h| = \sqrt{\sum h_i^2}$

(iv) $\quad$ If f is differentiable at a, then f has all the partial derivatives at a.

(v) $\quad$ If the partial derivatives of f are continuous at a, then f is differentiable at a.

Partial Differential Equations: An equation containing an unknown function of two or more variables and its partial derivatives with respect to these variables is known as a partial differential equation (p.d.e.).

Usually, we take z as an unknown function (called dependent variable) of two independent variables x and y. An equation of the form

$$f\left(x, y, z, \frac{\partial z}{\partial x}, \frac{\partial z}{\partial y}, \frac{\partial^2 z}{\partial x^2}, \frac{\partial^2 z}{\partial x \partial y}, \ldots\right) = 0$$

is a partial differential equation in two variables.

For example, $x\dfrac{\partial z}{\partial x}+y\dfrac{\partial z}{\partial y}=z^2,\left(\dfrac{\partial z}{\partial x}\right)^2+\left(\dfrac{\partial z}{\partial y}\right)^2=z,\ z=\left(\dfrac{\partial z}{\partial x}\right)\left(\dfrac{\partial z}{\partial y}\right),\dfrac{\partial^2 z}{\partial x^2}+\dfrac{\partial^2 z}{\partial y^2}=0,$

etc. are partial differential equations.

Order and Degree of a Partial Differential Equation: The order of a partial differential equation is the order of the highest-order partial derivative appearing in the equation.

The degree of a partial differential equation is the greatest exponent of the highest order partial derivative appearing in the equation.

For example:

- $x\dfrac{\partial z}{\partial x}+z=0,x^2\dfrac{\partial z}{\partial z}+y^2\dfrac{\partial z}{\partial y}=z^2$

    are partial differential equations of first order and first degree.

- $x^2\left(\dfrac{\partial z}{\partial x}\right)^2=z\left(z-y\dfrac{\partial z}{\partial y}\right),z=\left(\dfrac{\partial z}{\partial x}\right)^2+\left(\dfrac{\partial z}{\partial y}\right)^2$

    are partial differential equations of first order and second degree.

- $\left(\dfrac{\partial z}{\partial x}\right)^3+\left(\dfrac{\partial z}{\partial y}\right)^4=z$

    is a partial differential equation of first order and fourth degree.

- $\dfrac{\partial^2 z}{\partial x^2}=\dfrac{\partial z}{\partial y},\dfrac{\partial^2 z}{\partial x^2}+\dfrac{\partial^2 z}{\partial y^2}=x+y$

    are partial differential equations of second order and first degree.

Linear and non-linear PDEs: Just as in the case of ODEs, we say that a PDE is linear if (i) it is of the first degree in the unknown function (the dependent variable) and its partial derivatives, (ii) it does not contain the products of the unknown functions and either of its partial derivatives and (iii) it does not contain any transcendental functions. Otherwise, it is non-linear.

For example,

- $\dfrac{\partial^2 \phi}{\partial x^2}+\dfrac{\partial^2 \phi}{\partial y^2}+\dfrac{\partial^2 \phi}{\partial z^2}=0,\ \dfrac{\partial T}{\partial t}-K\dfrac{\partial^2 T}{\partial x^2}=0,$

    $x\dfrac{\partial f}{\partial x}+y\dfrac{\partial f}{\partial y}=0$ are linear PDEs.

- $\left(\dfrac{\partial f}{\partial x}\right)^3+\dfrac{\partial f}{\partial t}=0$ is non-linear PDE.

- $\dfrac{\partial^2 u}{\partial x^2} + \dfrac{\partial^2 u}{\partial y^2} = f(x,y)$ is linear PDE.

Homogeneous and non-homogeneous linear PDEs: If each term of a PDE contains either the unknown function or one of its partial derivatives, it is said to be homogeneous; otherwise it is non-homogeneous.

Second order partial differential equations: The most general form of Second order partial differential equations for a function u(x, y) is

$$a\frac{\partial^2 u}{\partial x^2} + b\frac{\partial^2 u}{\partial x \partial y} + c\frac{\partial^2 u}{\partial y^2} + d\frac{\partial u}{\partial y} + e\frac{\partial u}{\partial y} + fu = g(x,y) \qquad \text{...(ii)}$$

where a, b, c, d, e and f are functions of (x, y). If the coefficients a, b, c, d, e, f are constants, Eq. (ii) is termed a linear, second order, constant coefficient PDE. Equations of the form (ii) with constant coefficients, are further classified as elliptic, hyperbolic and parabolic, depending on the relationship between the second - order coefficients a, b, c:

if $ac - b^2 > 0$, the equation is elliptic,

if $ac - b^2 < 0$, the equation is hyperbolic

if $ac - b^2 = 0$, the equation is parabolic.

Hence, we can verify that the Laplace equation $\dfrac{\partial^2 \phi}{\partial x^2} + \dfrac{\partial^2 \phi}{\partial y^2} + \dfrac{\partial^2 \phi}{\partial z^2} = 0$ and

Poisson's equation $\dfrac{\partial^2 u}{\partial x^2} + \dfrac{\partial^2 u}{\partial y^2} = f(x,y)$ are elliptic. The diffusion equation

$\dfrac{\partial T}{\partial t} - K\dfrac{\partial^2 T}{\partial x^2} = 0$ is parabolic and equation $\dfrac{\partial^2 u}{\partial t^2} = c^2\dfrac{\partial^2 u}{\partial y^2}$ known as the wave

equation is hyperbolic.

Solution of a PDE: A solution of a PDE in some region R of the space of independent variables is a function, all of whose partial derivatives appearing in the equation exist in some domain containing R and which satisfies the equation everywhere in R.

Solved Practical Problems

Q1. Write down the order and degree of each of the PDEs listed below. Determine which of the PDEs are linear, non-linear. Classify the linear PDEs as homogeneous, non-homogeneous.

(i) $x^2 \dfrac{\partial^2 f}{\partial x^2} + y^2 \dfrac{\partial^2 f}{\partial y^2} = 0$

Ans. Order: 2;

Degree: 1:

Linear or non-Linear: Linear;

Homogeneous or non-homogeneous: Homogeneous.

(ii) $xy \dfrac{\partial^2 f}{\partial x^2} + x \dfrac{\partial f}{\partial x} \dfrac{\partial f}{\partial y} + y \dfrac{\partial^2 f}{\partial y^2} = x^2 + y^2$

Ans. Order: 2;

Degree: 1:

Linear or non-Linear: Linear;

Homogeneous or non-homogeneous: Non-homogeneous.

(iii) $\left(\dfrac{\partial y}{\partial x} \right)^3 + \dfrac{\partial y}{\partial t} = 0$

Ans. Order: 1;

Degree: 3:

Linear or non-Linear: Linear;

Homogeneous or non-homogeneous: Non-homogeneous.

(iv) $\dfrac{\partial^3 u}{\partial x^3} + 2 \dfrac{\partial^3 u}{\partial x \partial y^2} - 6 \left(\dfrac{\partial u}{\partial y} \right)^4 = 0$

Ans. Order: 3;

Degree: 1:

Linear or non-Linear: Non-Linear;

Homogeneous or non-homogeneous: Non-homogeneous.

Q2. **Determine** $\dfrac{\partial f}{\partial x}, \dfrac{\partial f}{\partial y}$ **and** $\dfrac{\partial^2 f}{\partial x \partial y}$ **for the function:** $f(x,y) = ln(x+y)$.

[June-2010,Q.No.-1(f)]

Ans. Given, $f(x,y) = ln(x+y) \ \Rightarrow \ \dfrac{\partial f}{\partial x} = \dfrac{1}{x+y}$ and $\dfrac{\partial f}{\partial y} = \dfrac{1}{x+y}$

and $\dfrac{\partial^2 f}{\partial x \partial y} = \dfrac{\partial}{\partial x}\left[\dfrac{\partial f}{\partial y} \right] = \dfrac{\partial}{\partial x}\left[\dfrac{1}{x+y} \right] = \left[\dfrac{(x+y)0 - 1.1}{(x+y)^2} \right] \Rightarrow \dfrac{\partial^2 f}{\partial x \partial y} = \dfrac{-1}{(x+y)^2}$.

Q3. **Show that** $\lim\limits_{(x,y)\to(0,0)} f(x,y)$ **does not exist for** $f(x,y) = \dfrac{y^2 - x^2}{y^2 + x^2}$.

Ans. Let $y = mx$. Then $\dfrac{y^2 - x^2}{y^2 + x^2} = \dfrac{m^2x^2 - x^2}{m^2x^2 + x^2} = \dfrac{m^2 - 1}{m^2 + 1}$

The value of $\dfrac{m^2 - 1}{m^2 + 1}$ will be different for different values of m. This means that $f(x, y)$ approaches different values along the lines corresponding to different values of m as (x, y) approaches $(0, 0)$. Hence, the $\lim\limits_{(x,y)\to(0,0)} f(x,y)$ does not exist.

Q4. Evaluate $\lim\limits_{(x,y)\to(-1,2)} \dfrac{x^3 + y^3}{x^2 + y^2}$.

Ans. We have $\lim\limits_{(x,y)\to(-1,2)} x = -1$ and $\lim\limits_{(x,y)\to(-1,2)} y = 2$

Using the formula, $\lim\limits_{(x,y)\to(x_0,y_0)} (fg)(x,y) = \lim\limits_{(x,y)\to(x_0,y_0)} f(x,y)\ \lim\limits_{(x,y)\to(x_0,y_0)} g(x,y)$

we get

$$\lim\limits_{(x,y)\to(-1,2)} x^3 = -1 \text{ and } \lim\limits_{(x,y)\to(-1,2)} y^3 = 8$$

$$\lim\limits_{(x,y)\to(-1,2)} x^2 = 1 \text{ and } \lim\limits_{(x,y)\to(-1,2)} y^2 = 4$$

Therefore, $\lim\limits_{(x,y)\to(-1,2)}$

$$\dfrac{x^3 + y^3}{x^2 + y^2} = \dfrac{\lim\limits_{(x,y)\to(-1,2)} x^3 + \lim\limits_{(x,y)\to(-1,2)} y^3}{\lim\limits_{(x,y)\to(-1,2)} x^2 + \lim\limits_{(x,y)\to(-1,2)} y^2} = \dfrac{-1+8}{1+4} = \dfrac{7}{5}.$$

Q5. (a) Show that $\lim\limits_{(x,y)\to(-1,1)} \dfrac{x^2 + 2xy^2 + y^4}{1 + y^2} = 0$

Ans. Here, $\lim\limits_{(x,y)\to(-1,1)} \dfrac{x^2 + 2xy^2 + y^4}{1 + y^2}$

$$= \dfrac{\lim\limits_{(x,y)\to(-1,1)} x^2 + 2 \lim\limits_{(x,y)\to(-1,1)} x \ \lim\limits_{(x,y)\to(-1,1)} y^2 + \lim\limits_{(x,y)\to(-1,1)} y^4}{1 + \lim\limits_{(x,y)\to(-1,1)} y^2}$$

$$= \dfrac{(-1)^2 + 2[-1][1]^2 + 1^4}{1 + 1^2} = \dfrac{1 - 2 + 1}{2} = 0$$

(b) Show that $\lim\limits_{(x,y)\to(0,0)} \dfrac{xy}{(x^2 + y^2)}$ **does not exist.**

Ans. Let $y = mx$, then $f(x,y) = \dfrac{xy}{x^2 + y^2} = \dfrac{mx^2}{x^2 + m^2x^2} = \dfrac{m}{1 + m^2}$

This will have different values for different values of m. This means that $f(x, y)$ approaches different values along the lines corresponding to different values of m as (x, y) approaches $(0, 0)$. Hence, $\lim\limits_{(x,y)\to(0,0)} f(x,y)$ does not exist.

Q6. **Show that $f(x,y) = \sin\dfrac{xy}{1+x^2+y^2}$ is a continuous function.**

Ans. Let $g(x,y) = \left(\dfrac{xy}{1+x^2+y^2}\right)$ and $u(t) = \sin t$

Then $f(x, y) = u(g)$, i.e. $f(x, y)$ is a composite of $g(x, y)$ and u. We know that $\lim\limits_{(x,y)\to(x_0,y_0)} x = x_0$ and $\lim\limits_{(x,y)\to(x_0,y_0)} y = y_0$. Since x_0 and y_0 can be any points in the domain of x and y, $p(x, y) = x$ and $q(x, y) = y$, are continuous. The sums, products and quotients of continuous functions are continuous. Hence, $g(x, y)$ is continuous. Similarly, we can verify that $u(t)$ is continuous. Therefore, their composite $f(x, y)$ is also continuous.

Q7. **(a) Verify that $u_1 = \cos x \cos cy$ and $u_2 = \sin x \sin cy$ are both solutions of the PDE $\dfrac{\partial^2 u}{\partial y^2} - c^2 \dfrac{\partial^2 u}{\partial x^2} = 0$. Show that $\cos(x+cy)$ and $\cos(x-cy)$ are also solutions of this PDE.**

Ans. The partial derivatives of $u_1 = \cos x \cos cy$ and $u_2 = \sin x \sin cy$ are

$$\frac{\partial u_1}{\partial x} = -\sin x \cos cy, \quad \frac{\partial^2 u_1}{\partial x^2} = -\cos x \cos cy$$

$$\frac{\partial u_1}{\partial y} = -c \cos x \sin cy, \quad \frac{\partial^2 u_1}{\partial y^2} = -c^2 \cos x \cos cy$$

$$\text{and} \quad \frac{\partial u_2}{\partial x} = \cos x \sin cy, \quad \frac{\partial^2 u_2}{\partial x^2} = -\sin x \sin cy$$

$$\frac{\partial u_2}{\partial y} = c \sin x \cos cy, \quad \frac{\partial^2 u_2}{\partial y^2} = -c^2 \sin x \sin cy$$

Substituting the relevant partial derivatives of u_1 and u_2 in the given PDE. We get two identities implying that both u_1 and u_2 are its solutions. Now, from the principle of superposition, a linear combination of linearly independent solutions of a PDE is also its solution. Since u_1 and u_2 are linearly independent, we get that

$$\cos(x+cy) = \cos x \cos cy - \sin x \sin cy = u_1 - u_2$$

and $\cos(x-cy) = \cos x \cos cy + \sin x \sin cy = u_1 + u_2$

are also solutions of the PDE. For excellent score, read GPH book.

(b) Show that for each integer n, the function $u_n = e^{-kn^2 y} \sin nx$ is a solution of the PDE $\dfrac{\partial u}{\partial y} - k\dfrac{\partial^2 u}{\partial x^2} = 0$. Deduce that for any positive integer N and real numbers, $a_1, a_2, ..., a_N,$ the function $\displaystyle\sum_{n=1}^{N} a_n e^{-kn^2 y} \sin nx$ is also a solution of the PDE.

Ans. Let us first compute the partial derivatives of u_n :

$$\frac{\partial u_n}{\partial y} = -kn^2 e^{-kn^2 y} \sin nx \quad \text{and} \quad \frac{\partial u_n}{\partial x} = n e^{-kn^2 y} \cos nx$$

$$\Rightarrow \frac{\partial^2 u_n}{\partial x^2} = -n^2 e^{-kn^2 y} \sin nx$$

Substituting $\dfrac{\partial u_n}{\partial y}$ and $\dfrac{\partial^2 u_n}{\partial x^2}$ in the PDE gives us an identity. Therefore, u_n is a solution of the PDE. Again, since $u_1, u_2, u_3, ... u_n$ are linearly independent functions, we get from the principle of superposition that their linear combination, i.e. $u = a_1 u_1 + a_2 u_2 + ... + a_n u_n$ is also a solution of the PDE.

In concise form, we may write $u = \displaystyle\sum_{n=1}^{N} a_n u_n = \sum_{n=1}^{N} a_n e^{-kn^2 y} \sin nx$.

Q8. Evaluate $\displaystyle\lim_{(x,y,z)\to(2,1,-1)} \frac{2x^2 y - xz^2}{y^2 - xz}$.

Ans. We can see that

$$\lim_{(x,y,z)\to(2,1,-1)} x = 2, \quad \lim_{(x,y,z)\to(2,1,-1)} y = 1, \quad \lim_{(x,y,z)\to(2,1,-1)} z = -1$$

Therefore, $\displaystyle\lim_{(x,y,z)\to(2,1,-1)} \frac{2x^2 y - xz^2}{y^2 - xz} = \frac{2\times 4\times 1 - 2(-1)^2}{1^2 + 2\times 1} = \frac{8-2}{3} = 2.$

Q9. Show that the function *ln* (x/y) is continuous at (e, 1).

Ans. Here, $\displaystyle\lim_{(x,y)\to(e,1)} ln(x/y) = ln(e/1) = 1.$

Let $f(x, y) = x/y$ and $g(t) = ln\,t.$ Using the quotient formula for limits

$$\lim_{(x,y)\to(e,1)} (x/y) = e.$$

Since $\displaystyle\lim_{t\to e} g(t) = ln(e) = 1 \equiv g(e),$ therefore $g(t)$ is continuous at $t = e.$

Thus, it follows that $\displaystyle\lim_{(x,y)\to(e,1)} ln(x/y) = g(e) = 1$.

Hence, the function *ln* (x/y) is continuous at (e, 1).

Q10. (a) Find all the first-order partial derivatives of $f(x,y,z) = x^4 - 2x^2y^2z^2 + 3yz^4$ and $h(x,y,t) = xe^t - y^2e^{2t}$. What are the values of $\dfrac{\partial f}{\partial y}(1,1,1)$ and $\dfrac{\partial h}{\partial t}(4,1,0)$?

Ans. We have $f(x,y,z) = x^4 - 2x^2y^2z^2 + 3yz^4$

$$\Rightarrow \frac{\partial f}{\partial x} = 4x^3 - 4xy^2z^2 \text{ and } \frac{\partial f}{\partial y} = -4x^2yz^2 + 3z^4; \frac{\partial f}{\partial y}(1,1,1) = -4 + 3 = -1$$

and $\dfrac{\partial f}{\partial z} = -4x^2y^2z + 12yz^3$

Now, $h(x,y,t) = xe^t - y^2e^{2t} \Rightarrow \dfrac{\partial h}{\partial x} = e^t$ and $\dfrac{\partial h}{\partial y} = -2ye^{2t}$

and $\dfrac{\partial h}{\partial t} = xe^t - 2y^2e^{2t} \Rightarrow \dfrac{\partial h}{\partial t}(4,1,0) = 4 \times 1 - 2 \times 1^2 \times 1 = 2$

(b) Show that the function $z = ln(x^2 + y^2)$ satisfies the equation

$$\frac{\partial^2 z}{\partial x^2} + \frac{\partial^2 z}{\partial y^2} = 0.$$

Ans. We have $z = ln(x^2 + y^2) \Rightarrow \dfrac{\partial z}{\partial x} = \dfrac{2x}{x^2 + y^2}, \dfrac{\partial z}{\partial y} = \dfrac{2y}{x^2 + y^2}$

$$\Rightarrow \frac{\partial^2 z}{\partial x^2} = \frac{2}{x^2 + y^2} - \frac{4x^2}{(x^2 + y^2)^2} = \frac{2y^2 - 2x^2}{(x^2 + y^2)^2}$$

and $\dfrac{\partial^2 z}{\partial y^2} = \dfrac{2}{x^2 + y^2} - \dfrac{4y^2}{(x^2 + y^2)^2} = \dfrac{2x^2 - 2y^2}{(x^2 + y^2)^2}$

hence, $\dfrac{\partial^2 z}{\partial x^2} + \dfrac{\partial^2 z}{\partial y^2} = \dfrac{2y^2 - 2x^2 + 2x^2 - 2y^2}{(x^2 + y^2)^2} = 0$

Thus, $z = ln(x^2 + y^2)$ satisfies the equation $\dfrac{\partial^2 z}{\partial x^2} + \dfrac{\partial^2 z}{\partial y^2} = 0$

(c) On a rainy day, we may have observed a rainbow in the sky. A rainbow is formed due to the refraction, reflection and another refraction of various monochromatic rays in the sunlight by water droplets suspended in air. The angle θ shown in following figure for one monochromatic ray is given as $\theta(\mu, i) = 4\sin^{-1}\left(\dfrac{\sin i}{\mu}\right) - 2i$

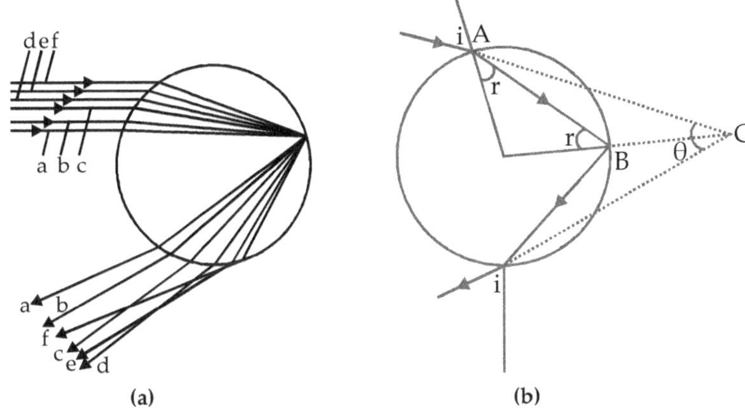

(a)   (b)

Fig. 5.4

where μ is the index of refraction of water for the ray and i, its angle of incidence. For any given μ, find the angle i_μ for which

$$\frac{\partial \theta}{\partial i}(\mu, i_\mu) = 0.$$

Ans. We have $\theta(\mu, i) = 4\sin^{-1}\left(\dfrac{\sin i}{\mu}\right) - 2i \;\Rightarrow\; \dfrac{\partial \theta}{\partial i} = \dfrac{4}{\sqrt{1 - \dfrac{\sin^2 i}{\mu^2}}} \dfrac{\cos i}{\mu} - 2$

$$= \frac{4\mu}{\sqrt{\mu^2 - \sin^2 i}} \cdot \frac{\cos i}{\mu} - 2 = \frac{4\cos i}{\sqrt{\mu^2 - \sin^2 i}} - 2$$

Since, $\dfrac{\partial \theta}{\partial i} = 0$ for $i = i_\mu$

Therefore, $\dfrac{4\cos i_\mu}{\sqrt{\mu^2 - \sin^2 i_\mu}} = 2$ or $4\cos^2 i_\mu = \mu^2 - \sin^2 i_\mu$

or $4\cos^2 i_\mu + 1 - \cos^2 i_\mu = \mu^2$ or $3\cos^2 i_\mu = \mu^2 - 1$

or $\cos i_\mu = \sqrt{\dfrac{\mu^2 - 1}{3}}$

$$\therefore i_\mu = \cos^{-1}\left(\sqrt{\frac{\mu^2 - 1}{3}}\right)$$

(d)   The entropy S of a gas is given by

$$S = C_v \ln P + C_p \ln V + A \qquad\qquad \dots(i)$$

where C_p, C_v and A are constants. We can substitute for V from the ideal gas law PV =RT to obtain

$$S = (C_v - C_p)\ln P + C_p \ln T + B \qquad \qquad ...(ii)$$

where B is a constant. Compute $\partial S/\partial P$ from (i) and (ii). Why do the two expressions differ?

Ans. From (i), $\dfrac{\partial S}{\partial P} = \dfrac{C_v}{P}$ and from (ii), $\dfrac{\partial S}{\partial P} = \dfrac{C_v - C_p}{P}$

In finding $\dfrac{\partial S}{\partial P}$ from (i), we keep V constant, whereas in computing $\dfrac{\partial S}{\partial P}$ from (ii), we keep T constant. Therefore, these two partial derivatives are different. The book you can believe most – GPH book.

Q11. Determine all the first and second order partial derivatives of the function $f(x,y) = x^2 - 5xy^3$　　　　　　**[June-2012, Q.No.-1(c)]**

Ans. Given equation is $f(x,y) = x^2 - 5xy^3$

Now, $\dfrac{\partial f}{\partial x} = 2x - 5y^3$ and $\dfrac{\partial f}{\partial y} = -15xy^2$

Similarly, $\dfrac{\partial^2 f}{\partial x^2} = \dfrac{\partial}{\partial x}\left(\dfrac{\partial f}{\partial x}\right) = \dfrac{\partial}{\partial x}\left(2x - 5y^3\right) = 2$;

$\dfrac{\partial^2 f}{\partial y^2} = \dfrac{\partial}{\partial y}\left(\dfrac{\partial f}{\partial y}\right) = \dfrac{\partial}{\partial y}(-15xy^2) = -30\,xy$;

$\dfrac{\partial^2 f}{\partial x \partial y} = \dfrac{\partial}{\partial x}\left(\dfrac{\partial f}{\partial y}\right) = \dfrac{\partial}{\partial x}\left(-15xy^2\right) = -15y^2$ and

$\dfrac{\partial^2 f}{\partial y \partial x} = \dfrac{\partial}{\partial y}\left(2x - 5y^3\right) = -15y^2$.

Q12. Show that $\cos(x+y)$ **is differentiable at the point** $\left(\dfrac{\pi}{4}, \dfrac{\pi}{4}\right)$.

Ans. Let $f(x,y) = \cos(x+y)$.

Consider,

$$f\left(\dfrac{\pi}{4}+h, \dfrac{\pi}{4}+k\right) - f\left(\dfrac{\pi}{4}, \dfrac{\pi}{4}\right) = \cos\left(\dfrac{\pi}{4}+h+\dfrac{\pi}{4}+k\right) - \cos\left(\dfrac{\pi}{4}+\dfrac{\pi}{4}\right)$$

$$= \cos\left(\dfrac{\pi}{2}+h+k\right) - \cos\left(\dfrac{\pi}{2}\right)$$

$$= -\sin(h+k)$$

$$= -h - k + h\left[1 - \frac{\sin(h+k)}{h+k}\right] + k\left[1 - \frac{\sin(h+k)}{(h+k)}\right]$$

$$= Ah + Bk + h\phi(h,k) + k\psi(h,k),$$

where $A = -1, B = -1, \phi(h,k) = \psi(h,k) = 1 - \dfrac{\sin(h+k)}{(h+k)}$

Now, $\lim\limits_{(h,k)\to(0,0)} \phi(h,k) = \lim\limits_{(h,k)\to(0,0)} \psi(h,k) = 1 - \lim\limits_{(h,k)\to(0,0)} \dfrac{\sin(h+k)}{(h+k)}$

$$= 1 - 1 = 0,$$

Since, $\lim\limits_{(h,k)\to(0,0)} \dfrac{\sin(h+k)}{(h+k)} = \lim\limits_{t\to 0} \dfrac{\sin t}{t} = 1$ where $t = h + k$.

Therefore, f is differentiable at $\left(\dfrac{\pi}{4}, \dfrac{\pi}{4}\right)$

Q13. According to Newton's law of gravitation, the magnitude of the force of attraction between two particles of mass m is $F = -\dfrac{Gm^2}{r^2}$ where $r = \sqrt{(x-x_0)^2 + (y-y_0)^2 + (z-z_0)^2}$ is the distance between the two particles. Determine whether F is continuous and differentiable at all points in space. The potential of this gravitational force field is given as $f(x,y,z) = -\dfrac{Gm^2}{r}\,(r > 0)$

Show that f satisfies the equation $\dfrac{\partial^2 f}{\partial x^2} + \dfrac{\partial^2 f}{\partial y^2} + \dfrac{\partial^2 f}{\partial z^2} = 0$

Ans. F is not continuous and therefore not differentiable at the point $r = 0$.

Now here, $\dfrac{\partial f}{\partial x} = -\dfrac{\partial}{\partial x}\left[\dfrac{Gm^2}{\sqrt{(x-x_0)^2 + (y-y_0)^2 + (z-z_0)^2}}\right]$

$$= \frac{1}{2}\frac{2(x-x_0)Gm^2}{\left\{(x-x_0)^2 + (y-y_0)^2 + (z-z_0)^2\right\}^{3/2}} = \frac{(x-x_0)Gm^2}{r^3}$$

$$\frac{\partial^2 f}{\partial x^2} = -\frac{3}{4}\frac{4(x-x_0)^2 Gm^2}{\left\{(x-x_0)^2 + (y-y_0)^2 + (z-z_0)^2\right\}^{5/2}} + \frac{Gm^2}{r^3} = -\frac{3(x-x_0)^2 Gm^2}{r^5} + \frac{Gm^2}{r^3}$$

Similarly, $\dfrac{\partial^2 f}{\partial y^2} = -\dfrac{3(y-y_0)^2 Gm^2}{r^5} + \dfrac{Gm^2}{r^3}$ and $\dfrac{\partial^2 f}{\partial z^2} = -\dfrac{3(z-z_0)^2 Gm^2}{r^5} + \dfrac{Gm^2}{r^3}$

Thus, $\dfrac{\partial^2 f}{\partial x^2} + \dfrac{\partial^2 f}{\partial y^2} + \dfrac{\partial^2 f}{\partial z^2} = -\dfrac{3Gm^2}{r^5}\left[(x-x_0)^2 + (y-y_0)^2 + (z-z_0)^2\right] + \dfrac{3Gm^2}{r^3}$

$= -\dfrac{3Gm^2}{r^5}r^2 + \dfrac{3Gm^2}{r^3} \equiv 0$

Therefore, $f = -\dfrac{Gm^2}{r}(r > 0)$ satisfies the given PDE.

Q14. If $f(x, y) = x^2 \tan^{-1}\dfrac{y}{x} - y^2 \tan^{-1}\dfrac{x}{y}$, $x \neq 0$, $y \neq 0$,

then prove that $\dfrac{\partial^2 f}{\partial x\, \partial y} = \dfrac{x^2 - y^2}{x^2 + y^2}$.

Ans. Here, $\dfrac{\partial f}{\partial y} = x^2 \cdot \dfrac{1}{1 + y^2/x^2} \cdot \dfrac{1}{x} - 2y \tan^{-1}\dfrac{x}{y} - y^2 \cdot \dfrac{1}{1 + x^2/y^2}\left(-\dfrac{x}{y^2}\right)$

$= \dfrac{x^3}{x^2 + y^2} + \dfrac{xy^2}{x^2 + y^2} - 2y \tan^{-1}\dfrac{x}{y} = \dfrac{x(x^2 + y^2)}{x^2 + y^2} - 2y \tan^{-1}\dfrac{x}{y}$

$= x - 2y \tan^{-1}\dfrac{x}{y}$

Now, $\dfrac{\partial^2 f}{\partial x\, \partial y} = \dfrac{\partial}{\partial x}\left(x - 2y \tan^{-1}\dfrac{x}{y}\right)$

$= 1 - 2y \cdot \dfrac{1}{1 + x^2/y^2} \cdot \dfrac{1}{y} = 1 - \dfrac{2y^2}{x^2 + y^2} = \dfrac{x^2 - y^2}{x^2 + y^2}$

Q15. If $u(x,y,z) = e^{xyz}$, then show that $\dfrac{\partial^3 u}{\partial x\, \partial y\, \partial z} = (1 + 3xyz + x^2y^2z^2)\, e^{xyz}$.

Ans. Given, $u(x,y,z) = e^{xyz}$,

Therefore, $\dfrac{\partial u}{\partial z} = xy\, e^{xyz}$,

$\dfrac{\partial^2 u}{\partial y\, \partial z} = x\, e^{xyz} + x^2\, yz\, e^{xyz}$, and

$\dfrac{\partial^3 u}{\partial x\, \partial y\, \partial z} = e^{xyz} + xyz\, e^{xyz} + 2xyz\, e^{xyz} + x^2y^2z^2\, e^{xyz}$

$= (1 + 3xyz + x^2y^2z^2)\, e^{xyz}$.

Q16. If $z = f(x,y)$, $x = \ln u$, $y = \ln v$, show that $\dfrac{\partial^2 z}{\partial x\, \partial y} = uv \dfrac{\partial^2 z}{\partial u\, \partial v}$.

Ans. Given, $z = f(x,y), x = \ln u, y = \ln v$

Now,

$$\frac{\partial z}{\partial u} = \frac{\partial z}{\partial x}.\frac{\partial x}{\partial u} = \frac{\partial z}{\partial x}.\frac{1}{u}$$

$$\Rightarrow \frac{\partial^2 z}{\partial v\,\partial u} = \frac{\partial}{\partial v}.\left(\frac{\partial z}{\partial u}\right)$$

where, $\dfrac{\partial z}{\partial v} = \dfrac{\partial z}{\partial y}.\dfrac{\partial y}{\partial v} = \dfrac{\partial z}{\partial y}.\dfrac{1}{v}$

$$\therefore \quad \frac{\partial^2 z}{\partial v\,\partial u} = \frac{1}{uv}\frac{\partial z}{\partial x}.\frac{\partial z}{\partial y} \Rightarrow \frac{\partial^2 z}{\partial x\,\partial y} = \frac{uv}{\partial u\,\partial v}\frac{\partial^2 z}{}$$

Q17. Let $f:R^2 \to R$ be a function given by $f(x,y)=x^2+xy+y^3$. Find $f_x(x,y)$ and $f_y(x,y)$.

Ans. Let, $z = f(x,y) = x^2 + xy + y^3$

Now, $\dfrac{\partial z}{\partial x} = 2x + y$ (Treat y as constant)

Similarly,

$\dfrac{\partial z}{\partial y} = 3y^2 + x$ (Treat x as constant)

Hence, $f_x(x,y) = 2x+y$ and $f_y(x,y) = 3y^2 + x$.

Q18. If $f(x,y) = 2x^2 - xy + 2y^2$, find $\dfrac{\partial f}{\partial x}$ and $\dfrac{\partial f}{\partial y}$ at the point (1, 2).

Ans. The function $f(x,y) = 2x^2 - xy + 2y^2$ is a polynomial in x and y. Therefore, the partial derivatives exist. By direct differentiation, we get,

$$\frac{\partial f}{\partial x} = 4x - y \text{ and } \frac{\partial f}{\partial y} = -x + 4y.$$

So, $\left(\dfrac{\partial f}{\partial x}\right)_{(1,2)} = 4 - 2 = 2$ and $\left(\dfrac{\partial f}{\partial y}\right)_{(1,2)} = -1 + 8 = 7.$

◈ ◈ ◈

Feedback is the breakfast of Champions.

Ken Blanchard

You can Help other students.
"Inform any error or mistake in this book."

We and Universe
will reward you for Your Kind act.

Email at : feedback@gullybaba.com
or
WhatsApp on 9350849407

Partial Differential Equations in Physics

An Overview

Partial differential equations (PDEs) play a central role in modern physics as a tool to model many fundamental physical processes.

Partial diferential equations are often used to construct models of the most basic theories underlying physics and engineering. For example, the system of partial diferential equations known as Maxwell's equations can be written on the back of a post card, yet from these equations one can derive the entire theory of electricity and magnetism, including light.

The Method of Separation of Variables: We consider a finite string AB of length L fixed at both ends, as shown in Fig. 6.1(a). Suppose that the string is plucked (initial displacement h(x)) and then released from rest, as shown in Fig. 6.1 (b). If we choose x-axis along the length of the string then the motion of the string is described by the 1 - D wave equation:

$$\frac{\partial^2 f}{\partial t^2} = v^2 \frac{\partial^2 f}{\partial x^2} \qquad\qquad \text{...(i)}$$

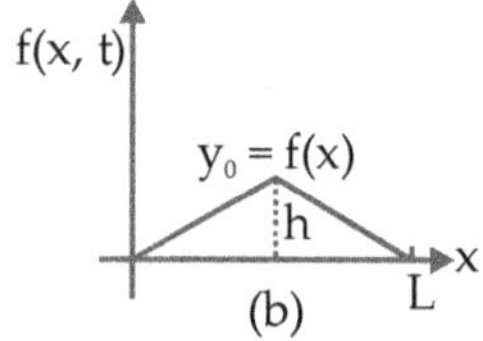

Fig. 6.1: Vibrations of a string fixed at both ends

We would note that there is no term containing mixed partials like $\frac{\partial^2 f}{\partial t \partial x}$ or $\frac{\partial f}{\partial t} \frac{\partial f}{\partial x}$ in Eq.(i). This is because this equation is obtained under the assumption that the string is displaced only slightly from its equilibrium position.

Now, we assume that the solution of Eq. (i) can be written in the form of a product as

$$f(x,t) = X(x)\ T(t) \qquad\qquad \text{...(ii)}$$

It means that the function X does not depend on t and the function T does depend upon x. For instance, the function

$$f(x,t) = x \sin \omega t \qquad\qquad \text{...(iii(a))}$$

is completely separable in x and t. On the other hand, the function

$$f(x,t) = x + t \qquad\qquad \text{...(iii(b))}$$

is inseparable in that the function cannot be written as a product of two functions.

Differentiating Eq. (ii) twice with respect to x. We get

$$\frac{\partial f}{\partial x} = X'T \ \text{ and } \ \frac{\partial^2 f}{\partial x^2} = X''T \qquad\qquad \text{...(iv)}$$

where prime(s) denote ordinary differentiation with respect to x.

Similarly, if we differentiate Eq. (ii) with respect to t, we obtain

$$\frac{\partial f}{\partial t} = X\dot{T} \quad \text{and} \quad \frac{\partial^2 f}{\partial t^2} = X\ddot{T} \tag{v}$$

where dot(s) denote ordinary differentiation with respect to t. We have used primes and dots just to distinguish the independent variables with respect to which differentiation has been carried out.

Using Eqs (iv) and (v) in Eq (i). We would obtain $X(x)\ddot{T}(t) = v^2 X''(x)T(t)$

Dividing throughout by $v^2 X(x)T(t)$, we get $\dfrac{\ddot{T}(t)}{v^2 T(t)} = \dfrac{X''(x)}{X(x)} \quad \text{...(vi)}$

The left hand side of this equation involves functions, which depend only on t whereas the expression on right-hand side is a function of x only. Thus, if we vary t and keep x fixed, the right-hand side cannot change. This means that $\ddot{T}(t)/v^2 T(t)$ must remain constant for all t. Similarly, if we vary x holding t fixed, the left-hand side must not change. That is, the quantity $X''(x)/X(x)$ must be the same for all x. Mathematically, we express this fact by saying that both sides must be equal to a constant, k say.

Hence, $\dfrac{\ddot{T}(t)}{v^2 T(t)} = k = \dfrac{X''(x)}{X(x)} \quad \text{...(vii)}$

This is the process of separation of variables.

Then from the right-hand side, we have $\dfrac{\partial}{\partial t}(k) = \dfrac{\partial}{\partial t}\left[\dfrac{X''(x)}{X(x)}\right] = 0$

and from the LHS, we have $\dfrac{\partial}{\partial x}(k) = \dfrac{\partial}{\partial x}\left[\dfrac{\ddot{T}(t)}{v^2 T(t)}\right] = 0$

Since the first order partial derivative of k with respect to t or x is zero, k must be a constant. It is called the separation constant. It means that if $y = a_0 \sin\omega t$ is a solution of the ODE $\ddot{y} + \omega^2 y = 0$ we will get an identity, for all values of t, on substituting the assumed form of the solution in the given equation.

Thus, we can now rewrite the given equation as two ordinary differential equations: $X''(x) - kX(x) = 0 \tag{viii(a)}$

and $\ddot{T}(t) - kv^2 T(t) = 0 \tag{viii(b)}$

That is, by assuming a separable solution, we have reduced a partial differential equation in two variables into two equivalent ordinary differential equations.

For instance, for a non-zero value of k, the solutions of Eqs. (viii(a)) and (viii(b)) are of the form exp(mx) and exp(nt) respectively. The characteristic equations are

$$m^2 - k = 0 \qquad \text{...(ix(a))}$$

and $\quad n^2 - kv^2 = 0 \qquad \text{...(ix(b))}$

which have roots

$$m_1 = \sqrt{k} = \mu, \ m_2 = -\sqrt{k} = -\mu \qquad \text{...(x(a))}$$

and $\quad n_1 = v\sqrt{k}, = v\mu, \ n_2 = -v\sqrt{k} = -\mu v \qquad \text{...(x(b))}$

The resulting solutions, therefore, are

$$X(x) = A\exp(\mu x) + B\exp(-\mu x) \qquad \text{...(xi(a))}$$

and

$$T(t) = C\exp(\mu vt) + D\exp(-\mu vt) \qquad \text{...(xi(b))}$$

which are sums of growing and decaying exponentials. If we calculate time derivative of T(t), we will obtain velocity, which too will increase or decrease with respect to time. This means that the kinetic energy of an element of the string will increase and decrease with time simultaneously, which is physically unacceptable.

We can now write the general solution as

$$f(x,t) = X(x)T(t) = [A\exp(\mu x) + B\exp(-\mu x)][C\exp(\mu vt) + D\exp(-\mu vt)]$$

$$\text{...(xii)}$$

However, in view of the argument given before Eq. (xii), this solution does not give the desired wave motion. So k cannot have positive values. Similarly, the value k = 0 leads to a trivial solution and is not acceptable. However, for $k < 0$, $\sqrt{k}$ will be imaginary. Therefore, we can write

$$\sqrt{k} = i\beta$$

where β is a real number and $i = \sqrt{-1}$. Then Eq. (xi(a)) becomes

$$X(x) = A\exp(i\beta x) + B\exp(-i\beta x) \qquad \text{...(xiii(a))}$$

and Eq. (11 b) takes the form

$$T(t) = C\exp(i\beta vt) + D\exp(-i\beta vt) \qquad \text{...(xiii(b))}$$

Using the Euler's relation, we can rewrite Eqs. (xiii(a)) and (xiii(b)) as

$$X(x) = A_1 \sin \beta x + A_2 \cos \beta x \qquad \text{...(xiv(a))}$$

and

$$T(t) = G_1 \sin \beta vt + G_2 \cos \beta vt \qquad \text{...(xiv(b))}$$

where A_1, A_2, G_1 and G_2 are new constants. We can easily verify that $A_1 = i(A - B)$, $A_2 = A + B$, $G_1 = i(C - D)$ and $G_2 = C + D$. The solutions given by Eqs. (14 a, b) are periodic in space and time. We can now write the general solution of 1 - D wave equation as

$$f(x, t) = X(x)T(t) = (A_1 \sin \beta x + A_2 \cos \beta x)(G_1 \sin \beta vt + G_2 \cos \beta vt) \quad ...(xv)$$

Rectangular Membrane: The function $f(x, y, t)$ satisfies the wave equation

$$\frac{\partial^2 f(x, y, t)}{\partial t^2} = v^2 \left(\frac{\partial^2}{\partial x^2} + \frac{\partial^2}{\partial y^2} \right) f(x, y, t) \qquad \qquad ...(xvi)$$

While solving this equation by the method of separation of variables, we expect to reduce it to three second order ODEs, which possess periodic solutions in space and time. We can do so in two ways:

(i)   By partial separation of Eq. (xvi) in space variables (x, y) taken together and the time variable by writing

$$f(x, y, t) = F(x, y)T(t) \qquad \qquad ...(xvii)$$

where F (x, y) is a function of space and T depends only on time.

This will result in an ODE in time and a PDE in space variables, which may then be further split to arrive at ODEs in x and y. This two-stage process is worthwhile to attempt as it invariably facilities mathematical steps.

(ii)   Separate all the three variables by writing

$$F(x, y, t) = X(x) \, Y(y) \, T(t) \qquad \qquad ...(xviii)$$

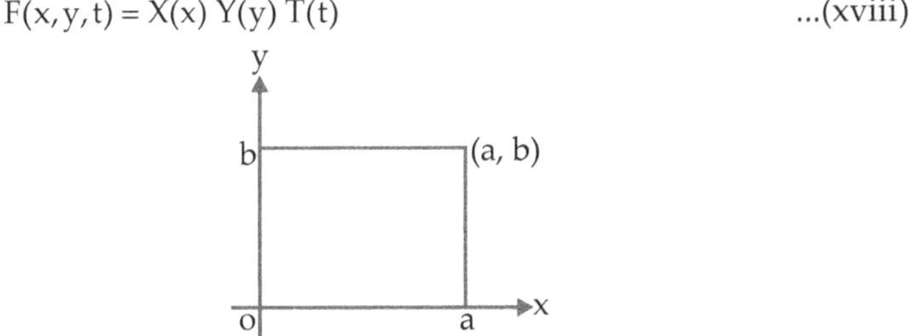

Fig. 6.2: A rectangular membrane fixed at edges

Substituting Eq.(xvii) in Eq. (xvi) we find that

$$F\ddot{T} = v^2 T \left(\frac{\partial^2}{\partial x^2} + \frac{\partial^2}{\partial y^2} \right) F(x, y)$$

Dividing throughout by $v^2 FT$, we get

   Mathematical Methods in Physics-II [PHE-05]

$$\frac{\ddot{T}}{v^2 T} = \frac{1}{F}\left(\frac{\partial^2}{\partial x^2} + \frac{\partial^2}{\partial y^2}\right) F(x,y) \qquad \text{...(xix)}$$

By comparing it with Eq. (vi), we can say that the expression on the left-hand side depends only on t, whereas the expression on the right-hand side depends only on space variables. Following the arguments used for wave equation in two variables, we can say that both sides must be equal to a constant. We now know that only negative values of this constant will lead to a non-trivial solution. If we denote this constant by $-p^2$, we have

$$\frac{\ddot{T}}{v^2 T} = \frac{1}{F}\left(\frac{\partial^2}{\partial x^2} + \frac{\partial^2}{\partial y^2}\right) F(x,y) = -p^2 \qquad \text{...(xx)}$$

This yields two differential equations:

$$\ddot{T} + p^2 v^2 T = 0 \qquad \text{...(xxi)}$$

and
$$\frac{\partial^2 F}{\partial x^2} + \frac{\partial^2 F}{\partial y^2} + p^2 F = 0 \qquad \text{...(xxii)}$$

We will note that whereas Eq. (xxi) is an ordinary differential equation, Eq. (xxii) still contains partial derivatives in x and y. That is, although we have separated the space and time variables, we have to separate space dependences. To do so, we assume that

$$F(x,y) = X(x)\,Y(y) \qquad \text{...(xxiii)}$$

Substituting it in Eq. (xxii), we get $\dfrac{d^2 X}{dx^2} Y = -X\left(\dfrac{d^2 Y}{dy^2} + p^2 Y\right)$

On dividing both sides by XY, we find that

$$\frac{1}{X}\frac{d^2 X}{dx^2} = -\frac{1}{Y}\left(\frac{d^2 Y}{dy^2} + p^2 Y\right) \qquad \text{...(xxiv)}$$

Note that the expression on LHS depends only on x, whereas the expression on RHS depends only on y. Therefore, both sides must be equal to a constant, which we take $-q^2$:

$$\frac{1}{X}\frac{d^2 X}{dx^2} = -\frac{1}{Y}\left(\frac{d^2 Y}{dy^2} + p^2 Y\right) = -q^2 \qquad \text{...(xxv)}$$

This immediately leads to two ordinary equations:

$$\frac{d^2 X}{dx^2} + q^2 X = 0 \qquad \text{...(xxvi)}$$

and $\dfrac{d^2Y}{dy^2}+\alpha^2Y=0$ ...(xxvii)

where $\alpha^2=p^2-q^2$.

We thus find that Eq. (xvi) which contained derivatives with respect to three independent variables has been reduced to three separate second order ODEs (xxi), (xxvi), and (xxvii). Thus, in the two-stage process of separation of variables, we separated the time dependence from the space dependence by clubbing them in one function, F(x,y), which is subsequently separated.

Now split Eq. (xvi) by taking f(x, y, t) as a product of three functions as in Eq. (xviii). Then we can write

$$\frac{\partial^2 f}{\partial t^2}=X(x)\,Y(y)\,\ddot{T}(t)\;;\frac{\partial^2 f}{\partial x^2}=X''(x)\,Y(y)\,T(t)\text{ and }\frac{\partial^2 f}{\partial y^2}=X(x)\,Y''(y)\,T(t)$$

On substituting these in Eq. (xvi), we get

$$X(x)\,Y(y)\,\ddot{T}(t)=v^2[Y(y)\,T(t)X''+X(x)\,Y''(y)T(t)]$$

On dividing throughout by $T(t)\,X(x)\,Y(y)$, this equation simplifies to

$$\frac{\ddot{T}(t)}{v^2T(t)}=\frac{X''(x)}{X(x)}+\frac{Y''(y)}{Y(y)}$$ ...(xxviii)

The left hand side of this identity is a function only of time and the right hand is a function only of the space variables. Therefore, we can write

$$\frac{1}{v^2}\frac{\ddot{T}}{T}=-k^2\text{ or }\ddot{T}+k^2v^2T=0$$ ...(xxix)

and $\dfrac{X''(x)}{X(x)}+\dfrac{Y''(y)}{Y(y)}=-k^2$ or $\dfrac{1}{X}\dfrac{d^2X}{dt^2}=-k^2-\dfrac{1}{Y}\dfrac{d^2Y}{dy^2}$ ...(xxx)

Here we have a function of x equated to a function of y. As before, we equate each side to another constant, $-m^2$. Therefore, we can split Eq. (xxx) into two ODEs:

$$\frac{1}{X}\frac{d^2X}{dt^2}=-m^2$$ ...(xxxi)

and $\dfrac{1}{Y}\dfrac{d^2Y}{dy^2}=-k^2+m^2=-n^2$ ...(xxxii)

where we have introduced a new constant by $k^2=m^2+n^2$ to produce a symmetric set of equations.

Circular Membrane: When we studied the one-dimensional wave equation we found that the method of separation of variables resulted in two simple harmonic oscillator (ordinary) differential equations. The solutions of these were relatively straightforward. Here we are interested in the next level of complexity – when the ODEs which arise upon separation may be different from the familiar SHO equation. This complexity arises when non-cartesian coordinate systems are used.

Let us separate wave equation in spherical coordinates.

For a circular membrane held fixed at the perimeter, as shown in Fig. 6.3, the wave equation takes the form

$$\frac{\partial^2 f}{\partial t^2} = v^2 \left(\frac{\partial^2}{\partial r^2} + \frac{1}{r}\frac{\partial}{\partial r} + \frac{1}{r^2}\frac{\partial^2}{\partial \theta^2} \right) f(r,\theta,t) \qquad \text{...(xxxiii)}$$

By assuming a solution in the separable form as

$$f(r,\theta,t) = F(r,\theta)T(t) \qquad \text{...(xxxiv)}$$

We can show that eq. (xxxiii) reduces to

$$\ddot{T} + \lambda^2 T = 0 \qquad \text{...(xxxv)}$$

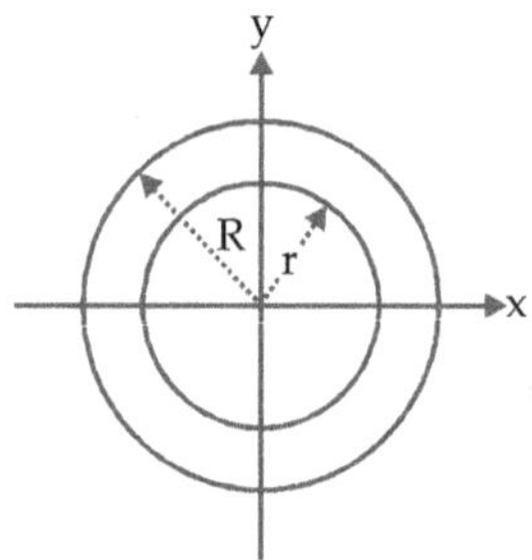

Fig. 6.3: A circular membrane fixed at the perimeter

and $\quad \dfrac{\partial^2 F}{\partial r^2} + \dfrac{1}{r}\dfrac{\partial F}{\partial r} + \dfrac{1}{r^2}\dfrac{\partial^2 F}{\partial \theta^2} + k^2 F(r,\theta) = 0 \qquad \text{...(xxxvi)}$

where $\lambda = vk; k$ being the separation constant. We will note that Eq. (xxxvi) still contains two variables. We separate these as well and write

$$F(r,\theta) = R(r)\,\Theta\,(\theta) \qquad \text{...(xxxvii)}$$

Substituting in Eq. (xxxvi), we obtain

$$\frac{1}{R}\left(r^2\frac{d^2 R}{dr^2} + r\frac{dR}{dr} + r^2 k^2 R \right) = -\frac{1}{\Theta}\frac{d\Theta}{d\theta^2} = p^2$$

so that Eq. (xxxvi) reduces to two ODEs; one involving R and the other one for Θ

$$r^2\frac{d^2 R}{dr^2} + r\frac{dR}{dr} + (r^2 k^2 - p^2)R = 0 \qquad \text{...(xxxviii)}$$

and $\dfrac{d^2\,\Theta}{d\theta^2} + p^2\,\Theta = 0$ ...(xxxix)

To put Eq. (xxxviii) in a more familiar form, we can change the variable by defining $s = kr$

Then $\dfrac{dR}{dr} = \dfrac{dR}{ds}\dfrac{ds}{dr} = k\dfrac{dR}{ds}$ and $\dfrac{d^2R}{dr^2} = k^2\dfrac{d^2R}{ds^2}$

Substituting these in Eq. (xxxviii), we will get

$$s^2\dfrac{d^2R}{ds^2} + s\dfrac{dR}{ds} + (s^2 - p^2)R = 0 \qquad \text{...(xxxx)}$$

which is Bessel's equation of order p.

Method of solving a boundary value problem using separation of variables: The method of solving a boundary value problem using separation of variables consists of the following basic steps.

- Write the function f as a product of two (or more) functions involving independent variables, i.e. $f(x,\ y) = X(x)Y(y)$ and insert it in the given PDE. We will obtain a set of ODEs. A PDE in two variables splits into two ODEs. If the number of independent variables is more, we get ODEs whose number is equal to the number of variables.

- Solve the separated ordinary differential equations. The solutions may be exponential functions, trigonometric functions or a power series.

- Substitute the solutions so obtained in the above product.

- Use boundary and/or the initial condition(s), and solve for the coefficients in the series.

Initial and boundary value problems in One-dimensional wave equation: Consider a one-dimensional wave equation for a string of length L, $\dfrac{\partial^2 f}{\partial t^2} = v^2\dfrac{\partial^2 f(x,t)}{\partial x^2}$ where v is wave speed. Since the string is fixed at $x = 0$ and $x = L$ for all times, the boundary conditions may be written as

$f(0,t) = 0$ and $f(L,t) = 0$ for all $t > 0$ ...(xxxxi)

Since the solution of the wave equation depends on t as well, we must also know as to what happens at $t = 0$, i.e. we have to specify initial conditions on displacement and velocity. Since the string is released from rest, the initial velocity is zero. In mathematical terms, we seek a function $f(x,\ t)$ which satisfies the initial conditions

$$f(x,0) = h(x) \qquad 0 < x < L$$

and $\left.\dfrac{\partial f(x,t)}{\partial t}\right|_{t=0} = 0$

Separating variables in wave equation, we will obtain

$$X'' + \mu^2 X(x) = 0 \quad \text{and} \quad \ddot{T}(t) + \mu^2 v^2 T(t) = 0.$$

whose solutions are given by

$$X(x) = A\cos\mu x + B\sin\mu x \text{ and } T(t) = C\cos\mu vt + D\sin\mu vt$$

Now, since $f(0,t) = X(0)\,T(t) = 0$ and $f(L,t) = X(L)T(t) = 0$, we must have $X(0) = 0$ and $X(L) = 0$. Using the first of these conditions, we find that $A = 0$. Therefore, $X(x) = B\sin\mu x$

The second condition now implies that $X(L) = B\,\sin\mu L = 0$

This equality will be satisfied if $B = 0$ or $\sin\mu L = 0$. If $B = 0$, then $X = 0$ so that $f = 0$, which is a trivial solution. Hence, we must have $B \neq 0$ and the only option is $\sin\mu L = 0$. This implies that $\mu L = n\pi$ or $\mu = n\pi/L$ for n = 0, 1, 2, 3, ... The solution for n = 0 is a trivial solution. For any arbitrary value of B, we obtain infinite solutions of the form

$$X(x) \equiv X_n(x) = \sin\left(\frac{n\pi}{L}\right)x \quad n = 1, 2, 3,\dots \qquad \dots\text{(xxxii)}$$

The value of $\mu = n\pi/L$ for n = 1, 2, 3, ... are called eigenvalues of Eq. (i). With B = 1, Eq. (xxxiv) is depicted in Fig. 6.4 for n = 1,2,3 and 4.

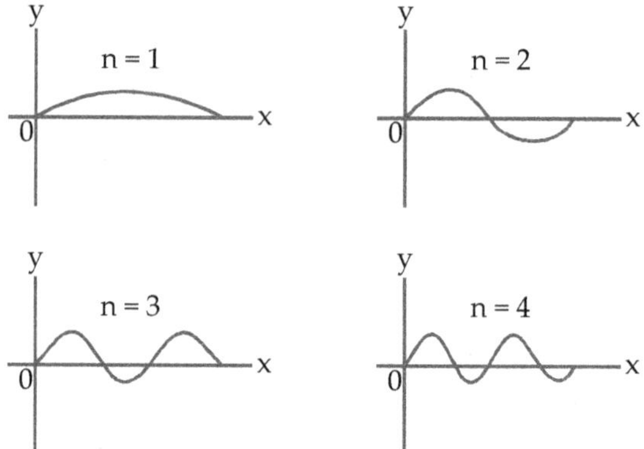

Fig. 6.4: A plot of Eq. (xxxv) for the first few modes

Hence, the solution of Eq. (ii) which satisfies the given boundary conditions can now be written as

$$f_n(x,t) = \left[C\cos\left(\frac{n\pi vt}{L}\right) + D\sin\left(\frac{n\pi vt}{L}\right) \right] \sin\left(\frac{n\pi x}{L}\right)$$

$$= \left[a_n \cos\left(\frac{n\pi vt}{L}\right) + b_n \sin\left(\frac{n\pi vt}{L}\right) \right] \sin\left(\frac{n\pi x}{L}\right) \qquad ...(\text{xxxxiii})$$

We would agree that $f_n(x,t)$ is not a solution of the given problem since initial conditions have not yet been imposed. Moreover, since the wave equation is linear and homogeneous, we expect that the most general solution, which satisfies the given boundary conditions, is given by the superposition principle:

$$f(x,t) = \sum_{n=1}^{\infty} f_n(x,t) = \sum_{n=1}^{\infty} \left[a_n \cos\left(\frac{n\pi vt}{L}\right) + b_n \sin\left(\frac{n\pi vt}{L}\right) \right] \sin\frac{n\pi x}{L} \qquad ...(\text{xxxxvi}$$

To match the initial conditions, we set t = 0 in the above equation. This gives $f(x,0) = \sum_{n=1}^{\infty} a_n \sin\left(\frac{n\pi x}{L}\right) = h(x)$ $\qquad ...(\text{xxxxv})$

To determine the constants a_n, we must know the form of the function h(x). Take $h(x) = \xi_0 \sin\frac{\pi x}{L}$. Then by comparison, we have $a_1 = \xi_0$

and $a_2 = a_3 = ... = 0$ $\qquad ...(\text{xxxxvi})$

To determine b_n, we first differentiate Eq. (xxxxiv) with respect to t and then set t = 0. We get

$$\frac{\partial f}{\partial t} = \sum_{n=1}^{\infty} \left[-a_n \left(\frac{n\pi v}{L}\right) \sin\left(\frac{n\pi vt}{L}\right) + b_n \left(\frac{n\pi v}{L}\right) \cos\left(\frac{n\pi vt}{L}\right) \right] \sin\left(\frac{n\pi x}{L}\right)$$

so that $\left. \dfrac{\partial f}{\partial t} \right|_{t=0} = 0 = \sum_{n=1}^{\infty} b_n \left(\frac{n\pi v}{L}\right) \sin\left(\frac{n\pi x}{L}\right)$

We will readily conclude by looking at this expression that

$b_n = 0;\ n = 1,2,.....$ $\qquad ...(\text{xxxvii})$

Hence, the unique solution of the one-dimensional wave equation on a string tied at both ends corresponding to the given initial and boundary conditions is given by $f(x,t) = \xi_0 \cos\omega t \sin\left(\frac{\pi x}{L}\right)$ $\qquad ...(\text{xxxxviii})$

where $\omega = \dfrac{\pi v}{L}$ is angular frequency and ξ_0 is amplitude.

Solved Practical Problems

Q1. **Use the method of separation of variables to reduce the following PDEs to a set of ODEs:**

(i) $\dfrac{\partial^2 T}{\partial r^2} + \dfrac{1}{r}\dfrac{\partial T}{\partial r} + \dfrac{\partial^2 T}{\partial z^2} = 0$

Ans. Let $\quad T(r,z) = R(r)Z(z)$ $\hfill$ ...(i)

Then, $\quad \dfrac{\partial T}{\partial r} = \dfrac{dR}{dr}Z; \dfrac{\partial^2 T}{\partial r^2} = \dfrac{d^2 R}{dr^2}Z$ and $\dfrac{\partial^2 T}{\partial z^2} = R\dfrac{d^2 Z}{dz^2}$ $\hfill$ ...(ii)

Substituting these in the given PDE, we obtain

$$Z\dfrac{d^2 R}{dr^2} + \dfrac{Z}{r}\dfrac{dR}{dr} + R\dfrac{d^2 Z}{dz^2} = 0$$

On dividing throughout by ZR, we get

$$\dfrac{1}{R}\left[\dfrac{d^2 R}{dr^2} + \dfrac{1}{r}\dfrac{dR}{dr}\right] = -\dfrac{1}{Z}\dfrac{d^2 Z}{dz^2} \hfill \text{...(iii)}$$

The LHS of this equality involves functions, which depend only on r, whereas the expression on RHS is a function of z only. Therefore, both sides must be equal to a constant, k. Hence, the given equation splits into the following two ODEs: $\dfrac{d^2 R}{dr^2} + \dfrac{1}{r}\dfrac{dR}{dr} - kR = 0$ $\hfill$ ...(iv)

and $\quad \dfrac{d^2 Z}{dz^2} + kZ = 0$ $\hfill$ ...(v)

(ii) $\dfrac{\partial}{\partial r}\left(r^2\dfrac{\partial V(r,\theta)}{\partial r}\right) + \dfrac{1}{\sin\theta}\dfrac{\partial}{\partial \theta}\left(\sin\theta\dfrac{\partial V}{\partial \theta}\right) = 0$

Ans. The given PDE can be rewritten as

$$r^2\dfrac{\partial^2 V}{\partial r^2} + 2r\dfrac{\partial V}{\partial r} + \cot\theta\dfrac{\partial V}{\partial \theta} + \dfrac{\partial^2 V}{\partial \theta^2} = 0 \hfill \text{...(i)}$$

Let us now write $\quad V(r,\theta) = R(r)\,\Theta(\theta)$ $\hfill$ ...(ii)

Then, differentiation with respect to r gives $\quad \dfrac{\partial V}{\partial r} = \dfrac{dR}{dr}\Theta$

and $\dfrac{\partial^2 V}{\partial r^2} = \dfrac{d^2 R}{dr^2}\Theta$ $\hfill$ ...(iii)

Similarly, differentiation with respect to θ gives

$$\dfrac{\partial V}{\partial \theta} = R\dfrac{d\Theta}{d\theta} \quad \text{and} \quad \dfrac{\partial^2 V}{\partial \theta^2} = R\dfrac{d^2\Theta}{d\theta^2} \hfill \text{...(iv)}$$

Substituting these results in the given equation, we obtain

$$r^2 \Theta \frac{d^2R}{dr^2} + 2r\, \Theta\, \frac{dR}{dr} + \cot\theta R \frac{d\,\Theta}{d\theta} + R \frac{d^2\,\Theta}{d\theta^2} = 0$$

Now, dividing throughout by $R\,\Theta$, we get

$$\frac{1}{R}\left[r^2 \frac{d^2R}{dr^2} + 2r\frac{dR}{dr} \right] = -\frac{1}{\Theta}\left[\cot\theta \frac{d\,\Theta}{d\theta} + \frac{d^2\,\Theta}{d\theta^2} \right] \qquad\qquad ...(v)$$

The LHS is a function of r only whereas RHS is a function of θ only. Hence, putting them equal to a constant, k, we get

$$r^2 \frac{d^2R}{dr^2} + 2r\frac{dR}{dr} - kR = 0 \quad\text{or}\quad \frac{d}{dr}\left(r^2 \frac{dR}{dr} \right) - kR = 0 \qquad\qquad ...(vi)$$

and $\quad \dfrac{d\,\Theta}{d\theta} + \dfrac{d^2\,\Theta}{d\theta^2} + k\,\Theta = 0 \quad\text{or}\quad \dfrac{1}{\sin\theta}\dfrac{d}{d\theta}\left(\sin\theta \dfrac{d\,\Theta}{d\theta} \right) + k\,\Theta = 0 \qquad ...(vii)$

(iii) $\quad \dfrac{\partial^2\psi}{\partial x^2} + \alpha \dfrac{\partial\psi(x,t)}{\partial t} = 0$

Ans.   The given equation is $\quad \dfrac{\partial^2\psi}{\partial x^2} + \alpha \dfrac{\partial\psi}{\partial t} = 0$

Express $\psi(x,t)$ as a product of two separable functions: $\psi(x,t) = X(x)T(t)$

Substituting it in the given PDE, we will obtain
$$X''(x)T(t) + \alpha\, X(x)\dot{T}(t) = 0$$

Dividing throughout by X(x) T(t), we find that $\quad \dfrac{X''(x)}{X(x)} = -\alpha\dfrac{\dot{T}(t)}{T(t)} = -k^2$

Hence, the Schrodinger equation splits into following equations:
$$X''(x) + k^2 X = 0 \quad\text{and}\quad \dot{T}(t) - \lambda^2 T(t) = 0$$

where $\qquad\qquad \lambda^2 = k^2/\alpha.$

Q2. Separate the following PDE into a set of two ODEs.

$$\frac{h^2}{2m}\left(\frac{\partial^2\psi}{\partial x^2} + \frac{\partial^2\psi}{\partial y^2} \right) + V\psi = E\psi. \qquad\qquad \text{[June-2010, Q.No.-1(d)]}$$

Ans. Given PDE is $\quad \dfrac{h^2}{2m}\left(\dfrac{\partial^2\psi}{\partial x^2} + \dfrac{\partial^2\psi}{\partial y^2} \right) + V\psi = E\psi$

$$\Rightarrow \quad \frac{h^2}{2m}\frac{\partial^2\psi}{\partial x^2} + \frac{h^2}{2m}\frac{\partial^2\psi}{\partial y^2} + V\psi - E\psi = 0 \qquad\qquad ...(i)$$

Let us put $\psi(x,y) = X(x)Y(y)$

$$\Rightarrow \qquad \frac{\partial \psi}{\partial x} = X'(x)\,Y(y)$$

$$\Rightarrow \qquad \frac{\partial^2 \psi}{\partial x^2} = X''(x)\,Y(y)$$

and $\quad \dfrac{\partial \psi}{\partial y} = X(x)\,\dot{Y}(y)$

$$\Rightarrow \qquad \frac{\partial^2 \psi}{\partial y^2} = X(x)\,\ddot{Y}(y)$$

Putting these values in eq.(i), we get

$$\frac{h^2}{2m}X''(x)\,Y(y) + \frac{h^2}{2m}X(x)\,\ddot{Y}(y) + VX(x)\,Y(y) - EX(x)\,Y(y) = 0$$

Dividing by $X(x)\,Y(y)$, we get $\dfrac{h^2}{2m}\left[\dfrac{X''(x)}{X(x)} + \dfrac{\ddot{Y}(y)}{Y(y)}\right] + V - E = 0$

$$\Rightarrow \qquad \frac{h^2}{2m}\frac{X''(x)}{X(x)} + \frac{h^2}{2m}\frac{\ddot{Y}(y)}{Y(y)} = E - V$$

$$\Rightarrow \qquad \frac{X''(x)}{X(x)} + \frac{\ddot{Y}(y)}{Y(y)} = \frac{2(E-V)m}{h^2}$$

$$\Rightarrow \qquad \frac{X''(x)}{X(x)} = \frac{2(E-V)m}{h^2} - \frac{\ddot{Y}(y)}{Y(y)} = -k^2$$

Hence, two ODEs are, $\dfrac{X''(x)}{X(x)} = -k^2$ or $X''(x) + k^2 X(x) = 0$

and $\quad \dfrac{2m(E-V)}{h^2} - \dfrac{\ddot{Y}(y)}{Y(y)} = -k^2 \Rightarrow \dfrac{\ddot{Y}(y)}{Y(y)} = \dfrac{2m(E-V)}{h^2} + k^2$

Putting $\dfrac{2m(E-V)}{h^2} + k^2 = A \Rightarrow \ddot{Y}(y) - AY(y) = 0$.

Q3. **The radial part of wave equation for a circular membrane of radius r_0 fixed at its circumference is $\dfrac{\partial^2 f}{\partial t^2} = v^2\left(\dfrac{\partial^2 f}{\partial r^2} + \dfrac{1}{r}\dfrac{\partial f}{\partial r}\right)$. Specify the boundary conditions and obtain a unique solution.**

Ans. The boundary conditions in this case are

$\qquad f(r, t) = 0 \quad$ for $r = r_0$ at all t

$\qquad\qquad = 0 \quad$ for $t = 0$ at all r

The wave equation describing the motion of circular membrane fixed at its perimeter can be reduced to the following ODEs:

$$\ddot{T} + \lambda^2 T = 0 \text{ where } \lambda = vk \qquad \qquad \text{...(i)}$$

and $\quad \dfrac{d^2R}{dr^2} + \dfrac{1}{r}\dfrac{dR}{dr} + k^2 R = 0$

$$\qquad \qquad \text{...(ii)}$$

By introducing a chance of variable through the relation $s = kr$ we find that $\quad \dfrac{dR}{ds} = \dfrac{dR}{dr}\dfrac{dr}{ds} = \dfrac{1}{k}\dfrac{dR}{dr}$ and $\dfrac{d^2R}{ds^2} = \dfrac{1}{k}\dfrac{d}{dr}\left(\dfrac{dR}{dr}\right)\dfrac{dr}{ds} = \dfrac{1}{k^2}\dfrac{d^2R}{dr^2}$

Hence, we can rewrite (ii) as

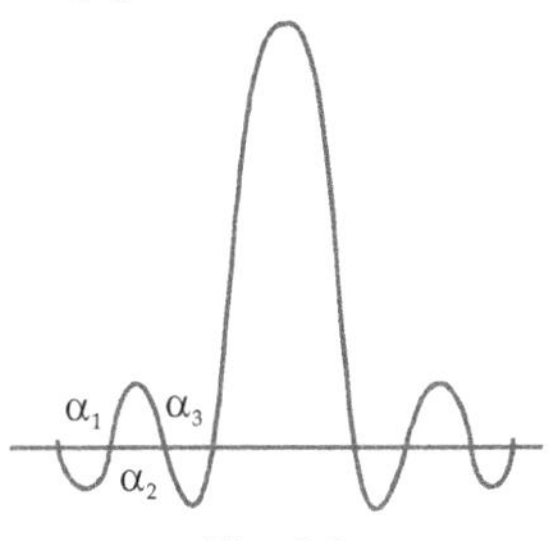

Fig. 6.5

$$k^2 \dfrac{d^2R}{ds^2} + \dfrac{k^2}{s}\dfrac{dR}{ds} + k^2 R = 0 \text{ or } \dfrac{d^2R}{ds^2} + \dfrac{1}{s}\dfrac{dR}{ds} + R = 0 \qquad \text{...(iii)}$$

This is zeroth order Bessel equation.

Its general solution is $R(s) = c_1 J_0(s) + c_2 Y_0(s)$

In terms of r, we can write $R(r) = c_1 J_0(kr) + c_2 Y_0(kr)$ ...(iv)

where J_0 and Y_0 are zeroth order Bessel's functions of the first and the second kind, respectively.

The Bessel's function of the second kind is known to tend to $-\infty$ as $r \to 0$. Therefore, we must choose $c_2 = 0$. Then (iv) reduces to

$$R(r) = c_1 J_0(kr) \qquad \qquad \text{...(v)}$$

Since the membrane is fixed at the perimeter $(r = r_0)$, the boundary condition $f(r, t) = 0$ implies that $R(r) = 0$ for $r = r_0$

Obviously, if we choose $c_1 = 0$ we will obtain a trivial solution. Therefore, we must choose $J_0(kr_0) = 0$. If we denote the zeros of $J_0(kr_0)$ by $\alpha_1, \alpha_2, ...,$ we get $kr_0 = \alpha_m$ or $k \equiv k_m = \dfrac{\alpha_m}{r_0}$ $\qquad \qquad$ ...(vi)

Hence, (v) takes the form $R(r) = c_1 J_0\left(\dfrac{\alpha_m}{r_0}\right)$

Q4. The Helmholtz equation in Cartesian coordinates can be written as

$$\left(\frac{\partial^2}{\partial x^2}+\frac{\partial^2}{\partial y^2}+\frac{\partial^2}{\partial z^2}\right)f(x,y,z)+k^2 f(x,y,z)=0$$

Reduce it to three ODEs using one-step process.

Ans. The Helmholtz equation is

$$\left(\frac{\partial^2}{\partial x^2}+\frac{\partial^2}{\partial y^2}+\frac{\partial^2}{\partial z^2}\right)f(x,y,z)+k^2 f=0 \qquad \text{...(i)}$$

Let $\quad f(x,y,z)=X(x)\,Y(y)\,Z(z)$ ...(ii)

Substituting it in the given PDE, we get

$$YZ\frac{d^2X}{dx^2}+XZ\frac{d^2Y}{dy^2}+XY\frac{d^2Z}{dz^2}+k^2\,XYZ=0$$

Dividing throughout by $X\,Y\,Z$ and rearranging terms, we obtain

$$\frac{1}{X}\frac{d^2X}{dx^2}=-k^2-\frac{1}{Y}\frac{d^2Y}{dy^2}-\frac{1}{Z}\frac{d^2Z}{dz^2} \qquad \text{...(iii)}$$

The LHS is a function of x alone, whereas the RHS depends only on y

and z. Let us choose $\quad \dfrac{1}{X}\dfrac{d^2X}{dx^2}=-l^2$ ...(iv)

Then we can write $\quad \dfrac{1}{Y}\dfrac{d^2Y}{dy^2}=-k^2+l^2-\dfrac{1}{Z}\dfrac{d^2Z}{dz^2}$ ...(v)

Here we have a function of y equated to a function of z. We now set

$$\frac{1}{Y}\frac{d^2Y}{dy^2}=-m^2 \qquad \text{...(vi)}$$

so that $\quad \dfrac{1}{Z}\dfrac{d^2Z}{dz^2}=-k^2+l^2+m^2=-n^2$ ...(vii)

where we have put $k^2=l^2+m^2+n^2$. Eqs. (iv), (vi) and (vii) are the three ODEs into which Helmholtz equation splits.

Q5. Separate the following PDE into two ODEs.

$$\left(E\frac{\partial}{\partial t}-p\frac{\partial}{\partial x}\right)\psi(x,t)=m\psi(x,t) \qquad \text{[June-2012, Q.No.-1(d)]}$$

Ans. Given PDE is $\left(E\dfrac{\partial}{\partial t}-p\dfrac{\partial}{\partial x}\right)\psi(x,t)=m\psi(x,t)$

$$\Rightarrow\ E\frac{\partial\psi}{\partial t}-p\frac{\partial\psi}{\partial x}=m\psi(x,t)$$

Let us write $\psi(x,t) = X(x)T(t)$

Substituting it in the given PDE, we obtain,

$$\left[E\, X(x)\dot{T}(t) - pX'(x)T(t)\right] = mX(x)T(t)$$

Dividing throughout by $X(x)T(t)$, we find that

$$E\frac{\dot{T}(t)}{T(t)} - p\frac{X'(x)}{X(x)} = m \;\Rightarrow\; E\frac{\dot{T}(t)}{T(t)} = m + p\frac{X'(x)}{X(x)}$$

L.H.S. depends on t only and R.H.S. depends on x only, So we can write,

$$E\frac{\dot{T}(t)}{T(t)} = m + p\frac{X'(x)}{X(x)} = -k^2$$

where k^2 is constant.

Hence, two ODEs are $E\dot{T}(t) + k^2 T = 0$ and $pX'(x) + k^2 x + m = 0$.

Q6 **Determine the constants a_n's occurring in equation**

$$f(x,t) = \sum_{n=1}^{\infty} f_n(x,t) = \sum_{n=1}^{\infty}\left[a_n\cos\left(\frac{n\pi vt}{L}\right) + b_n\sin\left(\frac{n\pi vt}{L}\right)\right]\cdot\sin\left(\frac{n\pi x}{L}\right), \text{ when}$$

$$h(x) = \xi_0\left[\sin\left(\frac{\pi x}{L}\right) + \sin\left(\frac{2\pi x}{L}\right)\right]$$

Ans. To determine the unknown constants, substitute the given form of $h(x)$ in equation $f(x,0) = \sum_{n=1}^{\infty} a_n\sin\left(\frac{n\pi x}{L}\right) = h(x)$. This gives

$$\sum_{n=1}^{\infty} a_n\sin\left(\frac{n\pi x}{L}\right) = \xi_0\left[\sin\frac{\pi x}{L} + \sin\left(\frac{2\pi x}{L}\right)\right]$$

On comparison of like terms on two sides of this expression, we find that $a_1 = \xi_0 = a_2$ and $a_3 = a_4 = \dots\dots a_n = 0$.

Q7. **Consider a solid cylindrical cooling tower as shown in given figure. The steady-state temperature distribution is described by Laplace's equation $\nabla^2 T = 0$**

(i) **Specify the boundary conditions, and**

(ii) **Determine the steady-state temperature.**

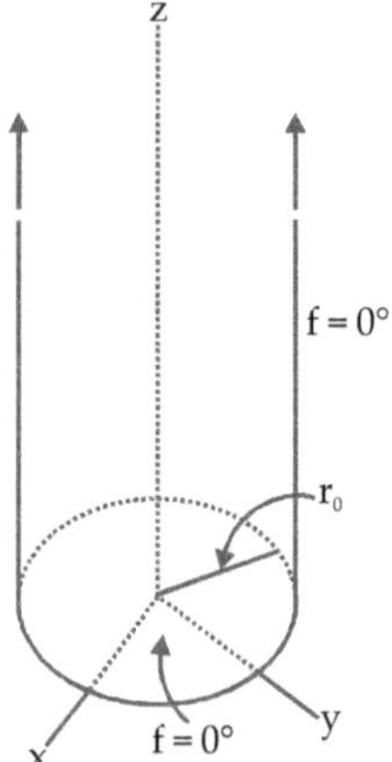

Fig. A cylindrical cooling tower

Ans. (i) We can express the boundary conditions as,

$$T(2,z)=0, \qquad\qquad 0 < z < 4,$$

$$T(\rho,0) = 0, \qquad\qquad T(\rho,4) = T_0, 0 < \rho < 2 \qquad\qquad ...(i)$$

(ii) To determine the steady-state temperature, we have to express the Laplacian in cylindrical polar coordinates. Since, the given geometry exhibits circular symmetry so we can write $\nabla^2 = \dfrac{\partial^2}{\partial\rho^2} + \dfrac{1}{\rho}\dfrac{\partial}{\partial\rho} + \dfrac{\partial^2}{\partial z^2}$

so that $\quad \dfrac{\partial^2 T}{\partial\rho^2} + \dfrac{1}{\rho}\dfrac{\partial T}{\partial\rho} + \dfrac{\partial^2 T}{\partial z^2} = 0 \qquad\qquad 0 < \rho < 2; 0 < z < 4$

Putting $\quad T = R(\rho)Z(z) \quad$ and separating variables, we get

$$\frac{R'' + \dfrac{1}{\rho}R'}{R} = -\frac{Z''}{Z} = -\lambda^2$$

which reduces to $\quad \rho R'' + R' + \lambda^2 \rho R = 0 \qquad\qquad ...(ii)$

and $\quad Z'' - \lambda^2 Z = 0 \qquad\qquad\qquad ...(iii)$

The negative separation constant is used since there is no reason to expect the solution to be periodic in z.

Eq. (ii) is the zeroth order parametric Bessel's equation. Its general solution is $R = c_1 J_0(\lambda\rho) + c_2 Y_0(\lambda\rho)$ where J_0 and Y_0 are Bessel's functions of the first and the second kind of order zero.

Since the solution of (iii) is defined on the finite interval, then we have $Z = c_3 \cosh\lambda z + c_4 \sinh\lambda z$.

In order to have a bounded temperature $T(\rho,z)=0$, we must define $c_2=0$. The condition $T(2,z)=0$ implies $R(2)=0$ or $J_0(2\lambda)=0$ ...(iv)

This equation will hold for $\lambda_1=\alpha_1/2,\ \lambda_2=\alpha_2/2,....,\lambda_n=\alpha_n/2$ where $\alpha_1,\alpha_2,....\alpha_n$ are zeros of the Bessel function. Lastly $Z(0)=0$ implies $c_3=0$. Hence, we have $R=c_1 J_0(\lambda_n\rho),\ \ Z=c_4\sin h\lambda_n z,$ and $u_n=A_n\sin h\lambda_n z\,J_0(\lambda_n\rho)$.

The general solution is therefore of the form

$$u(r,z)=\sum_{n=1}^{\infty}A_n\sin h\lambda_n z\,J_0(\lambda_n\rho)$$

Q8. Separate the following PDE into a set of two ODEs.

$$\left\{\frac{\partial^2}{\partial x^2}+\frac{\partial^2}{\partial y^2}-k^2+\left(\frac{\omega}{c}\right)^2\right\}E(x,y)=0 \qquad\qquad \text{[Dec-2010, Q.No.-1(e)]}$$

Ans. Given PDE is $\left\{\dfrac{\partial^2}{\partial x^2}+\dfrac{\partial^2}{\partial y^2}-k^2+\left(\dfrac{\omega}{c}\right)^2\right\}E(x,y)=0$

$$\Rightarrow \frac{\partial^2 E}{\partial x^2}+\frac{\partial^2 E}{\partial y^2}-k^2 E+\left(\frac{\omega}{c}\right)^2 E=0$$

Let us put $E(x,y)=X(x)Y(y)$

Hence, $\dfrac{\partial E}{\partial x}=X'(x)Y(y)\,;\dfrac{\partial^2 E}{\partial x^2}=X''(x)Y(y)\,;\dfrac{\partial E}{\partial y}=X(x)\dot{Y}(y)$

and $\dfrac{\partial^2 E}{\partial y^2}=X(x)\ddot{Y}(y)$

Putting these values in given PDE, we get

$$X''(x)Y(y)+X(x)\ddot{Y}(y)-k^2 X(x)Y(y)+\left(\frac{\omega}{c}\right)^2 X(x)Y(y)=0$$

Dividing throughout by $X(x)Y(y)$, we get

$$\frac{X''(x)}{X(x)}+\frac{\ddot{Y}(y)}{Y(y)}-k^2+\left(\frac{\omega}{c}\right)^2=0 \quad\Rightarrow\quad \frac{X''(x)}{X(x)}=k^2-\left(\frac{\omega}{c}\right)^2-\frac{\ddot{Y}(y)}{Y(y)}=m$$

Hence, ODE are $X''(x)-mX(x)=0$ and $k^2-m-\left(\dfrac{\omega}{c}\right)^2-\dfrac{\ddot{Y}(y)}{Y(y)}=0$

$$\Rightarrow \qquad \frac{\ddot{Y}(y)}{Y(y)}-l=0 \qquad\qquad\qquad \left[\text{put }k^2-m-\left(\frac{\omega}{c}\right)^2=l\right]$$

$$\Rightarrow \qquad \ddot{Y}(y)-l\,Y(y)=0$$

Q9. By substituting $f(r,\theta,t) = R(r)\,\Theta\,(\theta)T(t)$ in equation $\dfrac{\partial^2 f}{\partial t^2} = v^2\left(\dfrac{\partial^2}{\partial r^2} + \dfrac{1}{r}\dfrac{\partial}{\partial r} + \dfrac{1}{r^2}\dfrac{\partial^2}{\partial \theta^2}\right)f(r,\theta,t),$ show that it can be split into three ODEs.

Ans. The given equation is $\dfrac{\partial^2 f}{\partial t^2} = v^2\left(\dfrac{\partial^2}{\partial r^2} + \dfrac{1}{r}\dfrac{\partial}{\partial r} + \dfrac{1}{r^2}\dfrac{\partial^2}{\partial \theta^2}\right)f(r,\theta,t)$ ...(i)

By substituting $f(r,\theta,t) = R(r)\,\Theta\,(\theta)\,T(t)$ ...(ii)

We get, $\dfrac{\partial^2 f}{\partial t^2} = \ddot{T}R\,\Theta$ and $\dfrac{\partial^2 f}{\partial r^2} = \dfrac{d^2 R}{dr^2}\,\Theta\,T$ and

$$\dfrac{\partial^2 f}{\partial \theta^2} = RT\dfrac{d^2\,\Theta}{d\theta^2} \qquad \text{...(iii)}$$

Using these results in (i), we will find that

$$R\,\Theta\,\ddot{T} = v^2\left(\Theta\,T\dfrac{d^2 R}{dr^2} + \dfrac{\Theta\,T}{r}\dfrac{dR}{dr} + \dfrac{RT}{r^2}\dfrac{d^2\,\Theta}{d\theta^2}\right)$$

All the partial derivatives have now become ordinary derivatives. Dividing throughout by $R\,\Theta\,T$, we get

$$\dfrac{1}{v^2}\dfrac{\ddot{T}}{T} = \dfrac{1}{R}\dfrac{d^2 R}{dr^2} + \dfrac{1}{rR}\dfrac{dR}{dr} + \dfrac{1}{r^2}\dfrac{1}{\Theta}\dfrac{d^2\,\Theta}{d\theta^2} \qquad \text{...(iv)}$$

A function of t on the left equals a function of r and θ.

Let $\quad \dfrac{1}{v^2}\dfrac{\ddot{T}}{T} = -l^2$ ...(v)

so that $\quad \ddot{T} + v^2 l^2 T = 0 \quad$ or $\quad \ddot{T} + \lambda^2 T = 0$ ...(vi)

where $\lambda = vl$. Then (iv) can be rewritten as

$$\dfrac{1}{R}\dfrac{d^2 R}{dr^2} + \dfrac{1}{rR}\dfrac{dR}{dr} + \dfrac{1}{r^2}\dfrac{1}{\Theta}\dfrac{d^2\,\Theta}{d\theta^2} = -l^2 \quad \text{or} \quad -\dfrac{1}{\Theta}\dfrac{d^2\,\Theta}{d\theta^2} = r^2 l^2 + \dfrac{r}{R}\dfrac{dR}{dr} + \dfrac{r^2}{R}\dfrac{dR}{dr}$$

We may set the left hand side to m^2 so that

$$\dfrac{d^2\,\Theta}{d\theta^2} + m^2\,\Theta = 0 \qquad \text{...(vii)}$$

and $\quad r^2\dfrac{d^2 R}{dr^2} + r\dfrac{dR}{dr} + (r^2 l^2 - m^2)R = 0$ ...(viii)

Q10. **Consider a rod whose ends are kept at a constant temperature and the lateral surface is insulated. The heat flow is described by one-dimensional heat equation subject to the conditions**

$f(0, t) = 0, f(L, t) = 0$ for $t > 0$

and $f(x, t) = f(x)$ for $0 < x < L$

Obtain a unique solution.

Ans. Here, we wish to solve 1-D heat equation: $\dfrac{1}{v}\dfrac{\partial f}{\partial t} = \dfrac{\partial^2 f}{\partial x^2}$ subject to the conditions $f(0, t) = 0$, $f(L, t) = 0$ and $f(x, 0) = f(x)$ $0 < x < L$

We first write $f(x, t) = X(x)\, T(t)$ and substitute it back in the given equation. Then dividing by $X(x)\, T(t)$, we get $\dfrac{1}{v}\dfrac{1}{T}\dfrac{dT}{dt} = \dfrac{1}{X}\dfrac{d^2 X}{dx^2}$

The LHS depends only on t, whereas the RHS depends on x only. Therefore, we choose $\dfrac{1}{v}\dfrac{1}{T}\dfrac{dT}{dt} = \dfrac{1}{X}\dfrac{d^2 X}{dx^2} = -k^2$ so that $\dfrac{dT}{dt} + k^2 v\, T = 0$ and

$\dfrac{d^2 X}{dx^2} + k^2 X = 0$ which has solutions of the form

$$T(t) = A e^{-k^2 vt} \text{ and } X(x) = B\cos kx + C\sin kx \text{ so that}$$

$$f(x,t) = X(x)\, T(t) = (P\cos k x + Q\sin kx)e^{-k^2 vt}$$

The condition $f(0, t) = 0$ implies that $P = 0$ and $f(L, T) = 0$ demands that $k = n\pi/L$. Hence, the desired solution is given by

$$f(x,t) = \sum_{n=0}^{\infty} Q_n \sin\left(\frac{n\pi x}{L}\right)\exp\left[-vt\left(\frac{n\pi}{L}\right)^2\right]$$

Q11. Separate the following equation into two ordinary differential equations. $\dfrac{\partial^2 f}{\partial x^2} + C\dfrac{\partial f}{\partial t} = 0.$ **[Dec-2011, Q.No.-1(c)]**

Ans. Given equation is $\dfrac{\partial^2 f}{\partial x^2} + C\dfrac{\partial f}{\partial t} = 0$

Express $f(x, t)$ as a product of two separable functions: $f(x,t) = X(x)\, T(t)$

Substituting it in the given PDE, we obtain, $X''(x)T(t) + CX(x)\dot{T}(t) = 0$

Dividing throughout by $X(x)T(t)$, we find that $\dfrac{X''(x)}{X(x)} = -C\dfrac{\dot{T}(t)}{T(t)} = -k^2$

so that equation splits into following equations: $X''(x) + k^2 X = 0$

and $\dot{T}(t) - \lambda^2 T(t) = 0$ where $\lambda^2 = k^2/C$

Q12. Find the steady-state temperature $T(r,\theta)$ in the semi-circular plate shown in given figure

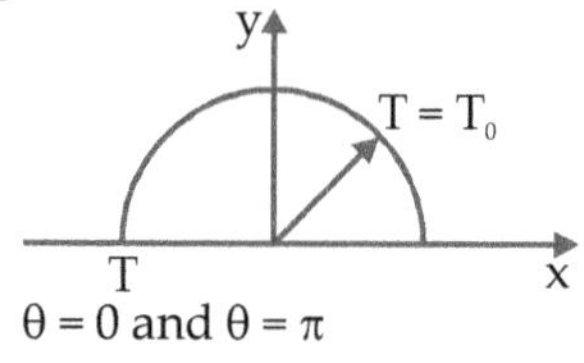

$$\theta = 0 \text{ and } \theta = \pi$$

A semi circular plate

Ans. We must solve $\dfrac{\partial^2 T}{\partial r^2}+\dfrac{1}{r}\dfrac{\partial T}{\partial r}+\dfrac{1}{r^2}\dfrac{\partial^2 T}{\partial \theta^2}=0 \quad 0<\theta<\pi; 0<r<a_0$

subject to the boundary conditions

$$T(a_0,\theta)=T_0 \sin\theta \qquad\qquad\qquad 0<\theta<\pi$$

$$T(r,0)=0, T(r,\pi)=0 \qquad\qquad\qquad 0<r<a_0$$

If we define $T=R(r)\,\Theta\,(\theta)$, then separation of variables gives

$$\frac{r^2 R''+rR'}{R}=-\frac{\Theta''}{\Theta}=\lambda^2$$

so that original PDE reduces to

$$r^2 R''+rR'-\lambda^2 R=0 \qquad\qquad\qquad\qquad\qquad ...(i)$$

and $\quad \Theta''+\lambda^2\,\Theta=0 \qquad\qquad\qquad\qquad\qquad\qquad ...(ii)$

Applying the boundary conditions $\Theta(0)=0$ and $\Theta(\pi)=0$ to the solution $\Theta=c_1\cos\lambda\theta+c_2\sin\lambda\theta$ of (ii) yields $c_1=0$ and $\lambda=n; n=1,2,3,...$.

Hence, $\Theta=c_2\sin n\theta$. For $\lambda=n$, (i) is Cauchy-Euler equation. It has the solution $R=c_3 r^n+c_4 r^{-n}$. In order that the solution $T(r,\theta)$ is finite as $r\to 0$ we must demand that $c_4=0$. Therefore,

$$T_n=A_n r^n\sin n\theta \text{ and } T(r,\theta)=\sum_{n=1}^{\infty}A_n r^n\sin n\theta.$$

The boundary condition at $r=a_0$ gives $T_0\sin\theta=\sum_{n=1}^{\infty}A_n a_0^n\sin n\theta$

so that $A_1=\dfrac{T_0}{a_0}$ and $A_2=A_3=0=......=A_n$

Hence, $T(r,\theta)=\dfrac{T_0}{a_0}r\sin\theta$. The book you can believe – GPH book.

Q13. A sinusoidal water wave having a maximum height of 7.4 cm above the equilibrium water level is propagating in the $-x$ direction with

a speed of $93\ \text{cm s}^{-1}$. The distance between two successive crests is 55 cm. Write the wave equation in terms of angular frequency and wave number. Also calculate the particle velocity.

Ans. A wave moving along x-direction is described by the equation

$$y(x,t) = a\sin(\omega_0 t - kx) \qquad\qquad \text{...(i)}$$

The angular frequency is connected to v and λ by the relation

$$\omega_0 = \frac{2\pi v}{\lambda}$$

Here $v = 93\ \text{cm s}^{-1}$ and $\lambda = 55$ cm.

$$\text{Hence, } \omega_0 = \frac{2\pi \times 93\,\text{cm s}^{-1}}{55\,\text{cm}} = \frac{584.34}{55}\,\text{s}^{-1} = 10.62\,\text{s}^{-1}$$

Similarly, the wave number is related to wavelength as

$$k = \frac{2\pi}{\lambda} = \frac{2 \times 22}{7 \times 55\,\text{cm}} = 0.11\,\text{cm s}^{-1}.$$

$$\text{Hence, } y(x,t) = (7.4\,\text{cm})\sin(10.62t + 0.11x) \qquad\qquad \text{(by equation (i))}$$

The particle velocity is given by

$$\frac{\partial y}{\partial t} = 7.4\,\text{cm} \times 10.62\,\text{s}^{-1}\cos(10.62t + 0.11x) = 78.6\ \text{cms}^{-1}\cos(10.62t + 0.11x).$$

Q14. (i) **The electrostatic potential in the exterior and interior of a spherical shell is calculated by using Laplace's equation: $\nabla^2 f = 0$. Use the method of separation of variables to split it into three ODEs.**

Ans. In spherical polar coordinates, the Laplace's equation can be written

$$\text{as } \frac{1}{r^2 \sin\theta}\left[\sin\theta\frac{\partial}{\partial r}\left(r^2\frac{\partial f}{\partial r}\right) + \frac{\partial}{\partial\theta}\left(\sin\theta\frac{\partial f}{\partial\theta}\right) + \frac{1}{\sin\theta}\frac{\partial^2 f}{\partial\phi^2}\right] = 0$$

In the method of separation of variables, we write $f(r,\theta,\phi) = R(r)\,\Theta(\theta)\Phi(\phi)$

By substituting back into the given equation and dividing by $R\Theta\Phi$,

$$\text{we have } \frac{1}{Rr^2}\frac{d}{dr}\left(r^2\frac{dR}{dr}\right) + \frac{1}{\Theta\, r^2\sin\theta}\frac{d}{d\theta}\left(\sin\theta\frac{d\Theta}{d\theta}\right) + \frac{1}{\Phi r^2\sin^2\theta}\frac{d^2\Phi}{d\phi^2} = 0$$

On multiplying throughout by $r^2\sin^2\theta$, we can isolate ϕ dependent term:

$$-\frac{1}{R}\sin^2\theta\frac{d}{dr}\left(r^2\frac{dR}{dr}\right) - \frac{\sin\theta}{\Theta}\frac{d}{d\theta}\left(\sin\theta\frac{d\Theta}{d\theta}\right) = \frac{1}{\Phi}\frac{d^2\Phi}{d\phi^2}$$

We will note that this equation relates a function of ϕ alone to a function of r and θ. Since r, θ, ϕ are independent variables, we can equate each side to a constant. Let us choose it to be $-m^2$. Then $\dfrac{1}{\Phi}\dfrac{d^2\Phi}{d\phi^2} = -m^2$ ...(i)

and $\dfrac{1}{R}\sin^2\theta \dfrac{d}{dr}\left(r^2\dfrac{dR}{dr}\right) + \dfrac{\sin\theta}{\Theta}\dfrac{d}{d\theta}\left(\sin\theta\dfrac{d\Theta}{d\theta}\right) = m^2$

or $\dfrac{1}{R}\dfrac{d}{dr}\left(r^2\dfrac{dR}{dr}\right) = \dfrac{m^2}{\sin^2\theta} - \dfrac{1}{\sin\theta}\dfrac{1}{\Theta}\dfrac{d}{d\theta}\left(\sin\theta\dfrac{d\Theta}{d\theta}\right)$

Again equating each side to a constant, we get the required result:

$$\dfrac{d}{dr}\left(r^2\dfrac{dR}{dr}\right) - nR = 0 \qquad\qquad \text{...(ii)}$$

and $\dfrac{1}{\sin\theta}\dfrac{d}{d\theta}\left(\sin\dfrac{d\Theta}{d\theta}\right) - \dfrac{m^2}{\sin^2\theta}\Theta + n\,\Theta = 0$ ...(iii)

where n is separation constant.

(ii) **The wave propagation in space is described by 3-D equation**

$$\nabla^2 f(\vec{r}, t) = \dfrac{1}{v^2}\dfrac{\partial^2 f}{\partial t^2}(\vec{r}, t)$$

Working in Cartesian coordinates, show that it can be reduced to four ODEs: $\ddot{T} + \omega^2 T = 0$

$X'' + l^2 X = 0$

$Y'' + m^2 Y = 0$

and $Z'' + n^2 Z = 0$

where $\omega = vk$ **and l, m, n are separation constants.**

Ans. The 3-D wave equation is $\nabla^2 f(\vec{r}, t) = \dfrac{1}{v^2}\dfrac{\partial^2 f(\vec{r}, t)}{\partial t^2}$ ...(i)

In Cartesian coordinates, the Laplacian can be written as

$$\nabla^2 = \dfrac{\partial^2}{\partial x^2} + \dfrac{\partial^2}{\partial y^2} + \dfrac{\partial^2}{\partial z^2} \qquad\qquad \text{...(ii)}$$

so that $\left(\dfrac{\partial^2}{\partial x^2} + \dfrac{\partial^2}{\partial y^2} + \dfrac{\partial^2}{\partial z^2}\right) f(x, y, z, t) = \dfrac{1}{v^2}\dfrac{\partial^2 f}{\partial t^2}$ ...(iii)

The function f depends on four variables. Hence, we can written as

$f(x, y, z, t) = X(x)Y(y)Z(z)T(t)$. On substituting back in the given equation and dividing by XYZT, we get

$$\frac{1}{X}\frac{d^2X}{dx^2} + \frac{1}{Y}\frac{d^2Y}{dy^2} + \frac{1}{Z}\frac{d^2Z}{dz^2} = \frac{1}{v^2}\frac{1}{T}\frac{d^2T}{dt^2} \qquad \text{...(iv)}$$

The LHS is a function of space variables whereas RHS is a function of time alone. Let us therefore choose $\dfrac{1}{v^2}\dfrac{1}{T}\dfrac{d^2T}{dt^2} = -k^2$

so that $\dfrac{d^2T}{dt^2} + \omega_0^2 T = 0$ $\qquad \text{...(v)}$

where $\omega_0 = kv$. Then, (iv) reduces to $\dfrac{1}{X}\dfrac{d^2X}{dx^2} = -k^2 - \dfrac{1}{Y}\dfrac{d^2Y}{dy^2} - \dfrac{1}{Z}\dfrac{d^2Z}{dz^2}$ ...(vi)

Again LHS is a function of x only, whereas the RHS depends only on y and z. We, therefore, choose $\dfrac{1}{X}\dfrac{d^2X}{dx^2} = -l^2$ so that $\dfrac{d^2X}{dx^2} + l^2X = 0$ ...(vii)

and $\dfrac{1}{Y}\dfrac{d^2Y}{dy^2} = l^2 - k^2 - \dfrac{1}{Z}\dfrac{d^2Z}{dz^2}$

Proceeding along the same lines, we can show that $\dfrac{d^2Y}{dy^2} + m^2Y = 0$

and $\dfrac{d^2Z}{dz^2} + n^2Z = 0$ where $n^2 = k^2 - l^2 - m^2$.

Q15. Reduce the following PDE into three ODEs: $\nabla^2\phi + k^2\phi = 0$

[June-2013, Q.No.-1(d)]

Ans. Given PDE is $\nabla^2\phi + k^2\phi = 0$

$$\Rightarrow \qquad \left(\frac{\partial^2\phi}{\partial x^2} + \frac{\partial^2\phi}{\partial y^2} + \frac{\partial^2\phi}{\partial z^2}\right) + k^2\phi = 0 \qquad \text{...(i)}$$

Let $\phi(x,y,z) = X(x)Y(y)Z(z)$ $\qquad \text{...(ii)}$

Substituting it in given PDE, we get

$$YZ\frac{d^2X}{dx^2} + XZ\frac{d^2Y}{dy^2} + XY\frac{d^2Z}{dz^2} + k^2XYZ = 0$$

Dividing throughout by XYZ and rearranging terms, we obtain

$$\frac{1}{X}\frac{d^2X}{dx^2} = -k^2 - \frac{1}{Y}\frac{d^2Y}{dy^2} - \frac{1}{Z}\frac{d^2Z}{dz^2} \qquad \text{...(iii)}$$

The LHS is a function of x above, whereas the RHS depends only on y and z. Let us choose $\dfrac{1}{X}\dfrac{d^2X}{dx^2} = -l^2$ $\qquad \text{...(iv)}$

Then we can write $\dfrac{1}{Y}\dfrac{d^2Y}{dy^2} = -k^2 + l^2 - \dfrac{1}{Z}\dfrac{d^2Z}{dz^2}$ ...(v)

Here we have a function of y equated to a function of z.

We now set $\dfrac{1}{Y}\dfrac{d^2Y}{dy^2} = -m^2$ ...(vi)

so that $\dfrac{1}{Z}\dfrac{d^2Z}{dz^2} = -k^2 + l^2 + m^2 = -n^2$ ...(vii)

where we have put $k^2 = l^2 + m^2 + n^2$.

Hence, equation (iv), (vi) and (vii) are the required three ODEs.

Q16. The one-dimensional wave equation for e.m. wave propagation in free space is given by $\dfrac{\partial^2 E_y}{\partial x^2} - \dfrac{1}{c^2}\dfrac{\partial^2 E_y}{\partial t^2} = 0$ **(for $\vec{E} \| \hat{y}$). Solve this equation and obtain the eigen frequencies of the cavity if $E_y = 0$ at $x = 0$ and $x = L$.**

Ans. The given equation describes e.m. wave propagation in free space:

$$\dfrac{\partial^2 E_y}{\partial x^2} - \dfrac{1}{c^2}\dfrac{\partial^2 E_y}{\partial t^2} = 0$$

Now, making the substitution $E_y = X(x)T(t)$ so that

$$X''T(t) - \dfrac{1}{c^2}X(x)\ddot{T} = 0$$

Dividing by $X(x)\,T(t)$, we get $\dfrac{X''}{X} = \dfrac{1}{c^2}\dfrac{\ddot{T}}{T} = -k^2$ so that $X'' + k^2 X = 0$

and $\ddot{T} + \omega_0^2 T = 0$ where $\omega_0 = ck$.

The solutions of these equations are of the form
$X = A\cos kx + B\sin kx$

and $T = C\cos\omega_0 t + D\sin\omega_0 t$

The condition $X(x)T(t) = E_y = 0$ at $x = 0$ and at $x = L$ implies that for all $t > 0$, $X(x) = 0$ at $x = 0$ and $x = L$. This leads to $X(L) = B\sin kL = 0$

For a non-trivial solution, the eigenvalues are $K_n L = n\pi$

or $k_n = (n\pi/L)$ with corresponding eigen functions $X_n(x) = B\sin\left(\dfrac{n\pi}{L}\right)x$

To get success in your studies, read only GPH book.

Fourier Series

An Overview

A Fourier series is an expansion of a periodic function $f(x)$ in terms of an infinite sum of sines and cosines. Fourier series make use of the orthogonality relationships of the sine and cosine functions. The computation and study of Fourier series is known as harmonic analysis and is extremely useful as a way to break up an arbitrary periodic function into a set of simple terms that can be plugged in, solved individually, and then recombined to obtain the solution to the original problem or an approximation to it to whatever accuracy is desired or practical.

Fourier series: In many physical investigations, it becomes important to express a given function $f(x)$, defined in the interval $(-L, L)$ in a series of sines and cosines of multiples of x, in the form

$$f(x) = a_0 + \sum_{n=1}^{\infty} \left(a_n \cos\frac{n\pi x}{L} + b_n \sin\frac{n\pi x}{L} \right) \qquad \ldots(i)$$

This series is called Fourier's series of $f(x)$ and a_0, a_n, b_n are called Fourier's coefficients for function $f(x)$.

For positive integers m and n, we have

$$\bullet \qquad \int_{-L}^{L} \sin\frac{m\pi x}{L} \cos\frac{n\pi x}{L} dx = 0 \qquad\qquad \ldots(ii(a))$$

$$\bullet \qquad \int_{-L}^{L} \sin\frac{m\pi x}{L} \sin\frac{n\pi x}{L} dx = 0 \quad (m \neq n) \qquad \ldots(ii(b))$$

$$\bullet \qquad \int_{-L}^{L} \cos\frac{m\pi x}{L} \cos\frac{n\pi x}{L} dx = 0 \quad (m \neq n) \qquad \ldots(ii(c))$$

$$\bullet \qquad \int_{-L}^{L} \sin\frac{m\pi x}{L} dx = \int_{-L}^{L} \cos\frac{m\pi x}{L} dx = 0 \qquad \ldots(ii(d))$$

$$\bullet \qquad \int_{-L}^{L} \sin^2\frac{m\pi x}{L} dx = \int_{-L}^{L} \cos^2\frac{m\pi x}{L} dx = L \qquad \ldots(ii(e))$$

Finding the coefficients: Let us first find a_0. Integrating both sides of Eqs. (i) from $-L$ to L, we get

$$\int_{-L}^{L} f(dx)dx = \int_{-L}^{L} a_0 dx + \int_{-L}^{L} \left[\sum_{n=1}^{\infty} \left(a_n \cos\frac{n\pi x}{L} + b_n \sin\frac{n\pi x}{L} \right) \right] dx \qquad \ldots(iii)$$

Now integrating Eq. (iii) term by term using Eq. (ii(d)). We find that all the terms in the second and third series in the RHS of Eq. (iii) are zero,

since $\displaystyle\int_{-L}^{L} \sin\frac{n\pi x}{L} dx = \int_{-L}^{L} \cos\frac{n\pi x}{L} dx = 0$, $\quad n=1,2,3,\ldots$.

Thus, we get $\displaystyle\int_{-L}^{L} a_0 dx = a_0 \int_{-L}^{L} dx = 2L a_0 = \int_{-L}^{L} f(x)dx$

or $\displaystyle a_0 = \frac{1}{2L} \int_{-L}^{L} f(x)dx \qquad\qquad \ldots(iv)$

We can determine $a_1, a_2, \ldots$ and $b_1, b_2, \ldots$ in a similar way. Let us multiply Eq. (i) throughout by $\sin\dfrac{m\pi x}{L}$ and integrate both sides from $-L$ to

L. We get $\displaystyle\int_{-L}^{L} f(x)\sin\frac{m\pi x}{L} dx = \int_{-L}^{L} \sin\frac{m\pi x}{L} \left[a_0 + \sum_{n=1}^{\infty} \left(a_n \cos\frac{n\pi x}{L} + b_n \sin\frac{n\pi x}{L} \right) \right] dx$

The right-hand-side of the equation can be simplified further as follows:

$$\int_{-L}^{L} f(x)\sin\frac{m\pi x}{L}\,dx = a_0 \int_{-L}^{L} \sin\frac{m\pi x}{L}\,dx + \sum_{n=1}^{\infty} a_n \int_{-L}^{L} \sin\frac{m\pi x}{L}\cos\frac{n\pi x}{L}\,dx$$

$$+\sum_{n=1}^{\infty} b_n \int_{-L}^{L} \sin\frac{m\pi x}{L}\sin\frac{n\pi x}{L}\,dx$$

We now use Eqs. (iid), (ii b) and (ii, e). The first term on the RHS of the above equation is zero, from Eq. (ii d). From Eq. (ii a), the integrals over all the terms in the first series on the RHS are zero. In the second series, there is only one term (for which n = m) that will survive. The remaining terms are zero by virtue of Eq. (ii b). Thus, we have

$$\int_{-L}^{L} f(x)\sin\frac{m\pi x}{L}\,dx = 0+0+b_m \int_{-L}^{L} \sin^2\frac{m\pi x}{L}\,dx = b_m L \qquad \text{[using (ii e)]}$$

Hence, $\quad b_m = \dfrac{1}{L}\displaystyle\int_{-L}^{L} f(x)\sin\frac{m\pi x}{L}\,dx, \quad m = 1,2,3,\ldots$

We can find a_m in the same way.

Multiplying equation $\quad f(x) = a_0 + \displaystyle\sum_{n=1}^{\infty}\left(a_n \cos\frac{n\pi x}{L} + b_n \sin\frac{n\pi x}{L}\right)\quad$ by

$\cos\dfrac{m\pi x}{L}$ and integrating from -L to L, we get

$$\int_{-L}^{L} f(x)\cos\frac{m\pi x}{L}\,dx = a_0 \int_{-L}^{L} \cos\frac{m\pi x}{L}\,dx + \sum_{n=1}^{\infty} a_n \int_{-L}^{L} \cos\frac{n\pi x}{L}\cos\frac{m\pi x}{L}\,dx$$

$$+\sum_{n=1}^{\infty} b_n \int_{-L}^{L} \sin\frac{n\pi x}{L}\cos\frac{m\pi x}{L}\,dx$$

Using Eqs. (ii d), (ii b), (ii c) and (ii e) we get

$$\int_{-L}^{L} f(x)\cos\frac{m\pi x}{L}\,dx = 0 + a_m \int_{-L}^{L} \cos^2\frac{m\pi x}{L}\,dx + 0,$$

$$= a_m L \quad \text{or} \quad a_m = \frac{1}{L}\int_{-L}^{L} f(x)\cos\frac{m\pi x}{L}\,dx \;.$$

Fourier coefficients of f(x) (Euler Formulas):- Let us put all results for a_n and b_n together. These are termed Euler formulas.

- $\quad a_0 = \dfrac{1}{2L}\displaystyle\int_{-L}^{L} f(x)\,dx \hspace{4cm}$ (iv a)

- $\quad a_n = \dfrac{1}{L}\displaystyle\int_{-L}^{L} f(x)\cos\frac{n\pi x}{L}\,dx, \quad n = 1,2,3,\ldots \hspace{1cm}$ (iv b)

$$\bullet \qquad b_n = \frac{1}{L}\int_{-L}^{L} f(x)\sin\frac{n\pi x}{L}dx, \quad n = 1,2,3,... \qquad\qquad \text{(iv c)}$$

The numbers a_0, a_n and b_n (for $n \geq 1$) given by Eqs. (4 a, b, c) are called the Fourier coefficients of $f(x)$.

Technique used to determine the Fourier series for any function f(x) defined on an interval -L < x < L: To find Fourier series, we must follow following steps:

Step 1: Write down the Fourier series for a function $f(x)$ defined on the

$$\text{interval } -L < x < L \text{ as } \quad f(x) = a_0 + \sum_{n=1}^{\infty}\left(a_n\cos\frac{n\pi x}{L} + b_n\sin\frac{n\pi x}{L}\right)$$

Step 2: Evaluate $\quad a_0 = \dfrac{1}{2L}\int_{-L}^{L} f(x)dx$

Step 3: Evaluate $\quad a_n = \dfrac{1}{L}\int_{-L}^{L} f(x)\cos\dfrac{n\pi x}{L}dx, \qquad n = 1,2,3,....$

$$\text{and } b_n = \frac{1}{L}\int_{-L}^{L} f(x)\sin\frac{n\pi x}{L}dx, \qquad n = 1,2,3,....$$

Use of Fourier series as an Approximation: Let us compare the graph of e^x with the graphs of functions obtained by adding an increasing number of terms in the Fourier series. The Fourier series for e^x on the given interval is $(e - e^{-1})\left[\dfrac{1}{2} + \displaystyle\sum_{n=1}^{\infty}\dfrac{(-1)^n}{1+n^2\pi^2}(\cos n\pi x - n\pi\sin n\pi x)\right]$

Now consider the sum of the first N terms of this series, which is called the Nth partial sum S_N :

$$S_N = (e - e^{-1})\left[\frac{1}{2} + \sum_{n=1}^{N}\frac{(-1)^n}{1+n^2\pi^2}(\cos n\pi x - n\pi\sin n\pi x)\right]$$

In Fig. 7.1, we compare the graph of e^x with the graphs of the partial sums S_2, S_5 and S_{10}, i.e. the sum of the first two, the first five and the first ten terms, respectively.

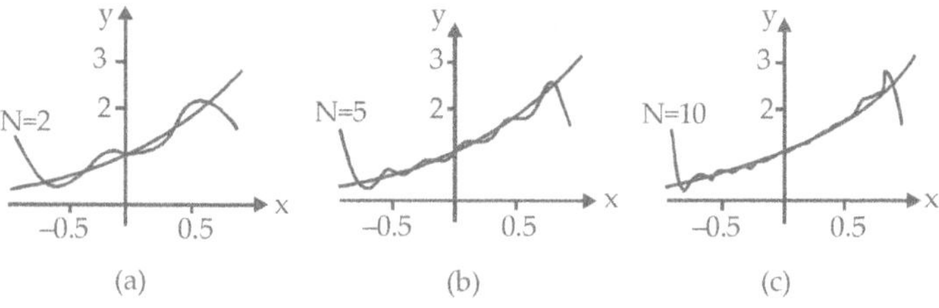

(a)   (b)   (c)

Fig 7.1: A comparison of e^x with the finite partial sums of its Fourier series for (a) N = 2 (b) N = 5, (c) N = 10.

We notice that with N = 10, we obtain better approximations to e^x at all points except the end points $x = \pm 1$.

We say that as N increases, the Fourier series approximation of the original function converges to e^x at all values of x such that $-1 < x < 1$.

Fourier series for even and odd functions: A Function f(x) defined on an interval $-L \leq x \leq L$ is said to be even if

$$f(-x) = f(x) \qquad \text{for all } x \in [-L, L]$$

and odd if

$$f(-x) = -f(x) \qquad \text{for all } x \in [-L, L]$$

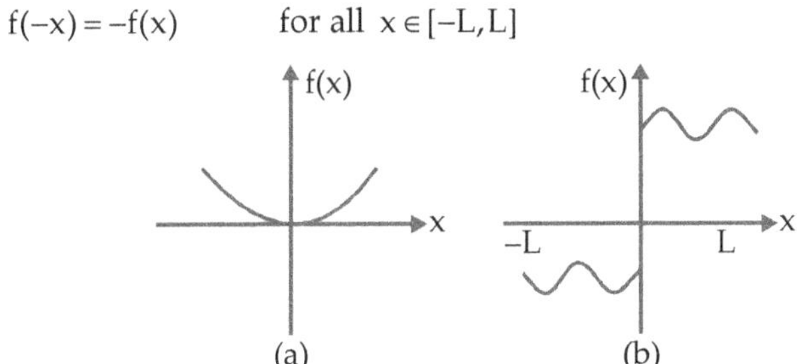

Fig.7.2: (a) An even and (b) an odd function

The graph of an even function can be obtained from its graph to the right of the vertical axis by reflection in that axis.

Similarly, the graph of an odd function is obtained by first reflecting its right half in the vertical axis, and then reflecting it in the horizontal axis.

Any function can be written as the sum of an even function and an odd function, as follows: $f(x) = \dfrac{1}{2}[f(x) + f(-x)] + \dfrac{1}{2}[f(x) - f(-x)]$

The first part on the RHS is even and the second part is odd.

For example, $e^x = \dfrac{1}{2}[e^x + e^{-x}] + \dfrac{1}{2}[e^x - e^{-x}] = \cosh x + \sinh x$

where $\cosh x$ is even and $\sinh x$ is odd.

Whether a function is odd or even, or neither odd nor even may depend merely on the choice of the origin and the coordinate axes.

Properties of Even and Odd Functions: Certain properties of even and odd functions that would be useful when we evaluate the Fourier coefficient are as follows:

(1)   If f (x) and g (x) are even (odd) functions then

       (a)   f (x) + g(x) is an even (odd) function.

(b) $f(x) - g(x)$ is an even (odd) function.

(2)   If f (x) and g(x) are both even functions or both odd functions, then f(x) g(x) is an even function.

(3)   If f(x) is an even function and g(x) is an odd function, then f (x) g(x) is an odd function.

(4)   If f (x) is an even function then $\displaystyle\int_{-L}^{L} f(x)dx = 2\int_{0}^{L} f(x)dx$

(5)   If f (x) is an odd function then $\displaystyle\int_{-L}^{L} f(x)dx = 0$

Fourier Sine and Cosine Series: The Fourier series for an even function f (x) on the interval $-L < x < L$ is a Fourier cosine series:

$$f(x) = a_0 + \sum_{n=1}^{\infty} a_n \cos\frac{n\pi x}{L} \qquad\qquad \text{(f even)}$$

with coefficients $\displaystyle a_0 = \frac{1}{L}\int_{0}^{L} f(x)dx, \quad a_n = \frac{2}{L}\int_{0}^{L} f(x)\cos\frac{n\pi x}{L}dx$

The Fourier series for an odd function on the interval $-L < x < L$ is a

Fourier sine series: $\displaystyle f(x) = \sum_{n=1}^{\infty} b_n \sin\frac{n\pi x}{L}$ (f odd)

with coefficients $\displaystyle b_n = \frac{2}{L}\int_{0}^{L} f(x)\sin\frac{n\pi x}{L}dx$

Extending the scope of Fourier series: Consider the solution of equation $\dfrac{\partial T}{\partial t} = k\dfrac{\partial^2 T}{\partial x^2}$, given the initial condition that $T(x,0) = f(x) \quad (0 < x < L)$

where f (x) is an arbitrary function. Since, the solution of this equation is of the form of equation $\displaystyle T(x,t) = \sum_{n=1}^{\infty} b_n \exp\left(-\frac{n^2\pi^2 kt}{L^2}\right)\sin\frac{n\pi x}{L}$, this initial condition will be satisfied only if we can express f (x) as a Fourier sine series, i.e. $\displaystyle f(x) = \sum_{n=1}^{\infty} b_n \sin\frac{n\pi x}{L} \quad (0 < x < L)$

Half-range Expansions: Consider a function f (x) defined on $0 < x < L$ so that we can represent it as a Fourier sine series. For this, we use f (x) to define a new odd function g(x) on the extended interval $-L < x < L$ by

$$g(x) = \begin{cases} -f(-x), & -L < x < 0 \\ 0, & x = 0 \\ f(x), & 0 < x < L \end{cases}$$

The function g(x) defined in this way is called the odd extension of f (x). If g(x) is periodic, it is termed the odd periodic extension. It is identical with f (x) on the interval $0 < x < L$. Graphically, the odd extension of f (x) is obtained simply by reflecting the graph of f (x) first in the vertical axis and then in the horizontal axis.

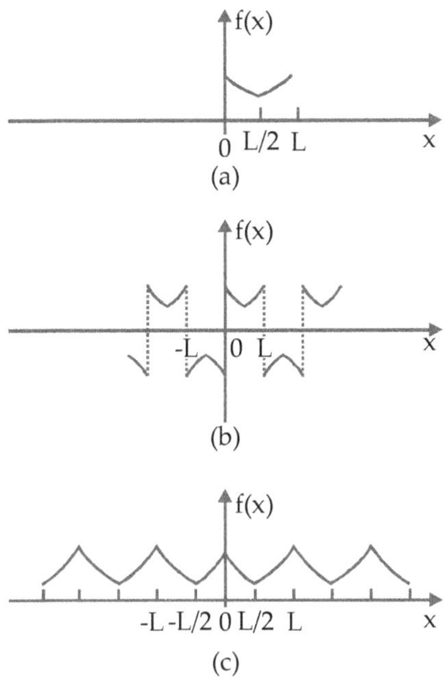

Fig. 7.3: (a) A given function f (x) extended as (b) an odd periodic function of period 2L and (c) an even periodic function of periodic 2L

Fig. 7.3 (b) shows the odd extension of a function f (x) of Fig. 7.3 (a). Since g(x) is odd on the interval $-L < x < L$, the cosine coefficients in its Fourier series are zero and the sine coefficients are given by

$$b_n = \frac{2}{L} \int_0^L g(x) \sin \frac{n\pi x}{L} dx, \quad n = 1,2,3,....$$

But for $0 < x < L$ we have g(x) = f (x), so that

$$b_n = \frac{2}{L} \int_0^L f(x) \sin \frac{n\pi x}{L} dx \qquad ...(v)$$

The resulting series is the Fourier sine series for the function f (x) on the interval $0 < x < L$. The series given by

Eq. $\left(f(x) = \sum_{n=1}^{\infty} b_n \sin \frac{n\pi x}{L} \quad (0 < x < L) \right)$ together with the coefficients given by

Eq. (v), is called the half-range expansion of the given function f (x).

Now suppose we develop a Fourier cosine series for a function f (x) defined on the interval $0 \le x < L$. Then we define the even extension g(x) of the function f (x) on the interval $-L < x < L$ as follows:

$$g(x) = \begin{cases} f(-x) & -L < x < 0 \\ f(x) & 0 < x < L \end{cases}$$

Again g(x) is identical with f (x) in $0 \le x < L$. Graphically, the even extension of f (x) is obtained by reflecting the graph of f (x) in the vertical axis (Fig. 7.3 c). If g(x) is periodic, it is termed the even periodic extension of f (x). Since g(x) is even, we get only the Fourier cosine series for f (x):

$$f(x) = \sum_{n=1}^{\infty} a_n \cos\frac{n\pi x}{L} \qquad \qquad ...(vi)$$

where $a_0 = \frac{1}{L}\int_0^L g(x)\,dx = \frac{1}{L}\int_0^L f(x)\,dx$, since g(x) = f (x) for $0 < x < L$ ...(vii a)

Similarly, $a_n = \frac{2}{L}\int_0^L g(x)\cos\frac{n\pi x}{L}\,dx, \qquad n = 1,2,....$

$$= \frac{2}{L}\int_0^L f(x)\cos\frac{n\pi x}{L}\,dx, \qquad n=1,2,...... \qquad ...(vii\ b)$$

The resulting Fourier cosine series (vi), along with Eqs. (vii a) and (vii b), is also termed as the half-range expansion of f(x).

Continuous Function: The word continuous means without any break or gap. Roughly speaking, a function f is continuous at a point c if f does not have a break or gap in its value at c, viz. f(c) when compared to the values at points near c. In other words, f is continuous at a point c if as x lies very near to c, f (x) also lies very near to f (c), i.e. if $|x-c|$ is made smaller and smaller, $|f(x)-f(x)|$ can also be made smaller and smaller. Consider a function

$$f(x) = x^2 \quad \text{if } 0 < x < 1$$
$$= 5 \quad \text{if } x = 1$$
$$= x^2 \quad \text{if } 1 < x < 2.$$

It may be seen that in the domain $[0,2], |x-1|$ may be as small as we please, yet $|f(x)-f(1)| = |f(x)-5| > 1$ for $x \ne 1$.

Hence, the function is not continuous at x = 1. However, if we take

$$f(x) = x^2 \quad \text{if } 0 < x < 1$$
$$= 1 \quad \text{if } x = 1$$

$$= x^2 \quad \text{if } 1 < x < 2,$$

then as $|x-1|$ is made smaller and smaller, $|f(x)-f(1)| = |f(x)-1|$ can also be made smaller and smaller. Hence, f is continuous at $x = 1$.

Now, the formal definition of the continuity of a function at a point is as follows:

A function f is said to be continuous at a point $x = c$ if as $x \to c, f(x) \to f(c)$, i.e. $\lim_{x \to c} f(x) = f(c)$.

Equivalently, f is continuous at $x = c$ if $\lim_{x \to c^-} f(x) = \lim_{x \to c^+} f(x) = f(c)$.

Piecewise continuous functions: A function can be called piecewise-continuous if its graph consists of a finite number of continuous pieces (see Figs. 7.4 and 7.5). We say that a function is piecewise continuous on the interval $a \le x \le b$, if there are a finite number of points $a = x_0 < x_1 < x_2 ... < x_n = b$

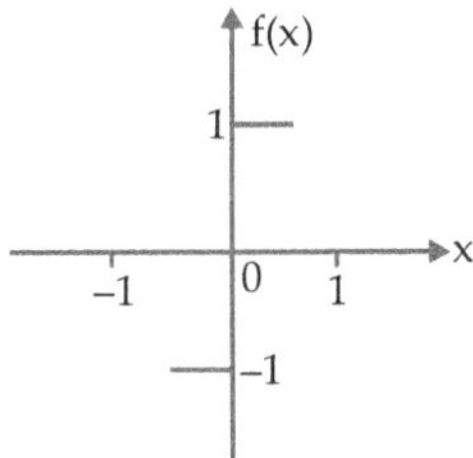

Fig. 7.4: This function is called the step function. It may represent the output signal of an electronic switch

such that:

(i) f is continuous on each subinterval

$$x_0 < x < x_1, x_1 < x < x_2, ..., x_{j-1} x < x_j, ..., x_{n-1} < x < x_n$$

(ii) f has finite limits as x approaches the end-points of each subinterval from within the subinterval.

Fig. 7.5 shows the graph of a typical piecewise continuous function, f. The dots on the graph represent the value of the function at each of the breakpoints.

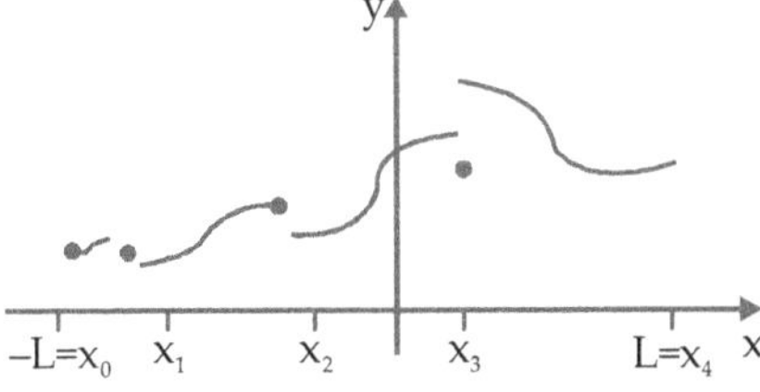

Fig. 7.5: The graph of a typical piecewise continuous function f on the interval (-L, L)

At each of the break-points, the value of the function f may or may not equal its left or right-hand limit. For example, in Fig. 7.5, we can see that $f(x_1^-) \neq f(x_1) \neq f(x_1^+)$, whereas $f(x_2^-) = f(x_2) \neq f(x_2^+)$

Convergence of Fourier series: Consider the sum of the first N terms of the series for a function f (x) on the interval $-L < x < L$ given by

$$S_N = a_0 + \sum_{n=1}^{N} \left(a_n \cos\frac{n\pi x}{L} + b_n \sin\frac{n\pi x}{L} \right) \qquad \text{...(viii)}$$

The Fourier series converges to f at a point $x = x_0$ if the partial sum given in Eq. (viii), with $x = x_0$, tends to a finite limit $f(x_0)$, in the limit as $N \to \infty$, i.e. $\lim_{N \to \infty} S_N(x_0) = f(x_0)$.

Dirichlet conditions: The Dirichlet conditions are sufficient conditions for a real-valued, periodic function f(x) to be equal to the sum of its Fourier series at each point where f is continuous.

Let the function f and its derivative f′ be piecewise continuous on the interval $-L < x < L$. Then, the Fourier series for f converges to f at all points in (-L, L) where f is continuous, and to the mean value $\dfrac{f(x_0^+) + f(x_0^-)}{2}$ at all points x_0 in (-L, L) where f is not continuous. At the end points, -L and L, the Fourier series converges to $\dfrac{[f(-L^+) + f(L^-)]}{2}$.

Solved Practical Problems

Q1. **(a) Is the waveform in following figure odd or even, when it is moved**

(i) **one unit vertically downwards, and**

(ii) **one unit vertically downwards and one unit to the left?**

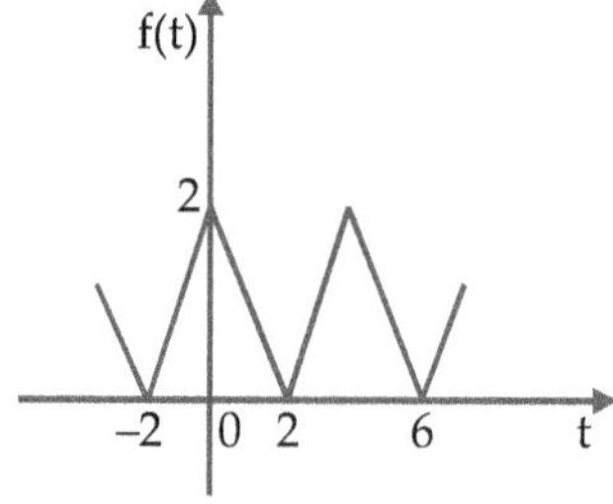

Triangular waveform

(b) An ac signal in the shape of triangular waveform is applied to an electrical circuit. Is it an odd or even function?

(c) Express each of the following functions as the sum of an even and an odd function

   (i) xe^x, **(ii)** $(1+x)(\sin x + \cos x)$

(d) Are the following functions even, odd or neither odd nor even?

   (i) $|x|$, **(ii)** $x \sin x$, **(iii)** e^x, **(iv)** x^{2n+1}, **(v)** $\sin nx + \cos nx$, **(vi)** $(\cos x)/x$

Ans. (a) (i) See Fig. 7.6 (a), this is an even function. (ii) See Fig. 7.6 (b), this is an odd function.

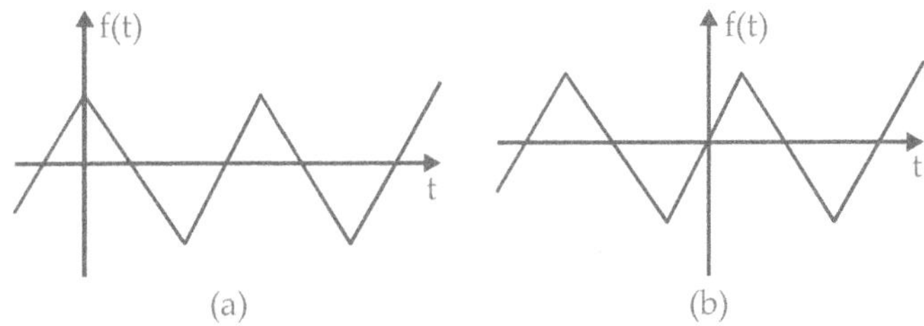

Fig. 7.6

(b) It is even, since $f(t) = f(-t)$

(c) **(i)** $\dfrac{xe^x - xe^{-x}}{2} + \dfrac{1}{2}[xe^x + xe^{-x}] = \dfrac{x}{2}[\sinh x + \cosh x]$

(ii) $\dfrac{1}{2}[(1+x)(\sin x + \cos x) + (1-x)(-\sin x + \cos x)]$

$+ \dfrac{1}{2}[(1+x)(\sin x + \cos x) - (1-x)(-\sin x + \cos x)]$

(d) (i) even (ii) even (iii) neither odd nor even (iv) odd (v) neither odd nor even (vi) odd.

Q2. Is the following function even, odd or neither? $x \cos nx$.

[June-2010, Q.No.-1(e)(ii)]

Ans. Let $f(x) = x \cos nx$

$\Rightarrow \qquad f(-x) = (-x)\cos n(-x)$

$\Rightarrow \qquad f(-x) = -x \cos nx$

$\Rightarrow \qquad f(-x) = -f(x)$

Hence, it is a odd function.

Q3. **(a) Determine the Fourier series for the function $e^{\alpha x}$ on the interval $-1 < x < 1$.**

Ans. In this case, $L = 1$.

Using equation, $a_0 = \dfrac{1}{2L}\displaystyle\int_{-L}^{L} f(x)\,dx$, we get

$$a_0 = \frac{1}{2}\int_{-1}^{1} e^{\alpha x}\,dx = \frac{1}{2\alpha}(e^{\alpha} - e^{-\alpha})$$

$$a_n = \int_{-1}^{1} e^{\alpha x} \cos n\pi x\,dx$$

Integrating by parts, we get $\quad a_n = \dfrac{\alpha(e^{\alpha} - e^{-\alpha})(-1)^n}{\alpha^2 + n^2\pi^2}, \qquad n = 1,2,3,\ldots$

Similarly, we get $\quad b_n = \displaystyle\int_{-1}^{1} e^{\alpha x} \sin n\pi x\,dx = \dfrac{-n\pi(e^{\alpha} - e^{-\alpha})(-1)^n}{\alpha^2 + n^2\pi^2}$

Thus, the Fourier series for the function $e^{\alpha x}$ on the interval $-1 < x < 1$ is

$$\frac{1}{2\alpha}(e^{\alpha} - e^{-\alpha}) + \sum_{n=1}^{\infty} \frac{\alpha(e^{\alpha} - e^{-\alpha})(-1)^n}{\alpha^2 + n^2\pi^2}\cos n\pi x - \sum_{n=1}^{\infty} n\pi \frac{(e^{\alpha} - e^{-\alpha})}{\alpha^2 + n^2\pi^2}(-1)^n \sin n\pi x$$

$$= (e^{\alpha} - e^{-\alpha})\left[\frac{1}{2\alpha} + \sum_{n=1}^{\infty} \frac{(-1)^n}{\alpha^2 + n^2\pi^2}(\alpha \cos n\pi x - n\pi \sin n\pi x)\right]$$

(b) **Find the Fourier series for the function $f(x)$ representing a periodic square wave of period 2π, defined as**

$$E(t) = \begin{cases} 0 & \text{if}-\pi < x < -\pi/2 \\ E & \text{if}-\pi/2 < x < \pi/2 \\ 0 & \text{if}\,\pi/2 < x < \pi \end{cases} \qquad\qquad \text{...(i)}$$

Functions of this type represent voltages impressed upon electrical circuits.

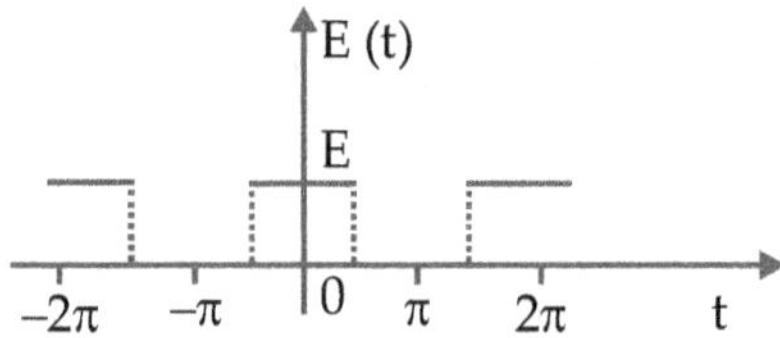

Fig. Periodic square wave of period 2π

Ans. Here $L = \pi$. Therefore, from equation $a_0 = \dfrac{1}{2L}\displaystyle\int_{-L}^{L} f(x)\,dx$,we have

$$a_0 = \frac{1}{2\pi}\int_{-\pi}^{\pi} E(t)\,dt = \frac{1}{2\pi}\int_{-\pi}^{-\pi/2}(0)\,dt + \frac{1}{2\pi}\int_{-\pi/2}^{\pi/2} E\,dt + \frac{1}{2\pi}\int_{\pi/2}^{\pi}(0)\,dt = \frac{E}{2\pi}\,\pi = \frac{E}{2}$$

From equation $a_n = \dfrac{1}{L}\int_{-L}^{L} f(x)\cos\dfrac{n\pi x}{L}\,dx$, $\qquad n = 1,2,3\ldots$

We have, $a_n = \dfrac{1}{\pi}\int_{-\pi}^{\pi} E(t)\cos nt\,dt = \dfrac{E}{\pi}\int_{-\pi/2}^{\pi/2}\cos nt\,dt$

$$= \frac{E}{n\pi}[\sin nt]_{-\pi/2}^{\pi/2} = \frac{2E}{n\pi}\sin\frac{n\pi}{2}$$

Thus, $a_n = 0$ if n is even $\Rightarrow a_n = \dfrac{2E}{n\pi}$, if $n = 1, 5, 9, \ldots$

and $a_n = -\dfrac{2E}{n\pi}$ $\quad$ if $n = 3, 7, 11, \ldots$

Similarly, from equation $b_n = \dfrac{1}{L}\int_{-L}^{L} f(x)\sin\dfrac{n\pi x}{L}\,dx$, $\qquad n = 1, 2, 3\ldots$

We get $b_n = \dfrac{1}{\pi}\int_{-\pi}^{\pi} E(t)\sin nt\,dt = \dfrac{E}{\pi}\int_{-\pi/2}^{\pi/2}\sin nt\,dt$

$$= \frac{E}{\pi}\left[-\frac{\cos nt}{n}\right]_{-\pi/2}^{\pi/2} = -\frac{E}{n\pi}\left[\cos\frac{n\pi}{2} - \cos\frac{n\pi}{2}\right] = 0.$$

Thus, $b_n = 0$ for all n.

Hence, the Fourier series for the periodic square wave of period 2π, represented by $E(t)$ is $E(t) = \dfrac{E}{2} + \dfrac{2E}{\pi}\left[\cos x - \dfrac{1}{3}\cos 3x + \dfrac{1}{5}\cos 5x + \ldots\right]$

Q4. **Find the Fourier series for the saw-tooth wave shown in given figure.**

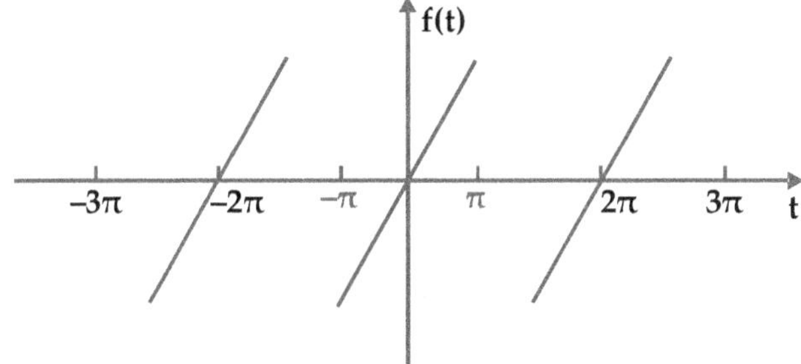

Ans. The function is algebraically expressed as: $f(t) = \dfrac{t}{\pi}$ $\quad -\pi < t < \pi$

and $\quad f(t+2\pi)=f(t)$

Thus, this saw-tooth function is odd and periodic with period 2π. It can be represented by a Fourier sine series.

$$f(t)=\sum_{n=1}^{\infty} b_n \sin\frac{n\pi t}{\pi}=\sum_{n=1}^{\infty} b_n \sin nt \text{ where}$$

$$b_n=\frac{2}{\pi}\int_0^\pi f(t)\sin nt\, dt=\frac{2}{\pi}\int_0^\pi \frac{t}{\pi}\sin nt\, dt$$

Integrating by parts, we get $\quad b_n=-\frac{2}{n\pi}(-1)^n=\frac{2}{n\pi}(-1)^{n+1}$

Thus, $f(t)=\frac{2}{\pi}\sum_{n=1}^{\infty}\frac{(-1)^{n+1}}{n}\sin nt=\frac{2}{\pi}\left[\sin t-\frac{1}{2}\sin 2t+\frac{1}{3}\sin 3t-\frac{1}{4}\sin 4t+...\right]$

Q4. Find the Fourier series for the saw-tooth wave shown in given figure.

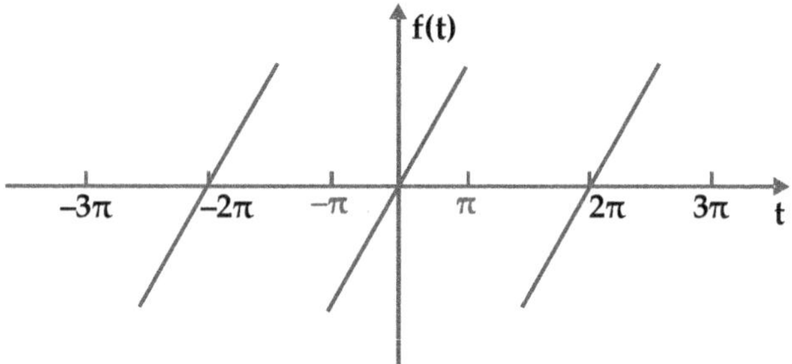

Ans. The function is algebraically expressed as: $f(t)=\dfrac{t}{\pi}\quad -\pi<t<\pi$ and

$f(t+2\pi)=f(t)$

Thus, this saw-tooth function is odd and periodic with period 2π. It can be represented by a Fourier sine series.

$$f(t)=\sum_{n=1}^{\infty} b_n \sin\frac{n\pi t}{\pi}=\sum_{n=1}^{\infty} b_n \sin nt \text{ where } b_n=\frac{2}{\pi}\int_0^\pi f(t)\sin nt\, dt=\frac{2}{\pi}\int_0^\pi \frac{t}{\pi}\sin nt\, dt$$

Integrating by parts, we get $\quad b_n=-\frac{2}{n\pi}(-1)^n=\frac{2}{n\pi}(-1)^{n+1}$

Thus, $f(t)=\frac{2}{\pi}\sum_{n=1}^{\infty}\frac{(-1)^{n+1}}{n}\sin nt=\frac{2}{\pi}\left[\sin t-\frac{1}{2}\sin 2t+\frac{1}{3}\sin 3t-\frac{1}{4}\sin 4t+...\right]$

Q5. Represent $f(x)=\begin{cases} 1 & 0<x<\dfrac{1}{2} \\[2mm] 0 & \dfrac{1}{2}<x<1 \end{cases}$ **in**

(a)　Fourier sine series and

Ans. In the first case, we need an odd extension g(x) of f(x) over the interval $-1 < x < 1$.

Thus, we can define $g(x) = \begin{cases} 0 & -1 < x < -\dfrac{1}{2} \\[2mm] -1 & -\dfrac{1}{2} < x < 0 \\[2mm] 0 & x = 0 \\[2mm] 1 & 0 < x < \dfrac{1}{2} \\[2mm] 0 & \dfrac{1}{2} < x < 1 \end{cases}$

The function g(x) is shown in Fig. 7.8 (b). Since it is odd, only the coefficient b_n will survive. Using equation $b_n = \dfrac{2}{L}\int_0^L f(x) \sin\dfrac{n\pi x}{L}\,dx$, we get

$$b_n = \frac{2}{1}\int_0^1 f(x)\sin n\pi x\,dx = 2\int_0^{1/2}\sin n\pi x\,dx = \frac{2}{n\pi}\big[\cos n\pi x\big]_0^{1/2} = -\frac{2}{n\pi}\left(\cos\frac{n\pi}{2} - 1\right)$$

or $b_1 = \dfrac{2}{\pi}, b_2 = \dfrac{4}{2\pi}, b_3 = \dfrac{2}{3\pi}, b_4 = 0,\dots$

Thus, the Fourier sine series for f (x) is

$$f(x) = \frac{2}{\pi}\left[\sin\pi x + \frac{2\sin 2\pi x}{2} + \frac{\sin 3\pi x}{3} + \frac{\sin 5\pi x}{5} + \frac{2\sin 6\pi x}{6} + \dots\right]$$

(b)　Fourier cosine series.

Ans. The even extension h(x) of f (x) over the interval $-1 \le x \le 1$ as shown in Fig. 7.7 (c) is

$$h(x) = \begin{cases} 0 & -1 \le x < -\dfrac{1}{2} \\[2mm] 1 & -\dfrac{1}{2} \le x \le \dfrac{1}{2} \\[2mm] 0 & \dfrac{1}{2} \le x \le 1 \end{cases}$$

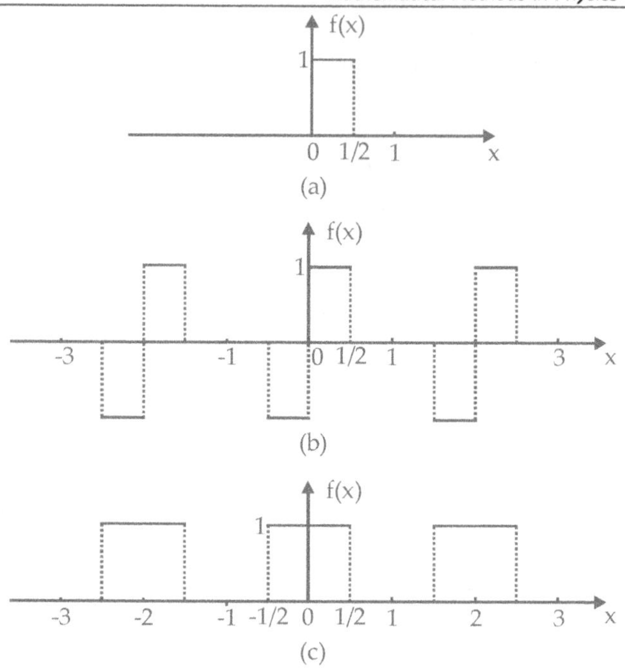

Fig. 7.7: Parts (b) and (c) show the odd and even extensions, respectively, of f(x) in (a)

In this case, using equations $a_0 = \dfrac{1}{L}\int\limits_0^L g(x)\,dx = \dfrac{1}{L}\int\limits_0^L f(x)\,dx$ and

$$a_n = \frac{2}{L}\int\limits_0^L f(x)\cos\frac{n\pi x}{L}\,dx,$$ we get the Fourier cosine series with coefficients:

$$a_0 = 2\int\limits_0^1 f(x)\,dx = 2\int\limits_0^{1/2} dx = 1$$

$$a_n = 2\int\limits_0^1 f(x)\cos n\pi x\,dx = 2\int\limits_0^{1/2}\cos n\pi x\,dx = \frac{2}{n\pi}[\sin n\pi x]_0^{1/2} = \frac{2}{n\pi}\sin\frac{n\pi}{2}$$

Thus, the Fourier cosine series for f (x) is

$$f(x) = \frac{1}{2} + \frac{2}{\pi}\left[\cos\pi x - \frac{1}{3}\cos 3\pi x + \frac{1}{5}\cos 5\pi x - \ldots\right].$$

Q6. Determine the period of the function $\sin\dfrac{2n\pi}{L}x$.

[Dec-2010, Q.No.-1(d)(i)]

Ans. Let $f(x) = \sin\dfrac{2n\pi}{L}x$

Now take, T = Period so that $f(T+x)=f(x)$

$$\Rightarrow \sin\left[\frac{2n\pi}{L}(T+x)\right]=\sin\frac{2n\pi}{L}x \Rightarrow \sin\left(\frac{2n\pi T}{L}+\frac{2n\pi x}{L}\right)=\sin\frac{2n\pi x}{L}$$

$$\Rightarrow \sin\left(\frac{2n\pi T}{L}\right)\cos\left(\frac{2n\pi x}{L}\right)+\cos\left(\frac{2n\pi T}{L}\right)\sin\left(\frac{2n\pi x}{L}\right)=\sin\frac{2n\pi x}{L}$$

$$\Rightarrow \cos\left(\frac{2n\pi T}{L}\right)=1 \text{ and } \sin\left(\frac{2n\pi T}{L}\right)=0 \Rightarrow \tan\left(\frac{2n\pi T}{L}\right)=0=\tan 2\pi$$

$$\Rightarrow \frac{2n\pi T}{L}=2\pi \Rightarrow \frac{nT}{L}=1 \Rightarrow T=\frac{L}{n} \Rightarrow \text{Period }=\frac{L}{n}.$$

Q7. **When a sound wave passes through the air and we hear it, the air pressure around us varies with time. Suppose the excess pressure above (and below) the atmospheric pressure in a sound wave is given by the graph in given figure. Represent this function in the form of a Fourier series and thus determine the frequencies we hear when we listen to this sound?**

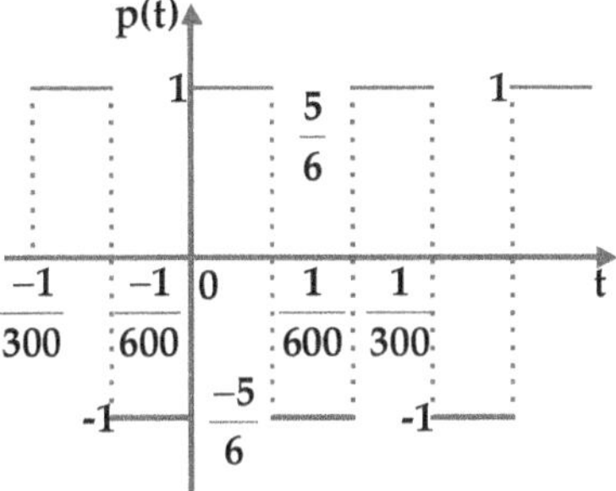

Ans. The function shown in given figure is an odd function, with L = 1/300. Therefore, we get only a Fourier sine series with coefficients

$$b_n = 2(300)\int_0^{1/300} p(t)\sin 300\, n\pi t\, dt$$

$$= 600\int_0^{1/600}\sin 300\, n\pi t\, dt-\frac{5}{6}(600)\int_{1/600}^{1/300}\sin 300\, n\pi t\, dt$$

$$\left[\therefore p(t)=\begin{cases}1, & 0<t<\dfrac{1}{600}\\[2mm]\dfrac{5}{6}, & \dfrac{1}{600}<t<\dfrac{1}{300}\end{cases}\right]$$

$$= 600\left(-\frac{\cos\dfrac{n\pi}{2}-1}{300\, n\pi}+\frac{5}{6}\frac{\cos n\pi-\cos\dfrac{n\pi}{2}}{300\, n\pi}\right)=\frac{2}{n\pi}\left(-\frac{11}{6}\cos\frac{n\pi}{2}+1+\frac{5}{6}\cos n\pi\right)$$

This gives $b_1 = \dfrac{2}{\pi}\left(1 - \dfrac{5}{6}\right) = \dfrac{1}{\pi}\cdot\dfrac{1}{3},$ $\qquad b_5 = \dfrac{2}{5\pi}\cdot\dfrac{1}{3}$

$b_2 = \dfrac{2}{2\pi}\left(\dfrac{11}{6} + 1 + \dfrac{5}{6}\right) = \dfrac{1}{2\pi}\cdot\dfrac{22}{3},$ $\qquad b_6 = \dfrac{1}{6\pi}\cdot\dfrac{22}{3}$

$b_3 = \dfrac{2}{3\pi}\left(1 - \dfrac{5}{6}\right) = \dfrac{1}{3\pi}\cdot\dfrac{1}{3},$ $\qquad b_7 = \dfrac{1}{7\pi}\cdot\dfrac{1}{3}$

$b_4 = \dfrac{2}{4\pi}\left(-\dfrac{11}{6} + 1 + \dfrac{5}{6}\right) = 0,$ $\qquad b_8 = 0,....\text{etc.}$

Thus, we have

$$p(t) = \dfrac{1}{3\pi}\left(\dfrac{\sin 300\pi t}{1} + \dfrac{22\sin 600\pi t}{2} + \dfrac{\sin 900\pi t}{3} + \dfrac{\sin 1500\pi t}{5}\right.$$
$$\left. + \dfrac{22\sin 1800\pi t}{6} + \dfrac{\sin 2100\pi t}{7} + ...\right)$$

We can see that the second harmonic at a frequency of 300 cps has the largest amplitude. Since the intensity is proportional to the square of the amplitude of a wave so that we would principally hear the second harmonic.

Q8. Find a Fourier's series for the function defined as

$\qquad$ **f(x) = -1, for $-\pi \le x < 0$**

$\qquad\quad$ **= 0, for x = 0**

$\qquad\quad$ **= + 1, for $0 < x \le \pi.$**

$\qquad$ **Hence, prove that** $\dfrac{1}{4}\pi = 1 - \dfrac{1}{3} + \dfrac{1}{5} - \dfrac{1}{7} + ...$

Ans. Here $a_0 = \dfrac{1}{2\pi}\displaystyle\int_{-\pi}^{\pi} f(x)\, dx = \dfrac{1}{2\pi}\left[\displaystyle\int_{-\pi}^{0} f(x)\, dx + \int_{0}^{\pi} f(x)\, dx\right]$

$\qquad = \dfrac{1}{2\pi}\lim_{\varepsilon\to 0}\left[\displaystyle\int_{-\pi}^{-\varepsilon} f(x)\, dx + \int_{-\varepsilon}^{\varepsilon} f(x)\, dx + \int_{\varepsilon}^{\pi} f(x)\, dx\right]$

$\qquad = \dfrac{1}{2\pi}\lim_{\varepsilon\to 0}\left[\displaystyle\int_{-\pi}^{-\varepsilon} (-1)\, dx + \int_{\varepsilon}^{\pi} 1\, dx\right] = \dfrac{1}{2\pi}\lim_{\varepsilon\to 0}\left[\{-x\}_{-\pi}^{-\varepsilon} + \{x\}_{\varepsilon}^{\pi}\right] = \dfrac{1}{2\pi}(-\pi + \pi) = 0.$

$a_n = \dfrac{1}{\pi}\displaystyle\int_{-\pi}^{\pi} f(x)\cos nx\, dx$

$\qquad = \dfrac{1}{\pi}\lim_{\varepsilon\to 0}\left[\displaystyle\int_{-\pi}^{-\varepsilon} (-1)\cos nx + \int_{\varepsilon}^{\pi} (1)\cos nx\, dx\right]$

$$= \frac{1}{n\pi}\lim_{\varepsilon\to 0}\{\sin n\varepsilon - \sin n\pi + \sin n\pi - \sin n\varepsilon\} = 0,$$

$$\text{and } b_n = \frac{1}{\pi}\lim_{\varepsilon\to 0}\left[\int_{-\pi}^{-\varepsilon}(-1)\sin nx\,dx + \int_{\varepsilon}^{\pi}(1)\sin nx\,dx\right]$$

$$= \frac{1}{\pi}\lim_{\varepsilon\to 0}\left[\left\{\frac{\cos nx}{n}\right\}_{-\pi}^{-\varepsilon} - \left\{\frac{\cos nx}{n}\right\}_{\varepsilon}^{\pi}\right] = \frac{2}{n\pi}(1 - \cos n\pi)$$

$$= 0, \text{ if n is even} \qquad\qquad (\because \cos n\pi = 1)$$

$$= \frac{4}{n\pi}, \text{ if n is odd} \qquad\qquad (\because \cos n\pi = -1)$$

$$\text{Hence, } f(x) = \frac{4}{\pi}\left[\frac{\sin x}{1} + \frac{\sin 3x}{3} + \frac{\sin 5x}{5} + \ldots\right]$$

The sum of the series when $x = \dfrac{\pi}{2} = \dfrac{1}{2}\left[f\left(\dfrac{\pi}{2} - 0\right) + f\left(\dfrac{\pi}{2} + 0\right)\right]$

$$= \frac{1}{2}\lim_{h\to 0}\left[f\left(\frac{\pi}{2} - h\right) + f\left(\frac{\pi}{2} + h\right)\right] = \frac{1}{2}\lim_{h\to 0}[1 + 1] = 1.$$

Hence, putting $x = \dfrac{1}{2}\pi$ on the right hand side of the series, we get

$$1 = \frac{4}{\pi}\left[\sin\frac{\pi}{2} + \frac{1}{3}\sin\frac{3\pi}{2} + \ldots\right] \text{ or } \frac{\pi}{4} = 1 - \frac{1}{3} + \frac{1}{5} - \frac{1}{7} + \ldots$$

Q9. **Complete parts (a) and (b) of given figure to trace even and odd extensions of these functions, respectively.**

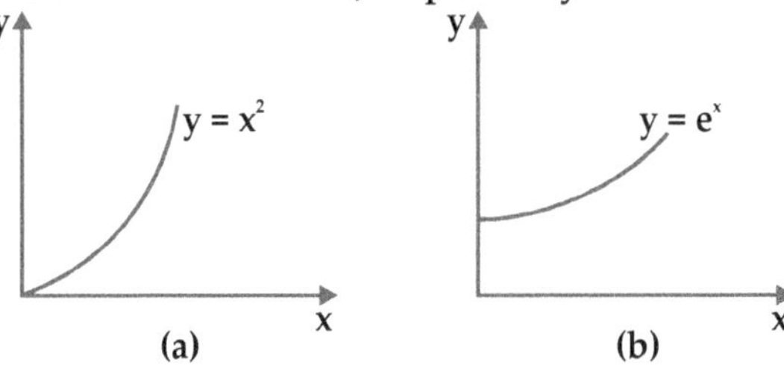

Ans. See Figs. 7.8(a) and 7.8(b).

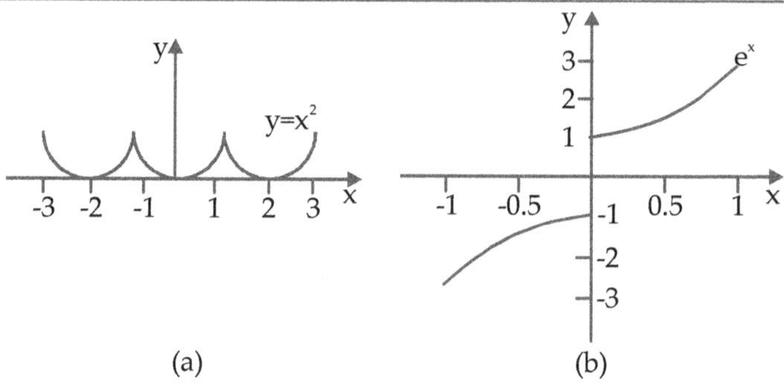

(a)　　　　　　　　　　　　　　(b)

Fig. 7.8

Q10. Is the following function even, odd or neither? $\sin x + \cos x; x\sin nx.$

[Dec-2010,Q.No.-1(d)(ii)]

Ans. Let $f(x) = \sin x + \cos x \Rightarrow f(-x) = -\sin x + \cos x = -(\sin x - \cos x)$

Hence, $f(-x) \neq f(x)$ and $f(-x) \neq -f(x)$

Hence, $f(x)$ is neither even nor odd.

Now let $g(x) = x\sin nx \Rightarrow g(-x) = (-x)\sin n(-x) \Rightarrow g(-x) = x\sin nx$

$\Rightarrow g(-x) = g(x)$

Hence, $g(x)$ is even.

Q11. Obtain the Fourier cosine series of the triangular pulse defined by

$$f(t) = \begin{cases} \dfrac{2k}{L}t & \text{when } 0 < t < \dfrac{L}{2} \\ \dfrac{2k}{L}(L-t) & \text{when } \dfrac{L}{2} < t < L \end{cases}$$

Ans. The even extension of the triangular pulse is shown in Fig. 7.9

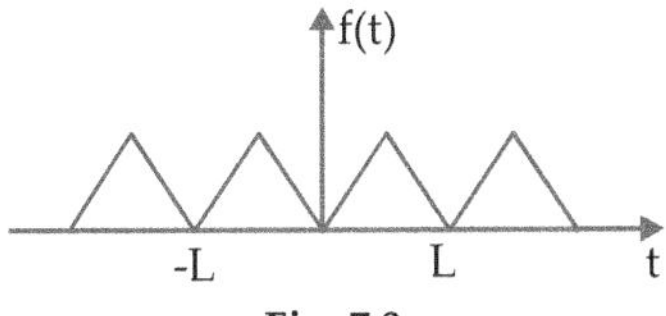

Fig. 7.9

From equations $b_n = \dfrac{2}{L}\int\limits_0^L f(x)\sin\dfrac{n\pi x}{L}\,dx$ and $a_n = \dfrac{2}{L}\int\limits_0^L f(x)\cos\dfrac{n\pi x}{L}\,dx$,

the coefficients of the Fourier cosine series representation of the given

function are $a_0 = \dfrac{1}{L}\left[\dfrac{2k}{L}\int\limits_0^{L/2} t\,dt + \dfrac{2k}{L}\int\limits_{L/2}^{L}(L-t)\,dt\right]$ $= \dfrac{1}{L}\cdot\dfrac{2k}{L}\left[\dfrac{t^2}{2}\right]_0^{L/2} + \left[Lt - \dfrac{t^2}{2}\right]_{L/2}^{L}$

$= \dfrac{2k}{L^2}\left(\dfrac{L^2}{8} + L^2 - \dfrac{L^2}{2} - \dfrac{L^2}{2} + \dfrac{L^2}{8}\right) = \dfrac{k}{2}$

$a_n = \dfrac{2}{L}\left[\dfrac{2k}{L}\int\limits_0^{L/2} t\cos\dfrac{n\pi t}{L}\,dt + \dfrac{2k}{L}\int\limits_{L/2}^{L}(L-t)\cos\dfrac{n\pi t}{L}\,dt\right]$

$= \dfrac{2}{L}\cdot\dfrac{2k}{L}\left(\left[\dfrac{Lt}{n\pi}\sin\dfrac{n\pi t}{L}\right]_0^{L/2} - \dfrac{L}{n\pi}\int\limits_0^{L/2}\sin\dfrac{n\pi t}{L}\,dt + \right.$

$\left.\left[(L-t)\dfrac{L}{n\pi}\sin\dfrac{n\pi t}{L}\right]_{L/2}^{L} + \dfrac{L}{n\pi}\int\limits_{L/2}^{L}\sin\dfrac{n\pi t}{L}\,dt\right)$

$= \dfrac{4k}{L^2}\left(\dfrac{L^2}{2n\pi}\sin\dfrac{n\pi}{2} + \dfrac{L^2}{n^2\pi^2}\left[\cos\dfrac{n\pi}{2}-1\right] - \dfrac{L^2}{2n\pi}\sin\dfrac{n\pi}{2} - \dfrac{L^2}{n^2\pi^2}\left[\cos n\pi - \cos\dfrac{n\pi}{2}\right]\right)$

$= \dfrac{4k}{n^2\pi^2}\left(2\cos\dfrac{n\pi}{2} - \cos n\pi - 1\right)$

Thus, $a_1 = 0,\, a_2 = -\dfrac{16k}{2^2\pi^2},\, a_3 = 0,\, a_4 = 0,\, a_5 = 0,$

$a_6 = -\dfrac{16k}{6^2\pi^2},\, a_7 = 0,\, a_8 = 0,\, a_9 = 0,\, a_{10} = -\dfrac{16k}{10^2\pi^2},\,......$

Thus, $a_n = 0$, when $n \neq 2,6,10,14,....$ The desired half-range expansion

of the triangular pulse is $f(t) = \dfrac{k}{2} - \dfrac{16k}{\pi^2}\left(\dfrac{1}{2^2}\cos\dfrac{2\pi t}{L} + \dfrac{1}{6^2}\cos\dfrac{6\pi t}{L} + ...\right)$

Q12. Determine the Fourier sine series for e^x on the interval $0 \leq x < 1$. How does the value of the series at $x = 0$ compare with the value of e^x at $x = 0$?

Ans. Since we have to determine the Fourier sine series of e^x on the interval $0 < x < 1$, we need an odd extension of e^x. Note that $g(0) = 0$. Then

the coefficient b_n are given by $b_n = 2\int\limits_0^1 e^x \sin n\pi x\,dx$

$$= 2\left[\frac{-e^x\cos n\pi x}{n\pi}\right]_0^1 + \frac{2}{n\pi}\int_0^1 e^x\cos n\pi x\, dx$$

$$= \frac{-2e\cos n\pi + 2}{n\pi} + \frac{2}{n\pi}\left[\frac{e^x\sin n\pi x}{n\pi}\right]_0^1 - \frac{2}{n^2\pi^2}\int_0^1 e^x\sin n\pi x\, dx$$

$$= \frac{-2e(-1)^n + 2}{n\pi} + 0 - \frac{b_n}{n^2\pi^2} \qquad\text{or}\qquad b_n\left(1+\frac{1}{n^2\pi^2}\right) = \frac{2-2e(-1)^n}{n\pi}$$

or $\qquad b_n = \dfrac{2n\pi(1-e(-1)^n)}{1+n^2\pi^2}$

Hence, the Fourier series for e^x on the interval $0 < x < 1$ is

$$2\pi\sum_{n=1}^{\infty}\frac{n[1-(-1)^n e]}{1+n^2\pi^2}\sin n\pi x$$

At $x = 0$, the value of Fourier sine series is zero. But $e^0 = 1$. Thus, the Fourier sine series for e^x does not give the value of the function e^x, at $x = 0$. However, it does give the value of the odd extension of e^x, at $x = 0$.

Q13. Find a half-range sine-series for $f(x) = x$ in $0 < x < 2$.

Ans. Here the interval is $(0, 2)$, therefore $c = 2$.

Hence, if $f(x) = \sum b_n\sin\dfrac{n\pi x}{2}$ then

$$b_n = \frac{1}{2}\int_0^2 f(x)\sin\frac{n\pi x}{2}\,dx = \int_0^2 x\sin\left(\frac{n\pi x}{2}\right)dx$$

$$= \left[x\left(-\frac{2}{n\pi}\cos\frac{n\pi x}{2}\right) + \frac{4}{n^2\pi^2}\sin\frac{n\pi x}{2}\right]_0^2 = -\frac{4}{n\pi}\cos n\pi = (-1)^{n+1}\cdot\frac{4}{n\pi}.$$

Hence, in $(0, 2)$, $\quad f(x) = x = \dfrac{4}{\pi}\left[\sin\dfrac{\pi x}{2} - \dfrac{\sin 2\pi x/2}{2} + \dfrac{\sin 3\pi x/2}{3} - ....\right].$

Q14. Obtain the Fourier series expansion of the output of the full-wave rectifier shown in given figure. The shape of the curve is the absolute value of a sine function. The maximum voltage is 100 V.

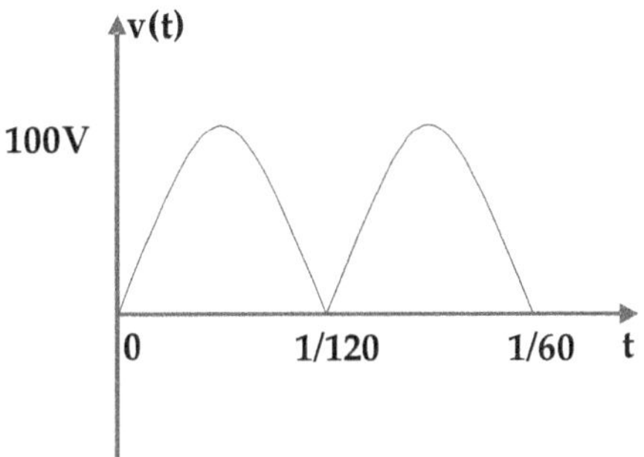

Ans. The output of a full-wave rectifier can be expressed as

$$v(t) = \begin{cases} 100 \sin \omega t & 0 < t < \pi \\ -100 \sin \omega t & -\pi < t < 0 \end{cases}$$

Since $v(t)$ is even, we can represent it by a Fourier cosine series. Here $L = \pi/\omega$. Therefore, from equation $a_0 = \dfrac{1}{L} \int_0^L f(x)dx$, $a_n = \dfrac{2}{L} \int_0^L f(x) \cos \dfrac{n\pi x}{L} dx$,

we have $a_0 = \dfrac{100\omega}{\pi} \int_0^{\pi/\omega} \sin \omega t \, dt = -\dfrac{100}{\pi}\left[\cos \omega t\right]_0^{\pi/\omega} = \dfrac{200}{\pi}$

and $a_n = \dfrac{200}{\pi} \int_0^{\pi/\omega} \sin \omega t \cos n\omega t \, dt$

After solving, we get $a_n = -\dfrac{400}{(n-1)(n+1)\pi}$, $\qquad n = 2,4,6,....$

Thus, $v(t) = \dfrac{200}{\pi} - \dfrac{400}{\pi} \sum_{m=1}^{\infty} \dfrac{\cos 2m\omega t}{4m^2 - 1}$, where we have put $n = 2m$.

We can see that the original frequency ω has been eliminated. The lowest surviving harmonic has frequency 2ω and amplitude $400/3\pi$. The amplitudes of higher harmonics (of frequencies $4\omega, 6\omega, ... 2m\omega, ...$) fall off as $1/m^2$. Thus, the full-wave rectifier does a fairly good job of approximating direct current. For excellent score, read GPH book.

Q15. Expand the function

$$f(x) = \frac{\pi}{2}, 0 < x < \frac{1}{2}$$

$$= 0, \; \frac{1}{2} < x < 1$$

in Fourier sine series. **[Dec-2010,Q.No.-2(c)]**

Ans. Given $f(x) = \dfrac{\pi}{2}$, $0 < x < \dfrac{1}{2}$

$$= 0, \quad \frac{1}{2} < x < 1$$

We need an odd extension $g(x)$ of $f(x)$ over the interval $-1 < x < 1$.

Thus, we can define

$$g(x) = \begin{cases} 0 & -1 < x < \dfrac{-1}{2} \\[2mm] -\pi/2 & \dfrac{-1}{2} < x < 0 \\[2mm] 0 & x = 0 \\[2mm] \dfrac{\pi}{2} & 0 < x < \dfrac{1}{2} \\[2mm] 0 & \dfrac{1}{2} < x < 1 \end{cases}$$

Now, $b_n = \dfrac{2}{L}\int_0^L f(x)\sin\dfrac{n\pi x}{L}dx = \dfrac{2}{1}\int_0^1 f(x)\sin n\pi x\, dx = 2\int_0^{1/2}\dfrac{\pi}{2}\sin n\pi x$

$$= \dfrac{-\pi}{n\pi}\Big[\cos n\pi x\Big]_0^{1/2} = -\dfrac{1}{n}\left(\cos\dfrac{n\pi}{2} - 1\right)$$

or $b_1 = 1, \quad b_2 = 1, \quad b_3 = \dfrac{1}{3}, \quad b_4 = 0, \dots$

Thus, the Fourier sine series for $f(x)$ is,

$$f(x) = \sin\pi x + \sin 2\pi x + \dfrac{\sin 3\pi x}{3} + \dfrac{\sin 5\pi x}{5} + \dots$$

Q16. To what values does the Fourier series representing e^x on the interval $-1 < x < 1$ converge at the points $x = \pm 1$? Do these values agree with the actual values of e^x at $x = \pm 1$?

Ans. According to the convergence theorem, the Fourier series for e^x on the interval $-1 < x < 1$ converges to $\dfrac{e^1 + e^{-1}}{2} \cong 1.5$.

At the points $x = \pm 1$. As we can see that this value does not agree with the actual values of e^x at $x = \pm 1$.

Q17. Expand $f(x) = \begin{cases} 0 & -\pi < x < 0 \\ \pi - x & 0 < x < \pi \end{cases}$ **in a Fourier series**

Verify whether the Fourier series representation of this function is valid.

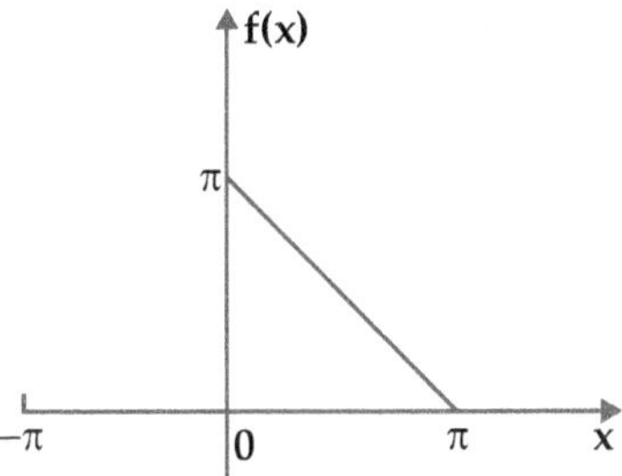

Ans. Here $L = \pi$ and the coefficients of Fourier series are

$$a_0 = \frac{1}{2\pi} \int_{-\pi}^{\pi} f(x)\,dx = \frac{1}{2\pi} \int_{0}^{\pi} (\pi - x)\,dx = \frac{1}{2\pi}\left[\pi x - \frac{x^2}{2}\right]_0^\pi = \frac{\pi}{4}$$

$$a_n = \frac{1}{\pi} \int_{-\pi}^{\pi} f(x)\cos nx\,dx = \frac{1}{\pi} \int_{0}^{\pi} (\pi - x)\cos nx\,dx$$

$$= \frac{1}{\pi}\left[(\pi - x)\frac{\sin nx}{n}\right]_0^\pi - \frac{1}{n^2\pi}\left[\cos nx\right]_0^\pi = -\frac{1}{n^2\pi}(\cos n\pi - 1) = \frac{1-(-1)^n}{n^2\pi};$$

$$b_n = \frac{1}{\pi} \int_{-\pi}^{\pi} f(x)\sin nx\,dx = \frac{1}{\pi} \int_{0}^{\pi} (\pi - x)\sin nx\,dx$$

$$= \frac{1}{\pi}\left[(\pi - x)\frac{\cos nx}{n}\right]_0^\pi + \frac{1}{\pi}\left[\frac{\sin nx}{n^2}\right]_0^\pi = \frac{1}{n}$$

Therefore, $\displaystyle f(x) = \frac{\pi}{4} + \sum_{n=1}^{\infty}\left\{\frac{1-(-1)^n}{n^2\pi}\cos nx + \frac{1}{n}\sin nx\right\}$

This series converges to the periodic extension of $f(x)$ onto the entire x-axis. At the points of discontinuity $(x = 0, \pm 2\pi, \pm 4\pi\ldots)$ the series converges to the value $\dfrac{f(0^+) + f(0^-)}{2} = \dfrac{\pi}{2}$

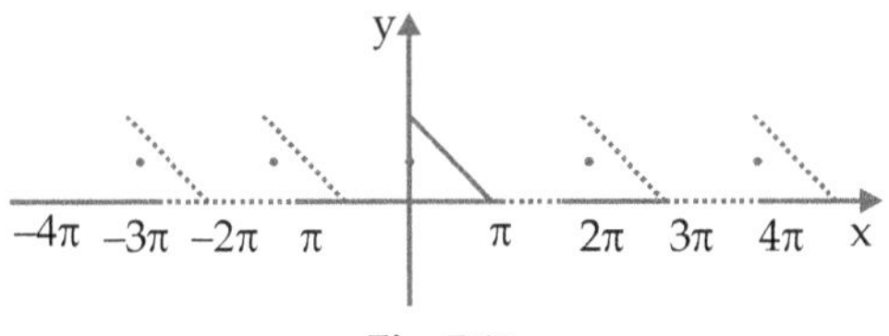

Fig. 7.10

These are shown by the solid dots in the figure.

At $n = \pm\pi, \pm 3\pi, \pm 5\pi,\ldots$ the series will converge to the value

$$\frac{f(\pi^-) + f(\pi^+)}{2} = 0$$

which is the value of the function at these points.

Q18. **Find series of sines and cosines of multiples of x, which will represent $x + x^2$ in the interval $-\pi < x < \pi$. Hence show that $\dfrac{\pi^2}{6} = 1 + \dfrac{1}{2^2} + \dfrac{1}{3^2} + ...$ Find the sum of the series when $x = \pm\pi$.**

Ans. Here, $f(x) = x + x^2$ in $(-\pi, \pi)$.

Let $f(x) = a_0 + \sum a_n \cos nx + \sum b_n \sin nx$ ...(i)

where $\quad a_0 = \displaystyle\int_{-\pi}^{\pi} f(x)\,dx = \frac{1}{2\pi}\int_{-\pi}^{\pi}(x + x^2)\,dx = \frac{1}{2\pi}\left[\frac{1}{2}x^2 + \frac{1}{3}x^3\right]_{-\pi}^{\pi} = \frac{1}{\pi}\frac{\pi^3}{3} = \frac{\pi^2}{3};$

$$a_n = \frac{1}{\pi}\int_{-\pi}^{\pi} f(x)\cos nx\,dx = \frac{1}{\pi}\int_{-\pi}^{\pi}(x + x^2)\cos nx\,dx$$

$$= \frac{1}{\pi}\left[\int_{-\pi}^{\pi} x\cos nx\,dx + \int_{-\pi}^{\pi} x^2\cos nx\,dx\right] \qquad = \frac{2}{\pi}\int_0^{\pi} x^2\cos nx\,dx,$$

$\because x\cos nx$ is odd function and $x^2\cos nx$ is even

$$= \frac{2}{\pi}\left\{(x^2)\left(\frac{\sin nx}{n}\right) - (2x)\left(-\frac{\cos nx}{n^2}\right) + (2)\left(-\frac{\sin nx}{n^3}\right)\right\}_0^{\pi}; \quad \text{on integrating by}$$

parts

$$= \frac{4}{\pi}\pi\frac{\cos n\pi}{n^2} = \frac{4\cos n\pi}{n^2} = \frac{4(-1)^n}{n^2},$$

$\because \cos n\pi = (-1)^n$

and $b_n = \dfrac{1}{\pi}\displaystyle\int_{-\pi}^{\pi}(x + x)^2\sin nx\,dx = \dfrac{2}{\pi}\int_0^{\pi} x\sin nx\,dx,$

$\because x^2\sin nx$ is odd function and $x\sin nx$ is even

$$= \frac{2}{\pi}\left\{x\left(-\frac{\cos nx}{n}\right) - (1)\left(-\frac{\sin nx}{n^2}\right)\right\}_0^{\pi} = -\frac{2}{n}\cos n\pi = \frac{2}{n}(-1)^{n+1}.$$

Hence, by (ii), $x + x^2 = \dfrac{\pi^2}{3} + \sum\dfrac{4(-1)^n}{n^2}\cos nx + \sum\dfrac{2}{n}(-1)^{n+1}\sin n\pi$

$$= \frac{\pi^2}{3} + 4\left\{-\frac{1}{1^2}\cos x + \frac{1}{2^2}\cos 2x - \frac{1}{3^2}\cos 3x + ...\right\}$$

$$+ 2\left\{\frac{\sin x}{1} - \frac{\sin 2x}{2} + \frac{\sin 3x}{3} - ......\right\} \qquad\qquad ...(2)$$

in $-\pi < x < \pi$. This is the required Fourier's series.

When $x = \pm\pi$, the sum of the series

$$= \frac{1}{2}[f(-\pi+0)+f(\pi-0)] = \frac{1}{2}\lim_{h\to 0}[f(-\pi+h)+f(\pi-h)]$$

$$= \frac{1}{2}\lim_{h\to 0}[(-\pi+h)+(-\pi+h)^2]+[(\pi-h)+(\pi-h)^2]$$

$$= \frac{1}{2}\lim_{h\to 0} 2(\pi-h)^2 = \pi^2.$$

Now putting $x = \pi$ on the right hand side of (ii) and equating the sum to π^2,

$$\pi^2 = \frac{\pi^2}{3}+4\left[-\frac{1}{1^2}\cos\pi+\frac{1}{2^2}\cos 2\pi-\frac{1}{3^2}\cos 3\pi+....\right]$$

$$+2\left[\sin\pi-\frac{\sin 2\pi}{2}+\frac{\sin 3\pi}{3}-....\right]$$

Hence, $\quad \dfrac{\pi^2}{6} = \dfrac{1}{1^2}+\dfrac{1}{2^2}+\dfrac{1}{3^2}+....$

Q19. Obtain the Fourier series expansion of the function

$\qquad f(x) = \pi - x$ **for** $0 < x < 2\pi$ $\qquad\qquad$ **[June-2011, Q.No.-2(b)]**

Ans. Given that $f(x) = \pi - x$ for $0 < x < 2\pi$

Here $L = 2\pi$ and the coefficients of Fourier series are

$$a_0 = \frac{1}{4\pi}\int_{-2\pi}^{2\pi} f(x)\,dx = \frac{1}{4\pi}\int_{0}^{2\pi}(\pi-x)\,dx = \frac{1}{4\pi}\left[\pi x-\frac{x^2}{2}\right]_0^{2\pi}$$

$$\Rightarrow a_0 = \frac{1}{4\pi}\left[\pi x-\frac{x^2}{2}\right]_0^{2\pi} = \frac{1}{4\pi}\left[\pi.2\pi-\frac{4\pi^2}{2}\right] = \frac{1}{4\pi}\left[2\pi^2-2\pi^2\right] = 0$$

Now, $\qquad\qquad a_n = \dfrac{1}{2\pi}\int_{-2\pi}^{2\pi} f(x)\cos\dfrac{n\pi x}{2\pi}\,dx$ or $a_n = \dfrac{1}{2\pi}\int_{-2\pi}^{2\pi} f(x)\cos\dfrac{nx}{2}\,dx$

$$= \frac{1}{2\pi}\int_{0}^{2\pi}(\pi-x)\cos\frac{nx}{2}\,dx$$

$$= \frac{1}{2\pi}\left[(\pi-x)\frac{2}{n}\sin\frac{nx}{2}\right]_0^{2\pi} - \frac{4}{2\pi n^2}\left[\cos\frac{nx}{2}\right]_0^{2\pi}$$

$$= \frac{1}{n\pi}\left[(\pi-2\pi)\sin\frac{n2\pi}{2}\right] - \frac{2}{\pi n^2}\left[\cos\frac{n2\pi}{2}-\cos 0\right]$$

$$= \frac{1}{n\pi}\left[(-\pi)\sin n\pi\right] - \frac{2}{n^2\pi}\left[\cos n\pi-1\right] = -\frac{2}{n^2\pi}(\cos n\pi-1) = \frac{2\left[1-(-1)^n\right]}{n^2\pi}$$

and $b_n = \dfrac{1}{2\pi}\int_{-2\pi}^{2\pi} f(x)\sin\dfrac{n\pi x}{2\pi}\,dx = \dfrac{1}{2\pi}\int_{-2\pi}^{2\pi} f(x)\sin\dfrac{nx}{2}\,dx = \dfrac{1}{2\pi}\int_{0}^{2\pi}(\pi-x)\sin\dfrac{nx}{2}\,dx$

$$= \frac{1}{2\pi}\left[(\pi-x)\cdot\frac{-2}{n}\cos\frac{nx}{2}\right]_0^{2\pi} + \frac{4}{2\pi n^2}\left[\frac{\sin nx}{2}\right]_0^{2\pi}$$

$$= \frac{1}{2\pi}\left[-\frac{2}{n}(\pi-x)\cos\frac{nx}{2}\right]_0^{2\pi} + 0$$

$$= \frac{1}{n\pi}\left[(x-\pi)\cos\frac{nx}{2}\right]_0^{2\pi} = \frac{1}{n\pi}\left[(2\pi-\pi)\cos\frac{n2\pi}{2} - (0-\pi)\cos 0\right]$$

$$= \frac{1}{n\pi}\left[\pi(-1)^n + \pi 1\right] = \frac{1}{n\pi}\left[\pi\left\{(-1)^n + 1\right\}\right] = \frac{1}{n}\left[(-1)^n + 1\right] = \frac{1+(-1)^n}{n}$$

Therefore, $f(x) = a_0 + \sum_{n=1}^{\infty} a_n \cos\frac{n\pi x}{L} + \sum_{n=1}^{\infty} b_n \sin\frac{n\pi x}{L}$

$$\Rightarrow f(x) = 0 + \sum_{n=1}^{\infty}\frac{2\left[1-(-1)^n\right]}{n^2\pi}\cos\frac{nx}{2} + \sum_{n=1}^{\infty}\frac{1+(-1)^n}{n}\sin\frac{nx}{2}$$

$$\Rightarrow f(x) = \sum_{n=1}^{\infty}\left[\frac{2\left[1-(-1)^n\right]}{n^2\pi}\cos\frac{nx}{2} + \frac{1+(-1)^n}{n}\sin\frac{nx}{2}\right]$$

Q20. Show that the series $2\left\{\sin x + \dfrac{\sin 2x}{2} + \dfrac{\sin 3x}{3} + \ldots\ldots\right\}$ **represents** $(\pi - x)$ **in the interval** $(0, 2\pi)$.

Ans. Here $f(x) = \pi - x$ in $(0, 2\pi)$.

Thus, $a_0 = \dfrac{1}{2\pi}\displaystyle\int_0^{2\pi} f(x)\, dx = \dfrac{1}{2\pi}\displaystyle\int_0^{2\pi} (\pi - x)\, dx$

$$= \frac{1}{2\pi}\left\{\pi x - \frac{1}{2}x^2\right\}_0^{2\pi} = \frac{1}{2\pi}(2\pi^2 - 2\pi^2) = 0;$$

$a_n = \dfrac{1}{\pi}\displaystyle\int_0^{2\pi} f(x)\cos nx\, dx = \dfrac{1}{\pi}\displaystyle\int_0^{2\pi}(\pi - x)\cos nx\, dx$

$$= \frac{1}{\pi}\left\{(\pi-x)\cdot\left(\frac{\sin nx}{n}\right) - (-1)\cdot\left(-\frac{\cos nx}{n^2}\right)\right\}_0^{2\pi}, \text{ on integrating by parts}$$

$$= \frac{1}{\pi}\left\{\frac{(-\pi)}{n}\sin 2n\pi - \frac{\cos 2n\pi}{n^2} + \frac{1}{n^2}\right\} = 0, \qquad \because \cos 2n\pi = 1,\ \sin 2n\pi = 0;$$

$b_n = \dfrac{1}{\pi}\displaystyle\int_0^{2\pi} f(x)\sin nx\, dx = \dfrac{1}{\pi}\displaystyle\int_0^{2\pi}(\pi - x)\sin nx\, dx$

$$= \frac{1}{\pi}\left\{(\pi-x)\left(-\frac{\cos nx}{n}\right) - (-1)\cdot\left(-\frac{\sin nx}{n^2}\right)\right\}_0^{2\pi}, \text{ on integrating by parts}$$

$$= \frac{1}{\pi}\left\{ \frac{\pi}{n}\cos 2n\pi - \frac{\sin 2n\pi}{n^2} + \frac{\pi}{n}\right\} = \frac{1}{\pi}\cdot\frac{2\pi}{n} = \frac{2}{n}.$$

Hence, the Fourier's series is given by

$$f(x) = (\pi - x) = \sum_{n=1}^{\infty} \frac{2}{n}\sin nx, \text{ as } a_0 = 0, a_n = 0$$

or $\pi - x = 2\left[\sin x + \frac{\sin 2x}{2} + \frac{\sin 3x}{3} + ...\right].$

Q21. Find the Fourier series to represent f(x), defined by

$$f(x) = 0, \text{ for } -2 < x < 0$$

$$= 1, \text{ for } 0 < x < 2.$$

Ans. Here the interval is (- 2, 2). Hence c = 2.

Therefore, let $f(x) = a_0 + \sum a_n, \cos\frac{n\pi x}{2} + \sum b_n \sin\frac{n\pi x}{2}$

where $a_0 = \frac{1}{2c}\int_{-c}^{c} f(x)\, dx = \frac{1}{4}\int_{-2}^{2} f(x)\, dx = \frac{1}{4}\left[\int_{-2}^{0} f(x)dx + \int_{0}^{2} f(x)\, dx\right] = \frac{1}{4}\left[0 + \int_{0}^{2} dx\right]$

$$= \frac{1}{2};$$

$$a_n = \frac{1}{c}\int_{-c}^{c} f(x)\cos\frac{n\pi x}{c}\, dx = \frac{1}{2}\left[\int_{-2}^{0} f(x)\cos\frac{n\pi x}{2}\, dx + \int_{0}^{2} f(x)\cos\frac{n\pi x}{2}dx\right]$$

$$= \frac{1}{2}\int_{0}^{2}\cos\frac{n\pi x}{2}\, dx \qquad \because f(x) = 0 \text{ in } -2 < x < 0 \text{ and } f(x) = 1 \text{ in } 0 < x < 2.$$

$$= \frac{1}{n\pi}[\sin n\pi - \sin 0] = 0,$$

$$b_n = \frac{1}{2}\int_{0}^{2}\sin\frac{n\pi x}{2}\, dx = \frac{1}{n\pi}[1 - \cos n\pi]$$

$$= \frac{1}{n\pi}[1 - (-1)^n] = 0, \text{ if n is even and } \frac{2}{n\pi}, \text{ if n is odd.}$$

Hence, Fourier series for f(x) in (- 2, 2) is given by

$$f(x) = \frac{1}{2} + \frac{2}{\pi}\left(\frac{\sin(\pi x/2)}{1} + \frac{\sin(3\pi x/2)}{3} + \frac{\sin(5\pi x/2)}{5} + ...\right).$$

Q22. Expand the square wave V(x) given by:

$$V(x) = 0 \quad -\pi < x < 0$$

$$= V_0 \quad 0 < x < \pi \text{ in Fourier series.} \qquad\qquad \text{[June-2012, Q.No.-2]}$$

Ans. Given that $V(x) = 0 \qquad\qquad -\pi < x < 0$

$$= V_0 \qquad 0 < x < \pi \qquad \qquad \text{...(i)}$$

Here $L = \pi$.

Therefore, from equation $a_0 = \dfrac{1}{2L} \displaystyle\int_{-L}^{L} f(x)\, dx$

We get $a_0 = \dfrac{1}{2\pi} \displaystyle\int_{-\pi}^{\pi} v(x)\, dx = \dfrac{1}{2\pi} \displaystyle\int_{-\pi}^{0} (0)\, dx + \dfrac{1}{2\pi} \displaystyle\int_{0}^{\pi} v_0\, dx$

$$= \dfrac{1}{2\pi} v_0 [x]_0^{\pi} = \dfrac{1}{2\pi} v_0 \pi = \dfrac{1}{2} v_0$$

Now, $a_n = \dfrac{1}{L} \displaystyle\int_{-L}^{L} f(x) \cos \dfrac{n\pi x}{L}\, dx \Rightarrow a_n = \dfrac{1}{\pi} \displaystyle\int_{-\pi}^{\pi} v(x) \cos nx\, dx$

$$= \dfrac{v_0}{\pi} \displaystyle\int_{0}^{\pi} \cos nx\, dx = \dfrac{v_0}{n\pi} \Big[\sin nx \Big]_0^{\pi} = 0$$

Thus, $a_n = 0$ for all n.

Now, $b_n = \dfrac{1}{L} \displaystyle\int_{-L}^{L} f(x) \sin \dfrac{n\pi x}{L}\, dx$

$$= \dfrac{1}{\pi} \displaystyle\int_{-\pi}^{\pi} v(x) \sin nx\, dx = \dfrac{1}{\pi} \displaystyle\int_{0}^{\pi} v_0 \sin nx\, dx = \dfrac{-v_0}{n\pi} \Big[\cos nx \Big]_0^{\pi} = \dfrac{-v_0}{n\pi} \Big[\cos n\pi - 1 \Big]$$

Hence, $b_n = 0$ iff $n = 0$ and $b_n = \dfrac{2v_0}{n\pi}$,   if $n = 1, 2, 3, \dots\dots$

Now, Fourier series, $V(x) = a_0 + \displaystyle\sum_{n=1}^{\infty} \left(a_n \cos \dfrac{n\pi x}{L} + b_n \sin \dfrac{n\pi x}{L} \right)$,

i.e. $V(x) = \dfrac{v_0}{2} + \dfrac{2v_0}{\pi} \left[\sin x + \dfrac{1}{2} \sin 2x + \dfrac{1}{3} \sin 3x + \dots \right]$

Q23. (a) Obtain the Fourier series expansion of the function

$$T(x,0) = \dfrac{100}{L} x, \text{ on the interval } -L < x < L.$$

Ans. The Fourier series representation of $T(x,0) = \dfrac{100x}{L}$ is given by

$$T(x,0) = a_0 + \displaystyle\sum_{n=1}^{\infty} a_n \cos \dfrac{n\pi x}{L} + \displaystyle\sum_{n=1}^{\infty} b_n \sin \dfrac{n\pi x}{L}$$

where $a_0 = \dfrac{1}{2L} \displaystyle\int_{-L}^{L} T(x,0)\, dx = \dfrac{1}{2L} \displaystyle\int_{-L}^{L} \dfrac{100x}{L} = \dfrac{100}{2L^2} \left[\dfrac{x^2}{2} \right]_{-L}^{L} = 0$,

$$a_n = \frac{1}{L} \int_{-L}^{L} T(x,0)\cos\frac{n\pi x}{L}\,dx = \frac{100}{L^2} \int_{-L}^{L} x\cos\frac{n\pi x}{2}\,dx$$

$$= \frac{100}{L^2}\left(\left[x\cdot\frac{L}{n\pi}\sin\frac{n\pi x}{L}\right]_{-L}^{L} - \frac{L}{n\pi}\int_{-L}^{L}\sin\frac{n\pi x}{L}\,dx\right) = \frac{100}{L^2}[0-0] = 0$$

and $\quad b_n = \dfrac{1}{L}\displaystyle\int_{-L}^{L} T(x,0)\sin\frac{n\pi x}{L}\,dx = \frac{100}{L^2}\int_{-L}^{L} x\sin\frac{n\pi x}{L}\,dx$

$$= \frac{100}{L^2}\left(\left[-x\frac{L}{n\pi}\cos\frac{n\pi x}{L}\right]_{-L}^{L} + \frac{L}{n\pi}\int_{-L}^{L}\cos\frac{n\pi x}{L}\,dx\right) = -\frac{100}{L^2}\cdot\frac{L}{n\pi}\,[2L\cos n\pi]+0$$

$$= -\frac{200}{n\pi}(-1)^n, \quad n = 1,2,\ldots (\because \cos n\pi = (-1)^n)$$

$$= \frac{200}{n\pi}(-1)^{n+1}$$

Thus, the Fourier series for T(x, 0) is $T(x,0) = \displaystyle\sum_{n=1}^{\infty} \frac{200}{n\pi}(-1)^{n+1}\sin\frac{n\pi x}{L}$

$$= \frac{200}{\pi}\left[\sin\frac{\pi x}{L} - \frac{1}{2}\sin\frac{2\pi x}{L} + \frac{1}{3}\sin\frac{3\pi x}{L} - \sin\frac{4\pi x}{L} + \ldots\right]$$

(b) Find the Fourier series of the periodic function

$$E(t) = \begin{cases} 0 & \text{if } -T/2 < t < 0 \\ E\sin\omega t & \text{if } 0 < t < T/2 \end{cases}' \qquad T = \frac{2\pi}{\omega}$$

which represents the output of a half-wave rectifier.

Ans. The Fourier series for E(t) is

$$E(t) = a_0 + \sum_{n=1}^{\infty} a_n\cos\frac{2\pi nt}{T} + \sum_{n=1}^{\infty} b_n\sin\frac{2\pi nt}{T} \quad (L = T/2)$$

$$= a_0 + \sum_{n=1}^{\infty} a_n\cos n\omega t + \sum_{n=1}^{\infty} b_n\sin n\omega t \quad \left(\omega = \frac{2\pi}{T}\right)$$

Here $a_0 = \dfrac{1}{T}\displaystyle\int_{-T/2}^{T/2} E(t)\,dt = \frac{E}{T}\int_0^{T/2}\sin\omega t\,dt \quad \left(E(t)=0\text{ for }\frac{-T}{2}<t<0\right)$

$$= \frac{E}{T}\left[-\frac{\cos\omega T}{\omega}\right]_0^{T/2} = \frac{E}{T\omega}\left(-\cos\frac{\omega T}{2}+\cos 0\right) = \frac{E}{2\pi}(2) = \frac{E}{\pi}$$

$$a_n = \frac{2}{T}\int_{-T/2}^{T/2} E(t)\cos n\omega t\,dt = \frac{2E}{T}\int_0^{T/2}\sin\omega t\cos n\omega t\,dt$$

$$= \frac{2E}{2T}\int_0^{T/2}[\sin(1+n)\omega t + \sin(1-n)\omega t]\,dt$$

$$\left(\because \sin x \cos y = \frac{1}{2}[\sin(x+y)+\sin(x-y)]\right).$$

We evaluate a_1, separately. For $n = 1$, the integral is zero.

$\therefore a_1 = 0.$ $\qquad\qquad$ For $n = 2,3,....$

$$a_n = \frac{E}{T}\left[-\frac{\cos(1+n)\omega t}{(1+n)\omega} - \frac{\cos(1-n)\omega t}{(1-n)\omega}\right]_0^{T/2}$$

$$= \frac{E}{\omega T}\left[-\frac{\cos(1+n)\pi}{(1+n)} - \frac{\cos(1-n)\pi}{(1-n)} + \frac{1}{1+n} + \frac{1}{1-n}\right]$$

$$= \frac{E}{2\pi}\left[\frac{-(-1)^{n+1}+1}{n+1} + \frac{-(-1)^{1-n}+1}{1-n}\right]$$

Thus, $a_n = 0$, for $n = 3,5,7,9,.....$

and $a_n = \dfrac{E}{2\pi}\left[\dfrac{2}{n+1} + \dfrac{2}{1-n}\right] = \dfrac{2E}{(n+1)(1-n)\pi}$, $\qquad n = 2,4,6,.....$

Similarly, $b_n = \dfrac{2}{T}\displaystyle\int_{-T/2}^{T/2} E(t)\sin n\omega t\, dt = \dfrac{2E}{T}\displaystyle\int_{-T/2}^{T/2}\sin \omega t \sin n\omega t\, dt$

From Eqs. $\displaystyle\int_{-L}^{L}\sin\frac{m\pi x}{L}\sin\frac{n\pi x}{L}dx = 0 \qquad (m \neq n)$

$\displaystyle\int_{-L}^{L}\sin\frac{m\pi x}{L}\sin\frac{n\pi x}{L}dx = 0 \qquad (m \neq n)$ and

$\displaystyle\int_{-L}^{L}\cos\frac{m\pi x}{L}\cos\frac{n\pi x}{L}dx = 0 \qquad (m \neq n)$ only b_1 is non-zero. Thus, we get

$b_1 = E/2,\; b_n = 0$ for $n = 2,3,4,.....$

Therefore, the Fourier series representation of $E(t)$ is

$$E(t) = \frac{E}{\pi} + \frac{E}{2}\sin\omega t - \frac{2E}{\pi}\left(\frac{1}{1\times3}\cos 2\omega t + \frac{1}{3\times5}\cos 4\omega t + ...\right)$$

Q24. Find the Fourier series to represent $f(x) = \begin{cases} \pi x & ,\quad \text{for } 0 \leq x < 1 \\ 0 & ,\quad \text{for } x = 1 \\ \pi(x-2) & ,\quad 1 < x \leq 2. \end{cases}$

Ans. Here interval is $(0,2)$ and we must convert it into $(0,2\pi)$.

Hence, $f(x) = a_0 + \sum a_n \cos n\pi x + \sum b_n \sin n\pi x$

where $\quad a_0 = \dfrac{1}{2}\displaystyle\int_0^2 f(x)\, dx = \dfrac{1}{2}\left[\displaystyle\int_0^{1-\varepsilon}\pi x\, dx + \displaystyle\int_{1+\varepsilon}^2 \pi(x-2)dx\right]$ as $\varepsilon \to 0$

$$= \frac{\pi}{2}\left[\frac{1}{2}(1-\varepsilon)^2 + \frac{1}{2}\{(2-2)^2 - (1+\varepsilon-2)^2\}\right] \text{ as } \varepsilon \to 0 = 0;$$

$$a_n = \int_0^2 f(x)\cos n\pi x\, dx = \lim_{\varepsilon \to 0}\left[\int_0^{1-\varepsilon} \pi x \cos n\pi x\, dx + \pi\int_{1+\varepsilon}^2 (x-2)\cos n\pi x\, dx\right]$$

$$= \lim_{\varepsilon \to 0} \pi\left[\left\{x\left(\frac{\sin n\pi x}{n\pi}\right) + \left(\frac{\cos n\pi x}{n^2\pi^2}\right)\right\}_0^{1-\varepsilon} + \left\{(x-2)\left(\frac{\sin n\pi x}{n\pi} + \frac{\cos n\pi x}{n^2\pi^2}\right)\right\}_{1+\varepsilon}^2\right]$$

$$= \pi\left[\frac{1}{n^2\pi^2}\{\cos n\pi - 1\} + \frac{1}{n^2\pi^2}\{\cos 2n\pi - \cos n\pi\}\right] = \frac{1}{n^2\pi}\{\cos 2n\pi - 1\} = 0;$$

$$\text{and } b_n = \int_0^2 f(x)\sin n\pi x\, dx = \lim_{\varepsilon \to 0}\left[\int_0^{1-\varepsilon} \pi x \sin n\pi x\, dx + \int_{1+\varepsilon}^2 \pi(x-2)\sin n\pi x\, dx\right]$$

$$= \lim_{\varepsilon \to 0} \pi\left[\left\{x\left(-\frac{\cos n\pi x}{n\pi}\right) + \left(\frac{\sin n\pi x}{n^2\pi^2}\right)\right\}_0^{1-\varepsilon} + \left\{(x-2)\left(-\frac{\cos n\pi x}{n\pi}\right) + \left(\frac{\sin n\pi x}{n^2\pi^2}\right)\right\}_{1+\varepsilon}^2\right]$$

$$= \pi\left[-\frac{\cos n\pi}{n\pi} + (1-2)\frac{\cos n\pi}{n\pi}\right] = \frac{-2}{n}\cos n\pi = \frac{(-1)^{n+1}2}{n}$$

$$\text{Hence, } f(x) = 2\left[\sin\pi x - \frac{\sin 2\pi x}{2} + \frac{\sin 3\pi x}{3} - \ldots\right].$$

Q25. Expand the function $f(t) = \begin{cases} 0 & -\pi \le t \le 0 \\ \sin t & 0 \le t \le \pi \end{cases}$ **in Fourier series.**

[June-2013,Q.No.-2(b)]

Ans. Given function is $f(t) = \begin{cases} 0, & -\pi \le t \le 0 \\ \sin t, & 0 \le t \le \pi \end{cases}$

$$\text{Now } f(t) = a_0 + \sum_{n=1}^{\infty}\left(a_n\cos\frac{n\pi t}{L} + b_n\sin\frac{n\pi t}{L}\right)$$

$$\Rightarrow f(t) = a_0 + \sum_{n=1}^{\infty}\left(a_n\cos\frac{n\pi t}{\pi} + b_n\sin\frac{n\pi t}{\pi}\right)$$

$$\Rightarrow f(t) = a_0 + \sum_{n=1}^{\infty}(a_n\cos nt + b_n\sin nt)$$

$$\Rightarrow f(t) = a_0 + \sum_{n=1}^{\infty}a_n\cos nt + \sum_{n=1}^{\infty}b_n\sin nt$$

$$\text{Here, } a_0 = \frac{1}{2L}\int_{-L}^{L} f(t)dt \Rightarrow a_0 = \frac{1}{2\pi}\int_{-\pi}^{\pi}\sin t\, dt = 0 \qquad [\because \sin t \text{ is odd function}]$$

$$\text{Now } a_n = \frac{1}{L}\int_{-L}^{L} f(t)\cos\frac{n\pi t}{L}dt = \frac{1}{\pi}\int_{-\pi}^{\pi}\sin t\cos nt\, dt = \frac{2}{\pi}\int_0^{\pi}\sin t\cos nt\, dt = 0$$

Similarly, $b_n = \dfrac{1}{L}\int_{-L}^{L} f(t)\sin\dfrac{n\pi t}{L}dt \Rightarrow b_n = \dfrac{1}{\pi}\int_{-\pi}^{\pi}\sin t\sin nt\,dt$

$\Rightarrow b_n = \dfrac{2}{\pi}\int_0^{\pi}\sin t\sin nt\,dt = \dfrac{2}{\pi}\int_0^{\pi}\dfrac{1}{2}\left[\cos t(1-n)-\cos t(1+n)\right]dt$

$= \dfrac{1}{\pi}\left[\dfrac{\sin(1-n)t}{1-n}-\dfrac{\sin(1+n)t}{1+n}\right]_0^{\pi}$

$\Rightarrow \quad b_n = \dfrac{1}{\pi}\left[0-0-0+0\right] \Rightarrow \quad b_n = 0$, for all n.

Therefore, the Fourier series representation of f(t) is

$f(t) = a_0 + \displaystyle\sum_{n=1}^{\infty} a_n \cos nt + \sum_{n=1}^{\infty} b_n \sin nt = 0$.

The main aim of GPH book is to provide knowledge as well as good marks in exams.

$\Diamond \ \Diamond \ \Diamond$

Applications of Fourier Series to PDEs

An Overview

In many important physical problems, there are two or more independent variables, so the corresponding mathematical models involve partial, rather than ordinary, differential equations.

In many cases, we ultimately need to deal with a series of sines and/ or cosines, so the chapter is devoted to a discussion of such series, which are known as Fourier series. With the necessary mathematical background in place, we then illustrate the use of separation of variables in a variety of problems arising from heat conduction, wave equation, and Laplace's equation.

Diffusion Equation: The diffusion equation is a partial differential equation which describes density fluctuations in a material undergoing diffusion.

In its most general form, the diffusion equation is expressed as

$$\nabla^2 u + G(x,y,z,t) = \frac{1}{k}\frac{\partial u}{\partial t} \qquad \qquad \text{...(i a)}$$

where $\nabla^2 \equiv \dfrac{\partial^2}{\partial x^2} + \dfrac{\partial^2}{\partial y^2} + \dfrac{\partial^2}{\partial z^2}$ is the Laplacian and G is an arbitrary function

of x, y, z and t. The function u(x, y, z, t) could represent temperature in a body so that Eq. (i a) models heat flow in that body. If I is the current in the wire and R its resistance, an additional amount of heat $\left(\equiv I^2 R\,\Delta x\right)$ will be accumulated in the portion of the wire between x and $x + \Delta x$. Thus, we

have $\dfrac{\partial^2 T}{\partial x^2} = \dfrac{1}{k}\dfrac{\partial T}{\partial t} - \dfrac{I^2 R}{KA}$ \qquad \qquad ...(i b)

where k is the thermal diffusivity and K, the thermal conductivity of the wire.

When Eq. (i a) is used to model the diffusion of dissolved substances in a solution, u(x, y, z, t) represents the concentration of the liquid, for example, the PDE

$$\nabla^2 u = \frac{1}{k}\frac{\partial u}{\partial t} + \gamma^2 u \qquad \qquad \text{...(i c)}$$

can be used to model the loss (diffusion) of moisture from a porous object through its surface. Here γ is constant and u represents the moisture concentration.

Heat conduction: Heat conduction is the flow of internal energy from a region of higher temperature to one of lower temperature by the interaction of the adjacent particles (atoms, molecules, ions, electrons, etc.) in the intervening space.

Here, we consider an example of heat flow, where the Fourier series can be applied. This is a slightly different application.

Consider the flow of heat in a uniform bar of length L, insulated along its length. As we know, the temperature of the bar is modelled by the diffusion equation

$$\frac{\partial T(x,t)}{\partial t} = k\frac{\partial^2 T(x,t)}{\partial x^2}, \left(0<x<L, t>0\right) \qquad \qquad \textit{...(ii a)}$$

One end of the block is immersed in a block of ice, maintained at $0^\circ C$, while the other end is insulated (Fig. 8. 1 a). This gives rise to the boundary conditions

$$T(0,t)=0 \text{ and } \frac{\partial T(L,t)}{\partial x}=0, t\geq 0 \qquad \dots(ii\ b)$$

If the initial temperature distribution is given by

$$T(x,0)=\frac{x}{2}(2L-x) \qquad (0<x<L) \qquad \dots(ii\ c)$$

(see Fig. 8. 1 b), then solve the heat equation (ii a). (Note that the initial condition is physically consistent with the boundary conditions at x = 0 and x = L).

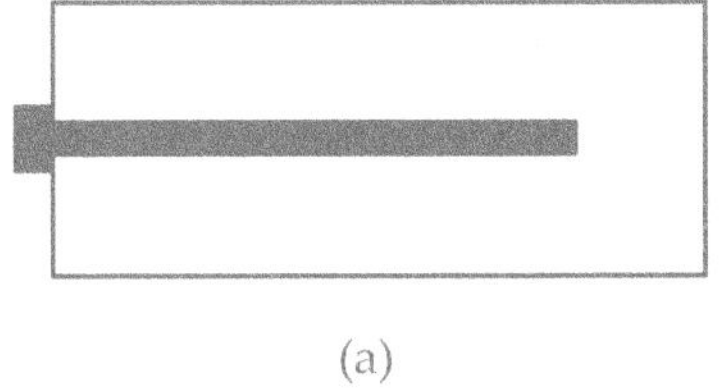

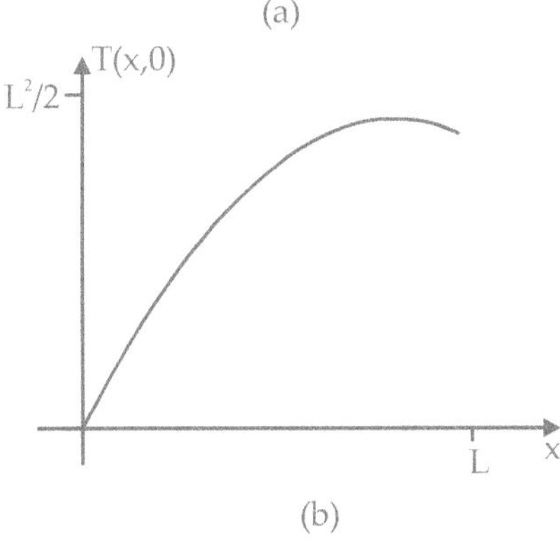

Fig. 8.1: (a) An insulated bar with its left end immersed in ice, (b) The initial temperature distribution of the bar

Using the method of separation of variables, we write T(x, t) as a product of two terms: T(x, t) = X(x) Y(t). Taking $-\lambda^2$ as the separation constant, we get

$$\frac{X''}{X}=\frac{Y'}{kY}=-\lambda^2 \qquad (1)$$

or $\qquad X''+\lambda^2 X=0 \qquad (2)$

and $\qquad Y'+k\lambda^2 Y=0 \qquad (3)$

The solutions of (ii) and (iii) for X(x) and Y(t) are well known

$$X(x)=C_1 \cos\lambda x+C_2 \sin\lambda x \qquad (4)$$

and $\qquad Y(t)=C_3 e^{-k\lambda^2 t} \qquad (5)$

From the boundary conditions for T(x, t) we have

$$T(0,t)=X(0)Y(t)=0$$

and $\quad \dfrac{\partial T}{\partial x}(L,t)=\left[\dfrac{d(L)}{dx}\right]Y(t)=0$

Since $Y(t)\neq 0, X$ must satisfy the conditions

$X(0)=X'(L)=0$

Application of the first of this condition gives us $C_1=0$.

Thus, $X(x)=C_2\sin\lambda x$

The second boundary condition gives us $X'(L)=C_2\cos\lambda'L=0$

For a non-trivial solution, for which $C_2\neq 0$, we have $\cos\lambda L=0$

or $\lambda L=\left(n+\dfrac{1}{2}\right)\pi,\qquad n=0,1,2,....$

We call these values of λ as λ_n. The solutions can thus be written as

$$X_n(x)=C_{2n}\sin\left[\dfrac{(2n+1)\pi}{2L}x\right],\qquad n=0,1,2,3,....$$

From (v), we have $Y_n(t)=C_{3n}\exp\left[-\left(\dfrac{(2n+1)\pi}{2L}\right)^2 kt\right]$

Thus

$$T_n(x,t)=X_n(x)Y_n(t)=b_n\exp\left[-\left(\dfrac{(2n+1)\pi}{2L}\right)^2 kt\right]\sin\left[\dfrac{(2n+1)\pi x}{2L}\right],\qquad n=0,1,2,3,....$$

where we have put $b_n=C_{2n}C_{3n}$.

From the principle of superposition, the most general solution is

$$T(x,t)=\sum_{n=0}^{\infty}b_n\exp\left(-\left[\dfrac{(2n+1)\pi}{2L}\right]^2 kt\right)\sin\dfrac{(2n+1)\pi x}{2L}\qquad\text{(iii)}$$

Applying the initial condition (2 c) we have

$$T(x,0)=\sum_{n=0}^{\infty}b_n\sin\left[\dfrac{(2n+1)\pi x}{2L}\right]=f(x),\qquad 0<x<L\qquad\text{(iv a)}$$

where $\quad f(x)=\dfrac{x}{2}(2L-x).$

We can determine b_n in Eq. (iv a) using the half-range expansion of $f(x)$. Since $f(x)$ is defined on $0<x<L,$ and $T(x,0)$ is the sum of a sine series,

we can take $g(x)$ to be the odd extension of $f(x)$. Multiplying the LHS of Eq. (iv a) by $\sin\left[\dfrac{(2m+1)\pi x}{2L}\right]$ and integrating from $-L$ to L, we have

$$\sum_{n=0}^{\infty} b_n \int_{-L}^{L} \sin\left[\frac{(2m+1)\pi x}{2L}\right]\sin\left[\frac{(2n+1)\pi x}{2L}\right]dx = \int_{-L}^{L} g(x)\sin\left[\frac{(2m+1)\pi x}{2L}\right]dx$$

then, $b_n = \dfrac{2}{L}\int_{0}^{L} f(x)\sin\left[\dfrac{(2n+1)\pi x}{2L}\right]dx = \dfrac{2}{L}\int_{0}^{L}\dfrac{x}{2}(2L-x)\sin\left[\dfrac{(2n+1)\pi x}{2L}\right]dx$

We can integrate by parts twice and show that $b_n = \dfrac{16L^2}{(2n+1)^3\pi^3}$

Hence, the solution is given by

$$T(x,t) = \frac{16L^2}{\pi^3}\sum_{n=0}^{\infty}\frac{1}{(2n+1)^3}\exp\left(-\left[\frac{(2n+1)\pi}{2L}\right]^2 kt\right)\sin\left[\frac{(2n+1)\pi x}{2L}\right]$$

Diffusion of Particles: A common phenomenon observed from the movement of particles is diffusion. Diffusion of particles plays an important role in many industrial applications. The removal of pollutants from plant discharge streams, the stripping of gases from waste water, acid concentration, salt production and sugar solution concentration through continuous evaporation, drying of industrial products, such as concrete slabs, wood, etc. are some examples of diffusion of particles.

Here we will apply the diffusion equation, to a typical example of drying of a porous material.

A porous rod containing moisture with one of its ends (for which $x = 0$) sealed is left to be dried. The other end of the rod is in contact with a dry medium, and it loses moisture through its surface to dry air. The concentration of moisture, $u(x, t)$, satisfies the following boundary value problem,

$$\frac{\partial^2 u}{\partial x^2} = \frac{1}{k}\frac{\partial u}{\partial t} + \gamma^2 u, \qquad 0 < x < L, \quad t > 0 \tag{v a}$$

$$\frac{\partial u}{\partial x}(0,t) = 0, \quad u(L,t) = 0, \qquad t > 0 \tag{v b}$$

$$u(x,0) = u_0, \qquad 0 < x < L \tag{v c}$$

Here, we need to find $u(x,t)$ and determine the concentration at $x=0$, i.e. $u(0,t)$ explicitly.

Using the method of separation of variables, we seek a solution of the form $u(x,t) = X(x)T(t)$. The PDE becomes

$$X''(x)T(t)=\frac{1}{k}X(x)T'(t)+\gamma^2 X(x)T(t)$$

Dividing by $X(x)T(t)$, we get $\dfrac{X''(x)}{X(x)}=\dfrac{T'(t)+k\gamma^2 T(t)}{kT(t)}=-\lambda^2$

Thus, we get two ODEs

$$X''(x)+\lambda^2 X(x)=0, \qquad 0<x<L \tag{1}$$

$$T'(t)+k\left(\gamma^2+\lambda^2\right)T=0, \qquad t>0 \tag{2}$$

The solution of (1) is $X(x)=C_1 \cos \lambda x+C_2 \sin \lambda x$

Applying the boundary conditions, we have

$$X'(0)=0, \qquad X(L)=0$$

$$X'(0)=\lambda C_2 =0, \text{i.e.,} C_2 =0$$

and $X(L)=C_1 \cos \lambda L=0$

Since $C_1 \neq 0$, this gives $\cos \lambda L=0$

or $\lambda_n L=\dfrac{(2n+1)\pi}{2}, \qquad n=0,1,2,...$

or $\lambda_n =\dfrac{(2n+1)\pi}{2L}, \qquad n=0,1,2,...$

Thus, $X_n(x)=C_{1n} \cos \lambda_n x$, where $\lambda_n =\dfrac{(2n+1)\pi}{2L}, \qquad n=0,1,2,...$

The solution of (ii) is

$$T_n(t)=C_{3n} \exp\left[-k\left(\gamma^2+\lambda_n^2\right)t\right]=C_{3n}e^{-\gamma^2 kt}\,e^{-\lambda_n^2 kt}$$

Therefore, the general solution of Eq. (5 a) is

$$u(x,t)=e^{-\gamma^2 kt}\sum_{n=0}^{\infty}a_n \cos \lambda_n x\,e^{-\lambda_n^2 kt}$$

where we have put $a_n =C_{1n}C_{3n}$. To determine these unknown constants, we note form the initial condition that $\displaystyle\sum_{n=0}^{\infty}a_n \cos \lambda_n x=u_0, \qquad 0<x<L$

Then, the coefficients a_n, $\quad a_n =\dfrac{2}{L}\displaystyle\int_0^L u_0 \cos \lambda_n x\,dx$

$$=\frac{2u_0}{L}\left(\frac{\sin \lambda_n L}{\lambda_n}\right)=\frac{4u_0 \sin \lambda_n L}{(2n+1)\pi}, \qquad n=0,1,2,....$$

Thus,

$$u(x,t)=\frac{4u_0}{\pi}e^{-\gamma^2 kt}\sum_{n=0}^{\infty}\frac{1}{(2n+1)}\sin\left[(2n+1)\frac{\pi}{2}\right]\cos\left[\frac{(2n+1)\pi x}{2L}\right]e^{-(2n+1)^2\pi^2 kt/4L^2}$$

We can find the value of $u(0,t)$ by putting $x=0$ in this solution

$$u(0,t)=\frac{4u_0}{\pi}e^{-\gamma^2 kt}\sum_{n=0}^{\infty}\frac{\sin\left[(2n+1)\frac{\pi}{2}\right]}{(2n+1)}e^{-(2n+1)^2\pi^2 kt/4L^2}$$

$$=\frac{4u_0}{\pi}e^{-\gamma^2 kt}\left[e^{-\tau}-\frac{e^{-9\tau}}{3}+\frac{e^{-25\tau}}{5}-...+...\right]$$

where $\tau=\pi^2 kt/4L^2$.

The Wave Equation: The wave equation is an important second-order linear partial differential equation for the description of waves – as they occur in physics – such as sound waves, light waves and water waves. It arises in fields like acoustics, electromagnetics, and fluid dynamics. Historically, the problem of a vibrating string such as that of a musical instrument was studied by Jean le Rond d'Alembert, Leonhard Euler, Daniel Bernoulli, and Joseph-Louis Lagrange.

Wave equations are examples of hyperbolic partial differential equations, but there are many variations. In its simplest form, the wave equation concerns a time variable t, one or more spatial variables x_1, x_2, …, x_n, and a scalar function u = u (x_1, x_2, …, x_n; t), whose values could model the displacement of a wave.

The wave equation for u is $\dfrac{\partial^2 u}{\partial x^2}=\dfrac{1}{v^2}\dfrac{\partial^2 u}{\partial t^2}$ $0<x<L,$ $t>0$

with given initial and boundary conditions. Let us solve this equation by applying Fourier series to two specific categories of physical problems related to (i) vibrating strings, and (ii) torsional vibrations.

(i) Vibrating Strings: A vibration in a string is a wave. Usually a vibrating string produces a sound whose frequency in most cases is constant. Therefore, since frequency characterises the pitch, the sound produced is a constant note. Vibrating strings are the basis of any string instrument like guitar, cello, or piano. When a sitarist plucks the sitar string, several other tones called overtones or harmonics, are generated along with the fundamental frequency. The richness of musical sound is related to the number of harmonics that can be detected by the human ear. The larger the amplitude of each harmonic, the more likely it is to be detected. The

amplitude of each harmonic depends, in turn, on where exactly the string is plucked. Therefore, if we know the point at which a sitar string is plucked, we can get a fair idea of the richness of the sound produced. To mathematically model this physical situation, we have to determine a unique solution of Eq.

$$\frac{\partial^2 u}{\partial x^2} = \frac{1}{v^2}\frac{\partial^2 u}{\partial t^2} \qquad 0<x<L, \quad t>0$$

for the "plucked string" problem which we consider in the following example.

A string is plucked at its mid-point and then released from rest from this position (Fig. 8.2). The resulting vibrations are modelled by equation $\dfrac{\partial^2 u}{\partial x^2} = \dfrac{1}{v^2}\dfrac{\partial^2 u}{\partial t^2}, 0<x<L, t>0$ *along with the following boundary and initial conditions.*

$$u(0,t)=0, \quad u(L,t)=0$$

$$u(x,0)=\begin{cases} \dfrac{2hx}{L,} & 0<x<\dfrac{L}{2} \\[2mm] 2h\left(1-\dfrac{x}{L}\right) & \dfrac{L}{2}\le x<L \end{cases}$$

$$\left.\frac{\partial u}{\partial t}\right|_{t=0}=0$$

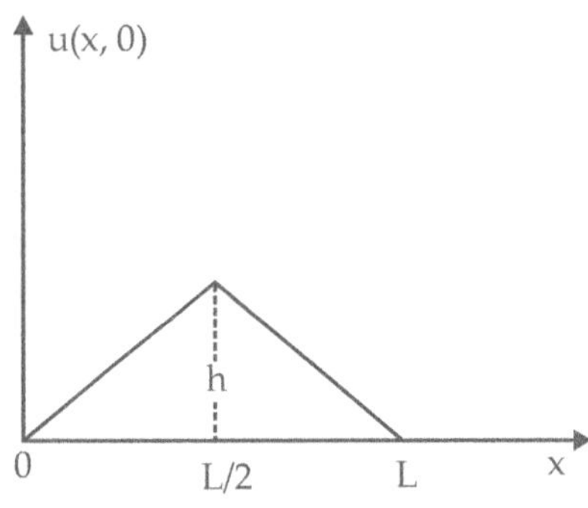

Fig. 8.2

where h is a positive constant which is small compared to L.

These conditions correspond to an initial triangular deflection and zero initial velocity. The general solution of the wave equation for given boundary conditions is

$$u(x,t) = \sum_{n=1}^{\infty}\left(a_n\cos\frac{n\pi vt}{L} + b_n\sin\frac{n\pi vt}{L}\right)\sin\frac{n\pi x}{L} \qquad \ldots(1)$$

Let us now apply the initial conditions to (1):

$$u(x,0)=\sum_{n=1}^{\infty}a_n\sin\frac{n\pi x}{L}=\begin{cases}\dfrac{2hx}{L}, & 0<x<\dfrac{L}{2}\\[2mm] 2h\left(1-\dfrac{x}{L}\right), & \dfrac{L}{2}\le x<L\end{cases}\qquad\ldots(2)$$

$$\left.\frac{\partial u}{\partial t}\right|_{t=0}=\left[\sum_{n=1}^{\infty}\left(-a_n\sin\frac{n\pi v}{L}\sin\frac{n\pi vt}{L}+b_n\frac{n\pi v}{L}\cos\frac{n\pi vt}{L}\right)\sin\frac{n\pi x}{L}\right]_{t=0}$$

$$=\sum_{n=1}^{\infty}b_n\frac{n\pi v}{L}\sin\frac{n\pi x}{L}=0\qquad\ldots(3)$$

Eq. (iii) will be satisfied only if $b_n=0$ for all n. Therefore, now we have to determine a_n, i.e. we have to expand u(x, 0) in a Fourier sine series. In effect, we have to obtain the odd periodic extension of u(x, 0) and hence its half-range expansion in a Fourier sine series.

Here, Half-range expansion of u(x, 0) in a Fourier sine series gives

$$a_n=\frac{2}{L}\int_0^L u(x,0)\sin\frac{n\pi x}{L}dx$$

$$=\frac{2}{L}\int_0^{L/2}\frac{2hx}{L}\sin\frac{n\pi x}{L}dx+\frac{2}{L}\int_{L/2}^{L}2h\left(1-\frac{x}{L}\right)\sin\frac{n\pi x}{L}dx$$

$$=\frac{4h}{L^2}\left(\left[-\frac{xL}{n\pi}\cos\frac{n\pi x}{L}\right]_0^{L/2}+\frac{L^2}{n^2\pi^2}\left[\sin\frac{n\pi x}{L}\right]_0^{L/2}\right)$$

$$-\frac{4h}{L}\frac{L}{n\pi}\left[\cos\frac{n\pi x}{L}\right]_{L/2}^{L}-\frac{4h}{L^2}\left(\left[-\frac{xL}{n\pi}\cos\frac{n\pi x}{L}\right]_{L/2}^{L}+\frac{L^2}{n^2\pi^2}\left[\sin\frac{n\pi x}{L}\right]_{L/2}^{L}\right)$$

$$=-\frac{4h}{L^2}\frac{L^2}{2n\pi}\cos\frac{n\pi}{2}+\frac{4h}{L^2}\frac{L^2}{n^2\pi^2}\sin\frac{n\pi}{2}-\frac{4h}{n\pi}\left(\cos n\pi-\cos\frac{n\pi}{2}\right)$$

$$+\frac{4h}{L^2}\left(\frac{L^2}{n\pi}\cos n\pi-\frac{L^2}{2n\pi}\cos\frac{n\pi}{2}\right)-\frac{4h}{n^2\pi^2}\left(\sin n\pi-\sin\frac{n\pi}{2}\right)=\frac{8h}{n^2\pi^2}\sin\frac{n\pi}{2}\text{ Thus,}$$

the solution of the 'plucked string' problem is

$$u(x,t)=\frac{8h}{\pi^2}\sum_{n=1}^{\infty}\frac{1}{n^2}\sin\frac{n\pi}{2}\cos\frac{n\pi vt}{L}\sin\frac{n\pi x}{L}$$

$$=\frac{8h}{\pi^2}\left[\frac{1}{1^2}\sin\frac{\pi x}{L}\cos\frac{\pi vt}{L}-\frac{1}{3^2}\sin\frac{3\pi x}{L}\cos\frac{3\pi vt}{L}+\ldots\right]$$

Torsional Vibrations: Another interesting application of the wave equation is in torsional vibrations. Such vibrations can result from unbalanced torques on shafts in a wide variety of machinery in cars, aircraft, turbines, railway engines, etc.

Consider a uniform, undamped torsionally vibrating shaft of finite length, subject to given initial conditions of angular displacement and angular velocity (Fig. 8.3). This means that we have to find solutions of the equation

$$\frac{\partial^2 \theta}{\partial x^2} = \frac{1}{v^2}\frac{\partial^2 \theta}{\partial t^2} \qquad \text{...(vi)}$$

where θ is the angle of twist of the shaft and $v^2 = E_s/\rho$; Here E_s is the modulus of elasticity in shear, and ρ, the mass per unit volume of the shaft. Here we use the method of separation of variables to express $\theta(x,t)$ as

$$\theta(x,t) = X(x)T(t)$$

In the case of a vibrating string, we reduce Eq. (6) to a set of two ODEs:

$$T'' = \frac{\lambda^2}{v^2}T, \qquad X'' = -\lambda^2 X$$

where $\left(-\lambda^2\right)$ is the separation constant. The solutions of these ODEs are

$$T = A\cos\lambda vt + B\sin\lambda vt \text{ and } X = C\cos\lambda x + D\sin\lambda x$$

Thus, the solution is

$$\theta(x,t) = X(x)T(t) = \left(C\cos\lambda x + D\sin\lambda x\right)\left(A\cos\lambda vt + B\sin\lambda vt\right) \quad \text{...(i)}$$

We can see that the solution is periodic, repeating itself for every increase in time t by $\frac{2\pi}{\lambda v}$. In other words, $\theta(x,t)$ represents a torsional motion of period $\frac{2\pi}{\lambda v}$ or frequency $\lambda v/2\pi$. It remains now to find the values of λ, A, B, C and D. The values of λ are determined by the given boundary conditions which define how the shaft is constrained at its ends. There are three cases, which occur most often in physical systems:

(I)   Both ends of the shaft are fixed so that no twisting can take place (Fig. 8.3 a)

(II)   Both ends of the shaft are free to twist (Fig. 8.3 b)

(III)   One end of the shaft is fixed, while the other is free to twist (Fig. 8.3 c).

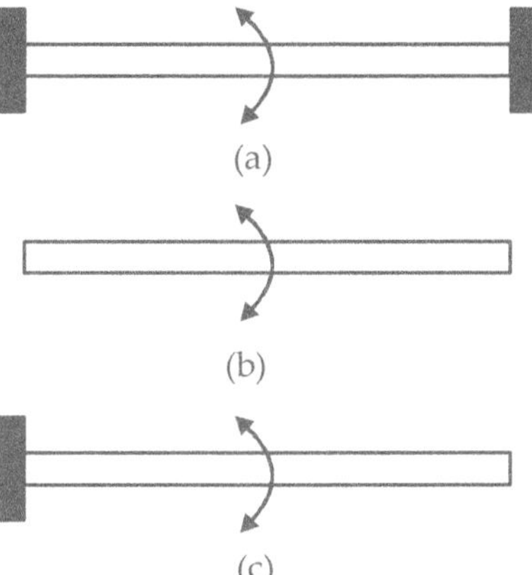

Fig. 8.3: A torsionally vibrating shaft with (a) both ends fixed (b) both ends free (c) one end fixed and one end free

Case I

The boundary conditions in this case are

$$\theta(0,t)=\theta(L,t)=0, \qquad t>0$$

Applying these conditions, we get the general solution which is the familiar result obtained for the vibrating string

$$\theta(x,t)=\sum_{n=1}^{\infty}\left(a_n\cos\frac{n\pi vt}{L}+b_n\sin\frac{n\pi vt}{L}\right)\sin\frac{n\pi x}{L}$$

This solution has to satisfy the given initial conditions on angular displacement and angular velocity. If we set $t=0$ in the equation for $\theta(x,t)$ and its derivative, we get

$$\theta(x,0)\equiv f(x)=\sum_{n=1}^{\infty}a_n\sin\frac{n\pi x}{L}$$

and

$$\left.\frac{\partial\theta}{\partial t}\right|_{t=0}\equiv g(x)=\sum_{n=1}^{\infty}\left(\frac{n\pi v}{L}b_n\right)\sin\frac{n\pi x}{L}$$

where $f(x)$ and $g(x)$ are some functions of x, representing the initial angular displacement and angular velocity of the shaft. We can then use the half-range sine expansions of $f(x)$ and $g(x)$. This gives

$$a_n=\frac{2}{L}\int_0^L f(x)\sin\frac{n\pi x}{L}dx$$

and

$$b_n=\frac{L}{n\pi v}\frac{2}{L}\int_0^L g(x)\sin\frac{n\pi x}{L}dx=\frac{2}{n\pi v}\int_0^L g(x)\sin\frac{n\pi x}{L}dx$$

Thus, a uniform shaft with both ends restrained against turning vibrates torsionally at any one of the infinite number of natural frequencies

$$f_n = \frac{nv}{2L} \text{ cycles per unit time,} \qquad\qquad n=1,2,3,....$$

Case II

When both ends of the shaft are free, no torque acts through the end section $\left(\text{i.e., at } x=0 \text{ and at } x=L\right)$ since there is no shaft material beyond these points. Thus, the torque transmitted through these ends is zero, i.e.

$$\tau = E_s I \frac{\partial \theta}{\partial x}\bigg|_{end\,points} = 0$$

where I is the moment of inertia of the rod, and E_s is the shear modulus of elasticity. Both E_s and I are non-zero. Thus, for a free-end, the boundary

conditions are $\dfrac{\partial \theta}{\partial x}=0 \qquad$ at $x=0$ and at $x=L$

The solution (i) for the PDE for a vibrating shaft is

$$\theta(x,t)=X(x)T(t)=\left(C\cos\lambda x+D\sin\lambda x\right)$$

$$\left(A\cos\lambda vt+B\sin\lambda vt\right)$$

The boundary conditions for a shaft with both ends free,

$$\frac{\partial \theta}{\partial x}=0 \qquad \text{at } x=0 \text{ and at } x=L$$

imply that for all $t>0$

$$\frac{\partial X}{\partial x}=0 \qquad \text{at } x=0 \text{ and at } x=L$$

This gives $D=0 \quad$ and $\quad C\sin\lambda L=0$

where, $\lambda_n = \dfrac{n\pi}{L}, \qquad n=1,2,....$

Thus, the general solution for $\theta(x,t)$ is

$$\theta(x,t)=\sum_{n=1}^{\infty}\left(a_n \cos\lambda_n vt+b_n \sin\lambda_n vt\right)\cos\lambda_n x$$

where $a_n = A_n C_n$ and $b_n \equiv B_n C_n$.

At $t=0$, $\theta(x,0)$ is proportional to $\left(2x-L\right)/2$.

$$\therefore \ \theta(x,0)=\sum_{n=1}^{\infty}a_n \cos\lambda_n x=k\frac{\left(2x-L\right)}{2}, \qquad 0<x<L$$

Using the half-range expansion technique, we get

$$a_n = \frac{2k}{L}\int_0^L \left(x - \frac{L}{2}\right)\cos\frac{n\pi x}{L}\,dx = \frac{2k}{L}\int_0^L x\cos\frac{n\pi x}{L}\,dx - k\int_0^L \cos\frac{n\pi x}{L}\,dx$$

$$= \frac{2k}{L}\left(\left[\frac{L}{n\pi}x\sin\frac{n\pi x}{L}\right]_0^L + \frac{L^2}{n^2\pi^2}\left[\cos\frac{n\pi x}{L}\right]_0^L\right) - \frac{Lk}{n\pi}\left[\sin\frac{n\pi x}{L}\right]_0^L$$

$$= \frac{2k}{L}\frac{L^2}{n^2\pi^2}\left(\cos n\pi - 1\right) = \frac{2Lk}{n^2\pi^2}\left(\cos n\pi - 1\right)$$

Since the shaft starts vibrating from rest, its initial velocity is zero giving the condition $\dfrac{\partial\theta}{\partial t}(x;0) = 0$ or $\displaystyle\sum_{n=1}^{\infty} b_n \lambda_n v\cos\lambda_n x = 0$

This will be satisfied only if $b_n = 0$ for all n. Thus, the solution for the given BVP is $\theta(x,t) = \dfrac{2Lk}{\pi^2}\displaystyle\sum_{n=1}^{\infty}\frac{1}{n^2}\left(\cos n\pi - 1\right)\cos\frac{n\pi vt}{L}$

Case III

A typical example of a shaft fixed at one end and free at the other is the drill pipe used in oil wells. A drill collar (C) containing the cutting bit (B) is attached to the lower end of the pipe (Fig. 8.4). The boundary conditions for such a shaft are $\theta(0,t) = 0$ and $\left.\dfrac{\partial\theta}{\partial x}\right|_{L,t} = 0$, $\qquad t > 0$

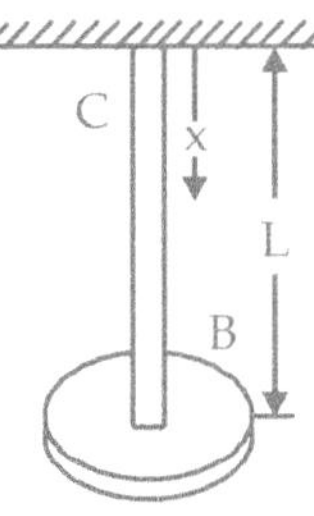

Fig. 8.4

When we impose these conditions on Eq. (i), we get

$C = 0, \cos\lambda L = 0$, which gives

$$\lambda_n L = (2n-1)\frac{\pi}{2}, \qquad n = 1,2\ldots$$

and $\qquad \lambda_n = \dfrac{(2n-1)\pi}{2L}, \qquad n = 1,2\ldots$

The general solution is, therefore,

$$\theta(x,t)=\sum_{n=1}^{\infty}(\sin\lambda_n x)(A_n\cos\lambda_n vt+B_n\sin\lambda_n vt)$$

Now suppose we have the initial conditions that

$$\theta(x,0)=f(x)\quad\text{and}\quad\left.\frac{\partial\theta}{\partial t}\right|_{x,0}=g(x)$$

These initial conditions yield

$$f(x)=\sum_{n=1}^{\infty}A_n\sin\left[\frac{(2n-1)\pi x}{2L}\right]$$

and

$$g(x)=\sum_{n=1}^{\infty}\left[\frac{(2n-1)\pi v}{2L}B_n\right]\sin\left[\frac{(2n-1)\pi x}{2L}\right]$$

Here, the half-range sine expansions of $f(x)$ and $g(x)$ yield

$$A_n=\frac{2}{L}\int_0^L f(x)\sin\left[\frac{(2n-1)\pi x}{2L}\right]dx$$

and $B_n=\dfrac{4}{(2n-1)\pi v}\displaystyle\int_0^L g(x)\sin\left[\frac{(2n-1)\pi x}{2L}\right]dx$

These coefficients can be obtained for any function $f(x)$ and $g(x)$ integrable on the interval $0<x<L$.

Laplace's Equation: A Laplace's equation is a second-order partial differential equation named after Pierre-Simon Laplace who first studied its properties. This is often written as: $\Delta\phi=0$ or $\nabla^2\phi=0$ where $\Delta=\nabla^2$ is the Laplace operator and ϕ is a scalar function.

To illustrate the applications of Fourier series, we will consider steady-state heat flow and the potential problems.

Steady-state Heat Flow

We consider first the following example:

A thin rectangular metal plate is sandwiched between sheets of insulation (Fig. 8.5 a). Since the plate is very thin and insulated at two of its surfaces, one may assume that the temperature does not vary in the z-direction. In the steady state, the temperature of the plate obeys the two-dimensional Laplace equation:

$$\frac{\partial^2 T(x,y)}{\partial x^2}+\frac{\partial^2 T(x,y)}{\partial y^2}=0,\quad 0<x<L,\quad 0<y<B \qquad ...(vii)$$

where L is the length and B is the width of the plate.

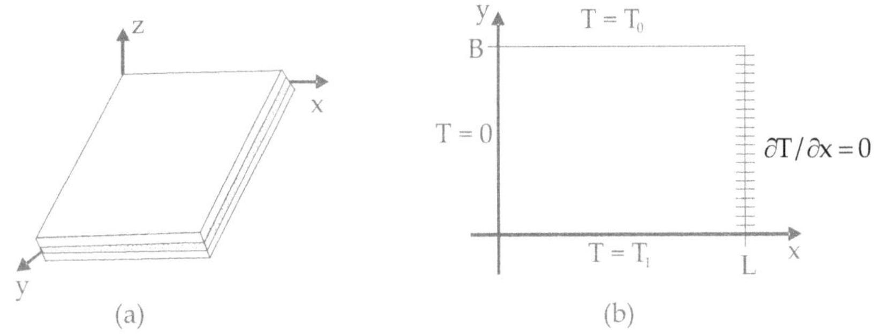

Fig. 8.5: (a) A thin plate between sheets of insulation (b) the boundary conditions for T(x, y)

Suppose that the temperature of the plate is held at T_0 at its top edge, T_1 at its bottom edge and $0°C$ on the left edge. The plate is insulated on the right edge, so that no heat flows in that direction, and the partial derivative of T in the x – direction is zero. We can write down these boundary conditions mathematically. These are,

(i)　　　$T(0,y)=0$,　　$\dfrac{\partial T(L,y)}{\partial x}=0$,　　$0<y<B$

(ii)　　　$T(x,0)=T_1$　　$T(x,B)=T_0$,　　$0<x<L$

We wish to determine T(x, y) by solving Laplace's equation subject to these boundary conditions.

For a non-trivial solution, we write $T(x,y)=X(x)\,Y(y)$ and using the method of separation of variables, we get $\dfrac{X''(x)}{X(x)}+\dfrac{Y''(y)}{Y(y)}=0.$

Since $X(x)$ vanishes at the boundaries, the ratio $\dfrac{X'(x)}{X(x)}$ cannot be positive. Hence, we get the two ODEs:

$$X''+\lambda^2 X=0\qquad 0<x<L$$

and　　$Y''-\lambda^2 Y=0\qquad 0<y<B$

The solutions are

$$X(x)=A\cos\lambda x+B\sin\lambda x$$

and　$Y(y)=C\cosh\lambda y+D\sinh\lambda y$

Applying the boundary conditions (i) and (ii), we get

$$A=0, \quad \cos \lambda L=0$$

or $\lambda_n = \dfrac{(2n-1)\pi}{2L}, \qquad n=1,2...$

which gives $X_n(x)=B_n \sin \lambda_n x$

and $Y_n(y)=C'_n \cosh \lambda_n y + D'_n \sinh \lambda_n y$

The general solution for T(x, y) is

$$T(x,y)=\sum_{n=1}^{\infty}\left(C_n \cosh \lambda_n y + D_n \sinh \lambda_n y\right)\sin \lambda_n x$$

with $\lambda_n = \dfrac{(2n-1)\pi}{2L}, \qquad n=1,2,...$

and $\qquad C_n = C'_n B_n, \quad D_n = D'_n B_n.$

The coefficients C_n and D_n are determined by applying the boundary condition (ii).

At y =0,

$$T(x,0)=C_n \sin \lambda_n x = T_1, \qquad 0<x<L$$

from which we can determine C_n to be

$$C_n = \frac{2}{L}\int_0^L T_1 \sin \lambda_n x\, dx = \frac{4T_1}{(2n-1)\pi}$$

At y = B,

$$T(x,B)=\sum_{n=1}^{\infty}\left(C_n \cosh \lambda_n B + D_n \sinh \lambda_n B\right)\sin \lambda_n x = T_0, \qquad 0<x<L$$

Now choose D_n so that the quantity within brackets is the Fourier sine coefficient of the function representing the given boundary value (T_0 in this case). Putting $C_n \cosh \lambda_n B + D_n \sinh \lambda_n B = G_n$

Then, the coefficients G_n are given by the relation

$$G_n = \frac{2}{L}\int_0^L T_0 \sin \lambda_n x\, dx = \frac{4T_0}{(2n-1)\pi}$$

This gives the coefficients D_n in terms of the known coefficients C_n and G_n:

$$D_n = \frac{G_n - C_n \cosh \lambda_n B}{\sinh \lambda_n B} = \frac{4}{(2n-1)\pi}\frac{T_0 - T_1 \cosh \lambda_n B}{\sinh \lambda_n B}$$

Thus, the unique solution of this problem is

$$T(x,y)=\frac{4}{\pi}\sum_{n=1}^{\infty}\left(\frac{T_1\cosh\lambda_n y}{2n-1}+\frac{T_0-T_1\cosh\lambda_n B}{(2n-1)\sinh\lambda_n B}\sin\lambda_n y\right)\sin\lambda_n x$$

The solution for the case $B=2L, T_1=10^\circ C, T_0=20^\circ C$ is shown in Fig. 8.6.

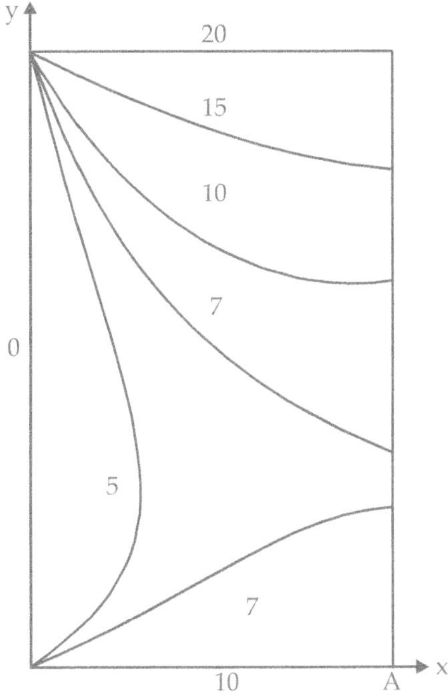

Fig. 8.6: The isotherms $T(x,y)=T_c$ for various values of T when

$$B=2L, T_1=10^\circ C, T_0=20^\circ C$$

The curves shown are the isotherms $T(x,y)=T_c$ for various values of T.

The Potential at a Point due to a Circular Disc

Here, we will solve Laplace's equation for the potential on a circular metallic disc. For a circular disc, it is natural to use plane-polar coordinates (r,θ). The problem is as follows:

$$\frac{1}{r}\frac{\partial}{\partial r}\left(r\frac{\partial u}{\partial r}\right)+\frac{1}{r^2}\left(\frac{\partial^2 u}{\partial\theta^2}\right)=0, \qquad 0\le r<L, \ -\pi<\theta\le\pi \qquad ...(viii)$$

$$u(L,\theta)=f(\theta), \qquad\qquad -\pi<\theta\le\pi \qquad\qquad ...(ix)$$

There are two special features of this problem:

- The points $\theta=-\pi$ and $\theta=\pi$ coincide. Therefore, the value of u and its angular derivative should match there:

$$u(r,-\pi)=u(r,\pi), \quad \frac{\partial u}{\partial \theta}(r,-\pi)=\frac{\partial u}{\partial \theta}(r,\pi), \quad\quad 0\le r<L$$

- The point $r=0$ is singular; the coefficient of $\dfrac{\partial^2 u}{\partial r^2}$ in Eq. (viii) is 1, while the coefficients of other terms are $1/r$ and $1/r^2$. We must, therefore, enforce a condition of boundedness:

  $u(r,\ \theta)$ tends to a finite value, i.e. it is bounded, as $r\to 0$.

Here, we can solve the potential problem using the method of separation of variables.

Let $u(r,\ \theta)=R(r)\Theta(\theta)$

Substituting $u(r,\ \theta)$ in Eq. (viii) and taking into account the special continuity conditions, we get

$$\frac{1}{r}\left[rR'(r)\right]'\Theta(\theta)+\frac{1}{r^2}R(r)\Theta''(\theta)=0, \quad\quad 0\le r<L,\ \ -\pi<\theta\le\pi \quad\quad\quad ...(1)$$

and

$$R(r)\Theta(-\pi)=R(r)\Theta(\pi), \quad\quad R(r)\Theta'(-\pi)=R(r)\Theta'(\pi) \quad 0\le r<L \quad\quad\quad ...(2)$$

Multiplying Eq. (i) by r^2, dividing it by $R(r)\,\Theta(\theta)$, and eliminating $R(r)$ in (ii), we get

$$\frac{r\left[rR'(r)\right]'}{R(r)}=-\frac{\Theta''(\theta)}{\Theta(\theta)}=\lambda^2 \quad\quad 0\le r<L, \quad\quad -\pi<\theta\le\pi$$

$$\Rightarrow\ \Theta(-\pi)=\Theta(\pi)\,\text{and}\,\Theta'(-\pi)=\Theta'(\pi), \quad\quad\quad\quad\quad ...(3i)$$

Thus, $\Theta''+\lambda^2\Theta=0$ which gives $\Theta=A\cos\lambda\theta+B\sin\lambda\theta$

The continuity conditions (2) for Θ gives us

$A\cos\lambda\pi-B\sin\lambda\pi=A\cos\lambda\pi+B\sin\lambda\pi$

$A\lambda\sin\lambda\pi+B\lambda\cos\lambda\pi=-A\lambda\sin\lambda\pi+B\lambda\cos\lambda\pi$

or $2B\sin\lambda\pi=0$

and $2\lambda A\sin\lambda\pi=0$

which gives $\lambda_n=n, \quad n=0,1,2,3,....$

Thus, we have $\Theta_n(\theta)=A_n\cos n\theta+B_n\sin n\theta, \quad\quad n=0,1,2,3,...$

The ODE for $R(r)$ is $\dfrac{r\left(rR_n'\right)'}{R_n}=\lambda_n^2$ or $r^2R_n''+rR_n'-\lambda_n^2R_n=0$

This is an Euler Cauchy equation with linearly independent solutions

$$R_n(r)=r^n \quad \text{and} \quad R_n(r)=r^{-n}$$

The second of these is physically unacceptable as it tends to ∞ in the limit as $r \to 0$. Thus, we have the general solution for $u(r,\theta)$:

$$u(r,\theta)=A_0+\sum_{n=1}^{\infty} r^n\left(A_n \cos n\theta+B_n \sin n\theta\right)$$

The boundary condition on $r=L$ yields

$$A_0+\sum_{n=1}^{\infty} L^n\left(A_n \cos n\theta+B_n \sin n\theta\right)=f(\theta) \quad -\pi<\theta\leq\pi$$

This is a Fourier series problem and the coefficients in the series are

$$A_0=\frac{1}{2\pi}\int_{-\pi}^{\pi} f(\theta)d\theta$$

$$L^n A_n=\frac{1}{\pi}\int_{-\pi}^{\pi} f(\theta)\cos n\theta d\theta \quad\quad L^n B_n=\frac{1}{\pi}\int_{-\pi}^{\pi} f(\theta)\sin n\theta d\theta$$

We can solve these three integrals for any given form of $f(\theta)$ provided they exist.

Solved Practical Problems

Q1. **Obtain the steady-state temperature for the rectangular plate of following figure given the following boundary conditions:**

$$u(0,y)=\frac{U_0 y}{B}, \frac{\partial u}{\partial x}(L,y)=-S, \quad\quad 0<y<B$$

$$u(x,0)=0, \quad u(x,B)=0, \quad\quad\quad 0<x<L$$

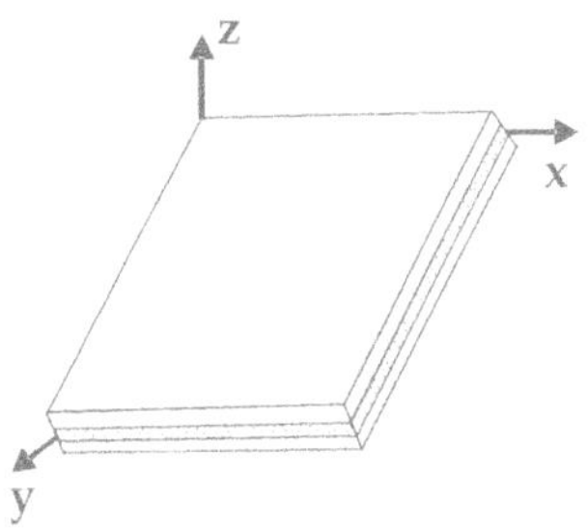

Ans. Putting $u(x,y)=X(x)Y(y)$ and applying the method of separation of variables we get $\dfrac{X''(x)}{X(x)}+\dfrac{Y''(y)}{Y(y)}=0, \quad 0<x<L, \quad 0<y<B$

with the boundary conditions

$$X(x)Y(0)=0, \quad X(x)Y(B)=0, \quad 0<x<L$$

or $\quad Y(0)=0, \quad Y(B)=0$

Since Y has to vanish at the boundaries $y = 0$ and $y = B$, the ratio $\dfrac{Y''}{Y}$ cannot be positive. Thus, we get the ODEs: $X''-\lambda^2 X=0, \quad Y''+\lambda^2 Y=0$

Hence, $X(x)=A\cosh\lambda x+B\sinh\lambda x$

$Y(y)=C\cos\lambda y+D\sin\lambda y$

The boundary conditions on Y yield the following values of C and λ:

$$C=0, \quad \lambda_n=\frac{n\pi}{B}, \quad n=1,2,3,....$$

Thus, $Y_n(y)=D_n\sin\dfrac{n\pi y}{B}, \quad n=1,2,3,....$

Thus, the general solution is

$$u(x,y)=\sum_{n=1}^{\infty}\left(a_n\cosh\lambda_n x+b_n\sinh\lambda_n x\right)\sin\lambda_n y$$

where $a_n=A_n D_n, b_n=B_n D_n$.

Applying the remaining boundary conditions, we get

$$At\, x=0, \quad \sum_{n=1}^{\infty}a_n\sin\lambda_n y=\frac{U_0 y}{B}, \quad 0<y<B$$

Using the half-range expansion technique, we get

$$a_n=\frac{2}{B}\int_0^B\frac{U_0 y}{B}\sin\lambda_n y\,dy =\frac{2U_0}{B^2}\left(\left[-\frac{y}{\lambda_n}\cos\lambda_n y\right]_0^B +\frac{1}{\lambda_n}\left[\frac{\sin\lambda_n y}{\lambda_n}\right]_0^B\right)$$

$$=\frac{2U_0}{B^2}\left(-\frac{B^2}{n\pi}\cos n\pi+0\right) =-\frac{2U_0\cos n\pi}{n\pi}$$

$$At\, x=L, \quad \frac{\partial u}{\partial x}(L,y)=-S, \quad 0<y<B$$

Differentiating the series for $u(x,y)$ term by term and applying the given boundary conditions, we get

$$\frac{\partial u}{\partial x}(L,y)=\sum_{n=1}^{\infty}\lambda_n\left(a_n\sinh\lambda_n L+b_n\cosh\lambda_n L\right)\sin\lambda_n y=-S, \quad 0<y<B$$

So we must choose b_n such that the coefficient of $\sin\lambda_n y$ will be

$$C_n=\lambda_n\left(a_n\sinh\lambda_n L+b_n\cosh\lambda_n L\right)$$

where $C_n = \dfrac{2}{B}\displaystyle\int_0^B (-S\sin\lambda_n y)\,dy$

$$= \frac{2S}{B}\left[\frac{\cos\lambda_n y}{\lambda_n}\right]_0^B = \frac{2S}{B\lambda_n}\left[\cos n\pi - 1\right] = \frac{2S}{n\pi}\left(\cos n\pi - 1\right)$$

Thus, $b_n = \dfrac{\dfrac{C_n}{\lambda_n} - a_n \sinh\lambda_n L}{\cosh\lambda_n L}$ is the required complete solution.

Q2. Solve the heat/diffusion problem stated below in terms of dimensionless variables

$$\frac{\partial^2 u}{\partial x^2} = \frac{\partial u}{\partial t}, \qquad 0<x<1, \qquad t>0$$

$$\frac{\partial u}{\partial x}(0,t)=0, \qquad \frac{\partial u}{\partial x}(1,t)=0, \qquad t>0$$

$$u(x,0)=1+2x, \qquad 0<x<1.$$

Ans. For solving heat/diffusion problem, we have

$$\frac{\partial^2 u}{\partial t^2} = \frac{\partial u}{\partial t}, 0<x<1, t>0$$

$$\frac{\partial u}{\partial x}(0,t)=0, \frac{\partial u}{\partial x}(1,t)=0, t>0$$

$$u(x,0)=1+2x, 0<x<1$$

We take $u(x,t) = X(x)\,T(t)$

and so that $\dfrac{\partial u}{\partial x} = T\dfrac{dX}{dx} \Rightarrow \dfrac{\partial^2 u}{\partial x^2} = T\dfrac{d^2 X}{dx^2}$ and $\dfrac{\partial u}{\partial t} = X\dfrac{dT}{dt}$

$\therefore$ Putting in $\dfrac{\partial^2 u}{\partial x^2} = \dfrac{\partial u}{\partial t}$, we have, $T\dfrac{d^2 X}{dx^2} = X\dfrac{dT}{dt} \Rightarrow \dfrac{1}{X}\dfrac{d^2 X}{dx^2} = \dfrac{1}{T}\dfrac{dT}{dt} = -\lambda^2$

Therefore, two ODEs are $\dfrac{d^2 X}{dx^2} + \lambda^2 X = 0.$

Its solution is $X = C_1\cos\lambda x + C_2\sin\lambda x$

By differentiating, we get $X' = -C_1\lambda\sin\lambda x + C_2\lambda\cos\lambda x$ and putting

$X'(1) = X'(0) = 0$, we get $C_2\lambda G_0 - 0 = 0 \Rightarrow C_2 = 0$

and $-C_1\lambda\sin\lambda = 0 \Rightarrow C_1\sin\lambda = 0$

As $C_1 \neq 0$ for a non-Trivial solution, we have

$\lambda = 0$ or $\lambda_n = n\pi$ for $n = 0, 1, 2, 3,...$

and for $\dfrac{1}{T}\dfrac{d^2T}{dt^2}=-\lambda^2 \Rightarrow \dfrac{d^2T}{dt^2}+\lambda^2 T=0$

$T_n(t)=C_3 e^{\left[-\pi^2 n^2 t\right]}$

Therefore, the general solution is

$$u(x,t)=a_0+\sum_{n=1}^{\infty}a_n \exp\left[-n^2\pi^2 t\right]\cos n\pi x,$$

At t = 0, we have $u(x,0)=a_0+\sum_{n=1}^{\infty}a_n \cos n\pi x=1+2x,\qquad 0<x<1$

The coefficients are $a_0=\int_0^1(1+2x)dx=\left[x+x^2\right]_0^1=2$;

$$a_n=2\int_0^1(1+2x)\cos n\pi x\,dx \;=\;\dfrac{4}{n^2\pi^2}(\cos n\pi-1)$$

Thus, the particular solution is

$$u(x,t)=2+4\sum_{n=1}^{\infty}\left(\dfrac{\cos n\pi-1}{n^2\pi^2}\right)\exp\left(-n^2\pi^2 t\right)\cos n\pi x$$

$$=2-\dfrac{8}{\pi^2}\left(\cos\pi e^{-\pi^2 t}+\dfrac{1}{9}\cos 3\pi x\, e^{-9\pi^2 t}+\dfrac{1}{25}\cos 5\pi x\, e^{-25\pi^2 t}+....\right)$$

Q3. **A cylindrical elastic bar (e.g. steel bar) of natural length L is initially stretched by an amount cL and is at rest. The initial Longitudinal displacement of any section of the bar is proportional to the distance from the fixed end x = 0. At the instant t = 0, both ends are released and left free. The longitudinal displacement y(x, t) of the bar satisfies the following BVP**

$$\dfrac{\partial^2 y(x,t)}{\partial x^2}=\dfrac{1}{v^2}\dfrac{\partial^2 y(x,t)}{\partial t^2}$$

where $v^2=E/\rho$, E is the modulus of elasticity and ρ is the density of the material of the bar. Since the ends are free, the force per unit area on the ends of the bar is zero and we get

$$\dfrac{\partial y}{\partial x}(0,t)=0,\qquad \dfrac{\partial y}{\partial x}(L,t)=0$$

Further $y(x,0)=cx,\qquad \dfrac{\partial y}{\partial t}(x,0)=0$

Solve the BVP and obtain $y(x,t)$.

Ans. Using the method of separation of variables, we write $y(x,t)=X(x)T(t)$ and obtain the ODEs for X and T with the corresponding boundary conditions:

$$X''(x)+\lambda^2 X(x)=0, \quad X'(0)=0, \quad X'(L)=0$$

and $\quad T''(t)+\lambda^2 v^2 T(t)=0, \quad T(0)=cx, \quad T'(0)=0$

The solutions are $X(x)=A\cos\lambda x+B\sin\lambda x$ and $T(t)=C\cos\lambda vt+D\sin\lambda vt$

Applying the boundary conditions on X and T we get $B=0$, $\sin\lambda L=0$ which yields the eigen values $\lambda_0=0$, $\quad \lambda_n=\dfrac{n\pi}{L}$, $\quad n=1,2,...$ and $D=0$.

Thus, the general solution is $y(x,t)=a_0+\displaystyle\sum_{n=1}^{\infty} a_n \cos\dfrac{n\pi x}{L}\cos\dfrac{n\pi vt}{L}$

where $a_n=A_n C_n$.

Applying the initial condition, we have

$$a_0+\sum_{n=1}^{\infty} a_n \cos\dfrac{n\pi x}{L}=cx \qquad 0<x<L$$

We can expand cx in a Fourier cosine series using the half-range expansion technique. Thus, $a_0=\dfrac{c}{L}\displaystyle\int_0^L x\,dx=\dfrac{c}{L}\dfrac{L^2}{2}=\dfrac{cL}{2}$; $a_n=\dfrac{2c}{L}\displaystyle\int_0^L x\cos\dfrac{n\pi x}{L}dx$

$$=\dfrac{2cL}{\pi^2}\left[\dfrac{\cos n\pi-1}{n^2}\right]=\dfrac{2cL}{\pi^2}\left(\dfrac{(-1)^n-1}{n^2}\right), \qquad n=1,2,....$$

Hence, the solution is

$$y(x,t)=\dfrac{cL}{2}-\dfrac{4cL}{\pi^2}\sum_{n=1}^{\infty}\dfrac{1}{(2n-1)^2}\cos\dfrac{(2n-1)\pi x}{L}\cos\dfrac{(2n-1)\pi vt}{L}.$$

Q4. Write the two dimensional Laplace equation in Cartesian coordinates and separate it into 2 ordinary differential equations.

[June-2011,Q.No.-1(b)]

Ans. Two dimensional Laplace equation in Cartesian coordinates is

$$\dfrac{\partial^2\phi}{\partial x^2}+\dfrac{\partial^2\phi}{\partial y^2}=0 \qquad\qquad ...(i)$$

This is a partial differential equation in two independent variables. This is accomplished by the method of separation of variables. It consists of assuming solutions with the special space dependence

$$\phi(x,y) = X(x)\,Y(y) \qquad \qquad \text{...(ii)}$$

In (ii), X is assumed to be a function of x alone and Y is a function of y alone. If need be, a general space dependence is then recovered by superposition of these special solutions. Substitution of (ii) into (i) and division by ϕ then gives

$$\frac{1}{X(x)}\frac{d^2X(x)}{dx^2} = -\frac{1}{Y(y)}\frac{d^2Y(y)}{dy^2} \qquad \qquad \text{...(iii)}$$

In (iii), we see that the left hand side is a function of x alone and the right hand side is a function of y alone. The equation can be satisfied independent of x and y only if each of these expressions is constant. We denote this "separation" constant by k^2, and it follows that

$$\frac{d^2X}{dx^2} = -k^2X \qquad \qquad \text{...(iv)}$$

and $\quad \dfrac{d^2Y}{dy^2} = k^2Y \qquad \qquad \text{...(v)}$

(iv) and (v) are the required two ordinary differential equations.

Q5. Obtain the solution of the two-dimensional diffusion equation, in the region $0 < x < a$, $0 < y < b$, $t > 0$

$$\frac{\partial^2 z}{\partial x^2} + \frac{\partial^2 z}{\partial y^2} = \frac{1}{k}\frac{\partial z}{\partial t}. \qquad \qquad \text{...(i)}$$

with boundary and initial conditions:

z (x, y, t) = 0 on ∂D,   ...(ii)

where ∂D is the boundary of the rectangle defined by $0 \le x \le a$, $0 \le y \le b$ and

z (x, y, 0) = f (x, y), $0 < x < a$, $0 < y < b$.   ...(iii)

Ans. Let the solution of (i) be $z(x,y,t) = X(x)\,Y(y)\,T(t) \neq 0$.

Then (ii) takes the form $X''YT + XY''T = \dfrac{1}{k}XYT'$.

Dividing both sides by $XYT \neq 0$, we obtain $\dfrac{X''}{X} + \dfrac{Y''}{Y} = \dfrac{1}{k}\dfrac{T'}{T}$

We take $\dfrac{X''}{X} = -\lambda^2$, $\dfrac{Y''}{Y} = -\mu^2$, $\dfrac{T'}{kT} = -v^2$, where $\lambda^2 + \mu^2 = v^2$.

(For non-negative constants, separable solution with given boundary data leads only to a trivial solution $z(x,y,t) \equiv 0$)

The boundary conditions given in (2) are

$$\left. \begin{array}{l} z\,(0,y,t) = 0 = z\,(a,y,t) \\ z\,(x,0,t) = 0 = z\,(x,b,t) \end{array} \right\} \quad \text{for } t \geq 0$$

$$\Rightarrow\ X(0) = 0 = X(a), \text{ and } \quad Y\,(0) = 0 = Y\,(b).$$

Now $X'' + \lambda^2 X = 0$ implies that $X(x) = A\cos \lambda x + B\sin \lambda x$.

$$\therefore \quad X(0) = 0 \Rightarrow A = 0 \qquad \text{and} \qquad X(a) = 0 \Rightarrow B\sin \lambda a = 0$$

$$\Rightarrow\ \sin \lambda a = 0 \ (\because B \neq 0) \Rightarrow \lambda a = m\pi, \text{ where } m = 1,\,2,\,3,\ldots$$

$$\therefore\ \lambda = \lambda_m = \frac{m\pi}{a}.$$

Thus, $\qquad X_m\,(x) = B_m \sin\left(\frac{m\pi x}{a}\right).$ $\qquad\qquad$ ...(iv)

Similarly, $\mu = \mu_n = \dfrac{n\pi}{b},\qquad$ where $n = 1,\,2,\,3,\ldots$

and $Y_n\,(y) = D_n \sin\left(\dfrac{n\pi y}{b}\right).$ $\qquad\qquad$ ...(v)

Now $v^2 = \lambda^2 + \mu^2 = \left(\dfrac{m\pi}{a}\right)^2 + \left(\dfrac{n\pi}{b}\right)^2 = \pi^2\left(\dfrac{m^2}{a^2} + \dfrac{n^2}{b^2}\right) = v_{mn}^2,$ say.

$$\therefore\ T' + v_{mn}^2\, kT = 0 \quad \Rightarrow\ T_{mn}\,(t) = E_{mn}\,e^{-v_{mn}^2\, kt} \qquad\qquad \text{...(vi)}$$

where $B_m,\, D_n$ and E_{mn} are integrating constants.

Using (4), (5) and (6); the solution of (1) is

$$z_{mn}(x,y,t) = b_{mn} \sin\left(\frac{m\pi x}{a}\right)\sin\left(\frac{n\pi y}{b}\right)e^{-v_{mn}^2\, kt},$$

where $\quad b_{mn} = B_m D_n E_{mn}$ is the new constant.

By the principle of superposition, the solution can be expressed as a double series $z\,(x,y,t) = \displaystyle\sum_{m=1}^{\infty}\sum_{n=1}^{\infty} b_{mn} \sin\left(\frac{m\pi x}{a}\right)\sin\left(\frac{n\pi y}{b}\right)e^{-v_{mn}^2\, kt}.$ $\qquad$ ...(vii)

To determine the constants b_{mn}, we use the given initial condition (iii). We have $f(x,y) = \displaystyle\sum_{m=1}^{\infty}\sum_{n=1}^{\infty} b_{mn} \sin\left(\frac{m\pi x}{a}\right)\sin\left(\frac{n\pi y}{b}\right),$ where $0 \leq x \leq a$ and $0 < y < b.$

This is a double Fourier-sine series, where

$$b_{mn} = \left(\frac{2}{a}\right)\left(\frac{2}{b}\right)\int_0^a\int_0^b f(x,y)\sin\left(\frac{m\pi x}{a}\right)\sin\left(\frac{n\pi y}{b}\right)dx\,dy. \qquad \text{...(viii)}$$

Hence, (vii) is the required solution, where b_{mn} is given by (viii).

Q6. **Use the method of separation of variables, determine the solution $V(x, y)$ of the problem which consists of Laplace's equation**

$$\frac{\partial^2 V}{\partial x^2} + \frac{\partial^2 V}{\partial y^2} = 0$$

and the boundary conditions:

$$V(x,0) = f(x), \qquad\qquad 0 \le x \le \pi$$

$$V(0,y) = 0 = V(\pi,y), \qquad 0 \le y \le \pi$$

$$V(x,\pi) = 0, \qquad\qquad 0 \le x \le \pi$$

where f is a specified function of x, $0 \le x \le \pi$.

Ans. By assuming a variable separable solution of the form

$$V(x,y) = X(x)\,Y(y) \ne 0, \text{ the given equation becomes}$$

$$X''Y + XY'' = 0 \text{ or } \frac{X''}{X} = -\frac{Y''}{Y} = -\alpha^2, \text{ say.}$$

$$\therefore \quad X'' + \alpha^2 X = 0,\, y'' - \alpha^2 Y = 0.$$

Their solutions are $X(x) = A\cos\alpha x + B\sin\alpha x$ and

$Y(y) = C\sinh\alpha\,(y + \varepsilon).$

We are given $X(0) = 0 = X(\pi)$. $(\because\ Y(y) \ne 0)$

$\therefore \quad A = 0$ and $\sin\alpha\pi = 0$ $(\Rightarrow \alpha = n)$.

Consequently, $X_n(x) = B_n \sin(nx);\ n = 1,2,3,...$

Similarly, on using $Y(\pi) = 0$, $(\because\ X(x) \ne 0)$

$Y_n(y) = C_n \sinh n\,(y - \pi).$

Hence, the general solution is given by

$$V(x,y) = \sum_{n=1}^{\infty} X_n Y_n = \sum_{n=1}^{\infty} b_n \sin(nx)\sinh n\,(y - \pi), \qquad\qquad ...(i)$$

where $b_n = B_n C_n.$

Using the boundary condition $V(x,0) = f(x),\ 0 \le x \le \pi$

$$f(x) = \sum_{n=1}^{\infty} b_n \sin(nx)\sinh(-n\pi),\ 0 \le x \le \pi,$$

where $b_n = -\dfrac{2}{\pi\sinh n\pi} \displaystyle\int_0^{\pi} f(x)\sin nx\,dx.$ ...(ii)

Hence, (i) and (ii) constitute the required solution.

Q7. Consider the initial temperature of the bar be a constant $T_0\,°C.$ Then solve the diffusion equation $\dfrac{\partial T(x,t)}{\partial t}=k\dfrac{\partial^2 T(x,t)}{\partial x^2}$, $(0<x<L,\, t>0)$ With $T(0,t)=\dfrac{\partial T}{\partial x}(L,t)=0,\;\;(t\geq 0)$ and $T(x,0)=T_0,$ $(0<x<L)$ Determine the expression for $T(x,t)$ and discuss its behaviour at large values of times.

Ans. The general solution of this problem is given by equation

$$T(x,t)=\sum_{n=0}^{\infty} b_n \exp\left[-\left\{\frac{(2n+1)\pi}{2L}\right\}^2 kt\right]\sin\left[\frac{(2n+1)\pi x}{2L}\right].$$ Applying the initial condition, we get $T(x,0)=\sum_{n=0}^{\infty} b_n \sin\left[\frac{(2n+1)\pi x}{2L}\right]=T_0,$ $0<x<L$

Using the half-range expansion of $T(x,0)$ we get

$$b_n=\frac{2}{L}\int_0^L T_0 \sin\left[\frac{(2n+1)\pi x}{2L}\right]dx = \frac{2T_0}{L}\left[-\frac{2L}{(2n+1)\pi}\cos\frac{(2n+1)\pi x}{2L}\right]_0^L$$

$$=-\frac{4T_0}{(2n+1)\pi}\left[\cos(2n+1)\frac{\pi}{2}-1\right]=\frac{4T_0}{(2n+1)\pi},$$

since $\cos(2n+1)\dfrac{\pi}{2}=0$ for all values of n.

Hence, $T(x,t)=\dfrac{4T_0}{\pi}\sum_{n=0}^{\infty}\dfrac{1}{(2n+1)}\exp\left(-\left[\frac{(2n+1)\pi}{2L}\right]^2 kt\right)\sin\left[\frac{(2n+1)\pi x}{2L}\right]$

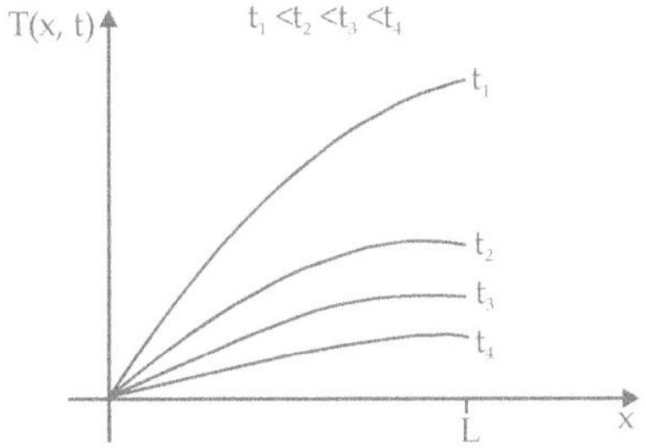

Fig. 8.7

As t increases, all the exponential terms tend to zero, hence $T(x,t)$ tends to zero. Fig. 8.7 shows the kinds of graphs expected for $T(x,t)$ vs. x for increasingly large values of t.

Q8. Solve one-dimensional wave equation:

$$\frac{\partial^2 z}{\partial x^2}=\frac{1}{c^2}\frac{\partial^2 z}{\partial t^2},\; 0<x<a,\; t>0 \qquad\qquad ...(i)$$

Deduce the expression for z satisfying the boundary conditions:

$$z(0,t) = 0 = z(a,t), \ \forall \ t > 0. \qquad \qquad \text{...(ii)}$$

Ans. Assume a separable solution of the form

$$z(x,t) = X(x)\,T(t) \neq 0, \qquad \qquad \text{...(iii)}$$

where X is a function of x only and T is a function of t only.

Substituting (iii) in (i) yields (after dividing by $XT \neq 0$),

$$\frac{1}{X}\frac{d^2X}{dx^2} = \frac{1}{c^2 T}\frac{d^2T}{dt^2}. \qquad \qquad \text{...(iv)}$$

The left-hand side of the eq. (iv) is a function of x only and the right-hand side is a function of t only. Since x, t are independent variables, it follows that (4) holds only if both sides are equal to the same constant.

Let $\dfrac{1}{X}\dfrac{d^2X}{dx^2} = \dfrac{1}{c^2 T}\dfrac{d^2T}{dt^2} = \lambda$, where λ is an arbitrary constant.

We get a pair of ordinary differential equations:

$$\frac{d^2X}{dx^2} - \lambda X = 0, \quad \frac{d^2T}{dt^2} - \lambda c^2 T = 0. \qquad \qquad \text{...(v)}$$

There are three possible cases:

(i) $\lambda > 0$, (ii) $\lambda = 0$ and   (iii) $\lambda < 0$.

Case I.

Let $\lambda = \alpha^2 > 0$. The solutions of equations in (v) are, respectively

$$X(x) = Ae^{\pm \alpha x}, T(t) = Be^{\pm \alpha ct}.$$

Thus, $z(x,t) = Ce^{\pm \alpha x \pm \alpha ct}, \qquad \qquad \text{...(vi)}$

where $C = AB$, is the required solution of (i).

Case II.

Let $\lambda = 0$. Then the solutions of equations in (v) are

$X(x) = Ax + B$ and $T(t) = Ct + D$, respectively

Thus, $z(x, t) = (Ax + B)(Ct + D) \qquad \qquad \text{...(vii)}$

is the required solution of (1).

Case III.

Let $\lambda = -\alpha^2 < 0$. The solutions of equations in (v) are

$$X(x) = Ae^{\pm i\alpha x}, \ T(t) = Be^{\pm i\alpha ct} \ \text{respectively.}$$

Thus, $z(x,t) = Ce^{\pm i\alpha x \pm i\alpha ct}$, where $C = AB \qquad \qquad \text{...(viii)}$

is the required solution of (i).

We shall now deduce the solution of (i) with the given boundary conditions (ii), which give

$z(0, t) = X(0) T(t) = 0,$ for $t > 0$

$z(a, t) = X(a) T(t) = 0,$ for $t > 0.$

But $T(t) \neq 0$, since otherwise $z(x, t) = 0$, which contradicts (iii).

$X(0) = 0 = X(a).$ ...(ix)

Using (ix), cases I and II for $\lambda \geq 0$ yield only the trivial solution $z(x,t) \equiv 0$. Hence, we take case III, when $\lambda = -\alpha^2 < 0$.

The solution of $\dfrac{d^2X}{dx^2} + \alpha^2 X = 0$ is $X(x) = A\cos\alpha x + B\sin\alpha x$

Using (ix) in the above equation, we get

$A = 0,$ $B\sin\alpha\, a = 0$ $\Rightarrow \sin\alpha\, a = 0$ $(\because B \neq 0)$

[Note that $B = 0$ $\Rightarrow X(x) \equiv 0$ and so $z(x,t) \equiv 0$]

Now $\sin\alpha\, a = 0 \Rightarrow \alpha a = n\pi$

$\therefore \quad \alpha = \alpha_n = \dfrac{n\pi}{a},\ n = 1, 2, 3\ldots$

[Note that $n = 0$ $(\Rightarrow \alpha = 0)$ leads to the trivial solution $z(x, t) = 0.$]

Thus, $X_n(x) = B_n \sin\left(\dfrac{n\pi x}{a}\right).$ ...(x)

Taking $\alpha = -\alpha_n^2$ in $\dfrac{d^2T}{dt^2} - \lambda c^2 T = 0$, we obtain $\dfrac{d^2T}{dt^2} + \alpha_n^2 c^2 T = 0.$

Its solution is given by $T_n(t) = C_n \cos(\alpha_n ct) + D_n \sin(\alpha_n ct),$ ...(xi)

where C_n and D_n are constants of integration.

Substituting (x) with (xi) in (iii), the solution of (i) is given by

$$z_n(x,t) = \left[a_n \cos\left(\frac{n\pi ct}{a}\right) + b_n \sin\left(\frac{n\pi\, ct}{a}\right)\right]\sin\left(\frac{n\pi x}{a}\right).$$

where $a_n = C_n B_n,\ b_n = D_n B_n$ are new arbitrary constants and $n = 1, 2, 3,\ldots$

These solutions $z_n(x,t)$, corresponding to the eigenvalues $\alpha_n = \dfrac{n\pi}{a}$, are called the eigenfunctions.

Since equation (i) is linear and homogenous, the most general solution of (i) is obtained, by the principle of superposition, in the form

$$z(x,t) = \sum_{n=1}^{\infty}\left(a_n \cos\frac{n\pi ct}{a} + b_n \sin\frac{n\pi ct}{a}\right)\sin\frac{n\pi x}{a},$$ ...(xii)

provided the series converges uniformly for $0 \leq x \leq a.$

Q9. Show that the function $\phi(x,y,z)=\dfrac{1}{\left(x^{2}+y^{2}+z^{2}\right)^{1/2}}$ satisfies Laplace's equation $\nabla^{2}\phi=0$ for $(x,y,z)\neq(0,0,0)$.　　　　[June-2013, Q.No.-1(c)]

Ans. Given equation is $\phi(x,y,z)=\dfrac{1}{\left(x^{2}+y^{2}+z^{2}\right)^{1/2}}$ and Laplace's equation is

$\nabla^{2}\phi=0$ for $(x,y,z)\neq(0,0,0)$.

We know that $\nabla^{2}\equiv\dfrac{\partial^{2}}{\partial x^{2}}+\dfrac{\partial^{2}}{\partial y^{2}}+\dfrac{\partial^{2}}{\partial z^{2}}$

Hence, $\nabla^{2}\phi\equiv\dfrac{\partial^{2}\phi}{\partial x^{2}}+\dfrac{\partial^{2}\phi}{\partial y^{2}}+\dfrac{\partial^{2}\phi}{\partial z^{2}}$

Hence, Laplace equation is $\dfrac{\partial^{2}\phi}{\partial x^{2}}+\dfrac{\partial^{2}\phi}{\partial y^{2}}+\dfrac{\partial^{2}\phi}{\partial z^{2}}=0$

Now, L.H.S. $=\dfrac{\partial^{2}\phi}{\partial x^{2}}+\dfrac{\partial^{2}\phi}{\partial y^{2}}+\dfrac{\partial^{2}\phi}{\partial z^{2}}=\dfrac{\partial}{\partial x}\left[\dfrac{\partial\phi}{\partial x}\right]+\dfrac{\partial}{\partial y}\left[\dfrac{\partial\phi}{\partial y}\right]+\dfrac{\partial}{\partial z}\left[\dfrac{\partial\phi}{\partial z}\right]$

$=\dfrac{\partial}{\partial x}\left[\dfrac{-1}{2}\left(x^{2}+y^{2}+z^{2}\right)^{-3/2}.2x\right]+\dfrac{\partial}{\partial y}\left[\dfrac{-1}{2}\left(x^{2}+y^{2}+z^{2}\right)^{-3/2}.2y\right]+\dfrac{\partial}{\partial z}\left[\dfrac{-1}{2}\left(x^{2}+y^{2}+z^{2}\right)^{-3/2}.2z\right]$

$=-\left[\left(x^{2}+y^{2}+z^{2}\right)^{-3/2}.1+x.\left(\dfrac{-3}{2}\right)\left(x^{2}+y^{2}+z^{2}\right)^{-5/2}.2x\right]-\left[\left(x^{2}+y^{2}+z^{2}\right)^{-3/2}.1+y.\left(\dfrac{-3}{2}\right)\left(x^{2}+y^{2}+z^{2}\right)^{-5/2}.2y\right]-$

$\left[\left(x^{2}+y^{2}+z^{2}\right)^{-3/2}.1+z.\left(\dfrac{-3}{2}\right)\left(x^{2}+y^{2}+z^{2}\right)^{-5/2}.2z\right]$

$=-3\left(x^{2}+y^{2}+z^{2}\right)^{-3/2}+3\left(x^{2}+y^{2}+z^{2}\right)^{-5/2}\left(x^{2}+y^{2}+z^{2}\right)$

$=-3\left(x^{2}+y^{2}+z^{2}\right)^{-3/2}+3\left(x^{2}+y^{2}+z^{2}\right)^{-3/2}$
$\qquad\qquad\qquad\qquad\qquad=0=\text{R.H.S.}$

Hence, given function satisfies Laplace's equation $\nabla^{2}\phi=0$ for $(x,y,z)\neq(0,0,0)$. The book you can believe most – GPH book.

Q10. The flow of electric current in a pair of telephone wires or power transmission lines and the emf across the wires can be modelled by equations similar to the diffusion equation provided the loss due to leakage of current is negligible and the inductance of the wires is negligible:

$$\dfrac{\partial^{2}i}{\partial x^{2}}=RC\dfrac{\partial i}{\partial t},\qquad\dfrac{\partial^{2}v}{\partial x^{2}}=RC\dfrac{\partial v}{\partial t}$$

Here R is the resistance per unit length and C the capacitance per unit length of the two wires. Solve this equation for a cable of length L for the following boundary and initial conditions

$$v(0,t)=0V, \qquad v(L,t)=0V, \quad t\geq 0$$

$$v(x,0)=(6x/L)V.$$

Ans. Since v satisfies an equation of the form of diffusion equation, we can use its solution with given boundary conditions, where k = 1/RC. The result is $v(x,t)=\sum_{n=1}^{\infty}b_n e^{-(n\pi/L)^2 t/RC}\sin\frac{n\pi x}{L}$

Applying the initial condition, we have

$$v(x,0)=\frac{6x}{L}=\sum_{n=1}^{\infty}b_n\sin\frac{n\pi x}{L}, \qquad 0<x<L$$

where $b_n=\frac{2}{L}\int_0^L\frac{6}{L}x\sin\frac{n\pi x}{L}dx=-\frac{12}{n\pi}(-1)^n=\frac{12}{n\pi}(-1)^{n+1}$

Therefore, the solution is $v(x,t)=\frac{12}{\pi}\sum_{n=1}^{\infty}\frac{(-1)^{n+1}}{n}\exp\left(-\frac{t}{RC}\frac{n^2\pi^2}{L^2}\right)\sin\frac{n\pi x}{L}.$

For excellent score, read GPH book.

Important Formulae

Important Formulae

(1) If a differential equation is of the form $Mdx + Ndy = 0$

and If $\dfrac{\partial M}{\partial y} = \dfrac{\partial N}{\partial x}$ then equation is an exact equation and the solution is

$$\int Mdx + \int (N \sim x)dy = c$$

(2) Wronskian of a differential equation is $W = \begin{vmatrix} y_1 & y_2 \\ y_1' & y_2' \end{vmatrix} \neq 0$

(3)

- If a second order D.E. has an auxiliary equation which has two distinct real roots then general solution or complementary function (C.F.) is $y(x) = c_1 e^{m_1 x} + c_2 e^{m_2 x}$ where m_1, m_2 are the roots of given equation.

- If equation has real equal roots then $y(x) = (c_1 + c_2 x)e^{mx}$

- If equation has complex conjugate pair of roots like $\alpha \pm i\beta$ then $y(x) = e^{\alpha x}(c_1 \sin \beta x + c_2 \cos \beta x)$

(4) Rules for finding particular integral for given D.E.:

Form of forcing function	Nature of root of A.E.	Form of Particular Integral
(i) Ae^{kx}	when k is not a root k is single root k is double root	Ce^{kx} Cxe^{kx} $Cx^2 e^{kx}$
(ii) Polynomial $Ax^n (n = 0, 1, ...)$	$k = 0$ is not a root $k = 0$ is single root $k = 0$ is double root	$c_0 + c_1 x + c_2 x^2 + ...$ $x(c_0 + c_1 x + ...)$ $x^2(c_0 + c_1 x + c_2 x^2 + ...)$
(iii) $A \cos kx$	ik is not a root	$C \cos kx + D \sin kx$
(iv) $A \sin kx$	ik is a single root	$x(C \cos kx + D \sin kx)$

(5) In the method of variation of parameter, the particular integral is given by $y_p = uy_1 + vy_2$

where $u = -\int \dfrac{y_2 R}{W} dx$ and $v = \int \dfrac{y_1 R}{W} dx$ where w is Wronskian.

(6)

- A function f of two variables is continuous at (x_0, y_0) if

$$\lim_{(x,y)\to(x_0,y_0)} f(x,y) = f(x_0,y_0)$$

- A function f of three variables is continuous at (x_0, y_0, z_0) if

$$\lim_{(x,y,z)\to(x_0,y_0,z_0)} f(x,y,z) = f(x_0,y_0,z_0)$$

(7) The sum, product and quotient rules for partial derivates are

- $$\frac{\partial}{\partial x}(f \pm g) = \frac{\partial f}{\partial x} \pm \frac{\partial g}{\partial x} \quad \text{and} \quad \frac{\partial}{\partial y}(f \pm g) = \frac{\partial f}{\partial y} \pm \frac{\partial g}{\partial y}$$

- $$\frac{\partial}{\partial x}(fg) = \frac{\partial f}{\partial x}g + f\frac{\partial g}{\partial x} \quad \text{and} \quad \frac{\partial}{\partial y}(fg) = \frac{\partial f}{\partial y}g + f\frac{\partial g}{\partial y}$$

- $$\frac{\partial}{\partial x}\left(\frac{f}{g}\right) = \frac{\frac{\partial f}{\partial x}g - f\frac{\partial g}{\partial x}}{g^2} \quad \text{and} \quad \frac{\partial}{\partial y}\left(\frac{f}{g}\right) = \frac{\frac{\partial f}{\partial y}g - f\frac{\partial g}{\partial y}}{g^2}$$

(8) Higher order partial derivatives are

- $$f_{xx}(x,y) = \frac{\partial}{\partial x}\left(\frac{\partial f}{\partial x}\right) = \frac{\partial^2 f}{\partial x^2}$$

- $$f_{yy}(x,y) = \frac{\partial}{\partial y}\left(\frac{\partial f}{\partial y}\right) = \frac{\partial^2 f}{\partial y^2}$$

- $$f_{xy}(x,y) = \frac{\partial}{\partial y}\left(\frac{\partial f}{\partial x}\right) = \frac{\partial^2 f}{\partial y\partial x}$$

- $$f_{yx}(x,y) = \frac{\partial}{\partial x}\left(\frac{\partial f}{\partial y}\right) = \frac{\partial^2 f}{\partial x\partial y}$$

(9) If a linear second order partial differential equation is of the form

$$a\frac{\partial^2 u}{\partial x^2} + b\frac{\partial^2 u}{\partial x\partial y} + c\frac{\partial^2 u}{\partial y^2} + d\frac{\partial u}{\partial x} + e\frac{\partial u}{\partial y} + fu = g(x,y)$$

then, if $ac - b^2 > 0$, the equation is elliptic

if $ac - b^2 < 0$, the equation is hyperbolic

if $ac - b^2 = 0$, the equation is parabolic

(10) Some important equations:

- $$\frac{\partial^2 u}{\partial t^2} - c^2\frac{\partial^2 u}{\partial x^2} + 2\beta\frac{\partial u}{\partial t} + \alpha u = 0$$

   This is the telegraph equation.

- $$\frac{\partial^2 u}{\partial t^2} - c^2 \frac{\partial^2 u}{\partial x^2} = 0$$

  This is the wave equation.

- $$-\frac{h^2}{2m}\left(\frac{\partial^2 \psi}{\partial x^2} + \frac{\partial^2 \psi}{\partial y^2} + \frac{\partial^2 \psi}{\partial z^2}\right) + V(r)\psi = ih\frac{\partial \psi}{\partial t}$$

  This is Schrodinger's time−dependent equation.

- $$\frac{\partial \rho}{\partial t} + \rho\left(\frac{\partial v}{\partial x} + \frac{\partial v}{\partial y} + \frac{\partial v}{\partial z}\right) = 0$$

  This is the continuity equation.

- $$\frac{\partial u}{\partial t} - k\left(\frac{\partial^2 u}{\partial x^2} + \frac{\partial^2 u}{\partial y^2}\right) = 0$$

  This is the two−dimensional diffusion equation.

- $$\frac{\partial^2 u}{\partial x^2} + \frac{\partial^2 u}{\partial y^2} + \frac{\partial^2 u}{\partial z^2} = \frac{1}{\varepsilon_0}\rho(x,y,z)$$

  This is Poisson's equation.

- $$\left(\frac{\partial^2}{\partial x^2} + \frac{\partial^2}{\partial y^2} + \frac{\partial^2}{\partial z^2}\right)f(x,y,z) + k^2 f(x,y,z) = 0$$

  This is Helmholtz equation.

(11) In Fourier series, Euler formulae are given as

- $$a_0 = \frac{1}{2L}\int_{-L}^{L} f(x)\,dx$$

- $$a_n = \frac{1}{L}\int_{-L}^{L} f(x)\cos\frac{n\pi x}{L}\,dx \quad, \; n = 1,2,3,....$$

- $$b_n = \frac{1}{L}\int_{-L}^{L} f(x)\sin\frac{n\pi x}{L}\,dx \quad, \; n = 1,2,3,....$$

(12) For finding Fourier series,

- Write down the Fourier series for a function f(x) defined on the interval −L<x<L as

  $$f(x) = a_0 + \sum_{n=1}^{\infty}\left(a_n\cos\frac{n\pi x}{L} + b_n\sin\frac{n\pi x}{L}\right)$$

- Evaluate $a_0 = \dfrac{1}{2L}\int_{-L}^{L} f(x)\,dx$

- Evaluate $a_n = \dfrac{1}{L}\int_{-L}^{L} f(x)\cos\dfrac{n\pi x}{L}\,dx \quad, \; n = 1,2,3,....$

$$\text{and } b_n = \frac{1}{L}\int_{-L}^{L} f(x)\sin\frac{n\pi x}{L}dx \quad , n = 1,2,3,....$$

(13)

- If f(x) is an even function then $\int_{-L}^{L} f(x)dx = 2\int_{0}^{L} f(x)dx$

- If f(x) is an odd function then $\int_{-L}^{L} f(x) = 0$

(14) Fourier sine and cosine series:

- The Fourier series for an even function f(x) on the interval – L<x<L is a Fourier cosine series,

$$f(x) = a_0 + \sum_{n=1}^{\infty} a_n \cos\frac{n\pi x}{L} \qquad \text{(f even)}$$

with coefficients $a_0 = \frac{1}{L}\int_{0}^{L} f(x)dx$, $a_n = \frac{2}{L}\int_{0}^{L} f(x)\cos\frac{n\pi x}{L}dx$

- The Fourier series for an odd function f(x) on the interval – L<x<L is a Fourier sine series,

$$f(x) = \sum_{n=1}^{\infty} b_n \sin\frac{n\pi x}{L} \qquad \text{(f odd)}$$

with coefficient $b_n = \frac{2}{L}\int_{0}^{L} f(x)\sin\frac{n\pi x}{L}dx$

(15) At a point of discontinuity, the Fourier series converges to the mean value $\dfrac{f(x_0^+) + f(x_0^-)}{2}$ where $f(x_0^+)$ and $f(x_0^-)$ denote, the right hand and left hand limits of f at x_0, respectively.

At the end points, the series converges to the mean value of the end point limits, $\dfrac{f(-L^+) + f(L^-)}{2}$

Question

Papers

MATHEMATICAL METHODS IN PHYSICS –II: PHE-5

June, 2010

Note: *Attempt all questions. The marks for each question are indicated against it.*
Symbols have their usual meaning.

Q1. Answer any three parts:

(a) Show that the following equation is exact: $e^y \, dx + (xe^y + 2y) \, dy = 0$.

Ans. Refer to Chapter-1, Q.No.-4

(b) Obtain the integrating factor and solve:

$$x\frac{dy}{dx} + y = 3x^2$$

Ans. Refer to Chapter-1, Q.No.-8

(c) Solve: $\dfrac{d^2y}{dx^2} + 4\dfrac{dy}{dx} + 4y = 0$

Ans. Refer to Chapter-2, Q.No.-2

(d) Separate the following PDE into a set of two ODEs.

$$\frac{h^2}{2m}\left(\frac{\partial^2 \psi}{\partial x^2} + \frac{\partial^2 \psi}{\partial y^2}\right) + V\psi = E\psi.$$

Ans. Refer to Chapter-6, Q.No.-2

(e) (i) Find the period of $\sin\dfrac{x}{4}$.

Ans. Same as Dec. 2010 Q No.-1(d)(i)

(ii) Is the following function even, odd or neither? $x\cos nx$.

Ans. Refer to Chapter-7, Q.No.-2

(f) Determine $\dfrac{\partial f}{\partial x}, \dfrac{\partial f}{\partial y}$ and $\dfrac{\partial^2 f}{\partial x \partial y}$ for the function: $f(x,y) = \ln(x+y)$

Ans. Refer to Chapter-5, Q.No.-2

(g)   Solve one-D diffusion equation $\dfrac{d^2 P}{dx^2} = \beta^2 P \quad 0 < x < \infty.$

for $P = 4\,Po$ at $x = 0$

$P = 0$ at $x = \infty.$

Ans. Refer to Gullybaba.com, "Download Section".

Q2.   **Answer any two parts:**

(a)   Obtain the singular point of $x^2 \dfrac{d^2 y}{dx^2} + x \dfrac{dy}{dx} + (x^2 - 4)\,y = 0$ and

determine the indicial equation and its roots.

Ans. Refer to Chapter-3, Q.No.-14

(b)   The general solution of one-dimensional wave equation $\dfrac{\partial^2 u(x,t)}{\partial x^2} = \dfrac{1}{C^2} \dfrac{\partial^2 u(x,t)}{\partial t^2} \quad 0 < x < L$ is   given   by:

$$u(x,t) = \sum_{n=1}^{\infty} \left(a_n \cos\frac{n\pi c t}{L} + b_n \sin\frac{n\pi c t}{L} \right) \sin\frac{n\pi x}{L}.$$ Obtain the solution

for a stretched string in equilibrium at $t = 0$ and having a constant velocity v, i.e. under the initial conditions.

$$u(x,0) = 0 \text{ for all } x \dfrac{\partial u}{\partial t}\Big|_{t=0} \ v$$

Ans. Refer to Chapter-8, [Vibrating strings]

(c)   A source of sinusoidal e.m.f $V = V_0 \cos \omega t$ is applied to a series LCR circuit. Determine the differential equation satisfied by current end charge in the circuit as a function of time.

Ans. Using Kirchoff's voltage law, we can model the circuit with the following non-homogeneous second order ODE with constant coefficients.

$$\frac{q}{C} + Ri + L\frac{di}{dt} = V = V_0 \cos\omega t$$

$$\Rightarrow \qquad L\frac{d^2 q}{dt^2} + R\frac{dq}{dt} + \frac{q}{C} = V_0 \cos\omega t \qquad \left[\because i(t) = \frac{dq(t)}{dt} \right]$$

Now we can find q(t) and i(t), same as Chapter-4, Q.No.-6.

◈ ◈ ◈

MATHEMATICAL METHODS IN PHYSICS –II: PHE-5

December, 2010

Note: *Attempt all questions. The marks for each question are indicated against it. Symbols have their usual meaning.*

Q1. Answer any five parts:

(a) Show that the following equation is exact: $\left(x+\dfrac{2}{y}\right)dy + y\,dx = 0$

Ans. Refer to Chapter-1, Q.No.-32

(b) Obtain the integrating factor and solve: $x\dfrac{dy}{dx} - 3y = x^4$

Ans. Refer to Chapter-1, Q.No.-10

(c) Obtain the particular integral of $\dfrac{d^2y}{dx^2} + \dfrac{dy}{dx} = \sin x.$

Ans. Refer to Chapter-2, Q.No.-15

(d) (i) Determine the period of the function $\sin\dfrac{2n\pi}{L}x.$

Ans. Refer to Chapter-7, Q.No.-6

(ii) Is the following function even, odd or neither? $\sin x + \cos;x \sin nx.$

Ans. Refer to Chapter-7, Q.No.-10

(e) Separate the following PDE into a set of two ODEs.
$$\left\{\frac{\partial^2}{\partial x^2} + \frac{\partial^2}{\partial y^2} - k^2 + \left(\frac{\omega}{c}\right)^2\right\} E(x,y) = 0$$

Ans. Refer to Chapter-6, Q.No.-8

(f) Solve $\dfrac{d^2y}{dx^2} - 2\dfrac{dy}{dx} + y = 0$

Ans. Refer to Chapter-2, Q.No.-11

(g)   Set up equation of motion for a particle of mass m falling under gravity in a water pond and subjected to a resistive force proportional to its velocity.

Ans. Refer to Dec. 2011, Q 1 (e).

Q2.   Answer any two parts:

(a)   Determine the singular points of the following equation

$$x(x-1)\frac{d^2y}{dx^2} + (3x-1)\frac{dy}{dx} + y = 0$$

Obtain the indicial equation, its roots and one solution of the equation.

Ans. Same as Chapter-3, Q.No.-14.

(b)   The electric potential v in a power, transmission line along x-axis satisfies the differential equation. $\dfrac{d^2y}{dx^2} = RC\dfrac{\partial v}{\partial t}$

Its general solution is given by $V = (a\cos\lambda x + b\sin\lambda x)\left(Ae^{-\frac{\lambda^2 t}{RC}} \right)$

$$V(0,t) = V(L,t) = 0 \quad t > 0$$

$$V(x,0) = V_0 \text{ at } t = 0$$

Ans. Same as Chapter-8, Q.No.-10.

(c)   Expand the function $f(x) = \dfrac{\pi}{2}, 0 < x < \dfrac{1}{2} = 0, \dfrac{1}{2} < x < 1$ in Fourier sine series.

Ans. Refer to Chapter-7, Q.No.-15

◈ ◈ ◈

MATHEMATICAL METHODS IN PHYSICS –II: PHE-5

June, 2011

Note: *Attempt all questions. The marks for each question are indicated against it. Symbols have their usual meaning.*

Q1. **Answer any three parts:**

(a) Solve the equation: $xy\,dy = -3\,(y^2 + 4)\,dx$

Ans. Refer to Chapter-1, Q.No.-14

(b) Write the two dimensional Laplace equation in Cartesian coordinates and separate it into 2 ordinary differential equations.

Ans. Refer to Chapter-8, Q.No.-4

(c) Show that the ordinary differential equation of the form: $(e^x + y - 1)\,dx + (3e^y + x - 7)\,dy = 0$ is an exact equation and hence solve it.

Ans. Refer to Chapter-1, Q.No.-12

(d) What do mean by linearly independent solutions of an ordinary differential equation? Show that the solutions of an undamped harmonic oscillator $y'' + \alpha y = 0$ are linearly independent.

Ans. Refer to Chapter-2, Q.No.-19

(e) A radioactive sample decays at a rate proportional to the number of nuclei present in it at a given time. Write down the equation of radioactive decay and solve it. Given that the number of nuclei at $t = 0$ is N_0.

Ans. Refer to Chapter-4, Q.No.-8

Q2. **Attempt any one part:**

(a) Obtain the general solution of the following ODE using the power series method

$$(x^2 + 1)\,y'' - 2x\,y' + 2y = 0$$

Ans. Refer to Chapter-3, Q.No.-19

(b)   **Obtain the Fourier series expansion of the function**

$$f(x) = \pi - x \quad \text{for} \quad 0 < x < 2\pi$$

Ans. Refer to Chapter-7, Q.No.-19

Q3.   **Attempt any one part:**

(a)   **Solve the equation** $\dfrac{\partial u(x,t)}{\partial t} = C^2 \dfrac{\partial^2 u}{\partial x^2}(x,t)$ **given that** $u(x,0) = \sin \pi x$

$$u(0,t) = 0 = u(L,t) \quad \text{for all t.}$$

Ans. Same as Chapter-8, Q.No.-2.

(b)   **Obtain the general solution of the following equation:** $\dfrac{\partial^2 u}{\partial t^2} = \dfrac{\partial^2 u}{\partial x^2}$

    for the boundary conditions $u(0,t) = 0$, $u(L,t) = 0$, **for all** $t > 0$.

Ans. Refer to Gullybaba.com, "Download Section".

◈ ◈ ◈

MATHEMATICAL METHODS IN PHYSICS –II: PHE-5

December, 2011

Note: *Attempt all questions. The marks for each question are indicated against it.*
Symbols have their usual meaning.

Q1. **Answer any three parts:**

(a) Solve the equation $\dfrac{y'}{y+1} = \dfrac{1}{x}$

Ans. Refer to Chapter-1, Q.No.-16

(b) Solve the equation $x^2 y' - 2xy = \dfrac{1}{x}$

Ans. Refer to Chapter-1, Q.No.-18

(c) Separate the following equation into two ordinary differential equations. $\dfrac{\partial^2 f}{\partial x^2} + C\dfrac{\partial f}{\partial t} = 0.$

Ans. Refer to Chapter-6, Q.No.-11

(d) Solve the equation $y'' - 4y' + 4y = 0$

Ans. Refer to Chapter-2, Q.No.-25

(e) A particle falls under gravity in a pool of water. A resistive force directly proportional to its velocity acts on it opposite to the force of gravity. Write its equation of motion. Solve it to obtain the particle's velocity as a function of time.

Ans. Refer to Chapter-4, Q.No.-3

Q2. **Answer any one part:**

(a) Determine the roots of the indicial equation and obtain the recurrence relation for the following ODE.

$$2x^2 \dfrac{d^2 y}{dx^2} - x\dfrac{dy}{dx} + (1 - x^2)\, y = 0$$

Ans. Given ODE is, $2x^2 \dfrac{d^2 y}{dx^2} - x \dfrac{dy}{dx} + (1-x^2)\, y = 0$ ...(i)

Now dividing by $2x^2$, we get $\dfrac{d^2 y}{dx^2} - \dfrac{1}{2x}\dfrac{dy}{dx} + \dfrac{(1-x^2)}{2x^2}\, y = 0$

$\Rightarrow\ P(x) = -\dfrac{1}{2x}$ and $Q(x) = \dfrac{(1-x^2)}{2x^2}$

Now, $xP(x) = x\left(-\dfrac{1}{2x}\right) = -\dfrac{1}{2}$ and $x^2 Q(x) = \dfrac{x^2(1-x^2)}{2x^2} = \dfrac{1-x^2}{2}$

Now $\displaystyle\lim_{x\to 0} x\,P(x) = -\dfrac{1}{2} = b(x)$ and $\displaystyle\lim_{x\to 0} x^2\,Q(x) = \dfrac{1}{2} = c(x)$

Here, $b(x)$ and $c(x)$ are analytic at $x = 0$. Thus, $x = 0$ is a regular singular point (RSP).

Now $y(x) = \displaystyle\sum_{n=0}^{\infty} a_n x^{n+r}$

Differentiating it with respect to x, we get $y'(x) = \displaystyle\sum_{n-0}^{\infty} a_n (n+r) x^{n+r-1}$

and $y''(x) = \displaystyle\sum_{n=0}^{\infty} a_n (n+r)(n+r-1) x^{n+r-2}$

On substituting these in given equation (i), we get

$$2\sum_{n=0}^{\infty}(n+r)(n+r-1)\,a_n\,x^{n+r} - \sum_{n=0}^{\infty}(n+r)\,a_n x^{n+r} + \sum_{n=0}^{\infty} a_n x^{n+r} - \sum_{n=0}^{\infty} a_n x^{n+r+2} = 0$$

For the indicial equation, we equate the coefficients of the lowest power of x, i.e. x^r to zero. This gives, $a_0\left[2r(r-1)-r+1\right]=0$

For $a_0 \neq 0$, the indicial equation takes form, $2r^2 - 2r - r + 1 = 0 \Rightarrow 2r^2 - 3r + 1 = 0$

Now $2r^2 - 2r - r + 1 = 0 \Rightarrow 2r(r-1) - 1(r-1) = 0 \Rightarrow (2r-1)(r-1) = 0$

$\Rightarrow\ r = 1/2\ ,\ 1$

Hence, $1/2\ ,\ 1$ are the required roots of indicial equation.

Now we can find recurrence relation same as Q.No-2(a) of June - 2011.

(b) **Obtain the Fourier series expansion of a function with periodicity 2π and defined as**

$$f(x) = \begin{cases} 0 & -\pi < x < 0 \\ x & 0 < x < \pi \end{cases}$$

Ans. Same as Chapter-7, Q.No.-17.

Q3. **Answer any one part:**

(a) **Both the ends of a uniform thin rod of length L units are kept at zero temperature and its lateral surface is insulated. Obtain its temperature distribution $T(x,t)$ if it is modelled by the equation**

$$\frac{\partial T(x,t)}{\partial t} = k\frac{\partial^2 T(x,t)}{\partial x^2}, \; (0 < x < L, \, t > 0)$$

Ans. Refer to Chapter-8, [Heat conduction]

(b) **A string at its two ends l metres apart. It starts its motion with the initial condition given as $y(x, 0) = a \sin\dfrac{\pi x}{l}$ and $\left(\dfrac{\partial y}{\partial t}\right)_{t=0} = 0$.**

Determine $y(x,t)$ using appropriate boundary conditions.

Ans. Refer to Chapter-8, [Vibrating Strings]

◇ ◇ ◇

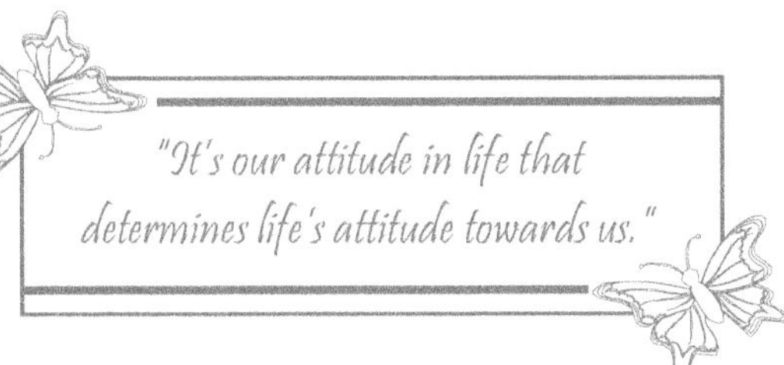

MATHEMATICAL METHODS IN PHYSICS –II: PHE-5

June, 2012

Note: *Attempt all questions. The marks for each question are indicated against it. Symbols have their usual meaning.*

Q1. **Attempt any three parts:**

(a) Show that the following equation is exact and solve it:
$e^y \, dx + (x e^y + 2y) \, dy = 0$

Ans. Refer to June-2010, Q.No.-1(a)

(b) Obtain the integrating factor of the following equation and solve it: $\dfrac{dy}{dx} + \dfrac{1}{x} y = 3x$

Ans. Refer to Chapter-1, Q.No.-6

(c) Determine all the first and second order partial derivatives of the function $f(x,y) = x^2 - 5xy^3$

Ans. Refer to Chapter-5, Q.No.-11

(d) Separate the following PDE into two ODEs.

$$\left(E \frac{\partial}{\partial t} - p \frac{\partial}{\partial x} \right) \psi(x,t) = m\psi(x,t)$$

Ans. Refer to Chapter-6, Q.No.-5

(e) Obtain the particular integral of

$$\frac{d^2 y}{dx^2} + \frac{dy}{dx} + 2y = 3x$$

Ans. Given equation is $\dfrac{d^2 y}{dx^2} + \dfrac{dy}{dx} + 2y = 3x \qquad \ldots(i)$

Using the method of undetermined coefficients, we have
$y_p = C_0 + C_1 x$ or $y = C_0 + C_1 x$

$$\Rightarrow \frac{dy}{dx} = C_1 \text{ and } \frac{d^2 y}{dx^2} = 0$$

Now from (i), we have

$$C_1 + 2C_0 + 2C_1 x = 3x$$

Equating the coefficients of like powers of x, we get $2C_1 = 3$

$\Rightarrow \quad C_1 = 3/2$ and $C_1 + 2C_0 = 0$

$$\Rightarrow \quad \frac{3}{2} + 2C_0 = 0 \Rightarrow \quad 2C_0 = \frac{-3}{2} \Rightarrow \quad C_0 = \frac{-3}{4}$$

Hence, P.I. is $y_p = C_0 + C_1 x \Rightarrow \quad y_p = \frac{-3}{4} + \frac{3x}{2}$

Q2. Expand the square wave V(x) given by:

$$V(x) = 0 \quad -\pi < x < 0$$

$$= V_0 \quad 0 < x < \pi$$

in Fourier series.

Ans. Refer to Chapter-7, Q.No.-22

Or

Obtain the singular point of the following ODE and specify its nature:

$$x\frac{d^2 y}{dx^2} - 2\frac{dy}{dx} + xy = 0$$

Determine the indicial equation and its roots.

Ans. Refer to Chapter-3, Q.No.-8

Q3. The electrical potential in a power transmission line along the x - axis satisfies the equation:

$$\frac{\partial^2 V}{\partial x^2} = RC\frac{\partial V}{\partial t}$$

Using the method of separation of variables, solve this equation for V under the following conditions:

$$V(x, t) = 0 \text{ at } x = 0$$

$$V(x, 0) = V_0 \qquad \text{at } t = 0$$

$$V(x, t) = 0 \text{ at } x = L$$

Ans. Same as Chapter-8 Q.No.10.

Or

A particle of mass m falls freely under gravity in a liquid that offers a resistive force proportional to its velocity:

$$f_{res} = -y\frac{dx}{dt}$$

Set up the equation of motion and solve it.

Ans. Refer to Chapter-4, Q.No.-14

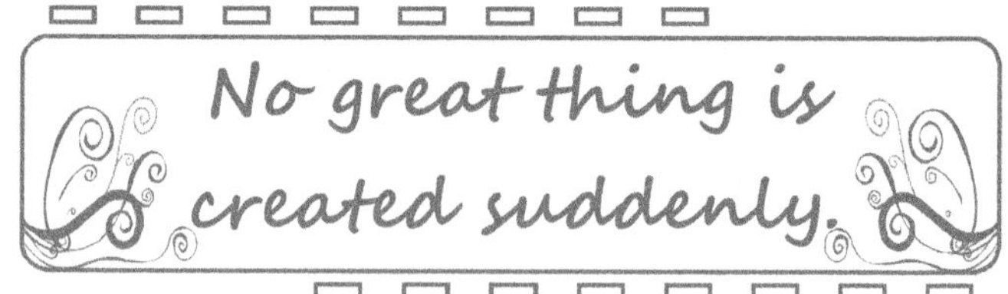

MATHEMATICAL METHODS IN PHYSICS –II: PHE-5

December, 2012

Note: *Attempt all questions. The marks for each question are indicated against it. Symbols have their usual meaning.*

Q1. Attempt any three parts:

(a) Show that the following equation is exact and then solve it:

$$\left(x+\frac{2}{y}\right)dy+y\,dx=0$$

Ans. Refer to Chapter-1, Q.No.-32

(b) Obtain the integrating factor and solve the equation: $x\dfrac{dy}{dx}-2y=x^4$

Ans. Refer to Chapter-1, Q.No.-2

(c) Determine all the first and second order partial derivatives of the function:

$$f(x,y)=xe^{y}+ye^{x}$$

Ans. Given equations is $f(x,y)=xe^{y}+ye^{x}$

Now $\dfrac{\partial f}{\partial x}=e^{y}+ye^{x}$ and $\dfrac{\partial f}{\partial y}=xe^{y}+e^{x}$

Hence, $\dfrac{\partial^{2}f}{\partial x^{2}}=ye^{x}$ and $\dfrac{\partial^{2}f}{\partial y^{2}}=xe^{y}$

Now $\dfrac{\partial^{2}f}{\partial x\partial y}=\dfrac{\partial}{\partial x}\left(\dfrac{\partial f}{\partial y}\right)\Rightarrow\quad\dfrac{\partial^{2}f}{\partial x\partial y}=\dfrac{\partial}{\partial x}\left[xe^{y}+e^{x}\right]=e^{y}+e^{x}$

and $\dfrac{\partial^{2}f}{\partial y\partial x}=\dfrac{\partial}{\partial y}\left[\dfrac{\partial f}{\partial x}\right]=\dfrac{\partial}{\partial y}\left[e^{y}+ye^{x}\right]=e^{y}+e^{x}$

(d)   Separate the following PDE into two ODEs:

$$-\frac{h^2}{2m}\left(\frac{\partial^2}{\partial x^2}+\frac{\partial^2}{\partial y^2}\right)\psi(x,y)+V\psi(x,y)$$

$$= E\psi(x,y).$$

Ans. Same as June-2010, Q.No.-1(d).

(e)   Find the particular solution of

$$\frac{d^2 y}{dx^2}+3\frac{dy}{dx}=4\sin x.$$

Ans. Refer to Chapter-2, Q.No.-6

Q2.   Determine the singular point of the following equation and specify its nature:

$$x^2\frac{d^2 y}{dx^2}-2x\frac{dy}{dx}+\left(x^2+2\right)y=0$$

Obtain the indicial equation and determine its roots.

Ans. Refer to Chapter-3, Q.No.-2

Or

A source of e.m.f E is connected to an LR circuit. Establish the differential equation governing the current I in the circuit. Solve it for the condition: $I=I_0$ at $t=0$.

Ans. Same as Chapter-4, Q. No.-1

Q3.   Expand the full wave rectified potential Fourier series:

$$V = V_0\sin\omega t \qquad 0<\omega t<\pi$$

$$= -V_0\sin\omega t \qquad -\pi<\omega t<0$$

Ans. Same as Chapter-7, Q. No.-23(b)

Or

The diffusion of particles in the atmosphere is governed by the diffusion equation:

$$\frac{\partial^2 u(x,t)}{\partial x^2}=\frac{1}{k}\frac{\partial u(x,t)}{\partial t}+\Upsilon^2 u(x,t) \quad \text{where } u(x,t) \text{ is the concentration}$$

density of particles. The general solution of this equation is given by $u(x,t)=(C_1\sin\lambda x+C_2\cos\lambda x)\,e^{-\left(\Upsilon^2+\lambda^2\right)kt}$

Obtain the particular solution under the following conditions.

$$u(x, 0) = u_0$$

$$\frac{\partial u(x,t)}{\partial x} = 0$$

$$u(L, t) = 0$$

Ans. Refer to Chapter - 8, [Diffusion of Particles]

◈ ◈ ◈

MATHEMATICAL METHODS IN PHYSICS –II: PHE-5

June, 2013

Q1. **Answer any three parts:**

(a) **Solve the equation** $(2y+2)dx + 2xdy = 0$

Ans. Refer to Chapter-1, Q.No.-20

(b) **Show that the ODE**

$$(4x^3 + 6e^y + 2y\cos 2x)dx + (3y^2 + 6xe^y + \sin 2x)dy = 0 \text{ is } \quad \text{an} \quad \text{exact}$$

equation and hence solve it.

Ans. Refer to Chapter-1, Q.No.-37

(c) **Show that the function** $\phi(x,y,z) = \dfrac{1}{\left(x^2 + y^2 + z^2\right)^{1/2}}$ **satisfies**

Laplace's equation $\nabla^2\phi = 0$ **for** $(x,y,z) \neq (0,0,0)$.

Ans. Refer to Chapter-8, Q.No.-9

(d) **Reduce the following PDE into three ODEs:** $\nabla^2\phi + k^2\phi = 0$

Ans. Refer to Chapter-6, Q.No.-15

(e) **What do you understand by 'ordinary' and 'singular' points of a differential equation? Determine the singularity of the equation** $x^3(1-x)y''(x) + (1-x)y'(x) - 4xy(x) = 0.$ **Is this singularity regular?**

Ans. See definitions of ordinary and singular points in Chapter-3.

Now, given equation is $x^3(1-x)y''(x) + (1-x)y'(x) - 4xy(x) = 0$

$$\Rightarrow \quad y''(x) + \frac{1}{x^3}y'(x) - \frac{4}{x^2(1-x)}y(x) = 0$$

Hence, $P(x) = \dfrac{1}{x^3}$ and $Q(x) = \dfrac{-4}{x^2(1-x)}$

Since, $P(x)$ and $Q(x)$ are not analytic at $x = 0$.

Hence, $x = 0$ is not ordinary point. Because $\lim\limits_{x \to 0} P(x) =$ does not exist

and $\lim\limits_{x \to 0} Q(x) =$ does not exist

Now $xP(x) = \dfrac{1}{x^2}$ and $x^2 Q(x) = \dfrac{-4}{1-x}$ $\Rightarrow$ $\lim\limits_{x \to 0} xP(x) =$ does not exist

and $\lim\limits_{x \to 0} x^2 Q(x) = -4$

Here $x\,P(x)$ is not analytic at $x = 0$ and $x^2 Q(x)$ is analytic at $x = 0$

Since $x = 0$ is not a regular singular point.

Hence, $x = 0$ is an irregular singular point

Q2. **Attempt any one part:**

(a) **Using the power series method, obtain the recurrence relation for the following equation:** $y'' - 2xy' + 2ny = 0$

Ans. Refer to Chapter-3, Q.No.-22

(b) $f(t) = \begin{cases} 0 & -\pi \le t \le 0 \\ \sin t & 0 \le t \le \pi \end{cases}$ **in Fourier series**

Ans. Refer to Chapter-7, Q.No.-25

Q3. **Attempt any one part:**

(a) **Solve the one-dimensional equation for an insulated wire of length** l: $\dfrac{\partial T(x,t)}{\partial t} = k\dfrac{\partial^2 T(x,t)}{\partial x^2}$. **Determine the temperature distribution given that** $T(x,0) = T_0 \sin^2\left(\dfrac{\pi x}{l}\right)$; **and** $\dfrac{\partial T}{\partial x}(x=0) = \dfrac{\partial T}{\partial x}(x=l) = 0$.

Ans. Same as Chapter-8, [Heat conduction]

(b) **Solve the wave equation** $\dfrac{\partial^2 u}{\partial t^2} = C^2 \dfrac{\partial^2 u}{\partial x^2}$ **under the boundary conditions** $u(0, t) = 0$ **and** $u(l, t) = 0$ **and the initial conditions** $u(x,0) = a\sin\left(\dfrac{\pi x}{l}\right)$ **and** $\left.\dfrac{\partial u}{\partial t}\right|_{t=0} = 0.$

Ans. Same as Chapter-8 [Vibrating strings]

MATHEMATICAL METHODS IN PHYSICS –II: PHE-5

December, 2013

Note: Attempt all questions. The marks for each question are indicated against it. Symbols have their usual meanings. Use of log tables or a non programmable calculator is allowed.

Q1. Answer any three parts:

(a) Solve the equation

$$xdy - ydx = \sqrt{x^2 - y^2}\,dx$$

(b) Show that the ODE of the form

$$\left(2xy + e^y\right)dx + \left(x^2 + xe^y\right)dy = 0$$ is an exact equation and hence solve it.

(c) Show that the function $T(x,y,z,t) = Ae^{-3kt}\sin x \sin y \sin z$, satisfies the three dimensional heat diffusion equation:

$$\nabla^2 T = \frac{1}{k}\frac{\partial T}{\partial t}$$

(d) Reduce the given PDE into two ODEs

$$\frac{\partial^2 \phi}{\partial r^2} + \frac{1}{r}\frac{\partial \phi}{\partial r} + \frac{1}{r^2}\frac{\partial^2 \phi}{\partial \theta^2} + k^2\phi = 0$$

(e) In an electric circuit, a resistance R and an inductance L are connected in series with a battery which provides the driving voltage E(t). Write down the differential equation for the electric current i in the circuit and solve it for $E(t) = E_0$.

Q2. Attempt any one part:

(a) Using the Frobenius method, determine the roots of the indicial equation for the following equation:

$$8x^2y''(x) + 10xy'(x) - (1+x)y(x) = 0$$

(b) Determine the Fourier series of the function

$$f(x) = \begin{cases} 1 & -\dfrac{1}{2} \le x < \dfrac{1}{2} \\[2mm] 0 & \dfrac{1}{2} \le x < \dfrac{3}{2} \end{cases}$$

Q3. Attempt any one part:

(a) Solve the heat diffusion equation

$$\alpha^2 \frac{\partial^2 T}{\partial x^2} = \frac{\partial T}{\partial t} \quad 0 < x < l,$$

0<t for a rod with both ends kept at $0°C$. The initial temperature distribution in the rod is given by

$$T(x,0) = \begin{cases} x & 0 < x < \dfrac{l}{2} \\[2mm] l - x & \dfrac{l}{2} \le x \le l \end{cases}$$ Determine the temperature distribution

in the rod.

(b) A uniform stretched string of length l is plucked at $x = \dfrac{l}{2}$ to a height 'h' and then released. Solve the wave equation for the string:
$$\frac{\partial^2 u}{\partial x^2} = \frac{1}{v^2}\frac{\partial^2 u}{\partial t^2} \quad \text{for the initial conditions:}$$

$$u(x,0) = \begin{cases} \dfrac{2hx}{l}, & 0 < x < \dfrac{l}{2} \\[3mm] 2h\left(1 - \dfrac{x}{l}\right), & \dfrac{l}{2} \le x < l \end{cases}$$

◈ ◈ ◈

MATHEMATICAL METHODS IN PHYSICS –II: PHE-5

June, 2014

Note: *Attempt all questions. The marks for each question are indicated against it. Symbols have their usual meaning.*

Q1. Answer any *three* parts:

(a) Show that the solution of the ODE:

$(y+4)y'+x=0$ is a family of concentric circles centred at (0, –4).

(b) Solve the ODE: $y''+3y'+2y=e^{x}$.

(c) If $z=ln(x^{2}+cy^{2})$, what should be the value of c so that z satisfies the equation

$$\frac{\partial^{2}z}{\partial x^{2}}+\frac{\partial^{2}z}{\partial y^{2}}=0$$

(d) Solve the initial value problem:

$y''+5y'+6y=0,\quad y(0)=1,\ y'(0)=4$

(e) Is the periodic function

$f(x)=x,\quad -1<x<1$

$f(x+2)=f(x)$

odd or even? Obtain its Fourier series expansion.

Q2. Answer any one part:

(a) Determine the roots of the indicial equation around the origin for the following differential equation:

$$x^{2}y''+xy'+\left(x^{2}-\frac{1}{9}\right)y=0$$

Also obtain the recurrence relation.

(b) A conductor of resistance R and inductance L is connected in series with an alternating voltage source $E = E_0 \sin \omega t$. Show that the current i(t) in the circuit is given by

$$i(t) = \frac{E_0 \sin(\omega t - \theta)}{\sqrt{R^2 + \omega^2 L^2}}$$

where $\theta = \tan^{-1}(\omega L / R)$.

Q3. Answer any one part:

(a) Obtain the Fourier series of the periodic function

$$E(t) = \begin{cases} 0, & \text{if } -T/2 < t < 0 \\ E_0 \sin \omega t, & \text{if } 0 < t < T/2 \end{cases}$$

where $T = 2\pi / \omega$

(b) The steady-state temperature distribution, $T(x, y)$, of a rectangular plate is governed by the following equation:

$$\frac{\partial^2 T(x, y)}{\partial x^2} + \frac{\partial^2 T(x, y)}{\partial y^2} = 0; \qquad\qquad 0 < x < L; \; 0 < y < B$$

Determine T(x, y) if the boundary conditions are

(i) $T(0, y) = 0, \; \dfrac{\partial T(L, y)}{\partial x} = 0, \; 0 < y < B$

(ii) $T(x, 0) = 0, \; \dfrac{T(x, B)}{9} = T_0, \; 0 < x < L$

◈ ◈ ◈

MATHEMATICAL METHODS IN PHYSICS –II: PHE-5

December, 2014

Note: *Attempt all questions. The marks for each question are indicated against it. Symbols have their usual meaning.*

Q1. Attempt any three parts:

(a) Solve the ordinary differential equation:

$$\frac{dy}{dx} = -\frac{1}{x}\frac{y^3+1}{3y^2}$$

(b) Obtain the general solution of the partial differential equation $y'' + 4y = 3\sin x$.

(c) Show that $u = \sum_{n=1}^{N} a_n e^{-kn^2 y} \sin nx$ is a solution of the partial differential equation

$$\frac{\partial u}{\partial y} - k\frac{\partial^2 u}{\partial x^2} = 0$$

(d) Using the method of separation of variables, reduce the following PDE to a set of ODEs:

$$\frac{\partial^2 f}{\partial r^2} + \frac{1}{r}\frac{\partial f}{\partial r} + \frac{\partial^2 f}{\partial z^2} = 0$$

(e) A body of mass M is attached to a spring of spring constant k. If this spring-mass system experiences a damping force linearly proportional to velocity, obtain the general solution of the equation governing the motion.

Q2. Answer any one part:

(a) For the Legendre's equation

$$\left(1-x^2\right)y'' - 2xy' + l(l+1)y = 0$$

Obtain the recurrence relations for the coefficients of the power series solution.

(b) Obtain the Fourier series expansion of a full-wave rectifier output given by

$$f(t) = \begin{cases} 100\sin\omega t; & 0 < t < \pi \\ -100\sin\omega t; & -\pi < t < 0 \end{cases}$$

Q3. Answer any one part:

(a) Solve the following equation for the given conditions:

$$\frac{\partial^2 u(x,t)}{\partial x^2} = \frac{\partial u(x,t)}{\partial t}, \quad 0 < x < 1, \ t > 0$$

$$\frac{\partial u(0,t)}{\partial x} = 0, \ \frac{\partial u}{\partial x}(1,t) = 0, \ t > 0$$

$$u(x,0) = 1 + 2x, \quad 0 < x < 1$$

(b) Solve the equation

$$\frac{\partial^2 u(x,t)}{\partial x^2} = \frac{1}{v^2}\frac{\partial^2 u(x,t)}{\partial t^2}, \quad 0 < x < 2, \ t > 0$$

For the following conditions:

$$u(0,t) = 0, \quad u(2,t) = 0$$

$$u(x,0) = \begin{cases} x & 0 < x < 1 \\ 2-x & 1 \le x < 2 \end{cases}$$

and $\left. \dfrac{\partial u}{\partial t} \right|_{t=0} = 0$

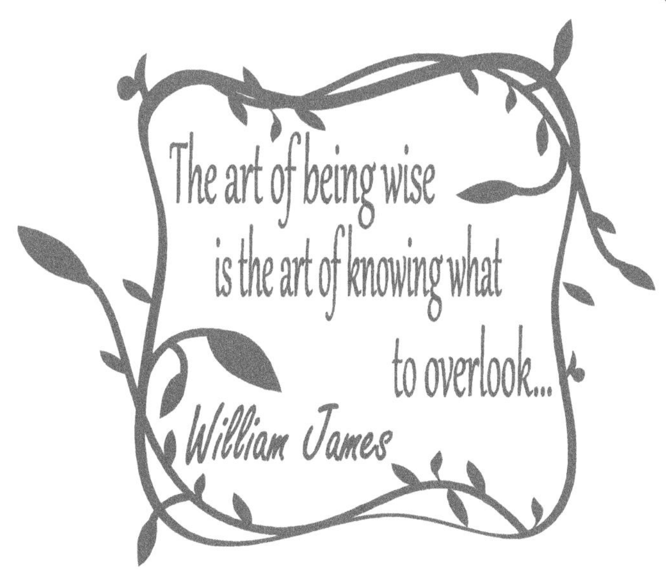

MATHEMATICAL METHODS IN PHYSICS –II: PHE-5

June, 2015

Note: *Attempt all questions. The marks for each question are indicated against it. Symbols have their usual meaning.*

Q1. Attempt any three parts:

(a) Show that the equation

$$3x(xy-2)dx + (x^3 + 2y)dy = 0 \text{ is exact and determine its solution.}$$

(b) Solve the following equation:

$$\frac{dy}{dx} = \frac{x^3 + y^3}{xy^2}$$

(c) Show that the function $f(x,t) = x^2 + 9t^2$ satisfies the wave equation $\dfrac{\partial^2 f}{\partial x^2} = \dfrac{1}{c^2}\dfrac{\partial^2 f}{\partial t^2}$. Hence, obtain the value of c.

(d) Find the particular integral of the following equation:

$$\frac{d^2 y}{dx^2} - y = x + \frac{x^2}{2}$$

(e) Use the method of separation of variables to reduce the Laplace's equation $\nabla^2 f = 0$ into three ODEs.

Q2. Write down the differential equation for a particle falling vertically from rest under a constant force of gravity $\left(\vec{F} = m\vec{g}\right)$ and a resistive force proportional to its velocity. Solve its equation of motion to obtain its velocity and position as a function of time.

Or

For the ODE, $\dfrac{d^2 y}{dx^2} - 2x\dfrac{dy}{dx} + 2xy = 0$, obtain the coefficients of the power series solution.

Q3. Plot the periodic function $f(x) = x \{ -\pi \le x \le \pi$ where $f((x + 2\pi) = f(x)$. Expand it in a Fourier series.

Or

Heat flow from an insulated bar of length L with both its ends at $0°C$ satisfies the following diffusion equation:

$$\frac{\partial T(x,t)}{\partial t} = k \frac{\partial^2 T}{\partial x^2}(x,t), \ (0 < x < L, \ t > 0)$$

Write down the boundary conditions for the problem and obtain the general solution.

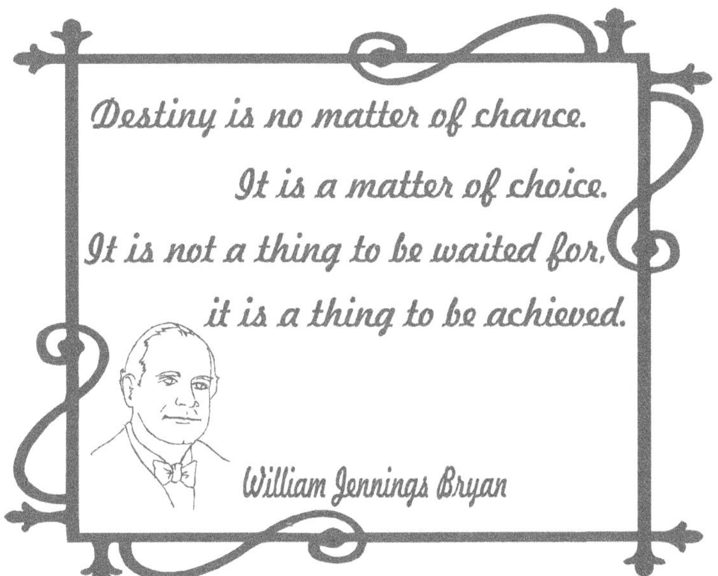

MATHEMATICAL METHODS IN PHYSICS –II: PHE-5
December, 2015

Note: *Attempt all questions. The marks for each question are indicated against it. Symbols have their usual meaning.*

Q1. **Answer any three parts:**

(a) Show that the function $z = \ln\left(x^2 + y^2\right)$ satisfies the equation

$$\frac{\partial^2 z}{\partial x^2} + \frac{\partial^2 z}{\partial y^2} = 0$$

(b) Show that the following equation is exact and solve it:

$$y^2 dx + 2xy\, dy = 0 \,.$$

(c) Solve the following differential equation:

$$y'' + 4y = 2\sin x$$

(d) Solve:

$$y' + y\tan x = \sin 2x$$

(e) Reduce the Helmholtz equation

$$\left(\frac{\partial^2}{\partial x^2} + \frac{\partial^2}{\partial y^2}\right) f(x,y) + k^2 f(x,y) = 0 \text{ to two ODEs.}$$

Q2. Write down the coupled differential equations for two identical pendulums, each having a mass m suspended on a rigid massless rod of length 1 m. The masses are connected by a spring of stiffness constant k. Uncouple these equations using suitable coordinates.

Or

Use power series method to solve the following equation:

$$\left(1 - x^2\right) y'' - 2xy' + 2y = 0$$

Q3. **Expand**

$$f(x) = x^2 \text{ for } -\pi \le x \le \pi$$

in a Fourier series.

Or

Solve the wave equation

$$\frac{\partial^2 u}{\partial t^2} = a^2 \frac{\partial^2 u}{\partial x^2}$$

under the conditions:

(i) $u = 0$, when $x = 0$ and $x = \pi$

(ii) $\dfrac{\partial u}{\partial t} = 0$, when $t = 0$ and

(iii) $u(x, 0) = x, \ 0 < x < \pi$.

◇ ◇ ◇

MATHEMATICAL METHODS IN PHYSICS –II: PHE-5

June, 2016

Note: *Attempt all questions. The marks for each question are indicated against it. Symbols have their usual meanings. Use of log tables or a non programmable calculator is allowed.*

Q1. Attempt any three parts:

(a) Show that the following ODE is exact and solve it:

$$\left(y - x^3\right)dx + \left(x + y^3\right)dy = 0$$

(b) Determine all the first and second order partial derivatives of the function $f(x,y) = \log(ax + by)$.

(c) Separate the following PDE into two ODEs:

$$\left\{\frac{1}{r}\frac{\partial}{\partial r}\, r\, \frac{\partial}{\partial r} + \frac{1}{r^2}\frac{\partial^2}{\partial \theta^2}\right\}\psi(r,\theta) = 0$$

(d) Obtain the integrating factor and solve the ODE:

$$\frac{dy}{dx} + \frac{1}{x}y = \frac{1}{x^2}$$

(e) Obtain the particular integral of the ODE:

$$\frac{d^2y}{dx^2} + 3\frac{dy}{dx} = 2\sin x$$

Q2. Determine the singular points of the ODE $x(x-1)\dfrac{d^2y}{dx^2} + (3x-1)\dfrac{dy}{dx} + y = 0.$ Obtain the indicial equation and one of the solutions of the differential equation.

Or

A sphere of mass 'm' is falling freely under gravity in a lake that offers a resistive force proportional to velocity i.e. $f_{res} = -\gamma \dfrac{dx}{dt}$, where γ is the constant of proportionality. Set up the equation of motion for the sphere and solve it.

Q3. The electric potential V(x, t) in a power transmission line along x-axis satisfies the equation:

$$\frac{\partial^2 V(x,t)}{\partial x^2} = RC \frac{\partial V(x,t)}{\partial t}$$

Using the method of separation of variables, solve the equation under the conditions:

V = 0	at	x = 0
V = V₀	at	t = 0
V = 0	at	x = L

Or

Draw the function $f(x) = \dfrac{\pi}{L}x$ defined in the interval $-L < x < L$ and obtain its Fourier series expansion.

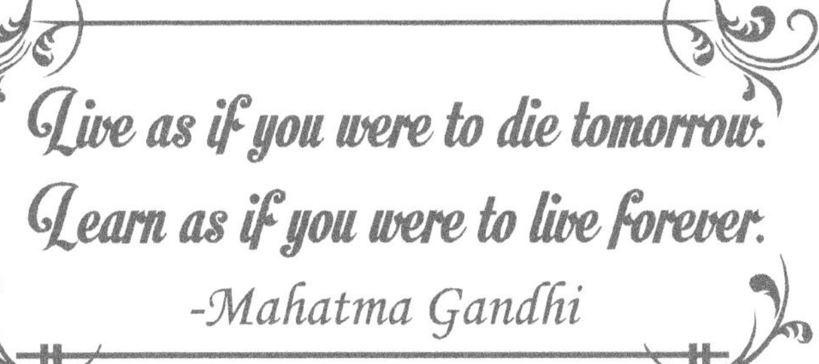

MATHEMATICAL METHODS IN PHYSICS –II: PHE-5

December, 2016

Note: *Attempt all questions. The marks for each question are indicated against it. Symbols have their usual meaning.*

Q1. Attempt any three parts:

(a) Determine which of the following ODEs are exact:

(i) $\cos x \cos^2 y \, dx + 2 \sin x \sin y \cos y \, dy = 0$

(ii) $\left(2xy^3 + y \cos x\right)dx + \left(3x^2y^2 + \sin x\right)dy = 0$

(b) Obtain the particular integral of the ODE:

$$\frac{d^2y}{dx^2} + \frac{dy}{dx} + 2y = 3x$$

(c) Obtain the integrating factor and solve the ODE

$$\frac{dy}{dx} + \frac{1}{x}y = 3x$$

(d) Separate the following PDE into two ODEs:

$$\frac{\partial}{\partial r}\left(r^2 \frac{\partial \psi}{\partial r}\right) + \frac{1}{\sin \theta}\frac{\partial}{\partial \theta}\left(\sin \theta \frac{\partial \psi}{\partial \theta}\right) = 0$$

(e) Classify the following PDEs by way of order and degree, linearity/non-linearity, homogeneity/non-homogeneity:

(i)
$$\frac{\partial^2 u}{\partial dt^2} - c^2 \frac{\partial^2 u}{\partial x^2} = 0$$

(ii)
$$\frac{\partial \rho}{\partial t} + \rho\left(\frac{\partial v}{\partial x} + \frac{\partial v}{\partial y} + \frac{\partial v}{\partial z}\right) = 0$$

Q2. Expand the square wave $V(x)$ defined by

$$V(x) = 0, \qquad\qquad -\pi < x < 0$$

$$= V_0, \qquad\qquad 0 < x < \pi$$

in Fourier series.

Determine the period of the function $\sin\dfrac{x}{4}$ and show whether the function is even or odd.

Or

The general solution of a PDE

$$\frac{\partial^2 f}{\partial x^2} = \alpha^2 \frac{\partial f}{\partial t} \quad \text{is given by}$$

$$f(x,t) = (a\ \cos\ kx + b\ \sin\ kx)\left(A\ e^{-\frac{k^2}{\alpha^2}t} + B\ e^{+\frac{k^2}{\alpha^2}t} \right)$$

Determine the particular solution under the conditions:

$$f(x, t) = 0, \ \text{at} \qquad x = 0 \qquad \text{and} \qquad x = L$$

$$f(x, t) = F_0, \ \text{at} \qquad t = 0$$

Q3. Determine the singular points of the ODE:

$$x(x-1)\frac{d^2 y}{dx^2} - x\frac{dy}{dx} + y = 0$$

Obtain the indicial equation and solve it. Determine the solution of the ODE for one of the roots of the indicial equation, namely, $r = 1$.

Or

A source of emf E is connected to an LR circuit. Establish the differential equation governing the current I in the circuit and solve for the case when $I = I_0$ at $t = 0$.

MATHEMATICAL METHODS IN PHYSICS –II: PHE-5

June, 2017

Note: *Attempt all questions. The marks for each question are indicated against it. Symbols have their usual meaning.*

Q1. **Attempt any three parts:**

(a) Show that the differential equation $x\dfrac{dy}{dx}+y+4=0$ is exact and hence, solve it.

Ans. Same as Chapter-1, Q.No.-19

(b) Obtain the general solution of the ODE $y''+y=2\sin x$.

Ans. Same as Chapter-1, Q.No.-9(a)

(c) Show that the function $z=e^{x}\cos y$ satisfies the equation

$$\frac{\partial^2 z}{\partial x^2}+\frac{\partial^2 z}{\partial y^2}=0.$$

Ans. Same as Chapter-5, Q.No.-10 (b)

(d) Reduce the following PDE into two ODEs:

$$\left(\frac{\partial^2}{\partial r^2}+\frac{1}{r}\frac{\partial}{\partial r}+\frac{1}{r^2}\frac{\partial^2}{\partial \theta^2}\right)f(r,\theta)=k^2 f(r,\theta)$$

Ans. Same as Chapter-6, Q.No.-5

(e) A source of emf $E(t)=E_0\cos\omega t$ is applied to a series RC circuit. Set up the differential equation for the variation of charge with time in the circuit. Solve the equation for $E(t)=0$.

Ans. Refer to Chapter-4, Q.No.-1

Q2. **Attempt any one part:**

(a) Consider the equation

$$2x^2\frac{d^2y}{dx^2}+3x\frac{dy}{dx}-\left(x^2+1\right)y=0.$$

(i) Locate the singularities and identify their nature.

Ans. Same as June-2013, Q.No.-1(e)

(ii) Obtain the indicial equation using the Frobenius series method and determine its roots.

Ans. Same as Chapter-3, Q.No.-13

(b) Solve the initial value problem

$$\frac{d^2x}{dt^2} - 3\frac{dx}{dt} - 10x = 0; \quad \frac{dx}{dt}(t=0) = 0,$$

$$x(0) = 1.$$

Ans. Same as Chapter-2, Q.No.-4

Q3. Attempt any one part:

(a) Expand the function $f(x) = x^2$ in Fourier series in the interval $(-\pi, \pi)$.

Ans. Since $f(x) = x^2$ is an event function, the sine coefficients b_n must be zero.

The cosine coefficients are given by

$$a_n = \frac{1}{\pi}\int_{-\pi}^{\pi} f(x).\cos(nx)\,dx$$

We get
$$a_0 = \frac{1}{\pi}\int_{-\pi}^{\pi} x^2\,dx = \frac{2x^2}{3},$$

and
$$a_n = \frac{1}{\pi}\int_{-\pi}^{\pi} x^2.\cos(nx)\,dx = \frac{4(-1)^n}{\pi n^2}$$

It follows that the Fouries series of f is given by

$$\frac{a_0}{2} + \sum_{n=1}^{\infty}\left(a_n\cos(nx) + b_n\sin(nx)\right) = \frac{\pi^2}{3} + 4\sum_{n=1}^{\infty}\frac{(-1)^n}{n^2}\cos(nx)$$

(b) A uniform bar of length L is insulated along its length. Both ends of the bar are maintained at 0°. Solve the one-dimensional heat flow equation $\frac{\partial T}{\partial t}(x,t) = k\frac{\partial^2 T}{\partial x^2}(x,t),$ for $(0 < x < L, t > 0)$ subjected to the boundary conditions

$$T(0,t) = T(L,t) = 0; \, t \geq 0.$$

The initial temperature distribution is $T(x,0) = 50\sin\dfrac{\pi x}{L}.$

Ans. Refer to Chapter-8, (Heat Conduction)

MATHEMATICAL METHODS IN PHYSICS –II: PHE-5

December, 2017

Note: *Attempt all questions. The marks for each question are indicated against it. Symbols have their usual meanings. You may use log tables or a non programmable calculator is allowed.*

Q1. Attempt any three parts:

(a) Show that the ODE

$$y^2 dx + 2xy\, dy = 0$$

is an exact equation and hence solve it.

(b) Solve the ODE $y'' + y = 2e^x$.

(c) Show that the function $z = y - \dfrac{y}{x^2 + y^2}$

satisfies the equation

$$\frac{\partial^2 z}{\partial x^2} + \frac{\partial^2 z}{\partial y^2} = 0.$$

(d) Reduce the following PDE into 3 ODEs:

$$\frac{\partial^2 \psi}{\partial x^2}(x, y, t) + \frac{\partial^2 \psi}{\partial y^2}(x, y, t) + \alpha \frac{\partial \psi}{\partial t}(x, y, t) = 0$$

(e) Solve the initial value problem

$$y'' - 2y' + y = 0, \quad y(0) = 0, \quad y'(0) = 1$$

Q2. Attempt any one part:

(a) Determine the power series solution for the ODE:

$$\frac{d^2 y}{dx^2} + x\frac{dy}{dx} + y = 0$$

(b) A stone of mass m is dropped in the sea where it experiences a resistive force proportional to its velocity. Determine the velocity of the stone as a function of time.

Q3. Attempt any one part:

(a) Expand the following function in a Fourier series:

$$f(x) = -1 \ (-\pi \le x \le 0)$$

$$= 1 \ (0 \le x \le \pi)$$

(b) A string of length L is plucked at its mid-point and then released from rest from this position. The resulting vibrations are modelled by the equation

$$\frac{\partial^2 u}{\partial x^2} = \frac{\partial^2 u}{\partial t^2}, 0 < x < L, t \ge 0$$

with the following initial and boundary conditions:

$$u = (0, t) = u(L, t) = 0$$

$$u(x, 0) = 0$$

$$\left. \frac{\partial u}{\partial t} \right|_{t=0} = 0.1 \sin \frac{2\pi x}{L}$$

Determine u (x, t).

MATHEMATICAL METHODS IN PHYSICS –II: PHE-5

June, 2018

Q1. **Answer any three parts:**

(a) **Solve the equation**

$$(y+2)\frac{dy}{dx}+x=0 \text{ and plot your result in x-y plane.}$$

Ans. Given DE is

$$(y+2)\frac{dy}{dx}+x=0$$

$$\Rightarrow (y+2)\frac{dy}{dx}=-x$$

$$\Rightarrow (y+2)\,dy=-x\,dx$$

Integrating both sides, we have

$$\int(y+2)dy=-\int x\,dx$$

$$\Rightarrow \frac{y^2}{2}+2y=\frac{-x^2}{2}+\frac{c_1}{2}$$

$$\frac{y^2+4y}{2}=\frac{-x^2+c_1}{2}$$

$$\Rightarrow y^2+4y=-x^2+c \qquad\qquad [\text{Putting } c_1=c]$$

Now, we will plot this result in $x-y$ plane as follows:

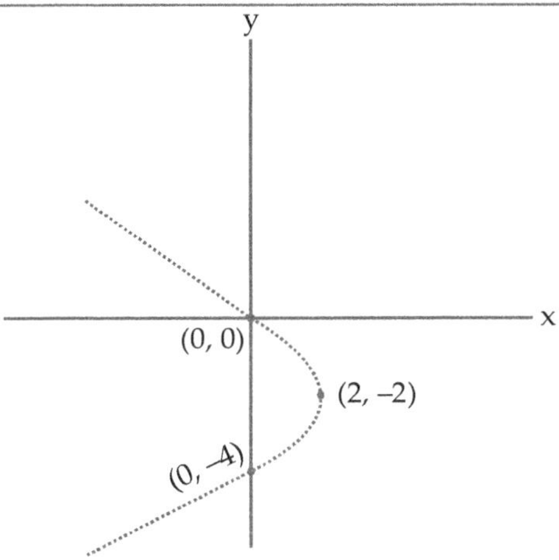

(b) **The general solution of the equation**

$$\frac{d^2y}{dx^2} + 9y = 0 \text{ is } y(x) = A \sin 3x + B \cos 3x.$$

Identify its two solutions and state the condition for their linear independence. Are these solutions linearly independent? Justify your answer by working out steps.

Ans. General solution of DE

$$\frac{d^2y}{dx^2} + 9y = 0 \qquad\qquad \text{...(i)}$$

is $y(x) = A \sin 3x + B \cos 3x$

Therefore, two solutions of Eq. (i) are

$$y_1 = \sin 3x$$

and $y_2 = \cos 3x$

Now, the wronskian is

$$W(x) = \begin{vmatrix} y_1 & y_2 \\ y_1' & y_2' \end{vmatrix}$$

$$= \begin{vmatrix} \sin 3x & \cos 3x \\ 3\cos 3x & -3\sin 3x \end{vmatrix}$$

$$= -3\sin^2 3x - 3\cos^2 3x$$

$$= -3(\sin^2 3x + \cos^2 3x)$$

$$= -3 \neq 0$$

Hence, y_1 and y_2 are linearly independent solutions.

(c)   Classify the singular points of the equation

$$x^2 \frac{d^2y}{dx^2} + x\frac{dy}{dx} + \left(x^2 - \frac{1}{4}\right)y = 0$$

and obtain the corresponding indicial equation.

Ans. Same as Chapter-3, Q.No.-2 (Pg. No.-55)

(d)   The steady state temperature distribution in a control rod in a nuclear reactor is given by

$$\frac{\partial^2 T}{\partial r^2} + \frac{1}{r}\frac{\partial T}{\partial r} + \frac{\partial^2 T}{\partial z^2} = 0$$

Use the method of separation of variables to reduce it to a set of ODEs.

Ans. Refer to Chapter-6, Q.No.-1 (Pg. No.-136)

(e)   Define the order and degree of a PDE. Write down the orders and degrees of the following PDEs:

$$\left(\frac{\partial y}{\partial x}\right)^3 + \left(\frac{\partial y}{\partial t}\right) = 0$$

$$x^2\left(\frac{\partial^2 u}{\partial x^2} + \frac{\partial^2 u}{\partial y^2}\right) - \frac{\partial u}{\partial x} - \frac{\partial u}{\partial y} = e^{xy}$$

$$\frac{\partial^3 u}{\partial x^3} + 2\frac{\partial^3 u}{\partial x\,\partial y^2} - 6\left(\frac{\partial u}{\partial y}\right)^4 = 0$$

Ans. Order of a PDE: The order of the highest derivative term in the equation is called the order of the PDE.

Degree of a PDE: The highest power of the highest order derivative in the equation is called the degree of a PDE:

Now, Same as Chapter-5, Q.No.-1 (Pg. No.-113)

Q2.   Consider two identical pendulums whose bobs are coupled by a spring of stiffness constant k. Write down the equations of motion of these pendulums and solve these by decoupling them. Show that the frequencies of their oscillation will be either equal to or greater than the natural frequency of their oscillation.

Ans. Refer to Chapter-4, Coupled differential equations (Pg. No.-86)

Or

Consider a series RC circuit. When a sinusoidally varying emf is applied to it. The charge in the circuit can be described by the equation

$$\frac{dq}{dt} + \frac{q}{RC} = \frac{E_0}{R} \sin \omega t$$

Show that the charge in the circuit is given by

$$q(t) = \frac{E_0 C}{\sqrt{1 + \omega^2 R^2 C^2}} \sin(\omega t - \theta) + C_1 e^{-t/RC}$$

Where C_1 is a constant.

Ans. Same as Chapter-4, Q.No.-1 (Pg. No.-91)

Q3. Obtain the Fourier sine series for exp (x) on the interval $0 \le x < 1$.

Ans. Refer to Chapter-7, Q.No.-12 (Pg. No.-171)

Or

The general solution of the wave equation

$$\frac{\partial^2 u}{\partial t^2} = v^2 \frac{\partial^2 u}{\partial x^2} \text{ is given by}$$

u (x, t) = (A cos mx + B sin mx) (C cos mvt + D sin mvt), where m is a constant.

Obtain the particular solution under the following conditions:

(i) u = 0, when x = 0 and $x = \pi$

(ii) $\dfrac{\partial u}{\partial t} = 0$, when t = 0

(iii) u (x, 0) = 2 sin x, $0 < x < \pi$

Ans. Same as Chapter-8, Q.No.-8 (Pg. No.-211)

MATHEMATICAL METHODS IN PHYSICS –II: PHE-5

December, 2018

Note: *All questions are compulsory. However, internal choices are given. The marks for each question are indicated against it. You may use log tables or non-programmable calculators.*

Q1. Answer any three parts:

(a) Show that the equation

$$\left(e^x + y - 2\right)dx + \left(e^y + x - 5\right)dy = 0$$

is exact and obtain its solution.

(b) What do you understand by the terms Initial Value Problem and Boundary Value Problem? Solve the equation

$$\frac{d^2y(x)}{dx^2} + 3\frac{dy(x)}{dx} + 2y(x) = 0$$

subject to the conditions $y(0) = 2$ and $\dfrac{dy(0)}{dx} = 4$.

(c) Define ordinary and singular points. When is a singularity said to be regular? Classify the singular points of the equation

$$\left(1 - x^2\right)\frac{d^2y}{dx^2} - 2x\frac{dy}{dx} + n(n+1)y = 0$$

(d) 1-D Schrodinger equation is written as

$$\left(\frac{\partial}{\partial x^2} + \alpha\frac{\partial}{\partial t}\right)\psi(x, t) = 0$$

Use the method of separation of variables and reduce it to a set of ODEs.

(e)   **(i) Show that the function**

$$z = ln\left(x^2 + y^2\right)$$

satisfies the equation

$$\frac{\partial^2 z}{\partial x^2} + \frac{\partial^2 z}{\partial y^2} = 0.$$

(ii)   Classify the following equations by way of order and degree:

$$\frac{\partial^2 u}{\partial t^2} - c^2 \frac{\partial^2 u}{\partial x^2} = 0 \text{ and}$$

$$\frac{\partial \rho}{\partial t} + \rho\left(\frac{\partial v}{\partial x} + \frac{\partial v}{\partial y} + \frac{\partial v}{\partial z}\right) = 0.$$

Q2.   A body dropped vertically from a height experiences air resistance. Its equation of motion can be written as $m\dfrac{dv}{dt} = mg - kv$, where k is a constant and v is instantaneous velocity. Show that the velocity of the body when it hits the ground is given by $v(t) = \dfrac{mg}{k} - \dfrac{mg}{k}\exp(-kt/m).$

OR

According to Newton's law of cooling, the rate at which a body cools is proportional to the temperature difference between the body and its surroundings. If the surroundings are at 300 K and the body cools from 370 K to 340 K in 15 minutes, calculate the time in which it will attain a temperature of 310 K.

Q3.   Express the function f(t) given below in a Fourier series:

$$f(t) = \frac{2}{T}t \qquad\qquad -\frac{T}{2} < t < \frac{T}{2}$$

and f(t + T) = f(t)

OR

The general solution of the diffusion equation

$$\frac{\partial T}{\partial t} = k \frac{\partial^2 T}{\partial x^2}$$

for heat flow in a uniform bar of length L is given by

$$T(x, t) = (C_1 \cos mx + C_2 \sin mx) e^{-km^2 t}.$$

Obtain the particular solution under the following conditions:

$$T(0, t) = \frac{\partial T}{\partial x}(L, t) = 0, (t \geq 0)$$

and $T(x, 0) = T_0 \, (0 < x < L)$

"Education is the most
powerful weapon
which you can use to
change the world."

–Nelson Mandela

MATHEMATICAL METHODS IN PHYSICS –II: PHE-5

June, 2019

Note: *All questions are compulsory. However, internal choices are given. The marks for each question are indicated against it. You may use log tables or non-programmable calculators. Symbols have their usual meanings..*

Q1. Answer any three parts :

(a) Determine all first and second order partial derivatives of the function

$f(x, y) = \log (ax + by)$.

(b) Solve the ODE

$y'' + 3y' + 2y = e^x$

(c) Solve the initial value problem

$y'' + 5y' + 6y = 0;\ y(0) = 1,\ y'(0) = 4$

(d) Show that the following ODE is exact and solve it :

$(y - x^3)dx + (x + y^3)dy = 0$

(e) Use the method of separation of variables to reduce the Laplace equation $\nabla^2 f = 0$ in three ODEs.

Q2. Determine the roots of the indicial equation around the origin for the following ODE :

$$x^2 y'' + xy' + \left(x^2 - \frac{1}{9} \right)y = 0$$

Also obtain the recurrence relation.

OR

A parachutist diving from an aeroplane from rest experiences an acceleration of g exp($-$ kt). Obtain expression for the distance travelled by the parachutist in time t given that $x(t = 0) = x_0$.

Q3. Obtain the Fourier series of the function

$$f(x) = \begin{cases} 0 & -\pi < x < 0 \\ \sin x & 0 < x < \pi \end{cases}$$

and $f(x + 2\pi) = f(x)$.

OR

Solve the $1 - D$ heat flow equation to obtain the general temperature distribution in a bar of length 20 cm at time t. The bar has insulated sides at temperatures of 100°C and its ends are at 0°C at $t = 0$.

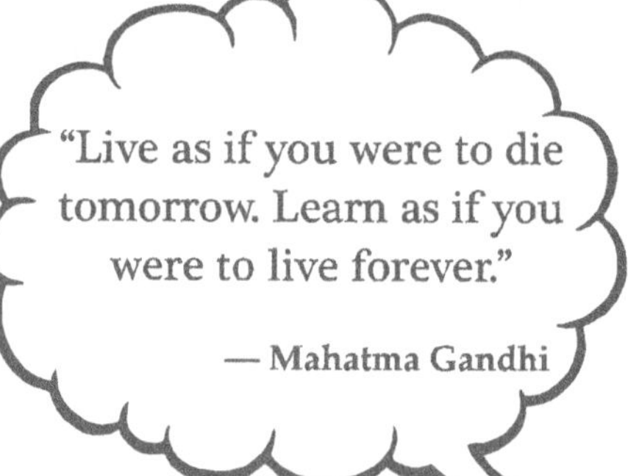

MATHEMATICAL METHODS IN PHYSICS –II: PHE-5

December, 2019

Note: *(i) Answer all questions.*

(ii) Marks for each question are indicated against it.

(iii) Symbols have their usual meaning.

(iv) You can use log tables or calculators.

Q1. Answer any three parts:

(a) Show that the following ODE is exact and solve it

$$\left(y - x^3\right)dx + \left(x + y^3\right)dy = 0.$$

(b) State the order and degree of the following differential equation

$$\frac{\partial u}{\partial t} = k\frac{\partial^2 u}{\partial x^2}$$

Also state whether it is linear or non-linear. Reduce it to a set of ODEs.

(c) Locate the singular points of the equation.

$$x^2\frac{d^2y}{dx^2} + x\frac{dy}{dx} + \left(x^2 - \frac{1}{9}\right)y = 0$$

Obtain the indicial equation around the origin and determine its roots.

Q2. Answer any three parts:

(a) According to Newton's law of cooling, the rate at which a substance cools in air is proportional to the difference between the temperature of the substance and that of the air. Set up the ODE that models this phenomenon. If the temperature of air is 300K and the substance cools from 370K to 340K in 15 minutes. determine the time it takes to attain 310K.

(b)   The vibrations of a rectangular membrane whose edges are fixed at $x = 0$, $x = a$, $y = 0$ and $y = b$ are given by the equation.

$$\frac{\partial^2 f(x,y,t)}{\partial t^2} = v^2 \left(\frac{\partial^2}{\partial x^2} + \frac{\partial^2}{\partial y^2} \right) f(x,y,t)$$

Reduce it to three ODEs using two step process.

(c)   Determine the Fourier sine series for e^x on the interval $0 \le x \le 1$.

(d)   The equations of motion of two identical simple pendulums coupled by a spring of stiffness constant K are

$$m \frac{d^2 x}{dt^2} = -mg\frac{x}{L} - k(x - y)$$

and $$m \frac{d^2 y}{dt^2} = -mg\frac{y}{L} + k(x - y)$$

Where m is mass of the bob and L is length of the simple pendulum. Uncouple these and solve them.

(c)   Solve the two-dimensional Laplace equation

$$\frac{\partial^2 f(x,y)}{\partial x^2} + \frac{\partial^2 f(x,y)}{\partial y^2} = 0, \qquad 0 < x < a; 0 < y < b$$

Write the general solution given that

$$f(0,y) = 0, \frac{\partial f(a,y)}{\partial x} = 0, 0 < y < b$$